Tomasz F. Bigaj
Non-locality and Possible Worlds

# EPISTEMISCHE STUDIEN
## Schriften zur Erkenntnis- und Wissenschaftstheorie

Herausgegeben von / Edited by

Michael Esfeld • Stephan Hartmann • Albert Newen

Band 10 / Volume 10

Tomasz F. Bigaj

# Non-locality and Possible Worlds

## A Counterfactual Perspective
## on Quantum Entanglement

**ontos**
**verlag**

Frankfurt I Paris I Ebikon I Lancaster I New Brunswick

**Bibliographic information published by Die Deutsche Bibliothek**
Die Deutsche Bibliothek lists this publication in the Deutsche Nationalbibliographie;
detailed bibliographic data is available in the Internet at http://dnb.ddb.de

North and South America by
Transaction Books
Rutgers University
Piscataway, NJ 08854-8042
trans@transactionpub.com

United Kingdom, Ire, Iceland, Turkey, Malta, Portugal by
Gazelle Books Services Limited
White Cross Mills
Hightown
LANCASTER, LA1 4XS
sales@gazellebooks.co.uk

Livraison pour la France et la Belgique:
Librairie Philosophique J.Vrin
6, place de la Sorbonne ; F-75005 PARIS
Tel. +33 (0)1 43 54 03 47 ; Fax  +33 (0)1 43 54 48 18
www.vrin.fr

©2006 ontos verlag
P.O. Box 15 41, D-63133 Heusenstamm
www.ontosverlag.com

ISBN 10: 3-938793-29-5
ISBN 13: 978-3-938793-29-9

2006

Printed on acid-free paper
ISO-Norm 970-6
FSC-certified (Forest Stewardship Council)
This hardcover binding meets the International Library standard

Printed in Germany
by buch bücher **dd ag**

# Table of Contents

# INTRODUCTION

This book is primarily intended as a philosophical analysis of the phenomenon of non-locality that so famously (or, one may say, infamously) unfolds in quantum theory. However, the scope of the proposed analysis is seriously limited by the adopted research methodology. It is not the purpose of the book to present the whole gamut of conceptions of how to interpret and deal with the problem of non-local causation—the causation that seems to propagate instantaneously from place to place—that apparently crops up in the quantum-mechanical realm. Instead, we will adopt a very specific perspective which may be dubbed the "counter-factual" approach to the problem of quantum non-locality and quantum entanglement. Thus, the main goal of the book will be to use the logic of counterfactual conditionals, i.e. expressions of the form "If it were (had been) *P*, then it would be (have been) *Q*", in order to shed a new light on the ontological issue of non-locality in quantum mechanics. Actually, a substantial portion of the book will be devoted to the preliminary task of constructing a logic (or logics) of counterfactuals suitable for the interpretative job that is called for within the foundations of quantum mechanics. Only after having satisfactory dealt with this challenge, we can venture to seek solutions to the perennial philosophical debate regarding fundamental quantum results such as various versions of Bell-like theorems, where the problem of non-locality plays a pivotal part.

Resorting to non-standard logical apparatuses in the foundational analysis of quantum mechanics is not an entirely novel idea. There is a well-established and highly regarded method of constructing a formal theory of quantum reality called "quantum logic" which was stimulated by the works of both mathematicians (G. Birkhoff, J. von Neumann) and philosophers (H. Reichenbach).[1] The most important feature of these logical ap-

---

[1] Classical texts on the subject of quantum logic are (Birkhoff, von Neumann 1936) and (Reichenbach 1944). A particularly nice and elegant introduction to various versions of quantum logic can be found in (Greechie, Gudder 1973). Other introductions to quantum logic that particularly accentuate its philosophical importance are (Putnam 1969), (van Fraassen 1973), (Haack 1996, chapter 8), (Bub 1997, chapter 1). For the recent developments of this subject see (Dalla Chiara *et al.* 2004). I took issue with some claims of Birkoff and von Neumann's version of quantum logic in (Bigaj 2001).

proaches—for there is actually more than one quantum logic—is that they are all underpinned by the strong conviction that the peculiar properties of quantum reality call for some change in classical logic. The proposed non-classical novelties of quantum logics range from multi-valency to the rejection of the law of distributivity. However, the task of constructing a counterfactual logic that would be helpful for describing quantum-mechanical phenomena is to be differentiated from these ambitious programs. The counterfactual approach to quantum mechanics does not aim to correct classical logic, but rather to extend its expressive powers by introducing some new non-truth-functional operators, similarly to the way modal logics extend, but do not reject classical logic by adding modal operators of possibility and necessity.

There are, in my opinion, three main reasons why counterfactual conditionals may prove themselves useful in the analysis of non-local quantum causality. The first reason is that causality itself admits a clear and intuitive analysis in terms of counterfactuals. It is commonly accepted that there are two predominant conceptions of causality: regularist and singularist. The regularist approach tries to reduce causation to a regular succession of events, thus subsuming singular causal agents under general types of events ("phenomena", in some terminology) and appealing to the general laws that connect these types of events. An alternative approach, famously developed by David Lewis, views causality as a relation between concrete token-events: this particular event $e$, as occurring in the actually obtaining circumstances, is a cause of another concrete event $e'$. Causation understood in such a way need not be based on regularities; another instance of event $e$ in different circumstances may not produce an effect of the same type as $e'$. The key to the relation between the cause and the effect in this case lies in counterfactuality: we say that if the cause $e$ had not occurred in those circumstances, the effect $e'$ would not have happened.

Even without an excursion into the analysis of causation it should be clear that counterfactual conditionals lend themselves naturally to the task of expressing the idea of the lack of influence between events which is so crucial to the notion of locality. For instance, if I want to make precise the idea that snapping my fingers cannot possibly repair my broken computer, I can resort to the simple counterfactual statement "If I snapped my fingers at this moment, the computer would still be broken". Incidentally, this statement may be claimed to remain true even if there is a slight chance for the computer to repair itself, as it sometimes happens with sophisticated electronic devices. For the fact is that the computer at this moment *is* actually broken, and when considering a possible situation in which I decided to snap my fingers we should, if possible, keep everything exactly as in the actual situation. We will return later to the detailed analysis of cases similar to this one.

The two remaining reasons why counterfactuals deserve to be considered a viable conceptual tool in the analysis of quantum non-localities have to do with the vagaries of quantum mechanics itself. Firstly, quantum theory famously places a severe restriction on the number of parameters whose values can be determined at a given time. Among several parameters that may separately characterize a given quantum system we can select only a handful of compatible (so-called "commuting") quantities, i.e. quantities such that the measurement revealing the value for one of them does not "destroy" the values of the other ones. Incompatible parameters, such as position and momentum, or various components of spin, cannot have their values jointly determined. Hence, if we decide to measure a particle's momentum, its position becomes undefined, and *vice versa*. And yet sometimes we want to talk about alternative measurement settings in which a parameter non-commuting with the one actually selected would have been put to an experimental test. For example, the widely analyzed EPR argument starts off with a situation in which a given parameter has been chosen for measurement on one of two entangled particles, but then it moves on to the analysis of what would have happened, had we decided to measure an alternative parameter that does not commute with the former one. To speak intelligibly of such situations one has to have a firm grasp of the meaning of counterfactual parlance.

Finally, there is yet another aspect of quantum-mechanical description beside the one given above that may require a counterfactual treatment. Quantum theory very sparsely attributes definite properties to physical systems, yet sometimes such property attributions are made, whether on the basis of a direct measurement, or as a result of an inference from the outcome of a measurement on another, correlated system.[2] In the mathematical jargon of quantum theory we speak in such cases of the system being in an *eigenstate* with respect to a particular observable. But the exact nature of such attributions is somewhat obscure, especially in the case when they are derived from measurements and observations done on objects different from those that the property is attributed to. And it turns

---

[2]  Sometimes the existence of such true property attributions is assumed as a consequence of more "metaphysical" conjectures, for instance the hidden-variable hypothesis, as is the case with Bell's theorem.

out that counterfactuals offer us an elegant and metaphysically uncommitting way of expressing those property attributions. We can treat the statement "System $x$ possesses the measurable property $a$ with respect to an observable $A$" as being equivalent to the "operational" counterfactual "If $A$ was measured on $x$, the outcome would be $a$".

Although the counterfactual reinterpretation of quantum-mechanical problems and paradoxes is a relatively new undertaking, it has already gained some prominence. Most famously, counterfactual semantics has been used by H.P. Stapp in his numerous attempts at strengthening Bell's theorem.[3] This strengthening, of which we will be talking extensively later in the book, amounts to eliminating the assumption of hidden variables from the derivation of Bell's inequality or its equivalent. If successful, this procedure would show that the assumption of locality on which Bell's argument relies is in itself untenable independently of the status of the hidden-variable hypothesis. But the use of the counterfactual logic in quantum mechanics is by no means limited to the issue of non-locality and Bell's theorems. Counterfactual conditionals have been employed to support particular non-standard interpretations of quantum-mechanical formalism, such as the consistent history approach (Griffiths 1999, 2001), or the time-symmetrized approach (Vaidman 1999a, 1999b). In the current monograph these uses of counterfactuals will play a limited role, as I don't want to restrict the application of the general counterfactual method to the task of defending specific (and often controversial) interpretations of quantum mechanics.

As it is often the case with new and non-standard conceptual tools, the counterfactual method of analysis in quantum mechanics has some formidable opponents too. John Earman, for instance, expressed his deep mistrust of the counterfactual analysis in philosophy of science in his (1986), where he said that:

> [...] it is more than slightly obscene to make ultimate judgments about the truth of such a noble doctrine as determinism on something as slippery as counterfactuals. If in the end the debate about whether or not the world is deterministic comes down to trading conflicting intuitions about nearness of possible worlds, then leave me out of it. (pp. 230-231)

I do hope that the analysis presented in the book can be seen as a step toward making the counterfactual analysis of quantum phenomena a bit less

---

[3] References to Stapp's works will be given later.

"slippery" and less prone to conflicting intuitions than Earman fears it to be.

## 0.1 THE OUTLINE OF THE BOOK

Below I will present a brief synopsis of this book's chapters. I hope that this will make it easier for the readers to select the fragments that best fit their interests without having to pore over uninteresting or obvious sections. The first chapter of the book offers a general introduction to the problem of non-locality and realism in quantum-mechanical description. It explains why quantum mechanics apparently displays non-local features even at the most fundamental level of description (with no reference to any entangled states whatsoever), and why the purported non-locality of quantum mechanics is so intimately connected with the issue of the ontological interpretation of quantum states and quantum probabilities. The reader will find there informal expositions of both the EPR argument and of Bell's theorem in its standard though somewhat simplified version, as well as some preliminary distinctions between different natural-language formulations of the locality condition. The main focus of the chapter is on the so-called generalized Bell theorem, which alleges to have established that the locality assumption leads to a logical clash with quantum-mechanical predictions. The locality assumption of the generalized Bell theorem takes on the form of the probabilistic requirement of independence, known as the factorization condition. This condition has been famously analyzed by J. Jarrett, who has proposed to split it into two independent conditions, today referred to as "parameter independence" and "outcome independence".

In section 1.5 an extensive analysis of Jarrett's two conditions is presented, and the thesis is advanced that the standard, commonly accepted ontological interpretation of the parameter independence condition is not sufficiently justified. The mathematical form of this condition does not legitimize the thesis that when parameter independence is violated, the choice of measurement in a remote system can "instantaneously" change the physical state of the local object. The latter fact could find a much better and uncontroversial formulation in the language which explicitly uses counterfactual conditions of the sort "if the distant setting were different, the state of the local system would be different, too" or similar. Consequently, due to the lack of a clear intuition regarding precisely what type of non-locality is necessitated by Bell's generalized theorem, it is claimed that we are still in need of further investigations of this issue in various alternative frameworks (including the counterfactual approach).

Chapter 2 is entirely devoted to the preliminary task of introducing the reader to the basics of the standard semantics of counterfactual conditionals. Starting with the historically prior conception of R. Stalnaker's, we will move on to the exposition of the standard possible-world semantics of counterfactuals based on the notion of relative similarity between possible worlds with respect to the actual world, as developed by D. Lewis. It will be stressed that it is imperative to reject the so-called principle of Conditional Excluded Middle (CEM), if one wants to apply counterfactual conditionals to the description of possible results of quantum measurements without committing oneself to the counterfactual definiteness of these results (which can be claimed to be equivalent to the realism of possessed values). Fortunately, the violation of CEM is one of the primary features of Lewis's logic, as opposed to Stalnaker's.

Having presented Lewis's informal criteria of similarity between possible worlds (whose main role is to achieve the temporal asymmetry of counterfactuals, i.e. the feature which implies that in typical true counterfactuals the consequent-event occurs after the antecedent-event and not *vice versa*) in subsection 2.3.2 I will formulate an argument showing that the notion of law-breaking events ("miracles") used in those criteria does not fare well with the way counterfactuals work in quantum mechanics. More specifically, it will be demonstrated that if we use the criterion of similarity according to which a possible world containing a small miracle is more similar to the actual world than a world in which there is a large and widespread difference in individual facts, then no counterfactual describing observable correlations between outcomes of distant measurements can come out true. For that reason it is suggested, in accordance with common practice, that in the context of quantum mechanics the only available criterion of similarity has to be based on the maximization of the area of perfect match with regard to individual facts. However, it remains to be seen if some facts will have to be excluded from the similarity criterion (and whether they should be excluded on the basis of their physical nature, or on the basis of their space-time locations relative to the location of the antecedent-event that is assumed to be true by the evaluated counterfactual).

Chapters 3 and 4 deal with Stapp's extensive project of proving the non-locality of quantum mechanics within the counterfactual framework. Stapp can rightfully claim the title of the pioneer of the counterfactual method of analysis in quantum physics. His first attempt to strengthen Bell's theorem (in the form known as CHSH) using informal counterfactual reasoning dates back to 1971, when he suggested that we could consider would-be outcomes of alternative measurements in spite of the fact that actually only one measurement setting can be selected and one outcome revealed (Stapp 1971). This early attempt was subsequently criticized by M. Redhead in (1987), which prompted Stapp to do a serious overhaul of his argument, with proper attention paid to the intricacies of the semantics of "would" and "might" counterfactuals (Stapp 1989). However, even this rectified argument did not avoid another serious criticism at the hands of R. Clifton, J. Butterfield and M. Redhead (1990). Chapter 3 presents the details of this early polemic between Stapp and his critics. Although my final assessment will be that Stapp cannot claim to have succeeded in achieving his goal, some of his opponents' criticisms have to be deemed unjustified. I will argue that one of the causes of the disagreement between the participants in the debate, regarding the status of the counterfactual locality requirement involved in Stapp's proof, is the fact that both sides use slightly different truth conditions for counterfactuals (they will be analyzed extensively later in the book). To avoid possible misunderstandings I will propose in section 3.3 a universal semantic locality condition (SLOC), which is expressed in terms of possible worlds only with no reference to counterfactual statements, and therefore is independent of one's intuitions regarding the semantics for counterfactuals.

Chapter 4 is divided into two parts, each of which is devoted to a particular new counterfactual proof of non-locality by Stapp. In section 4.1 our attention will be focused on the less well known derivation formalized by Stapp and D. Bedford which uses the so-called Greenberg-Horne-Zeilinger (GHZ) version of Bell's theorem (Bedford & Stapp 1995). A thorough analysis of this proof reveals that the principle "Elimination of Eliminated Conditions", used several times to justify crucial transitions of the proof, has no backing in counterfactual semantics and is indeed faulty. Moreover, a general semantic argument is produced showing that, contrary to Stapp's claim, his locality assumption is logically compatible with the quantum predictions regarding the GHZ case. Because this section of chapter 4 does not contain any new results that would be important in the further course of argumentation, it may be treated as a mere exercise in the logic of counterfactuals and can be skipped by the reader who is not particularly interested in that sort of practice. However, section 4.2 opens up some new perspectives which will prove important later. The main topic of this section is the most recent proof of the non-locality of quantum mechanics offered by Stapp in 1997 and later reformulated and improved upon. This proof is based on yet another thought experiment that has recently been proposed as a way of improving upon Bell's classical theorem, namely, the so-called Hardy example.

Stapp's derivation in this case is based on not one but two formulations of the locality condition. One of them is basically equivalent to my earlier condition (SLOC) and does not raise suspicions; the other one, however, has spurred a debate regarding its legitimacy. The difference of opinion between Stapp and his opponents comes from the fact that the locality condition in question alleges that the truth of a counterfactual statement whose components pertain to one spatiotemporal region should be preserved under alternative selections of measurements in a space-like separated region, and this can be questioned given the complex nature of counterfactual conditionals. In subsection 4.2.6 I argue that Stapp's claim regarding the *prima facie* plausibility of his second locality condition could be supported by a counterfactual version of the so-called Einstein's criterion of reality which so famously turns up in the EPR argument. However, I present an argument showing that Einstein's criterion of reality itself together with the unquestionable version of the locality condition entails a violation of the quantum-mechanical predictions in the Hardy case. This result not only undermines the legitimacy of Stapp's second notion of locality, but also constitutes an unquestionable strengthening of Bell's original theorem, in which the assumption of the hidden-variable hypothesis is replaced with the arguably weaker criterion of reality. Furthermore, I argue that Stapp's proof cannot possibly be recovered with the help of only one locality condition (SLOC), as (SLOC) turns out to be logically compatible with the quantum-mechanical predictions of the Hardy example.

Chapters 5 and 6 contain a detailed exposition of my proposal of how to exploit the logic of counterfactuals in the analysis of entangled states and their alleged non-local features. The main focus of chapter 5 is on developing a particular type of semantics for counterfactual conditionals that could give us some insight into the foundational debates on quantum mechanics. The starting point of these considerations is yet another possible approach to temporal counterfactuals considered by Lewis as an alternative to his own proposal. This approach builds the temporal asymmetry explicitly into the truth-condition of counterfactuals, stipulating that for a counterfactual to be true its consequent should be true in all the possible worlds that share with the actual world the past of the antecedent-event, while the future of this event is left open (within the limits of physical laws, naturally). We can notice at the outset that such a characteristic can be interpreted in two ways within the special theory of relativity where the notion of an event's past can be understood as covering either the exterior of its forward light cone (everything that according to the special theory of relativity cannot be causally affected by the event) or the interior of its backward light cone (everything that can causally influence the event). Thus we actually have two alternative semantic approaches to spatiotemporal counterfactuals. However, as Lewis has observed, the "asymmetry by fiat" approach is seriously undermined by its being limited to a narrow class of antecedents describing well-localized spatiotemporal events. Therefore, the question arises how to achieve a suitable generalization for each of the two above-mentioned truth conditions.

In section 5.2 I present a method of generalizing the truth-condition that requires the entire exterior of the forward light cone of the antecedent-event to be kept exactly as in the actual world. This generalization is based on the proposal put forward by J. Finkelstein, who used a specific similarity comparison between possible worlds defined solely in terms of their areas of divergence from the actual world. With a slight formal modification, the standard Lewis truth-condition for counterfactuals can then be applied to complement the entire procedure. However, in section 5.3 I present a proof of the somewhat surprising fact that an analogous generalization is impossible to accomplish in the case of the second counterfactual semantics that chooses to keep the interior of the backward light cone of the antecedent-event. As a result, an alternative method of its generalization is proposed that does not use a well-defined similarity relation, but instead follows a particular procedure described in the chapter in order to evaluate a given counterfactual. An interesting feature of this procedure is that it implies that the comparison between possible worlds with respect to the actual world may depend on what particular counterfactual is being considered, i.e. it is possible that a given world $w_1$ can be seen as more similar to the actual world than world $w_2$ when evaluating one counterfactual statement, but equally similar as $w_2$ when evaluating another one. Thus, the similarity comparison becomes antecedent-dependent. Finally, both generalized truth-conditions for counterfactuals are tested using the GHZ example of three correlated measurements. It is claimed that in spite of some clear differences between the two semantic approaches to counterfactuals there is no decisive argument that could tell us which one is superior, and consequently the choice between them may depend on individual "metaphysical" preferences, so in the remainder of the book both approaches will be given equal attention.

The main goal of chapter 6 is to use the formal apparatus developed in chapter 5 in the counterfactual reconstruction of the two fundamental results that were already discussed informally in chapter 1, that is the EPR argument and Bell's theorem. One of the prerequisites of a successful reconstruction of that sort is to formulate a precise criterion of local causality. For this criterion I shall choose the condition (SLOC) proposed earlier that basically demands that for every non-contradictory event there should be a possible world in which this event occurs and which agrees with the actual world everywhere outside the event's forward light cone. To make sure that this is a proper verbalization of the notion of locality I shall prove that (SLOC) when considered under the first of the two available interpretations of counterfactuals is equivalent to the counterfactual condition of locality used by Stapp in his latest proofs, and that under the second available semantics of counterfactuals it becomes nearly equivalent to another counterfactual requirement based on Lewis's definition of counterfactual dependence and adopted by Clifton, Butterfield and Redhead (1990). It is also necessary to stress that the condition (SLOC) should be limited to events that I call indeterministic (events not causally conditioned by their pasts). As it is well known, all considerations in quantum mechanics are typically carried out with the assumption that measurement selections are indeterministic in that sense, so (SLOC) can be directly applied to them. However, if we want to extend our analysis to events which could possibly turn out to be conditioned by their pasts (for instance outcome-events in hidden-variable theories), we have to resort to a generalized version of the locality condition (GLOC). I formulate and discuss this condition in section 6.6.

The counterfactual reinterpretation of the EPR argument aims to reconstruct all of its premises as well as its logical structure. The argument uses the quantum-mechanical predictions stemming from the mathematical form of the initial entangled state that the two particles are prepared in, in order to derive the existence of a definite quantum property of one particle from the result of the measurement of the other particle. However, we should notice that the two truth conditions for counterfactuals introduced in chapter 5 offer us two ways of interpreting quantum properties, and only under one of these interpretations the derivation is actually valid. Furthermore, it is argued that even if the counterfactual property attribution regarding one spin component can be made for one particle on the basis of the actual outcome revealed in the measurement on the distant particle, this does not imply that the "disappearance" of this attribution under the counterfactual supposition that the distant particle underwent a different measurement or no measurement at all constitutes a violation of the locality condition (SLOC). In order to argue, as Einstein, Podolsky and Rosen did, that there is a non-local influence at play here, another premise in the form of the counterfactual criterion of reality is needed. However, we already noted in chapter 4 that Einstein's criterion of reality is controversial, as it makes it possible to derive the conclusions that disagree with the quantum-mechanical predictions regarding the Hardy example. In section 6.4 I suggest that we could reject the supposition that a true counterfactual ascribing a definite outcome to a would-be measurement has to be based in a categorical property localized in one subsystem of the entangled system. Instead, I propose to use the notion of an irreducible disposition of the system in order to describe such a counterfactual property attribution. If we assume that quantum systems can display dispositional properties that are not reducible to categorical properties, then we can effectively rebut the EPR argument which purports to show that in standard quantum theory there are non-local influences induced by the act of measurement selection.

Another result of chapter 6 is a proof that Bell's theorem in its standard form retains its validity under both available interpretations of counterfactuals. It turns out that changing from a distance a counterfactual property attribution of a local system from one definite value to another does constitute a breach of the locality condition (SLOC), and hence it follows that the counterfactual hidden variable hypothesis has to assume measurement-induced non-locality if the quantum statistical predictions are to be preserved. However, when the counterfactual hidden variable hypothesis is rejected, no non-locality associated with the selection of the distant measurement follows suit. Yet, at the end of chapter 6, as well as in the final chapter 7, I argue that some form of non-locality related to the outcome-outcome link is present even in the standard formulation of quantum mechanics. To establish this fact I use the generalized formulation of the locality condition (GLOC), according to which a non-local effect induced by an event $E$ is present if in the closest possible $E$-world there occurs a space-like separated event $E'$ whose absolute past is exactly the same as in the actual world. It turns out that this condition cannot possibly be satisfied in the case of quantum entangled systems, so we have no choice but to accept that measurements performed in space-like separated locations may be able to "secretly" synchronize their outcomes with one another. But it is questionable whether such non-local correlations can strictly be said to violate the principle of local *causality*, as causality seems to require that one of the pair of linked events (labeled "the cause") be selected as a free variable (a variable that in principle can be controlled by an experimenter). And yet no outcome can actually be controlled in quantum-mechanical measurements, and the reciprocal relation between the correlated outcomes turns out to be symmetric, contrary to what typical causal relations are assumed to be.

*    *    *

I would like to acknowledge some of the numerous debts that I incurred during working on this book from my initial research into the existing literature to the moment of sending the final version of the manuscript to the publisher. To begin with, I would probably never have ventured into the muddy waters of the philosophical interpretations of quantum mechanics if it hadn't been for Rob Clifton and his enlightening seminar in the philosophy of quantum mechanics that I was lucky to attend in 1998 in Pittsburgh. I deeply regret the fact that Rob's untimely death deprived us all of the opportunity to learn more from his immense expertise in the subject. The choice of topic for the research whose results are presented in the book was suggested to me by Tomasz Placek; to him I also owe helpful advice regarding the most recent literature on the subject of counterfactuals in quantum mechanics, as well as extensive critical comments on the manuscript. At an early stage of my research, in 2001-2002 I visited the University of Michigan, where I had the opportunity to receive excellent advice from Larry Sklar, as well as from Jim Joyce, Rich Thomason and other members of the Philosophy Department in Ann Arbor. The years 2002-2004, which I spent as a visiting faculty member in Rowan University, Glassboro NJ, were also very productive for me. I benefited much from formal and informal conversations with members of both the Philosophy and Religion Department, and the Physics Department, especially with Abe Witonsky and Eduardo Florez. Most recently, I learned a lot from discussions with Martin Thomson-Jones, Wayne Myrvold and Mauro Dorato. I would like to thank Michael Esfeld for his kind suggestions regarding how to complement my general discussions of the problem of non-locality in quantum mechanics. To Konrad Talmont-Kaminski I owe thanks for correcting my English. Last but not least I would like to thank my wife, Małgorzata for her patience and unwavering support during all those years.

The final stage of writing the book was partly financed by the grant from the Polish State Committee for Scientific Research KBN 1 H01A 033 28.

# Chapter 1

# WHY DOES THE QUANTUM WORLD HAVE TO BE NON-LOCAL?

## 1.1 INTRODUCTION: REALISM AND LOCALITY

The classical picture of physical reality rests upon, among others, two intuitively compelling principles. The first of these reflects our natural belief in the objective and independent existence of the physical world. Skeptical arguments notwithstanding, we are inclined to believe that there are objects that constitute our physical environment, and that they possess certain properties independently of whether we are aware of them or not. In philosophical parlance this ontological intuition is typically presented under the multifarious heading of "realism". Of course realism need not be "naïve"—we know very well that the very act of observation can disturb or even destroy the elements of reality under consideration. However, although there is probably no such thing as an ideal observer or an ideal observation, realists would insist that we can either make the disturbances associated with observations arbitrarily small, or at least take them into account and modify the outcomes of our observations accordingly. To use a standard textbook example: if I observe a stick which is partly submerged in water, and it appears bent to me, I can take into account the fact that light bends upon hitting water and infer that the stick is actually straight. In general, the crux of realism lies in the conviction that it makes sense to speak about objects and their properties even if no one is currently perceiving them, measuring them or is in any other way directly aware of them.

The second classical principle concerns the structure of the external world and the law-like connections between its elements. We believe that objects furnishing our world influence one another in many different ways —changing their behavior, properties, etc. In other words, we perceive a multitude of causal interactions among elements of physical reality. Those interactions and correlations are not entirely chaotic or capricious. They seem to display certain patterns, and the most conspicuous one is that the ability to influence seems to be dependent on proximity. If I want to move an object—a chair for example—I have to come close to it. And if I want to act from a distance, I have to find a mediating tool, like a broomstick or a fully automated and computerized artificial arm. It seems, then, that the interactions we are familiar with display the feature of being "local"— roughly meaning that to influence a faraway object the causal chain has to somehow pass in a certain amount of time through the entire distance separating us from the object.

In spite of its intuitive appeal, the locality of cause-effect relations has not always been accepted unconditionally. Isaac Newton in his gravitational theory assumed, without much consideration, that the gravitational attraction between distant bodies is immediate and unmediated. The idea of action at a distance apparently wasn't a cause of concern for the founding father of classical physics. However, his followers were not so sure. Physicists felt that it is a legitimate question to ask whether, for example, the effects of the Sun's sudden disappearance would be felt instantaneously throughout the Solar system. Would the planets of the Solar system "feel" freed from the Sun's gravitational bonds immediately as a result of its vanishing or would they follow their usual paths until the disturbance in the gravitational field caused by the sudden annihilation of the Sun reached them? As is well known, Albert Einstein opted strongly for the second answer. He built into his theories of relativity a fundamental principle expressing the locality of the physical world. This principle, of an undoubtedly ontological character, can be formulated in terms of the special theory of relativity as the claim that all events causally relevant to a particular occurrence $O$ have to occupy a specific part of space-time, called "the absolute past of $O$" ("the past light cone of $O$") In other words, causal influences cannot propagate at arbitrary speeds, the speed of light being the upper limit for all transmissions of mass and energy.[1]

Quantum mechanics calls into question the validity of both of the aforementioned principles, however. Probably the most notorious feature

---

[1] We should mention, however, that there is a slightly different intuition associated with the notion of locality, which does not focus on the limitation of speed at which all causal interactions can propagate, but rather on the idea of the spatiotemporal contiguity of causal chains. This alternative sense of locality can be presented informally in the form of the requirement that for any event $e$, no matter how small a spatiotemporal interval stretching in $e$'s past and containing it we consider, there will be always a set of complete causes for $e$ occurring in this interval. This meaning of locality is obviously different from the one we are presenting in the text, for it is possible that no interactions propagate faster than the speed of light, and yet that there are "gaps" in causal chains leading from the cause to the effect. For more on that issue, see (Lange 2002), in particular pp. 13-17.

of quantum mechanics is that it casts doubt on the objective existence of properties that characterize a particular physical system. A complete quantum description of a state for a physical system consists not of functions ascribing precise values to all physical parameters, but rather of a probability distribution function over all possible values for the given parameters. The literature on this subject, professional as well as popular, offers numerous examples and thought experiments illustrating this particular feature of the quantum world. Thus, we learn that when we want to measure a property of light called "polarization", the result of this measurement for a particular photon is not determined, and we can only speak about a numerically given probability that the photon will pass through a specifically oriented polarizer or that it will get absorbed. However, after the measurement has been done and the photon has successfully passed through the polarizer, its polarization along that particular direction becomes well defined. Hence the idea of a photon having a particular polarization even when nobody is watching begins to fade away.

Even more astoundingly, the same disturbing phenomenon occur with mundane parameters such as position. The famous two-slit experiment teaches us that it makes no sense to ask exactly which slit the electron went through, even though it manages to reach the detecting screen where it "materializes". Again, the quantum mechanical description of this situation invokes the probability function known also as the wave function. The wave function enables us to calculate the probability of finding an object in any particular region of space. In the two-slit experiment the wave function consists of two components; one describing the electron passing through the first slit, and the other through the second one. A combination (or superposition) of these two components creates the famous interference pattern observed on the screen.[2]

However, it should be stressed that realism is not contradicted by the standard formulation of quantum mechanics. Quantum formalism operates with the probability function, but by itself offers no definitive answer to the question of how to interpret this probability. It is logically possible to maintain that quantum probability reflects only our ignorance regarding the exact state of a system, just as in statistical mechanics. This brings us to the perennial debate regarding the correct interpretation of quantum mechanics, with the choice being between the Copenhagen interpretation, the

---

[2] (Hughes 1989) offers an excellent and accessible, yet rigorous introduction to these problems. For a more historically-oriented exposition of the foundations of quantum mechanics, see (Jammer 1974).

various hidden variable theories and several other interpretations. Hidden variable theories, which claim that the physical parameters have objective values that go beyond what is given in the standard quantum-mechanical description, have been seriously undermined by several no-go results, some of which will be later analyzed. Still, no one has succeeded in showing their impossibility, so realist alternatives to quantum mechanics, such as David Bohm's famous mechanics, remain an option, albeit an unlikely one in the opinion of the majority of scientists.

The anti-realist leaning of quantum mechanics has been its hallmark almost since its inception. This wasn't the case with non-locality. Philosophical interest in the possibly non-local character of quantum mechanics arouse only after John Bell's groundbreaking studies of entangled systems in the sixties, even though the problem with locality in the context of the interpretation of quantum mechanics was suggested much earlier by Einstein and his collaborators. What is particularly fascinating is that these two apparently separate issues—the issue of realism and of locality—turn out to be deeply interconnected within the area of quantum physics. This connection can be hinted at with the help of the following, simple example. Let us suppose that we have an electron in the state in which its position is described by a wave function $\Psi$ that has only two non-zero components $\Psi_1$ and $\Psi_2$, one concentrated around a particular location $A$, and the other around a distant location $B$. We can imagine that location $A$ is situated in a lab on Earth, whereas distant location $B$ is on the Moon. No principle in quantum mechanics forbids the existence of such systems, although for obvious reason their practical realization would encounter serious difficulties. Translating this description into the language of probability, we can say that in these initial conditions the probability of detecting the electron on Earth equals the probability of detecting it on the Moon, which in turn equals one-half. Now let us suppose that we have set up some sort of a detecting device in our lab, and that the detector successfully localized our initially prepared electron as being in area $A$. What impact does this result of measurement have on the physical situation in area $B$? The answer depends on whether we interpret the initial wave function $\Psi$ as describing merely our ignorance, or as reflecting the fundamental property of the quantum world. In other words, we have to decide if we choose to embrace ontological realism with respect to quantum properties, or to reject it and admit that before the measurement the position of the electron was not objectively defined.

26

If we opt for the first solution, nothing mysterious follows. We detected the electron in our lab, because it had been there all along. The function $\Psi$ represents only our limited knowledge with regard to the exact position of the electron. The fact that after the measurement the second component $\Psi_2$ disappears reflects merely the change in our knowledge (we now know that the electron hadn't been on the Moon at all), not a change in the objective world, so there is no reason to believe that the measurement on Earth has had any physical impact on the Moon. However, things are different when we agree, as is suggested by the orthodox interpretation of quantum mechanics, that the function $\Psi$ affords a complete and objective description of all there is in the physical world. Suppose then—contrary to the realist stance—that before the measurement the electron wasn't physically in area $A$ or $B$ separately, but rather "in both", at least "partially".[3] Now we can agree that by detecting the electron in one location $A$, and by "forcing" it to reappear in our lab, we have made some change in the physical situation on the Moon—we have eliminated the "partial", or "incomplete" presence of the electron there. But the question is whether this change, whose nature is still somewhat mysterious, has to occur instantly, or maybe—as it was the case with the gravitational influence between the Sun and the planets—only after the time required for the signal carrying the information about the outcome of our experiment to travel the distance between the Earth and the Moon. A little thought reveals that the second option is not tenable. If we allowed for even the slightest delay in the flow of signal from the earthly lab to the Moon, we would open the possibility of detecting the electron on the Moon in the short period of time allowed before the signal was received and in spite of its detection on Earth, which is obviously impossible. The change in the physical situation on the Moon has to occur simultaneously with the detection on the Earth, otherwise it would be possible to end up with two electrons rather than one. This means, however, that this purported influence has all marks of non-locality; that is it does not obey the restrictions put forward by Einstein. It propagates at infinite speed, and it also seems not to be transported by any physical means. Hence, if this is correct, it seems that once we reject realism while accepting the quantum-mechanical formalism, we have to reject locality as well.

Interestingly, the foregoing example is rarely taken seriously by philosophers and physicist as a genuine case of non-locality implied by the orthodox interpretation of quantum mechanics. P. Gibbins for example re-

---

[3] Robert Griffiths describes this quantum state of a particle as "delocalized" (Griffiths 2001, p. 18).

*consistent*
*Q - Theory*

fers to a similar case as a "naïve" instance of non-locality (Gibbins, 1983, p. 191). The reason for this belittling remark is that the non-locality in this case supposedly follows only under an additional, unreasonable assumption of the physical character of the wave function. According to the standard presentation, quantum measurement is always accompanied by the so-called collapse of the wave function—i.e. the transformation of the initial probability distribution, which reflects the indeterminacy in the parameter to be measured, into a distribution representing the definite result of the measurement (in our situation the collapse transforms the initial function $\Psi = \Psi_1 + \Psi_2$ into its component $\Psi_1$). If the wave function were to be interpreted analogously to electromagnetic or gravitational fields, as some sort of a field-like entity, then an instantaneous disappearance of its distant part would obviously count as a genuine non-local phenomenon. However, most interpreters and commentators of quantum mechanics warn specifically against construing the wave function as having any objective physical existence. Instead, we are instructed to treat it merely as a "calculation device", a mathematical instrument used to compute probabilities.[4] Consequently, the collapse is not to be interpreted as a physical process, and the transition from the function $\Psi$ to its first component $\Psi_1$ ought not to be seen as involving any physical change in the distant area where $\Psi_2$ used to be non-zero.

However, I think that this argument against the genuineness of the non-locality in the case of a single particle is not conclusive, and that by drawing our attention to the issue of the ontological interpretation of the wave function it draws us away from the real source of non-locality here—the interpretation of probability. I can readily agree that the wave function is nothing more but a calculating device to obtain probabilities. The question, however, is how are we supposed to interpret the probabilities obtained in this way. I believe that one unquestionable way of avoiding non-locality is to admit that the probabilities are to be interpreted subjectively, as reflections of our ignorance. But, as Tim Maudlin rightly pointed out, if "these probabilities are not reflections of our ignorance but of a basic indeterminism in nature, then we must take an event's having a particular probability

---

[4]   John Bell, for example, wrote: "One of the apparent non-localities of quantum mechanics is the instantaneous, over all space, 'collapse of the wave function' on 'measurement'. But this does not bother us if we do not grant beable status to the wave function. We can regard it simply as a convenient but inessential mathematical device for formulating correlations between experimental procedures and experimental results" (Bell 1987, p. 23; see also Griffiths 2001, p. 17, p. 261).

as a basic *physical* fact" (Maudlin 1994, p. 147) And an instantaneous change in a basic physical fact on the Moon brought about by a measurement on Earth has to involve some type of non-local influence. Denying this, while accepting some sort of a non-subjective interpretation of quantum probabilities, seems to be intellectually dishonest (Maudlin 1994, p. 148).

The reluctance to see the single-electron case as a strong case of non-locality may also be due to the fact that we don't have here a clear ontological intuition regarding what entity physically constitutes a "bearer" of the property to be non-locally changed. If the probability of the occurrence of the electron on the Moon is an objective physical property, what is it a property of? An electron? This would only muddle the issue, because before the measurement the electron has no defined localization, so how could we be sure that the change in the probability happened on the Moon? After all, the localization of a property should be primarily tied to the localization of its bearer. The possibility of treating the wave function as the bearer of properties has to be excluded because of the above-mentioned arguments against the objective existence of a physical counterpart of the wave function. A possible response to this challenge could be that it is reasonable to accept space-time regions as bearers of the properties reflected in the appropriate ascription of probability. So, under this interpretation, it would count as a property of spatiotemporal region $B$ on the Moon that the probability of the occurrence of the electron there is one-half, and this property of region $B$ would be subsequently changed by the measurement on the Earth. Still, we should agree that the case for non-locality would look stronger, or at least more compelling, if we could find a material object whose physical property would be changed by action-at-a-distance. And this is exactly what happens in the famous EPR case involving two entangled particles.

## 1.2 THE EPR ARGUMENT: INCOMPLETENESS OR NON-LOCALITY?

As it is widely known, Albert Einstein was very keen on showing that quantum theory, although empirically accurate and amazingly fruitful, does not offer a complete description of physical reality. In other words, whenever a quantum formalism presents us with a (non-trivial) probability distribution over a set of possible values of a physical quantity as the ultimate description of a real physical system, we should expect that reality holds more—that the quantity in question is actually characterized by a unique value. In order to argue that this is the case, Einstein together with Podolsky and Rosen turned their attention to what is known as entangled quantum systems (Einstein *et al.* 1935). They noticed that the quantum formalism allows for the existence of pairs of objects whose parameters (observables) $A_1$ and $A_2$ are such that although $A_1$ and $A_2$ may not have separate determinate values, there is a strict functional dependence between their values. As an illustration, they chose two particles whose positions and momentums were correlated as follows: the difference between the location of the first particle $X_1$ and the location of the second particle $X_2$ was guaranteed to be constant ($X_1 - X_2 = a$), and the total momentum of two particles was constant as well ($P_1 + P_2 = b$).

Later, Nils Bohr suggested a thought experiment in which it would be possible to experimentally create a situation like that (Bohr 1935, p. 697). The experiment involves a macroscopic plate with two slits, suspended on springs attached to a rigid frame. When two electrons pass through the slits, their locations relative to the rigid frame are not defined, because the plate can move freely with respect to the frame, while the difference between their relative positions remains determined by the distance between the slits. Hence, if we put a detecting screen right behind the plate and record the position of one electron, we would be able to immediately derive the position of the other electron without detecting it directly. The same applies to the momentum: the recoil of the plate after the passing of the electrons can give us information regarding their total momentum along one axis, so measuring the momentum of one particle in this direction is sufficient to infer the value of the momentum for the second one.

In modern discussions of the EPR argument momentum and position are typically replaced with different components of spin or with polarizations of pairs of photons.[5] This is due to the fact that correlated systems involving position and momentum are very short-lived—the correlation between parameters quickly fades away with the evolution of the system (Dickson 2002). However, the basic idea remains the same. If we create a pair of electrons in the singlet state, in which their total spin equals zero, we can be sure that when we measure the spin of one of them along a specific direction, the spin of the other one in this direction will have to be the opposite. Using this example, we can now reconstruct the original EPR argument aiming to show that the quantum formalism is incomplete. The

---

[5] This reformulation of the EPR argument is due to David Bohm (1951, pp. 611-622).

logical structure of this argument is such that one of its premises expresses the locality assumption, and the conclusion is the thesis that there must be an element of physical reality not described by the standard quantum formalism. The authors invite us to imagine an experiment, performed on one of two electrons created in the singlet state, that measures its spin along an arbitrarily chosen direction $x$. Knowing the result of this experiment, which we can denote as $a$, we can now infer, using the assumption of the perfect correlation between the spins of both particles, that the second electron has to have the opposite spin value along the same direction, which we can write as $\sigma_x^2 = -a$. The crucial thing is that we have arrived at this conclusion without physically interacting with the second electron. In order to ensure that this is the case, we have to appeal to the principle of locality, which forbids the existence of instantaneous influences at a distance. So, at the exact time $t$ when the experiment was performed on the first particle no physical change could occur in the vicinity of the second one. Because the inferred property $\sigma_x^2 = -a$ of the second electron cannot be created by the distant measurement, it must have characterized the electron even before time $t$ (this is the essence of Einstein's so-called criterion of reality). But this plainly shows that the quantum-mechanical description is incomplete, because before the measurement both particles are supposed to be in a totally unpolarized state, i.e. in the state in which the objective probability of obtaining any value of spin in a given direction is ½.

The above sketch of the EPR argument can raise legitimate doubts. The main problem is that it implicitly assumes the existence of absolute simultaneity when it "transfers" the time $t$ of the experiment to the second particle. Yet absolute simultaneity violates the principles on which the entire Einstein's "local" worldview has been built. This drawback can be corrected by introducing the relativistic relation of space-like separation between distant particles. Now we can replace the statement about what property the second electron should possess at the time of the measurement, with the contention that the second electron has to have the $x$-component of its spin defined in all regions which are space-like separated from the measurement. Because according to the relativistic principle of locality no physical signal can connect two space-like separated regions, it can be conjectured that the second electron should have been characterized by the objective property even in the common past of the two particles (this being a relativistic equivalent of the non-relativistic notion of "the moment right before the measurement").

Alternatively, it can be claimed that the same physical characteristic of the second electron, which was inferred but not obtained by any physical interaction with the particle, should also exist in the possible situation in which no measurement was performed on the first particle. This should be intuitively clear when we take into account that, because of the locality assumption, the measurement on the first particle should not make any difference in the distant region of space-time; so it seems legitimate to assume that in a possible situation in which no measurement is performed, all the properties of the second particle would remain the same—including the previously derived element of physical reality pertaining to the $x$-component of spin. The second variant of the EPR argument notably makes use of counterfactual reasoning, entertaining a possible but not actual situation when no measurement is carried out. Whether this argument is in fact valid remains to be seen later, but for the moment let us accept it without further analysis. If we accept the above derivation, then it should be quite clear that it subsequently leads to the incompleteness of quantum mechanics, because with no measurements performed whatsoever the particles are not supposed to have their spins defined. Consequently, the net result of the EPR argument can be presented in the form of the following implication:

(EPR)    Locality $\Rightarrow$ Incompleteness

which is logically equivalent to

(EPR)    Completeness $\Rightarrow$ Non-locality

Let us be more specific as to what the meaning of the Completeness assumption is. It means, basically, that the probabilities provided by quantum-mechanical formalism are all there is to say about reality—that there is no physical reality beyond what is given in the quantum probability distribution. Consequently, quantum systems sometimes do not possess the definitive properties that might meaningfully characterize them at other times. But this amounts precisely to the non-realist viewpoint we talked about earlier. Hence, the result of the EPR argument can be presented as

(EPR)    Anti-realism $\Rightarrow$ Non-locality

If we give up realism, then quantum formalism forces us to abandon locality as well—that is the direct lesson of the EPR argument. However, there still seems to be room to keep both these cherished principles intact. Implication (EPR) does not exclude the possibility that both anti-realism and non-locality could be false. That is exactly what Einstein wanted to argue for. The only thing which is impossible in light of the EPR argument is to have locality while rejecting realism.

## 1.3 BELL'S THEOREM AND THE PLIGHT OF LOCALITY

Unfortunately for Einstein, it turns out that the possibility of the peaceful coexistence between realism, locality and the quantum-mechanical formalism vanishes as a consequence of the famous result achieved by Bell in (1964). Bell's argument proceeded from the hypothetical assumption of realism (in his terminology: hidden variable hypothesis) coupled with the locality principle. In the mathematically simplified version of Bell's argument, popularized by E. Wigner and B. d'Espagnat (Wigner 1970), we start with $N$ pairs of electrons prepared in the same quantum state—namely the previously mentioned singlet state. Let us now select three directions in space $\alpha$, $\beta$, $\gamma$ and consider three components of spin along those directions: $\sigma_\alpha$, $\sigma_\beta$ and $\sigma_\gamma$. According to the realist assumption, all particles in question have their spins pre-defined, so we can divide the sample into eight basic categories, depending on the ascription of one of two possible values (let's symbolize them with + and − signs) to each spin component $\sigma_\alpha$, $\sigma_\beta$, $\sigma_\gamma$. Let us now focus on the following three categories: $(\alpha, \beta)$, $(\beta, \gamma)$ and $(\alpha, \gamma)$, where $(\alpha, \beta)$ denotes all pairs of electrons such that the value of the $\alpha$-component of spin for the first electron is the same as the value of the $\beta$-component for the second one (either both are +, or − ), and the remaining $\gamma$-component has an arbitrary value (either + or −). The remaining symbols are to be interpreted in the same way. Now it is straightforward to notice that the number of the pairs in $(\alpha, \beta)$ can be presented in the following way:

$$N(\alpha, \beta) = N(+,-, +) + N(+,-,-) + N(-, +, +) + N(-, +, -)$$

where a combination of pluses and minuses $(a, b, c)$ denotes a pair of electrons for which the values of spin of the first electron in directions $\alpha$, $\beta$, $\gamma$ equal respectively $a$, $b$, $c$ (hence the values for the second electron are the opposite.) In the same way we can argue that the following equations have to hold:

$$N(\beta, \gamma) = N(+, +, -) + N(-, +, -) + N(+,-, +) + N(-,-, +)$$

and

$$N(\alpha, \gamma) = N(+, +, -) + N(+, -, -) + N(-, +, +) + N(-, -, +).$$

Noticing that each element constituting the definition of $N(\alpha, \beta)$ occurs either in the equation characterizing $N(\beta, \gamma)$ or the equation defining $N(\alpha, \gamma)$ we can arrive at the following inequality:

(1.1)     $N(\alpha, \gamma) \leq N(\alpha, \beta) + N(\beta, \gamma)$

This inequality consists of elements which are not jointly measurable. We have no means of determining simultaneously all spin components for the particles in question. Moreover, numbers like $N(\alpha, \gamma)$ cannot be directly determined by the quantum mechanical formalism, as they are defined in terms of hidden parameters, not described by the standard quantum theory. The only thing the theory is capable of predicting is the probability that if we decide to perform for a given pair of singlet-state electrons a combined measurement of spins $(\sigma_\alpha, \sigma_\beta)$ (or any other combination), the results on both electrons will be the same. This probability has an obvious empirical interpretation—namely it is equal to the relative frequency of cases with joint outcomes being either (+, +) or (−, −), *among all pairs of particles which underwent the joint measurements in the setting* ($\alpha$, $\gamma$). Now the most important question is: can we argue that the quantum mechanical probability (the relative frequency of the occurrence of the same outcomes with respect to the number of particles selected for a particular measurement) is numerically equal to the ratio $N(\alpha, \gamma)/N$, where $N$ denotes the total numbers of prepared electrons, and not only of those which were selected for the measurement? If that is the case, then we can replace the above, non-empirical inequality, with the following, empirically meaningful one:

(1.2)     $P(\alpha, \gamma) \leq P(\alpha, \beta) + P(\beta, \gamma)$

The last inequality can be confronted with quantum-mechanical predictions, as well as directly with experience. It has been verified that there are particular directions $\alpha$, $\beta$, $\gamma$ for which quantum-mechanical predictions significantly violate inequality (1.2). But the question remains, how can we justify the transition from (1.1) to (1.2)? It appears that we have to rely, among others, on a principle evoking the locality assumption. In order to make sure that the outcomes of particular joint measurements on both particles accurately reveal the possessed values that, according to the realist assumption, were already present before the measurement, we have to assume that a distant measurement is incapable of changing the spin value already possessed by the local electron. As unlikely as it may seem, if we allow for a possibility that every now and then when we measure spin in the direction $\alpha$ on the first particle, the second particle's spin suddenly "flips", then the transition from (1.1) to (1.2) is not justified, because what we measure does not reflect exactly what was objectively there before. On the other hand, if we accept locality, and if we add that the local undisturbed measurement always reveals the value objectively possessed by the system beforehand (which seems to be a necessary part of what we mean by a "faithful measurement" and "objectively possessed value"), then the transition from (1.1) to (1.2) is just a matter of a statistically valid inference from a smaller random sample to the whole ensemble. In other words, we can make the statistical error associated with the derivation of (1.2) arbitrarily small by selecting greater and greater numbers of measured particles. In conclusion, the Bell argument seems to lead to the following implication:

(Bell$_1$)   Realism + Locality $\Rightarrow$ Bell's inequality

Knowing that Bell's inequality is violated by quantum-mechanical predictions, we can rewrite (Bell$_1$) as follows

(Bell$_2$)   Realism + Locality $\Rightarrow$ Not-Quantum Mechanics

or, equivalently

(Bell$_2$)   Quantum Mechanics $\Rightarrow$ Anti-Realism or Non-Locality

The above implication expresses the common wisdom regarding the lesson taught by Bell's result. It is widely accepted, especially in popular presentations written by physicists, that Bell's theorem leaves us with two options: either to abandon realism, contrary to Einstein and following

Bohr, or to face non-locality.[6] Confronted with such a choice, physicists usually opt for the first of two evils, sometimes reluctantly adding that a small group of dissenters (with David Bohm in the forefront) decided to follow the second path, rescuing realism at the price of introducing mysterious non-local interactions (for example electrons that "know" instantaneously what is going on in remote parts of the universe). However, surprisingly many philosophers of physics claim that this popular view is deeply incorrect. Quoting Bell himself, who sympathized with the realistic point of view, they say that in fact Bell's proven contradiction with the quantum-mechanical formalism should be diffused by sacrificing locality, no matter what stance one takes regarding the issue of realism (see Maudlin 1994, p. 19; Hawthorn & Silberstein 1995, p. 100; Bell 1987a; 1987c, p. 150). This can be bewildering when we have the result like (Bell₂) above; however, when we couple it with the previously accepted (EPR) things begin to clarify a bit. As we remember, according to (EPR) anti-realism implies non-locality. This means that actually the dilemma given in (Bell₂) is illusory. Combining together (EPR) with (Bell₂), we obtain, with the help of elementary propositional logic, the following implication:

(Bell+EPR)    Quantum Mechanics $\Rightarrow$ Non-Locality

In other words, no matter what you decide about realism, locality has to go. If you opt for realism, the Bell result by itself shows that you have to accept non-locality. And if you reject realism in a futile attempt to rescue locality, the EPR argument moves in and forces you to abandon locality anyway. So it looks like we have eliminated the problem of realism altogether.

Accepting the above conclusion (at least as long as we accept the validity of both EPR and Bell arguments, of which more comes later), I don't think that it exhausts all that can be said regarding the relation between locality and realism in the context of quantum mechanics. True, it looks like locality in one or another form has to be abandoned, but a question remains: What exactly is the nature of the non-locality which is imposed on

---

[6]  Bell himself presented the conclusion of his theorem in the following way: "In a theory in which parameters are added to quantum mechanics to determine the results of individual measurements, without changing the statistical predictions, there must be a mechanism whereby the setting of one measuring device can influence the reading of another instrument, however remote" (Bell 1964, p. 20).

us by the combined forces of the EPR and Bell theorems? And I am going to argue that when we look more closely at the type of non-locality implied by the EPR result and by the Bell theorem, we reach the conclusion that the decision to choose or abandon realism can make a difference after all. But first we have to notice that the non-locality referred to in (EPR) differs significantly from the non-locality implied by the Bell result. Let us first have a look at the EPR case. Einstein claims that when we accept a non-realistic interpretation of quantum mechanics, we have to admit the existence of non-local interactions between distant elements of an entangled system. What kind of non-local influence is it? Remember that the crux of Einstein's argument is that by measuring a given parameter of one particle, we can learn about the value of this parameter for a distant particle. If we agree that before the measurement the value of the observable in question was not determined, then it means that our measurement was capable of changing the state of the distant particle from an indeterminate to a determinate one. Hence we can generally characterize the type of non-locality in question as follows:

(EPR-NonLoc)  A distant measurement can instantaneously alter the state of a particle $p$ from being undetermined with respect to the value of a given parameter $A$ to being characterized by a precise value.

Alternatively, we can formulate the above version of non-locality as admitting that a distant measurement can create an objective element of physical reality that was previously absent (or, alternatively, that was present only "potentially"). The word "distant" is to be understood as denoting the relativistically invariant space-like separation between the act of measurement and the appearance of the precise value on the second particle. As it should be clear, we characterize the type of non-local influences by identifying two elements: the kind of event which can exert non-local influence ("the cause") and the kind of physical change brought about by the non-local influence in question ("the effect"). In the EPR case, the cause is an act of measurement, whereas the effect is a transition from being undetermined to possessing a determinate value.

Let us now turn to the Bell case. In order for the argument to go through, we had to make sure that a distant measurement cannot change a possessed value which is already there. This was the case, because the Bell argument works under the assumption of realism. Hence, the non-locality occurring in the (Bell$_2$) formulation should be interpreted as follows:

(Bell-NonLoc)    A distant measurement can instantaneously alter the state of a particle $p$ from possessing one value of a given parameter $A$ to possessing a different one.[7]

Speaking loosely, Bell-nonlocality allows for changing elements of physical reality, and not just picking them out of the great number of initial possibilities. Now let us look at the consequences of the distinction we have just made. First, we have to observe that by combining (EPR) with (Bell$_2$) we now obtain the following dilemma:

(Bell+EPR′)    Quantum Mechanics $\Rightarrow$ EPR-NonLocality or Bell-NonLocality

Although this formula doesn't mention the viewpoint of realism, it appears that realism plays an important part in our decision as to which non-locality to choose. If we reject realism, then in order to rescue the quantum mechanical formalism we have the option of only accepting the EPR-type non-locality, and rejecting the Bell-type. However, when we opt for realism, we have to accept both types of non-locality—the Bell-type because

---

[7] The idea of distinguishing different versions of the locality condition in the contexts of the EPR argument and Bell's theorem is not a new one. M. Redhead in (1987) formulates one version of the locality condition LOC$_1$ as "An unsharp value for an observable cannot be changed into a sharp value by measurements performed 'at a distance'" (p. 77) which is very similar to my EPR-Loc, and locality condition LOC$_3$ as "A sharp value for an observable cannot be changed into another sharp value by altering the setting of a remote piece of apparatus" (p. 82), closely resembling my Bell-Loc. A. Fine, in turn, speaks directly about Bell-locality versus Einstein-locality; however his way of characterizing them differs somehow from the definitions I am proposing (Fine 1986, pp. 59-60). For Fine the main difference between these two types of locality lies in the fact that according to Einstein locality excludes the possibility of influencing the "real" physical state of a distant system, while in the context of Bell's theorem the locality implies only the impossibility of changing outcomes of measurements for quantum observables from a distance. Using his distinction Fine argues next that Bell's result does not directly affect Einstein's locality, as it may be maintained that quantum observables do not represent real physical states of systems. It seems to me that this is a pretty desperate way of defending Einstein, implying that quantum-mechanical "measurements" actually don't measure anything real.

of the dilemma contained in (Bell$_2$), and the EPR-type because of the implication (EPR). In conclusion, it looks like rejecting or accepting realism does make a difference to the issue of locality. This observation is all the stronger when we note that EPR-nonlocality seems to be weaker than Bell-nonlocality. In other words, the departure from the classical, local world is probably less radical in case of the acceptance of the former than the latter. EPR-nonlocality allows the determining of a parameter when it has no prior value; once this value is defined, however, EPR-nonlocality doesn't by itself allow changing it. To put it differently, EPR-nonlocality leaves room for a limited locality principle, in which it is maintained that no distant influence can instantaneously change a definite, existent element of reality. Using philosophical terminology we may say that non-local interactions can only transform potentiality into actuality, but not one actuality into another one.[8] On the other hand, the Bell-type non-locality goes further in violating our ontological intuitions: an objective, possessed characteristic of a physical system can be changed from far away. Later on we will see that this off-hand assessment can be supported by a counterfactual analysis of both the Bell and EPR versions of non-locality. If the above argument is correct, there may be a philosophical basis for rejecting realism and, thanks to that, admitting only a minimal version of non-locality.

## 1.4 GENERALIZED BELL'S THEOREM

The above conclusion from the joint EPR and Bell arguments does not exclude a possibility that there may be other arguments that directly show strong non-locality of quantum mechanics, with no reference to the realist assumption whatsoever. One such argument was actually proposed and analyzed by Bell himself (Bell 1987b, pp. 53-62; 1987c, pp. 150-153).[9] His goal was to produce the most general inference possible that would proceed from some version of the locality principle without any additional, philosophically "suspicious" premises, such as the principle of realism (in Bell's terminology "determinism")[10], the condition of perfect correlation,

---

[8]  Shimony uses the same terminology in (1986, p. 153).

[9]  A particularly elegant exposition of this version of Bell's theorem, with an extensive discussion of its consequences for the issue of non-locality, and containing a section illustrating experimental methods of its verification, can be found in (Shimony 1990).

[10]  The common, yet philosophically peculiar practice of using interchangeably the terms "determinism" and "realism" in the context of quantum mechanics can be

or even the assumption that there are some objective and physically separated particles involved. The conclusion of this inference was supposed to be a result (in the form of an inequality) that violated quantum-mechanical predictions. If successful, this argument would show unambiguously that the principle of locality is untenable, as the assumption of realism is actually irrelevant to the derivation of the contradiction, and that, therefore, one is free to accept or reject realism according to one's own ontological preferences.

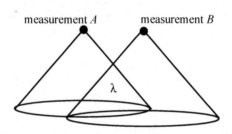

Figure 1.1 Spatiotemporal layout of measurements in the generalized Bell theorem.

The initial assumptions of the argument in question are very parsimonious indeed. We have to presuppose only that there are two spatially separated measuring devices, capable of recording outcomes of measurements for two sets of observables, each set associated with one measuring device. Let us denote by $A$ and $B$ the two particular observables that can be measured, respectively, by our two devices, and let us use lower-case let-

---

explained by pointing out that the apparent indeterministic character of quantum mechanics reveals itself only in measurements. As it is well known, quantum mechanics is a deterministic theory when it comes to the description of the state evolution of a system which is not subject to measurement, meaning that the initial state at time $t$ uniquely determines all later states, given the Hamiltonian governing all existing physical interactions. However, this determinism applies only to states understood as probability distributions. When a measurement which aims to reveal a precise value of a given parameter is performed, the transition from the initial state to the final state is believed to be stochastic. If, in spite of this, one insists that the value revealed in the measurement should have characterized the system beforehand (realism), then one is committed to the view that the measurement-induced transition is actually purely deterministic. (To avoid possible confusion, some authors use the term "determinateness" instead of "determinism"—cf Maudlin 2003, pp. 470-472).

ters $a$ and $b$ to indicate the results of the measurements (we assume that each measurement can yield one of two numerical values +1 or –1 as its outcome). The quantum system that is about to be subjected to this double measurement has to be created at a certain moment, lying in the absolute past of both acts of measurement (in other words, it has to be located in the intersection of the two backward light cones, each defined by the appropriate measurement) (see Fig. 1.1). Now let us assume that the letter $\lambda$ represents a complete description of the physical state of the quantum system at the moment of its creation. No specific hypothesis as to what this complete description can look like is necessary here. In fact, the generality of the result we are about to present relies on not deciding what kind of "hidden variables" the parameter $\lambda$ describes. In particular, $\lambda$ can be seen as determining completely and accurately outcomes of all of the measurements in question (so-called "deterministic hidden variables"), or only the objective probabilities of particular outcomes ("stochastic hidden variables"). One example of such a description $\lambda$ can simply be a standard quantum-mechanical state as given with the help of the wave function $\Psi$. In that case $\lambda$ would be obviously stochastic. Without deciding the particular nature of the description $\lambda$, we will nevertheless assume that $\lambda$ is *complete*, i.e. that there is nothing more in the physical situation of the common past that is relevant to the future outcomes of experiments.

The single mathematically formulated assumption on which the entire generalized argument hinges is the following relation concerning the probabilities of the measurements outcomes:

(F) $\qquad P(a, b| A, B, \lambda) = P(a| A, \lambda)\, P(b| B, \lambda)$[11]

We will call this equation the "factorization assumption", although it is known in the literature under various names.[12] It specifies that the probability of the joint results $a$, $b$ of measurements $A$ and $B$ for a system in the initial state $\lambda$ can be presented as the product of two independent probabilities: that the result of the first measurement $A$ is $a$, and the second $B$ is $b$. Equation (F) evokes the well-known definition of stochastically independ-

---

[11] The exact nature of the conditional probabilities used in this expression will be discussed later.

[12] It was A. Fine who coined the term "factorizability" to refer to condition (F) (Fine, 1981). J. Jarrett in turn calls it "strong locality" (Jarrett 1984, 1989). Some authors use the longer but obviously uncontroversial term "conditional stochastic independence".

ent events, and therefore can be seen as expressing the idea of the nonexistence of causal influences between the two measurements in question; however, we will have to return to the question of its proper interpretation later. For the moment let us examine where this equation leads us. It appears that (F) itself implies mathematically a simple restriction on the expectation values of the products of the two measurement outcomes. Suppose that we have chosen two observables (two "settings") $A$ and $A'$ for the left-hand side apparatus, and two observables $B$, $B'$ for the right-hand side. Let $E(A, B)$ denote the expectation value (the average) of the product of results for both observables. This expectation value is calculated as the sum

$$E(A, B) = \sum_{i,j} P(a_i, b_j \mid A, B) a_i b_j$$

where the probabilities $P(a_i, b_j \mid A, B)$ are given as the averages over all possible values of the parameter $\lambda$:

$$P(a, b \mid A, B) = \int P(a, b \mid A, B, \lambda) \rho(\lambda) d\lambda$$

With the help of the factorization assumption (F), it is a matter of a relatively simple derivation to arrive at the following inequality (known as the Clauser-Holt-Shimony-Horne inequality)[13]:

(CHSH)     $|E(A, B) + E(A, B') + E(A', B) - E(A', B')| \leq 2$

As was the case with the original Bell inequality, it turns out that there are observables $A$, $A'$, $B$, $B'$ for which quantum-mechanical predictions violate the above equation. In particular, we can choose suitable components of spin such that the right-hand side of the above inequality will have the numerical value of 2½, which is a significant departure from the predicted value of less or equal to 2. So the contradiction with the quantum-mechanical formalism has been achieved.

The above result can be significant for the purpose of proving the non-locality of quantum mechanics only if we are able to give a clear, unambi-

---

[13]   This inequality can be derived in a more standard way, using assumptions of locality and realism, exactly as in the original Bell theorem. See (Clauser *et al.* 1969; Redhead 1987, pp. 82-84) and sec. 3.1 in this book for more details.

guous interpretation of the condition (F) and its connections with the issue of non-locality. Unfortunately, this is not an easy matter. Let us start first with the original derivation of factorization proposed by Bell. Bell claims that (F) is a consequence of another ontological principle, which he dubs "the principle of local causality" (Bell 1987b, p. 54). Its non-mathematical expression can be presented as follows: all causes of a particular event must lie in its backward (past) light cone (see Maudlin 1994, p. 90). Due to the notorious ambiguity of the word "cause", the aforementioned principle has to be given a more precise formulation. The proposal here is to use once again the notion of the conditional probability. Suppose that we have a particular event $E$, and let us denote by $\Gamma$ the complete physical description of the entire past light cone of $E$. Then, once $\Gamma$ is assumed to be known, no additional information can be relevant to the probability of the occurrence of $E$—this can be expressed as:

(LC) $\quad P(E \mid \Gamma, \Delta) = P(E \mid \Gamma)$

where $\Delta$ denotes any additional information about physical reality. $\Delta$ can for instance include the complete description of a space-time region not overlapping with the past light cone of $E$. We should arguably exclude the possibility that $\Delta$ refers to the absolute future of event $E$, for conditionalizing on future, yet unrealized events may change the initial probability without violating the idea of non-locality (for example, taking into account the outcomes of future measurements could dramatically change my evaluations of the current probability distribution over possible values).[14] So, let us assume that $\Delta$ can refer only to the regions space-like separated from event $E$.

The condition (LC) obviously does not exclude the possibility that there may be observable statistical correlations between space-like separated systems. In other words, we can change our estimation of the probability for a given event on receiving information about distant systems. But this may happen only if we don't have the complete knowledge of the causal past of the event in question.[15] In other words, the only admissible reason

---

[14]   To put it more succinctly: if we agreed that the symbol $\Delta$ is to be interpreted as referring to future events as well, then the only way of satisfying (LC) would be by postulating deterministic hidden variables which would imply that $P(E \mid \Gamma)$ equals either 0 or 1.

[15]   To illustrate this point, we may use Jarrett's example (1989, p. 72). When we estimate the probability that a particular person will have a heart attack, the

for such pseudo non-local correlations may be that they are due to a common cause in the absolute past. Once all the relevant facts from the past are taken into account, the space-like separated events should become statistically "screened-off".[16] In connection with this point we can raise the question about the nature of the probability function used in (LC): should we interpret it subjectively, objectively, as the relative frequency, or maybe in an entirely different fashion? It seems natural that if we conditionalize on the complete physical state of the system in the absolute past of $E$, then we do not have to restrict our interpretation of probability to a subjective one. Hence, we will accept that the probabilities in (LC) are to be interpreted objectively, as the only and ultimate description available which is relevant to the occurrence of event $E$. Subjective probabilities reflect our ignorance, but probabilities conditional on complete knowledge should reflect no less than the objective "propensities" or tendencies existing in physical reality.[17]

Now, we have to make sure that the factorization condition (F) is derivable from (LC). Let us start with the left-hand side of the equation (F), which can be presented equivalently as

$$P(a, b| A, B, \lambda) = P(a \mid A, B, b, \lambda)\, P(b \mid A, B, \lambda)$$

(by the rules of the probability calculus, including the definition of conditional probability). We would like to take out the conditionalization on $B$ and $b$ from the first factor in the product, as well as the conditionalization on $A$ from the second one. Can we do this on the basis of the local causality principle (LC)? In order to appeal directly to (LC) we have to assume

---

information that the person regularly buys jogging shoes may influence our judgment. However, the negative statistical correlation in question is not due to a causal connection between buying a pair of jogging shoes and avoiding a heart attack, but is a result of the existence of a common factor, namely regular exercising, which at the same time causally lowers the probability of a heart attack and is statistically positively correlated with possessing athletic equipment.

[16] Hans Reichenbach (1956) was the first to introduce the notion of the "common cause" using the screening-off condition. See also (van Fraassen 1982, Bigaj 2003a).

[17] This agrees with the standard way of treating probabilities in quantum mechanics (see e.g. Jarrett 1985, p. 586, footnote 6). However, we have to admit that probability interpreted as a dispositional property creates many conceptual difficulties, as presented in (Sklar 1970 and 1979). For an excellent survey of other interpretations of probability, see a chapter in the same author's book (Sklar 1993, pp. 96-120) .

that the complete description $\Gamma$ of the absolute past of the outcome $a$ is given by totally specifying the common past of the two measurements (parameter $\lambda$) and by specifying the setting of the measurement $A$: $\Gamma = \lambda + A$. Maudlin in (1994, p. 91) seems to agree that we can make use of (LC) only if we assume that the sole physical event statistically relevant to the outcome and located in the part of the backward light cone of the measurement outside the common past is the choice of the setting of the first detector (observable $A$). Once we agree on that, we can eliminate factors $B$ and $b$ from $P(a \mid A, B, b, \lambda)$. Obviously, by symmetry the same applies to the second measurement and outcome $b$. However, this seemingly insignificant detail can in fact ruin the entire generalized argument against locality, as an ardent proponent of the local causality principle (LC) may claim that the resulting inequality (CHSH) contravening quantum mechanics is not due to the failure of (LC), but due to the above-mentioned minor assumption. After all, it is quite reasonable (and compatible with the relativity) to expect that physical processes that take place in the proximity of the measurement may affect its outcome, even if they do not belong to the common past of both measurements. If that is the case, then (LC) can be applied only when we take as our complete description $\Gamma$ not only $\lambda + A$, but also all possibly relevant states of affairs localized in the absolute past of measurement $A$ but outside $\lambda$. However, the expression $P(a \mid A, B, b, \lambda)$ conditionalizes only on $A$ and $\lambda$, so (LC) is not directly applicable, and therefore the derivation of the factorization condition (F) fails.

There is no question that the factorization principle (F) by itself represents an intuition bordering on the locality of causal influences, and the CHSH inequality shows that this intuition has to be abandoned. But, in the light of the above-mentioned difficulties associated with an attempt to derive (F) from the more fundamental principle (LC), the question about the proper interpretation of (F) becomes more pressing. Precisely what kind of non-local influences has to be admitted? As we recall, with the Bell and EPR arguments we had a choice between the weaker EPR-nonlocality and the stronger Bell-nonlocality. Now it appears that it is possible to analyze the principle (F) into similar components. In what follows we will review and discuss the famous attempt to distinguish two elements in the general factorization condition developed by Jon Jarrett.

It is easy to prove that the factorization is equivalent to the conjunction of the two following principles:

(I)     $P(a \mid A, B, \lambda) = P(a \mid A, \lambda)$
        $P(b \mid A, B, \lambda) = P(b \mid B, \lambda)$

(II)    $P(a \mid A, B, b, \lambda) = P(a \mid A, B, \lambda)$
        $P(b \mid A, B, a, \lambda) = P(b \mid A, B, \lambda)$

Obviously, when we combine (I) and (II) we can take out all conditionalization on distant measurements and outcomes without changing the numerical values of the probabilities: $P(a \mid A, B, b, \lambda) = P(a \mid A, \lambda)$ and $P(b \mid A, B, a, \lambda) = P(b \mid B, \lambda)$. Hence, the factorization (F) follows immediately. But the crucial thing is to analyze the physical meaning of these two principles. The most commonly used nomenclature already reveals the meaning typically associated with those conditions: condition (I) is namely referred to as "parameter independence", and (II) as "outcome independence".[18] Parameter independence supposedly expresses the idea that the physical state of one system (encapsulated in the objective probabilities of the possible measurement outcomes) cannot be influenced by the choice of an observable ("parameter") to be measured for the other, distant system. The principle (II), on the other hand, seemingly amounts to the assertion that the outcome of the distant measurement cannot influence the physical state of the local system. Under this interpretation, both principles (I) and (II) represent some instances of the general locality principle. Surprisingly, however, this is not quite the way Jarrett interpreted them originally. According to his terminology, the first condition bears the name of "the locality condition", but he calls the second "completeness". Jarrett's point is that only violation of the principle (I) poses a threat to the fundamental principles of the relativity, as it allows for the possibility of the existence of superluminal signaling. The violation of completeness, on the other hand, does not allow for any signaling, for we have no control over what outcome will be revealed by a particular measurement.

The motivation behind Jarrett's choice of the term "completeness" may be that when (II) is violated, it means that the separate descriptions of the two components of the system in terms of outcome probabilities are going to be incomplete, as they will not contain any information about the mutual correlations between the distant outcomes. This can be illustrated with the help of the standard case of two electrons in the singlet spin state. Assuming, for the sake of argument, that the hidden variable $\lambda$ contains only the

---

[18]    This terminology was introduced by A. Shimony in his (1986).

usual quantum-mechanical state, we can notice that the probability functions $P(a \mid A, \lambda)$ and $P(b \mid B, \lambda)$ do not contain the entire available information about the system, for they totally ignore the fact that the outcome $a$ of the measurement of $A$ will be always correlated with the opposite outcome $b$ of the measurement of $B$.

These above remarks may explain the motivation behind the terminology proposed by Jarrett, but his terminology seems to suggest that it is possible to avert the inevitable demise of the locality principle at the price of rejecting "completeness".[19] This may look (intentionally or not) like a repetition of the EPR argument, but this impression is thoroughly misguided. Jarrett's completeness has in fact very little in common with Einstein's one, in spite of his own remarks in this matter (see Jarrett 1989, p. 73; Hughes p. 243). Moreover, no terminology can obscure the fact that the denial of the principle (II) entails some ontological non-locality. If (II) is false, it means that the complete state of the absolute past of the measurement does not fully determine the probability distribution of the possible outcomes but that this objective probability distribution depends ultimately (and not through a common cause) on some physical facts space-like separated from the measurement itself. Hence, we have to agree with the common view that both principles (I) and (II) are relevant to the issue of locality, although it may be argued that the negation of (I) constitutes a greater departure from the idea of locality than the negation of (II).

## 1.5 OUTCOME-LOCALITY AND PARAMETER-LOCALITY

Tim Maudlin seems to agree with the view that both principles (I) and (II) involve ideas that bear on the issue of locality. However, he is generally suspicious as to the correctness of their standard interpretations. His main argument against treating (I) as expressing "parameter independence", and (II) "outcome independence", as well as—as I see it—generally against splitting the factorization principle (F) into two components, is that the combination (I) and (II) does not offer a unique way of representing (F). Maudlin points out that we can formulate two alternative principles, different from (I) and (II), whose conjunction is logically equivalent to (F), and

---

[19] This is precisely the conclusion in Jarrett's 1984 article (p. 585). In his later paper (1989) however, while still maintaining that only completeness should be abandoned, he admits that "incompleteness [...] appears to represent a connectedness of some sort between spatially distant events, which nevertheless does not directly contradict relativity" (p. 77)

which supposedly can express the ideas of "parameter independence" and "outcome independence" equally well as (I) and (II). Here is what they look like according to Maudlin (1984, p. 95):

(I')     $P(a \mid A, B, b, \lambda) = P(a \mid A, b, \lambda)$
         $P(b \mid A, B, a, \lambda) = P(b \mid B, a, \lambda)$

(II')    $P(a \mid A, b, \lambda) = P(a \mid A, \lambda)$
         $P(b \mid B, a, \lambda) = P(b \mid B, \lambda)$

To see that with equations (I') and (II') we can get (F), we should observe that they allow us to take out the conditionalization on $A$ from $P(b \mid A, B, \lambda)$. According to the law of total probability we have

$$P(b \mid A, B, \lambda) = \sum_i P(b \mid A, B, a_i, \lambda) P(a_i \mid A, B, \lambda)$$

(where $a_i$'s are different outcomes of the measurement of $A$, and therefore constitute a set of mutually exclusive and jointly exhaustive events). But using (I') and (II') we can replace $P(b \mid A, B, a_i, \lambda)$ with $P(b \mid B, \lambda)$, and because the sum $\Sigma_i P(a_i \mid A, B, \lambda)$ equals 1, we finally get $P(b \mid A, B, \lambda) = P(b \mid B, \lambda)$. Once we have this result, we can see that (F) is easily derivable from the formula $P(a, b \mid A, B, \lambda) = P(a \mid A, B, b, \lambda) P(b \mid A, B, \lambda)$.

Having proven that (I') and (II') imply (F), we have now to turn to the issue of their proper "physical" interpretation. Maudlin maintains that (I') deserves to be named "parameter independence", because it allows us to eliminate conditionalization on the distant measurement, and (II') can be seen as expressing the outcome independence, because it shows that conditionalization on the distant outcome is irrelevant for the probability of the local outcome. However, (I') is not equivalent to (I), and (II') is not equivalent to (II). As Maudlin points out, standard quantum mechanics (under the supposition that $\lambda$ contains only available quantum-mechanical description of the state) violates (I') but obeys (I), and violates (II) but obeys (II'). Hence if Maudlin is right, our basic ideas of what constitutes outcome independence and parameter independence are fundamentally ambiguous.

I don't agree with the aforementioned conclusion for quite straightforward reasons. It seems to me quite clear that equations (I') and (II') do not represent any physically significant conditions which could be interpreted in an analogous way to the way principles (I) and (II) are commonly interpreted. To see this, let us first focus on equations (II′), supposedly expressing the idea of independence on the distant outcome. Equations (II′) state that the information about the outcome of an *unspecified* distant measurement is statistically irrelevant to the probability of a given outcome of the local measurement. In other words, if we considered all cases of combined measurements such that the first apparatus is set to measure $A$, but the second apparatus records a given value $b$ no matter what the setting is (what observable $B$ is being measured), then the outcome $a$ will occur in the same fraction of cases as in the entire population of cases. But now the question is: what is the physical significance of the outcome of an unspecified measurement? To say that the second apparatus registered the value $-1$, without mentioning what particular observable was being measured carries no meaningful physical information. *The very notion of an outcome is meaningful only when it is coupled with the specification of what it is an outcome of.* Hence if we look for a clear-cut, physically meaningful description of a distant factor which may be responsible for an instantaneous, non-local change, we should not use the notion of the outcome of an unknown measurement. Such outcomes simply don't constitute legitimate physical events.[20]

Similar objections can be raised against principle (I′). Taken at face value, (I′) says that conditionalization on a distant measurement (setting) is statistically irrelevant, provided that the result of this measurement is fixed. In other words, we are comparing cases in which a particular measurement is performed and the result is such and such, with cases in which any possible measurement is taken, *but the result remains numerically the same*. But, once again this means that we assign physical significance to "dangling" outcomes; outcomes detached from their appropriate measuring procedures. After all, that is exactly what happens on the right-hand side of equations (I′): we are asked to entertain the probability of a given outcome under the supposition that the distant result is known, but without specifying the procedure leading to this result. It is, therefore, highly doubtful that the principles (I′) and (II′) could express any clear idea of locality with respect to distant outcomes and distant settings.

However, this is not to say that conditions (I) and (II) are crystal-clear. On the contrary—Maudlin's example teaches us that we should be extremely careful in attaching physical or philosophical meaning to otherwise

---

[20] A similar point is emphasized in (Dickson 1998, pp. 135, 137).

meaningful mathematical formulas. And it appears that there is certain amount of confusion associated with the proper interpretation of the statistical independence conditions given in (I) and (II). For example, Maudlin himself gives the following characteristics of (I) and (II), apparently reporting them as a commonly accepted interpretation: "parameter independence holding if the act of setting the distant device has no distant causal role; outcome independence holding if the measurement event itself has no distant effects." (Maudlin 1994, p. 95) However, this is somewhat surprising. Usually, when we talk about outcome independence, we have in mind the fact that somehow the last phase of the measurement process, i.e. that the recording or determining in any way of *a particular* outcome has no bearing on the distant state of affairs. And yet Maudlin speaks about the whole process of measurement. But, if this is correct, why call this "outcome independence", and not "measurement independence"? The proposed characteristic of parameter independence is no less confusing, in spite of being quite persistent in the literature. What do we mean by "setting the distant device" or, as it is sometimes put, "preparing the device"? The usual interpretation is that this setting amounts, for example, to the spatial orientation of a Stern-Gerlach magnet, so that it is ready to measure the spin of an incoming electron in a suitable direction. But let us suppose that for some reason the right-hand electron didn't get to the measuring device (it was absorbed by an atom, or scattered away by some passing particle). Would we count such a case in order to empirically calculate the probability given in the left-hand side of equations (I)? It seems that in order to calculate $P(a \mid A, B, \lambda)$, we have to make sure not only that the distant apparatus was ready to measure $B$, but that it *actually* measured it (that the electron was fed in, and got reflected either up or down, although we don't know which).[21]

It appears then that we have to devote more effort to the task of properly interpreting the formulas given in (I) and (II) than it has been thus far. We have to make precise the meaning associated with the different conditionalizations of the probabilities on various parameters that we have taken for

---

[21] It speaks volumes that other authors display a certain amount of hesitation when characterizing physically both conditions (I) and (II). For example R.I.G. Hughes interprets explicitly symbol $A$ as "$A$-measurement is performed on an electron" (Hughes 1989, p. 244); however, when he explains the meaning of the conditionalization in (I) he uses the notorious phrase "given certain settings of the measurement apparatuses" (ibid.). One cannot help but wonder whether authors like Hughes intentionally blur the distinction between preparing measuring devices and actually performing the measurement.

granted so far. We will start this clarification with a confession: the formulas which have been used throughout our current discussion have actually been oversimplified in comparison with Jarrett's original article (1984). This oversimplification is quite common in the literature, nevertheless it can obscure certain important issues and cause misunderstandings. In order to have a firm grasp on expressions like $P(a, b| A, B, \lambda)$, used freely in all discussions on the Bell theorem, we have to precisely define our probability space and probability function first. As we remember, our experimental setup consists of two measuring devices, each of which may be prepared in different settings. Let us denote by $A_i$ $(B_i)$ all the possible settings of the measuring devices (left and right, respectively). To these we will have to add one more state of the devices: it is possible that a device is simply turned off—not prepared for measuring any observable (any component of spin). We will symbolize by $0^A$ and $0^B$ the states of the left-hand side and the right-hand side apparatuses in which they do not measure any observable. Hence the set of all states for the left-hand side device will be $M^A = \{0^A, A_i\}$ (and $M^B = \{0^B, B_i\}$ for the right-hand side apparatus).

Analogously, we will define the sets of possible outcomes. Each device can record two "normal" outcomes $+1$ and $-1$. To this we will once again add a non-standard "outcome" 0, associated with the non-measuring state of the apparatus. Hence the set of possible outcomes for the left-hand side device will be $O^A = \{+1^A, -1^A, 0^A\}$ (and $O^B = \{+1^B, -1^B, 0^B\}$ for the other system). Subsequently, we will omit superscripts whenever it doesn't lead to ambiguities. Any theory that aspires to give a complete description of the physical reality in our example should produce probabilities of the following sort:

(P)      $P(a, b| A_i, B_j, \lambda)$

where $\lambda$, as usual, denotes the complete initial state of the system. The formula above uses the standard mathematical symbol for conditional probability, but the actual meaning of this conditionalization has to be quite non-standard. In particular, we cannot resort to the formal definition of the conditional probability in order to explain the meaning of the probability function given above. The standard definition gives the following explication for (P):

$$\frac{P(a,b,A_i,B_j \mid \lambda)}{P(A_i,B_j \mid \lambda)}$$

but the probabilities $P(A_i, B_j \mid \lambda)$ cannot be calculated within the underlying theory. The decision to choose a particular setting of the device is made freely by an experimenter, and although in principle it is possible to select settings $A_i$ and $B_j$ randomly according to a previously defined statistical distribution, the resulting probabilities will be essentially extraneous with respect to the theory governing the behavior of the system in question (see Dickson 1998, p. 136 for a similar appraisal). For that reason it is better to interpret the conditionalization given in (P) as merely amounting to a *parameterization* of the probability function.[22] In other words, the formula (P) should be actually read as describing a class of independent probability functions, each of which defines the probabilities of particular outcomes *in a given experimental setting*, as in the following notation:

(P′)     $P_\lambda^{ij}(a,b)$

Remembering that only (P′) provides the proper interpretation for the formulas (P), we will nevertheless continue using the conditionalization symbol ("the stroke"), as it is commonly done in literature. The domain on which functions (P′) are defined consists obviously of four values: $\{\langle+1, +1\rangle, \langle+1, -1\rangle, \langle-1, +1\rangle, \langle-1, -1\rangle\}$. Now, as we remember, the formulation of both locality conditions (I) and (II) requires probabilities "conditionalized" only on one measurement: $P(a \mid A_i, \lambda)$. How are we supposed to interpret these expressions? Let us start by presenting the standard interpretation of probabilities for only one selected outcome, given two settings of the measuring devices: $P(a \mid A_i, B_j, \lambda)$. This function is obtained by simply summing the function (P) over all possible results of measurement $B_j$: $\Sigma_b P(a, b \mid A_i, B_j, \lambda)$. However, the question remains how we can "eliminate" the second conditionalization on measurement $B_j$. The standard probabilistic equation

$$P(a \mid A_i, \lambda) = \sum_j P(a \mid A_i, B_j, \lambda) P(B_j \mid a, A_i, \lambda)$$

---

[22] In the 1984 article Jarrett used no conditional probabilities. However, he adopted a terminology based on conditional probabilities in his later 1989 paper without much explanation.

won't work for the purpose of explicating the expression $P(a|\ A_i,\ \lambda)$, because of meaningless probabilities $P(B_j|\ a,\ A_i,\ \lambda)$ of particular settings of the apparatus. In order to give the function $P(a|\ A_i,\ \lambda)$ an acceptable interpretation we have to make use of the extra state of the measuring devices, the non-measuring setting, and to stipulate that $P(a|\ A_i,\ \lambda)$ is meant to actually represent the following probability: $P(a|\ A_i,\ 0^B,\ \lambda)$, which in turn is identical to $P(a,\ 0|\ A_i,\ 0^B,\ \lambda)$. Hence, our class of probability functions has to be extended to include the following:

(P″)    $P(a,\ 0|\ A_i,\ 0^B,\ \lambda)$
         $P(0,\ b|\ 0^A,\ B_j,\ \lambda)$

Functions (P″) are defined on the following domains: $\{\langle +1, 0\rangle, \langle -1, 0\rangle\}$ and $\{\langle 0, +1\rangle, \langle 0, -1\rangle\}$, respectively. Their empirical meaning is quite straightforward – they numerically represent relative frequencies of a particular outcome of one measurement in case the other measuring device is simply turned off.

With these preparatory stipulations in hand, we can now turn to the task of the reinterpretation of the two components (I) and (II) of the factorization condition. The full version of the so-called parameter independence condition can now be expressed as follows:

(PI)    $P(a,\ 0|\ A_i,\ 0^B,\ \lambda) = \sum_b P(a, b\ |\ A_i, B_j, \lambda)$

The formula expressing the outcome independence will be a little more complicated. In order to avoid possible confusion, let us proceed in steps. The original version of the principle was:

(II)    $P(a|\ A_i, B_j, b, \lambda) = P(a|\ A_i, B_j, \lambda)$

The right-hand side of the equation has a suppressed summation over all the possible results of measurement $B_j$. The left-hand side in turn contains the new element on which the probability is conditional (namely the outcome $b$), and as it turns out it can be interpreted with the help of the usual definition of conditional probability (all elements in the definiens are meaningful). This brings us to the following reformulation:

(OI)   $$\frac{P(a,b \mid A_i, B_j, \lambda)}{P(b \mid A_i, B_j, \lambda)} = \sum_b P(a,b \mid A_i, B_j, \lambda)$$

Now, we can introduce the suppressed summation in the denominator of the left-hand side fraction. The resulting equation will look like this (compare Howard 1997, p. 127):

(OI)   $$P(a, b \mid A_i, B_j, \lambda) = \sum_a P(a,b \mid A_i, B_j, \lambda) \sum_b P(a,b \mid A_i, B_j, \lambda)$$

Finally, we can give the full version of the factorization condition. You can easily verify that its precise formulation should look like this:

(F)   $$P(a, b \mid A_i, B_j, \lambda) = P(a, 0 \mid A_i, 0^B, \lambda)\, P(0, b \mid 0^A, B_j, \lambda)$$

So we have achieved our first goal: we have presented all three conditions in a uniform language containing only well defined, empirically meaningful probabilistic functions of the kind presented in (P) and (P''). This should help us to gain a better understanding of the physical and philosophical meaning behind these conditions.

However, the task is not yet complete. The problem is that we would like to understand exactly what types of non-local influence are associated with the negation of each condition (PI) and (OI). The analysis of these influences should preferably be given, as was the case with Bell-locality vs. Einstein-locality, in terms of "what causes what" (what kind of action on the distant system triggers what changes in the local one). Let us start with parameter independence (or the "proper" locality, as Jarrett would put it). The left-hand side of the equation (PI) represents, most typically, the objective probability ("propensity") of obtaining outcome $a$ of measurement $A_i$ when no measurement is performed on the other system (with the "null" outcome). The right-hand side is usually interpreted, as we already indicated several times, as the probability of the same outcome $a$ given that the measurement of $B_j$ is performed on the distant particle. Hence, the typical interpretation associated with the negation of (PI) is that by selecting a particular observable for measurement we can change the objective state of the distant system (represented by the probability function) as compared with the situation when no measurement is performed. But is this really the correct interpretation? Several objections against this standard elucidation can be put forward. To begin with, we already know that the probability

$P(a|\ A_i, B_j, \lambda)$ is not a probability 'in its own right', but, rather, is defined as the sum of two more basic probabilities: $P(a, +1|\ A_i, B_j, \lambda) + P(a, -1|\ A_i, B_j, \lambda)$. Hence, it can hardly be seen as an objective characterization of the state of the distant system in the case where the observable $B_j$ is chosen to be measured. A more accurate explication would be that $P(a|\ A_i, B_j, \lambda)$ can represent our subjective estimation of the probability of outcome $a$ when we know that the measurement $B_j$ has been performed, but we don't know its outcome. In other words, $P(a|\ A_i, B_j, \lambda)$ would merely reflect our ignorance rather than the objective propensity determining the likelihood of obtaining outcome $a$. But if that is the case, then the above "ontological" interpretation of not-(PI) has to be reconsidered.

Let us illustrate this point with an artificially created example. Suppose that the "initial" probability of a particular outcome $a$ for the measurement $A_i$ when no measurement is performed on the other system (given all the available knowledge about the past of both systems, of course) equals $P(a, 0|\ A_i, 0^B, \lambda) = \frac{1}{2}$. Moreover, let us assume that when the distant measurement of $B_j$ reveals +1 the probability of obtaining $a$ in the situation is given the numerical value

$$P(a|\ A_i, B_j, b = +1, \lambda) = \frac{3}{4},$$

and let's similarly stipulate that, when $B_j$ yields $-1$,

$$P(a|\ A_i, B_j, b = -1, \lambda) = \frac{3}{8}.$$

Finally, we will assign particular values to the conditional probabilities of obtaining the results +1 and −1 in the $B_j$ measurement:

$$P(b = +1|\ A_i, B_j, \lambda) = \frac{1}{3} \text{ and } P(b = -1|\ A_i, B_j, \lambda) = \frac{2}{3}$$

(these numbers obviously have to add up to one). With these numerical values of the probabilities in question, it is not difficult to verify that the probabilities $P(a, +1|\ A_i, B_j, \lambda)$ and $P(a, -1|\ A_i, B_j, \lambda)$ will both equal ¼, so $P(a|\ A_i, B_j, \lambda) = \frac{1}{2}$. Thus the equation (PI) remains satisfied, which may be interpreted as expressing the fact that the choice of a distant measurement has no influence on the local outcome. But let us consider the individual case of two particles, such that the first underwent the measurement of $A_i$ with the result $a$, and the second was subject to the measurement of $B_j$. Are we justified in the claim that in this particular, singular case the state of the first particle just before its measurement is exactly the same as in the situation when no measurement is made on the other particle? After all, measurement $B_j$ has to reveal some precise outcome, even if we don't know what it will be. And it may be pointed out that if the outcome of $B_j$ is +1 then the objective probability of revealing $a$ equals ¾, which is different than ½; and when the outcome of $B_j$ is −1, the objective probability of $a$ takes the value ⅜, which again differs from ½. So no matter which is the case (and one of them has to be the case) the probability of the outcome $a$ for the measurement $A_i$ will be different from the probability given that no measurement is performed on the distant system. But doesn't this amount to saying that the distant measurement is capable of changing the objective state of the local system? Yet this conclusion does not agree with our initial reading of the condition (PI). Hence the association of (PI) with the lack of influence between the act of measurement on one particle and the outcome of the other one seems to be unjustified.

Jarrett in his article (1984) has proposed a particular argument in favor of the standard interpretation of the condition (PI). His idea was to prove that when the condition (PI) is violated, it is in principle possible to send information regarding the distant choice of measurement setting to the other, spatiotemporally separated experimenter, thus violating the relativistic restrictions. However, his example involves a large number of correlated pairs of particles, all prepared in the same initial state $\lambda$.[23] The information about the distant setting can be "decoded" only when sufficiently many independent measurements $(A_i, B_j)$ have been made. In such a case the statistical distribution of result $a$ for measurement $A_i$ in the ensemble will reflect the probability $P(a| A_i, B_j, \lambda)$ (different from $P(a, 0| A_i, 0^B, \lambda)$ by assumption) because the impact of individual outcomes of $B_j$ will be statistically "filtered out". This will allow the local experimenter to learn that the distant collaborator chose to measure $B_j$ rather than making no measurement at all. However, it is not at all clear whether this proves that the supposed non-local correlation takes place in each pair independently. My point is that in order to prove that a non-local influence between the choice of setting and the particular outcome obtains when (PI) is violated, we would have to devise a method which would allow us to transfer super-

---

[23] Jarrett's argument obviously proceeds under the assumption that it is possible to create quantum systems in a desired state $\lambda$. However, it may be the case that the laws of nature forbid this. In this case the direct violation of Einstein's restriction on superluminal signaling would not threaten.

luminally the information about the distant setting *for a single pair of correlated particles*. And the only conceivable way of accomplishing this would be to make a sufficient number of identical copies of the left-hand side particle, and then to measure the relative frequency of obtaining *a* as the result of the measurement of observable $A_i$ within the prepared ensemble However, in that way we would not obtain a measure of the required probability $P(a|\ A_i, B_j, \lambda)$ but rather one of the following: $P(a|\ A_i, B_j, +1, \lambda)$ or $P(a|\ A_i, B_j, -1, \lambda)$, depending on what the actual outcome of measurement $B_j$ was. Hence, in some cases it would be impossible to tell whether the other particle underwent measurement $B_j$ or not. This means that information transfer appears to be unattainable in the case when we have at our disposal only one pair of entangled particles.

This problem does not occur when we consider the second component of the factorization condition, namely outcome independence. Here it turns out that the violation of the principle (OI) amounts to the change of the outcome of one measurement having an instantaneous impact on the physical situation of the other system. To see this, let us first present the condition (OI) in a different, but equivalent form:

(OI′)     $P(a|\ A_i, B_j, b, \lambda) = P(a|\ A_i, B_j, b', \lambda)$ for all $b \ne b'$

That (OI′) follows from the original formulation (II) should be seen as pretty obvious when we take into account that there is actually a suppressed universal quantification over all possible outcomes $b$ in (II). To see the reverse implication (OI′) $\Rightarrow$ (II) let us note that the right-hand side of (II) can be presented as

$$P(a|\ A_i, B_j, \lambda) = \sum_b P(a\ |\ A_i, B_j, b, \lambda) P(b\ |\ A_i, B_j, \lambda)$$

by the law of total probability (outcomes $b$ constitute a set of mutually exclusive and jointly exhaustive events). Using assumption (OI′) and the fact that $\Sigma_b\ P(b|\ A_i, B_j, \lambda) = 1$ we arrive at the required equation $P(a|\ A_i, B_j, \lambda) = P(a|\ A_i, B_j, b, \lambda)$. We can see now that the violation of (OI′) means that a change of the outcome in the measurement $B_j$ from $b$ to $b'$ changes the objective probability of obtaining outcome $a$ in the distant system. Or, using Jarrett's approach, we can argue that it is possible to let the faraway experimenter know what the result of the local measurement $B_j$ was. In order to decipher the information about the outcome, the experimenter has to make a sufficient number of copies of his particle and then measure the relative frequency of the occurrence of outcome $a$. If this number approaches $P(a|\ A_i,\ B_j,\ +1,\ \lambda)$, the experimenter learns that the other end of the apparatus recorded $+1$; if the number approximates $P(a|\ A_i,\ B_j,\ -1,\ \lambda)$ (and by the negation of (OI′) this has to be different from $P(a|\ A_i,\ B_j,\ +1,\ \lambda)$), he knows that the result was $-1$.[24]

To sum up, we have argued that the first of the two "locality" conditions considered here gives rise to some interpretive problems.[25] This is not to say that the idea of separating the two types of possible non-local influence—one triggered by an experimenter's choice of an observable to measure, and the other linked to the outcome received in the course of the measurement—is unreasonable. The only thing that is questionable is the connection between these ontological ideas and particular mathematical formulas, such as formula (PI). And, ultimately, if we agree that it is by no means clear what condition is expressed in (PI), then the philosophical lesson from the generalized Bell theorem becomes quite ambiguous. Hence, it may be argued that there is still a need for a more decisive result showing the untenability of the notion of locality in the context of quantum-mechanical phenomena. This is precisely the task taken up by Henry Stapp, among others, and which we will scrutinize at length later in this book. One idea of approaching such a task may be to express "parameter locality" in the language of counterfactual conditionals rather than in the probability calculus language; for example in the form of a sentence stating that if we had chosen a setting of the measuring apparatus different from the actual one, no physical change would have occurred in the distant system. If we were able to derive Bell's inequality from such a condition coupled with quantum-mechanical predictions, without any explicit or implicit reference to the realist condition, then we would unambiguously

---

[24] Jarrett does not see this possibility as violating the prohibition of superluminal signaling, because, as he argues, the outcome of the measurement $B_j$ does not depend on the other experimenter's will, so he cannot use the outcome dependence as a means for sending meaningful messages to his partner. Regardless of this practical setback, the outcome dependence definitely allows for superluminal exchange of physical information about a distant system, and therefore counts as a non-local influence.

[25] Dickson (1998, pp. 134-139) is similarly skeptical about the philosophical significance of Jarrett's analysis. However, he has no objections to treating the factorization condition (F) as a direct representation of the locality requirement. I, on the other hand, am inclined to look for more appealing and straightforward representations of the principle of local causality than the statistical condition (F).

show that quantum mechanics is non-local. However, we will argue throughout this book that this ambitious task has never been accomplished to a satisfactory degree, and there are even some grounds for thinking that it may simply be incapable of being accomplished.

### 1.5.1 Non-locality and non-separability

It can easily be verified that when the hidden variable $\lambda$ is interpreted as consisting only in the standard quantum-mechanical state, quantum theory implies that parameter independence (PI) is satisfied, but outcome independence (OI) turns out to be violated. This fact is commonly seen as indicating that in standard quantum theory there is no measurement-induced non-locality, while some sort of non-local influence between outcomes revealed in distant wings of the measuring apparatus is present. Yet this last conclusion has been questioned. Some authors argue that the violation of (OI) (or (II)) has nothing to do with the existence of superluminal causal links, but instead is a consequence of the failure of an altogether different classical intuition, i.e. the assumption of separability. In what follows we will take a closer look at this claim.

The most ardent proponent of this way of interpreting the failure of outcome independence is Don Howard, who claims on the basis of the available historical evidence that Einstein himself distinguished separability from locality as two different metaphysical principles.[26] Roughly speaking, the principle of separability asserts that complex systems can be broken up into smaller components, each of which is endowed with its own physical properties, and such that the properties of the entire system are somehow "reducible" to or "supervenient" on the properties of its parts. In the context of quantum mechanics it is claimed that entangled systems do not satisfy the requirement of separability, as the state of the complex system is not a simple combination of states of the components. For instance, the single spin state of the system of two spin-½ particles is given as the following (up to the normalization constant) superposition of pure states: $\psi_{singlet} = \psi_1^+ \otimes \psi_2^- - \psi_1^- \otimes \psi_2^+$, where $\psi_i^j$ represents the pure state of the $i$th particle in which the value of this particle's spin in a given direction equals $j$ (either + or –). It turns out that $\psi_{singlet}$ cannot be represented as a simple product of pure states of the two components $\psi_1 \otimes \psi_2$, which is sometimes interpreted as indicating that entangled particles do not possess

---

[26] Howard presented his position in a series of publications, including (1985), (1989) and (1997). Other authors subscribing to similar views on non-separability of quantum mechanics are R. Healey (1991), (1994), (2004) and M. Esfeld (2001), (2004).

well-defined states of their own. On the other hand, each particle taken separately does have a well-defined *mixed* state, i.e. there exists a probability distribution over all possible results of spin-measurements in every direction, however this state cannot be represented with the help of a vector (a ray) in the Hilbert space, but rather as a density operator on the same space (or alternatively as a weighted sum of pure states—for mathematical details see Hughes 1989, chapter 5).

I think that at this point we should distinguish two separate although closely related problems. The first issue is whether it is generally justified to claim that quantum entangled systems violate the metaphysical principle of separability; the second is the more specific question whether the outcome independence condition can be seen as a legitimate explication of separability. In terms of the first issue, Michael Esfeld points out that although technically it makes sense to speak of separate states of the components of an entangled system, still these states taken together do not determine the total state of the system, for the important information about the correlations between outcomes is lost (Esfeld 2001, 2004). To use the singlet spin example, the two mixed states that reduce the state $\psi_{singlet}$ can be combined in an infinite number of ways to create entirely different complex states, of which $\psi_{singlet}$ is only one. However, one may wonder if this underdetermination of the complex state by the component states is by itself sufficient to conclude that the metaphysical principle of separability is violated here (and that instead we have to adopt some sort of quantum holism). For example Richard Healey in (2004) gives one possible characterization of separability in terms of the "property determination" condition:

> Every qualitative intrinsic physical property and relation of a set of physical objects from any domain $D$ subject only to type $P$ processes supervenes on qualitative intrinsic physical properties and *relations* in the supervenience basis of their basic physical facts relative to $D$ and $P$ [italics mine]

It is important to notice that the above condition does not assert that intrinsic base properties alone should determine the properties of the compound system, but rather that base properties plus base *relations* should accomplish this determination. But if that's the case, then the singlet spin state clearly satisfies the condition of separability, for the specification of each particle's own mixed state plus the perfect anti-correlation relation between outcomes of spin-measurements uniquely determine that the state of the entire system is $\psi_{singlet}$. It has to be added that Howard as well as Esfeld adopt a stronger requirement of separability in which it is demanded that the joint state of entangled systems be wholly determined by their separate states (Healey calls this requirement "state separability"). But it is open to a debate whether this is a reasonable claim, given that there may be some non-local relations between elements of the system that do not enter into their separate states.

Nevertheless, Howard maintains that the statistical condition of outcome independence that we presented in the form of the equations $P(a \mid A, B, b, \lambda) = P(a \mid A, B, \lambda)$ and $P(b \mid A, B, a, \lambda) = P(b \mid A, B, \lambda)$ represents the condition of separability rather than locality. To show this, he rewrites the outcome independence condition in an equivalent form as $P(a, b \mid A, B, \lambda) = P(a \mid A, B, \lambda) P(b \mid A, B, \lambda)$, and then argues that this is essentially the assumption of the factorizability of the joint state represented by $P(a, b \mid A, B, \lambda)$ into the component "contextual" states $P(a \mid A, B, \lambda)$ and $P(b \mid A, B, \lambda)$, equivalent to the assumption that the joint state is a tensor product of the separate states (see Howard 1997, pp. 126-127). However, Howard's claim is countered by Maudlin, who points out that it is possible to construct models of the EPR situation which violate outcome independence and which explicitly employ superluminal signals while arguably conforming to the separability requirement (Maudlin 1994, p. 98). The violation of outcome independence does not *per se* imply non-separability, as the probability distributions for each particles separately may be well-defined, although due to non-local interactions those distributions may not uniquely determine the joint distributions for the outcomes of the entire system.

Finally, we may voice more general concerns regarding the proposed holistic interpretation of quantum entangled systems. As Dickson emphasizes (1998, p. 156), it is unclear what is precisely gained by postulating that the two parts of the entangled system are in fact one unseparable whole possessing joint and irreducible states. As long as we continue to use the notions of localized measurements and outcomes, there will always be a problem of how to explain apparent correlations between spatially separated readings of the measuring apparatuses. The very notion of a measurement is *local*: it is always a result of interaction of the separated measuring device with whatever we take as the measured system. Unless we change radically our ontology of events, allowing for instance for the existence of events that are simultaneously localized in two space-like separated regions, the measurement-events are local and separated, and hence any correlations between them call for some explanation in terms of influences, even if we subscribe to the holistic vision of the quantum world.[27]

## 1.6 A PROVISIONAL TAXONOMY OF QUANTUM NON-LOCALITIES

At the end of this opening chapter we will try to introduce some order into the untidy world of the multitude of non-local influences. Earlier, we suggested that the most intuitive way to characterize any type of causal correlation is in terms of "what causes what": what type of action precipitates what effects. We now know that in the context of quantum entangled systems there are two basic candidates for a cause of non-local interactions: the choice of a particular observable to be measured on one component of an entangled system, and the revealed outcome of the measurement. As far as the potential effects of these factors are concerned, we have the following possibilities, mentioned already before. First of all, one can try to non-locally induce a transition from an "unsharp" state of the particle to a sharp one (i.e. from a state with no defined value for a given observable to a state in which the observable takes a precise value). Another type of non-local interaction would lead to a transition from one definite value to a different one. We should also allow for a possibility, albeit to my knowledge only a theoretical one, of changing the state of the distant particle from possessing a determined value to an undetermined one. The non-locally induced change may also be of a more subtle kind,

---

[27] It should be stressed that our brief survey of the problem of non-locality in quantum mechanics and various approaches to it is by no means exhaustive. Many attempts to solve the problem of non-locality stem from adopting particular non-standard interpretations of quantum mechanics. Let me mention one such attempt: in a recently proposed variant of the many worlds interpretation, known as the many minds interpretation, the problem of the non-local correlations between distant outcomes in the EPR situation disappears altogether. According to the many minds interpretation, the physical evolution of quantum systems is always deterministic, and measurements are no exceptions (hence, there are no wave collapses). However, upon interacting with the measuring device, the mind of the experimenter "splits" into an infinity of different minds, each associated with a particular possible outcome. Of course under this interpretation there is no problem of how to explain the correlation between outcomes obtained in space-like separated locations, as there are physically no definite outcomes. The correlations predicted by the theory come into being only when two experimenters communicate the results of their respective measurements, thus interacting physically and locally with one another (see Albert & Loewer 1988; Albert 1992)

expressed in terms of probabilities, or relative frequencies only. We would definitely call it non-locality, if it were possible to instantaneously change from a distance the objective probability of revealing particular values of an observable.

| | Choice of a measured observable $A$ | Obtained outcome of $A$ |
|---|---|---|
| Change from an undefined value of $B$ to a defined one | Non-Loc$_{11}$ | Non-Loc$_{21}$ |
| Change from a defined value of $B$ to an undefined one | Non-Loc$_{12}$ | Non-Loc$_{22}$ |
| Change from one defined value of $B$ to a different one | Non-Loc$_{13}$ | Non-Loc$_{23}$ |
| Change from one probability measure on all values of $B$ to a different one | Non-Loc$_{14}$ | Non-Loc$_{24}$ |

Tab. 1.1. Classification of quantum non-localities

All this can be summarized conveniently in a table, where the columns indicate different causes precipitating non-local effects, and rows indicate the different effects of the causes. We assume that the causes relate to cases of measuring an observable $A$ on the left-hand side particle of a two-particle EPR system, while the effects involve a correlated observable $B$ and its values, characterizing the right-hand side particle of the same system.

So, for example, Non-Loc$_{13}$ represents a non-local influence such that by choosing a particular observable to be measured on a distant particle we can change an already possessed definite quantum property of another system (a sharp value of an observable) to another definite property, and Non-Loc$_{21}$ characterizes a situation in which by "forcing" a particular outcome to appear for one particle we could give some value to a previously undefined observable. It should not be difficult to identify in this table the versions of non-locality known from our previous discussion of the EPR and Bell theorems. The EPR non-locality will obviously be identical to Non-Loc$_{11}$, and Bell non-locality to Non-Loc$_{13}$. On the other hand, intended interpretations of "parameter non-locality" and "outcome non-locality" would coincide, respectively, with Non-Loc$_{14}$ and Non-Loc$_{24}$. However, as we recall from the previous section, at least the first interpretation raises serious concerns.

Non-localities Non-Loc$_{14}$ and Non-Loc$_{24}$ can be given a narrow interpretation, under which probability measures are only permitted to assume values other than 1, or a broad interpretation in which the probability distributions which give measure 1 to one value of the observable $B$ and 0 to the rest are included. However, in the latter case all of the remaining types of non-localities would count as subspecies of the broad categories Non-Loc$_{14}$ or Non-Loc$_{24}$, so we will opt for a narrow interpretation which uses only "non-trivial" probability distributions.

We can now use the classification of non-localities given in Tab 1.1 in order to attach different "weights" to particular types of non-local interactions. It has already been remarked several times that not all cases of violation of the locality intuition are equal. The departure from the common-sense ontological view regarding the propagation of causal influences varies depending on the "severity" of accepted non-locality. It seems natural to treat one type of non-locality as being less "severe" than another, depending on two factors: on the degree to which the effect makes a difference in the world (for example, whether the effect can be observed, or detected), and on the ease with which the cause required to obtain such an effect can be produced. Regarding the latter factor, it can be argued that all non-localities placed in the first column under the heading of "Choice of a measured observable" are stronger than their counterparts in the second column. This is the case, because the choice to measure a particular observable can be made freely by an experimenter (or, more cautiously, because there are no strong arguments against such a contention), whereas the outcome obtained in the course of the experimenter's action seems to be independent of their will. Hence, superluminal signaling is in principle possible in the first case, while the second case does not offer us such an opportunity. It may be also pointed out that "outcome non-locality" offends our common sense to a lesser degree, because it resembles cases of spurious non-causal correlations of the sort we discussed in footnote 14. According to this intuition, it may be tempting to explain away a correlation between outcomes of space-like separated experiments by pointing to a possible hidden factor which causally determines both outcomes and hence secures their connection. In other words, an outcome revealed in one experiment would reflect certain "preordained" mechanism, which is also responsible for the other result. Such a move is plainly impossible in the case of a correlation between a choice of experiment on one system and a physical state of the other, because by assumption the experimenter's decision doesn't depend causally on any physical factor in the past of the system. However, we should not forget that this strategy of explaining away non-local correlations between outcomes has been seriously undermined by Bell-like results (see e.g. van Fraassen 1983). Therefore, we have to accept that there is an irreducible element of non-locality in the correlation between the outcome of one experiment and a physical situation leading to the outcome of the other experiment.

Let us now turn to looking at how the strength of a particular type of non-locality depends upon the sort of effects brought about. No effect given in the left-hand side column of the table can be seen as literally observable, yet it should be quite clear that changing one definite value into another one comes close. If we could only monitor a particular physical magnitude over an extended period of time, we would definitely be able to notice that this magnitude "switched" between two values at a certain instant. On the other hand, there is no easy way to detect an "undefined" or "superposed" state of a particular observable. Any properly conducted measurement in quantum physics has to reveal a particular value, regardless of whether the system was initially in an eigenstate for a given observable or not (in short: there is no "superposition" label on the measuring device). We can only indirectly conclude that the initial state was not an eigenstate when we conduct the same measurement on a statistical ensemble of identically prepared objects. Hence, all transitions involving quantum "potentialities" seem to be at least epistemologically less radical than the transition from one actuality to another (once again this relates to the possibility of sending and receiving signals at a superluminal speed). For that reason we may argue that the strongest type of non-locality is Non-Loc$_{13}$ (identical to Bell non-locality!) and next is Non-Loc$_{11}$ along with Non-Loc$_{12}$. The weakest variant of non-locality seems to be associated with the statistical transition from one probability distribution to a different one, and combining this with the analysis from the previous paragraph, we can see that the best candidate for the least radical departure from locality is Non-Loc$_{24}$.

This ordering can also be confirmed by considerations of a more ontological nature. There is a quite commonly accepted intuition which attaches greater ontological importance to well-defined states of a particular observable rather than undefined ones. According to this intuition, a genuine property attribution happens only when a system possesses a definitive value $a$ for a given observable $A$. When, on the other hand, the system is not in an eigenstate with respect to $A$, it is claimed that the system *lacks* certain physical characteristics, rather than *possesses* a property of a different sort. Although this approach is not entirely uncontroversial, it seems that probabilistic *propensities* or *dispositions* are less clear-cut attributes of physical objects than sharp values of magnitudes, like position, momentum, or charm.[28] Hence, a switch from, and to a state characterized only by some sort of "fuzziness" should count as less conspicuous compared with a transition between definitive properties.[29]

Finally, a word about how to understand the causal relation connecting causes to effects in different types of non-local influences. Causality is often associated with repeatability: every time a cause occurs, it is followed by the appropriate effect. However, this approach ignores the fact that causal relations are highly sensitive to external conditions, meaning that the alleged repeatability holds only under certain strict conditions (an example: striking a match causes flames to occur only if there is enough oxygen in the atmosphere, if the match is not wet, if we strike at the proper angle, etc.). These conditions are typically difficult to characterize properly and exhaustively, so it is argued that a better approach is to define causality in terms of "necessary" conditions: if a cause hadn't occurred, the effect wouldn't have occurred. This characterization is a "singular" one; it defines a cause for a particular event in the context of its actual realization in particular conditions, and not as the regularity "events of type $A$ always cause events of type $B$".[30] Here we will be following this second method of

---

[28] M. Redhead would probably disagree. See (Redhead 1987, pp. 48-49). However, this intuition can be further supported by the tendency within science to reduce dispositional properties, such as fragility or water-solubility, to more fundamental physico-chemical properties of objects. The only problem in quantum mechanics is that quantum propensities cannot be reduced to anything more fundamental. We will talk more about this issue in sec. 6.4.

[29] Once again, as it happened previously, the following intuition may have influenced this particular judgment. Someone could namely interpret the "undefined" state merely epistemologically—as a reflection of our subjective ignorance regarding the exact value of the magnitude in question. Of course in such a situation a "transition" from such state to a fully defined state would not count as something that happens objectively "there". However, we should remember that the ignorance interpretation of the quantum state is essentially equivalent to the hidden variable hypothesis, and as such is seen as highly improbable.

[30] It is almost impossible to give here an exhaustive list of the relevant texts that deal with the philosophical problems of causation, so huge is the literature of this topic. An introductory survey of the main conceptions of causality can be found in the an-

interpreting causality, thus adding one more area for applying counterfactual conditionals to the problems analyzed in this book. Because locality conditions are given in terms of the non-existence of causal connections between space-like separated events, no wonder that counterfactuals will play a role in the precise formulation of the locality assumption. Hence it may be a good idea to look more closely at the logical analysis of counterfactual conditionals in order to prepare logical tools necessary for our undertaking. The next chapter will be entirely devoted to this task.

thology edited by E. Sosa and M. Tooley (1993), which includes, among others, D. Lewis's classical text "Causality" (Lewis 1986b). Lewis's counterfactual analysis of causation has been directly applied to the correlations of quantum entangled systems in (Butterfield 1992), as well as (Esfeld 2001). One of the most recent monographs on causality worth recommending is (Pearl 2000). The most comprehensive and up-to-date collection of essays regarding counterfactual theories of causation is (Collins *et al.* 2004), which contains Lewis's latest improvement on his counterfactual approach to causality (Lewis 2000).

# Chapter 2

# POSSIBLE-WORLD SEMANTICS FOR COUNTERFACTUALS

Counterfactual conditionals are statements asserting that something happens under certain conditions, which are presupposed not to be satisfied in reality. In natural language counterfactuals are typically expressed in the so-called subjunctive mode, indicated by an appropriate form of the verb ("If it were..." or "If it had been..."). Counterfactual statements seem quite unproblematic in certain contexts—like, for example, when we assert self-evident statements of the sort "If John were older than Mary, then Mary would be younger than John"—but we are at a loss when we have to decide whether it is true that if Kennedy hadn't been assassinated, the war in Vietnam would have lasted shorter. It is well known that a nice and clean truth-functional analysis cannot do justice to the semantics and pragmatics of counterfactuals, and when we add to this the abundance of controversial cases like the one above, it may be tempting to dismiss counterfactual talk altogether as unscientific and illogical gibberish. Yet this move seems to be too radical. After all, counterfactual statements occur in many situations in science. In fact, almost every general problem considered in science may be interpreted as a question about the truth of a particular counterfactual. For instance, the three-body problem in physics (the problem of determining the motion of three massive bodies under the influence of their mutual gravitation only) can be formulated as the question "What would the movements of the Sun, the Earth and the Moon look like if there was no other body in the Solar System?"

Under what circumstances, then, does a statement "If it were $P$, then it would be $Q$" become true? Or, in other words, what is the truth condition for the counterfactual? Let us first consider an example. Suppose that we look at a massive body at rest (for example a stationary billiard ball on a table). According to what is prescribed by ordinary laws of dynamics, if we exerted a non-zero force on this ball, it would accelerate. Now, it may be tempting to propose that the truth of the above-mentioned counterfactual amounts to the fact that the consequent (the statement about the acceleration) is derivable from the antecedent (the statement about the acting force) plus a set of applicable laws (in this case Newton's second law of dynamics). According to this approach, true counterfactuals are backed by enthymematic arguments, where the missing premises are the laws of nature. However, there is a slight problem with this solution. First of all, it may be pointed out that in our case the consequent does not, strictly speaking, follow from the antecedent plus the laws of dynamics. It is conceivable that a counteracting force could appear (in the form of someone's hand, for instance), preventing the ball from moving. One possible way of responding to this objection could be to claim that physics, strictly speaking, supports only the counterfactual with the antecedent stating that the *total* force acting upon the body is non-zero.

But this defense has two negative consequences. Firstly, it ignores the linguistic fact that contrary to the postulated restriction, we are still inclined to accept the counterfactual belief that if I pushed this ball a little, it would move. The fact that there is a possible situation in which my pushing is not accompanied by the ball's movement does not seem to undermine this belief, because our intention is to imagine a situation which is almost exactly like the actual one (and in reality we believe that there are no extra forces acting upon the ball), with the exception that I push the ball. And secondly, if we insist that the foregoing linguistic intuition is nonetheless inadequate, and the only true counterfactuals are those whose consequents follow nomologically from the antecedents, then the class of true non-analytic counterfactuals will be reduced to a narrow group of statements of a very limited practical use, where the antecedent has to describe the complete state of a physical system in a minute detail and taking into account all conceivable external influences and disturbances.[1]

Moreover, there are examples of intuitively true counterfactuals which clearly do not satisfy the requirement that the consequent follow nomologically from the antecedent. Suppose that in our example with the billiard ball there is actually another stationary ball on the table, at a considerable distance from the former one. Intuitively, we would accept it as an uncontroversial truth that if I pushed the first ball, the second ball would remain at rest (at least for some time). The truth of this counterfactual expresses our belief that there is no known physical connection between the

---

[1]    To use our example: the meaning of the expression "the total force acting upon the ball is non-zero" presupposes that we can discern all possible known and unknown interactions which may manifest themselves in this case. But this postulate is highly idealistic, and barely realizable in scientific practice. For a similar example from outside science, see (Bennett 2003, p. 162).

two balls which would force one to move instantaneously when the other is touched. And yet no law connects the fact of exerting a force on the first ball with the fact that the second one is stationary.[2] The reason for accepting the above-mentioned counterfactual is not the existence of a connection between the antecedent and the consequent, but rather the fact that the consequent had already belonged to our stock of beliefs, and we have no reason to suspect that making the antecedent true would alter this situation. This example illustrates the fact that counterfactuals are highly contextual: their truth cannot be ascertained without a broad context, including beliefs regarding the actual states of affairs, as well as beliefs about the nomological connections between events.

The contextuality of counterfactual conditionals is responsible for the violation of some logical principles which are satisfied by other types of conditionals, e.g. material implication or strict implication.[3] For example, the principle of antecedent strengthening is violated, meaning that if we add an extra condition to the antecedent of a true counterfactual, the resulting counterfactual may very well turn out false. This may be illustrated with the help of our previous example: it is true that if I pushed the ball, it would move, but if I pushed the ball while somebody was holding it tight, it would not budge. As a consequence, another cherished principle—the transitivity principle—has to go (see Bennett 2003, p. 160). This follows directly from the fact that there are statements $P$, $Q$ and $R$ such that it is true that $P \mathbin{\Box\!\!\rightarrow} Q$ but it is false that $(P \wedge R) \mathbin{\Box\!\!\rightarrow} Q$, when we take into account that obviously $(P \wedge R) \mathbin{\Box\!\!\rightarrow} P$ is true (the symbol "$\Box\!\!\rightarrow$" will represent the counterfactual operator).[4] Yet another case of counterfactual

---

[2] You may point out that the laws of nature predict that if the second ball was originally stationary, it will remain so under the assumption that the first ball was moved. However, this means that the argument backing the counterfactual "If I pushed one ball, the other would be at rest" requires more than laws of nature—it requires an additional assumption about the behavior of the second ball in the actual world.

[3] Material implication is defined with the help of the usual truth-table. Strict implication (strict conditional) is characterized by the modal expression $\Box\,(P \supset Q)$, where $\supset$ stands for the material implication, and the box "$\Box$" is read "it is necessary that".

[4] However, E.J. Lowe in (1995) rejects the cases of "counterfactual fallacies", arguing that they are the result of the high context-sensitivity of counterfactual conditionals. In particular, Lowe explains away the cases that apparently violate transitivity $[(P \mathbin{\Box\!\!\rightarrow} Q) \wedge (Q \mathbin{\Box\!\!\rightarrow} R)] \supset (P \mathbin{\Box\!\!\rightarrow} R)$ by pointing out that the truth of

fallacy involves the violation of transposition (or contraposition, as it is sometimes called).[5] We have agreed that it is true that if I pushed one ball, the other one would remain at rest, this does not imply, however, that if the other ball started moving for some reason, I would definitely not push the first ball. These violations show that without codifying the formal rules of inference for the counterfactual conditional we could have significant difficulties with its application in any context, including the context of quantum mechanics.

## 2.1 STALNAKER'S COUNTERFACTUAL LOGIC AND THE LAW OF CONDITIONAL EXCLUDED MIDDLE

The first step towards a formalization of the counterfactual operator should focus on giving a general account of what its assertibility conditions may look like. Robert Stalnaker (1968) gave the following, intuitive exposition of how to evaluate a counterfactual conditional:

> First, add the antecedent (hypothetically) to your stock of beliefs; second, make whatever adjustments are required to maintain consistency (without modifying the hypothetical belief in the antecedent); finally, consider whether or not the consequent is then true. (p. 169)

This procedure can be seen as giving a pragmatic criterion for the acceptance or rejection of a particular counterfactual, but we are more interested in finding an objective truth condition for the counterfactual, independent of anybody's particular beliefs. An objective, "ontological" counterpart of a collection of hypothetical beliefs is typically encompassed by the notion of *possible world*. A possible world can be seen either as a complete and consistent description of a given reality, or as the reality itself. For our purposes this distinction is insignificant, although it gave rise to a heated metaphysical debate regarding the status of possible worlds.[6] What is im-

---

both statements $P \,\square\!\!\rightarrow Q$ and $Q \,\square\!\!\rightarrow R$ is typically asserted in such cases in different contexts (using different similarity measures between possible worlds).

[5]  In the case of material implication the law of contraposition states that the formula $P \supset Q$ is equivalent to $\sim\!Q \supset \sim\!P$.

[6]  David Lewis is the most ardent proponent of the second, "realistic" interpretation of possible worlds, according to which all possible worlds are no less "real" entities than our world (see Lewis 1973, pp. 84-91; Lewis 1986d). For a metaphysical development of Lewis's views see also (Unger 1984). Some of his critics include R. Stalnaker (1976), A. Plantinga (1976) and P. van Inwagen (1986).

portant is that possible worlds form a convenient structure for referring to the ways things could have been different. As a formal tool, possible worlds have been used extensively for the task of explicating the semantics of modal logics (S. Kripke's systems). In the context of the counterfactual conditional they will play an analogous role.

According to Stalnaker's pioneering approach, the semantic structure for a language containing the counterfactual operator $\square\rightarrow$ consists of a set $S$ of possible worlds, together with an accessibility relation $R$ ($xRy$ means that $x$ is a world which is possible relatively to $y$). To this standard structure for modal logic, Stalnaker adds one extra element in the form of a function $f$ (called the selection function), taking pairs ($w$, $P$) consisting of a world $w$ and a sentence $P$ as arguments, and a possible world as its corresponding value. The intuitive interpretation of the formula $f(w, P)$ is that it represents the world in which $P$ is true, and which differs minimally from $w$ in comparison to all other $P$-worlds. The minimality requirement amounts to the assumption that the only differences between $f(w, P)$ and $w$ are those that are necessary for making $P$ true without introducing a contradiction. So, for example, when $w$ is the actual world containing two stationary billiard balls, and $P$ is the statement "The first ball is pushed", the second ball will remain stationary in $f(w, P)$, for the supposition that it also moves is not needed in order for $P$ to be true. Now it is not difficult to guess that the truth condition proposed by Stalnaker for the counterfactual conditional will be as follows:

(S)     $P \square\rightarrow Q$ is true in $w$ iff $Q$ is true in $f(w, P)$

Stalnaker imposes several conditions on the selection function $f$, to ensure that it properly represents the intuitions associated with it. He postulates, among other things, that if $P$ is true in $w$, then the selection function picks out the world $w$ itself: $f(w, P) = w$. This amounts to saying that a world is always more similar to itself than any other world. Stalnaker also makes sure that the ordering of possible worlds defined by the selection function is consistent, i.e. if function $f$ determines for a given statement $P$ that a particular world $w'$ is "closer" to $w$ than $w''$, then no other selection made for a different statement $Q$ can establish that $w''$ is closer than $w'$. This condition can be expressed in the form of a stipulation that there are no statements $P$ and $Q$ such that $Q$ is true in $f(w, P)$, $P$ is true in $f(w, Q)$, and $f(w, P) \neq f(w, Q)$. If there were such statements, then $f(w, P)$ would obviously be closer to $w$ than $f(w, Q)$ from the perspective of the $P$-

selection, but $f(w, Q)$ would be closer than $f(w, P)$ from the perspective of the $Q$-selection.

The formal structure defined by Stalnaker determines the validity of formulas containing the counterfactual connective (characterized, standardly, as truth in all models). In particular, it entails the violation of the "classical" laws of transitivity and contraposition, as explained earlier. However, one significant law remains valid within Stalnaker's theory. It is the so-called Law of Conditional Excluded Middle:

(CEM)     $(P \; \Box\!\!\rightarrow Q) \lor (P \; \Box\!\!\rightarrow \sim Q)$

The validity of the above formula follows directly from the truth condition (S) plus the assumption that all possible worlds are complete, i.e. that for every sentence $P$ and every world $w$, either $P$ or $\sim P$ is true in $w$. The main reason for the validity of (CEM) is that the truth of the counterfactual $P \; \Box\!\!\rightarrow Q$ depends on *exactly one* possible world selected by $f(w, P)$. But there are strong arguments against the principle (CEM). Let us use the following famous example:

> If Bizet and Verdi were compatriots, they would be French, or if they were compatriots, they would be Italian.

According to Stalnaker's semantics, exactly one of the above disjuncts has to be true (granted, of course, that any possible world in which both composers have a nationality different than French or Italian is farther from the actual one than those in which they are both French or both Italian). And yet our commonsensical knowledge does not give us any clue as to which one may be true. It seems that both worlds—one in which the composers are French and the other in which they are Italian—are equally distant from the actual one, in which Bizet is French and Verdi Italian. Perhaps further investigation into their respective biographies could reveal that for some reason one of them got closer to be born of parents of the other nationality, which could give an argument in favor of one of the disjuncts, but is should be quite clear that other examples of that sort can be produced in great numbers. In particular, an example showing that the logic of counterfactuals that assumes (CEM) is inadequate for the description of quantum measurements can be given very easily. Suppose that we have a physical system $x$, and that we consider one of its measurable discreet properties $A$ with $n$ possible values $a_1, ..., a_n$. One of the main assumptions of experimental physics is that a proper measurement of $A$ should reveal one of these values as its outcome. We can call this thesis the Definite Response principle, which can be represented in the form of the following counterfactual:

(DR)     $M(A) \,\square\!\!\rightarrow (A = a_1 \vee \,...\, \vee A = a_n)$,

where $M(A)$ is an abbreviation of "Observable $A$ was measured". The intuitive and unquestionable reading of (DR) is that if I'd measured $A$ (even when I hadn't done it in reality), then my measurement would have revealed one of its admissible values. In other words, proper measurements cannot be left without an outcome.

Taking into account that the truth condition (S) implies that in order for (DR) to be true, one of the formulas $A = a_i$ has to be true in a selected world $f(w, M(A))$, we derive from this the conclusion that the following principle of Counterfactual Definiteness has to hold:

(CD)     $[M(A) \,\square\!\!\rightarrow A = a_1] \vee \,...\, \vee [M(A) \,\square\!\!\rightarrow A = a_n]$

But this claim is much stronger than (DR). It amounts to the presupposition that, even before the measurement, it is already determined for a given value $a_i$ that if I were to measure $A$, $a_i$ would be revealed. It is hard to interpret this statement otherwise than as a counterfactual expression of the realism of possessed values which we talked about in the previous chapter. But this means that a highly controversial ontological presumption, rejected by the standard interpretation of quantum mechanics, is a direct logical consequence of the uncontroversial and indeed quite trivial statement (DR). Surely, a logic that allows for this to happen should be treated with high suspicion.

Bas van Fraassen (1991, pp. 122-125) argues that Counterfactual Definiteness leads directly to Bell's inequality (in its Bell-Wigner version, cf. sec. 1.3). He points out that for all three components of spin $\sigma_\alpha$, $\sigma_\beta$, $\sigma_\gamma$ (CD) predicts that one of the counterfactuals $M(\sigma_i) \,\square\!\!\rightarrow \sigma_i = a$ will be true. To be precise, because the principle of Definite Response can be strengthened to the form in which the consequent contains not ordinary disjunctions, but exclusive ones (there is exactly one outcome that is revealed in each measurement), (CD) can also be reformulated to ensure that exactly one counterfactual is true. This means that for each spin component there is a unique value which would be revealed, had this component been chosen. From this point we can continue the usual Bell-Wigner derivation which leads to Bell's inequality. Van Fraassen admits that his result is avoidable in an alternative semantics for the counterfactual which was developed by Lewis, and which does not license the law of Conditional Excluded Middle (we will present the basic assumptions of Lewis's semantics in the subsequent section); nevertheless he expresses skepticism as to the possibility of a fruitful application of counterfactual logic in quantum mechanics:

> The violation of Bell's Inequalities demonstrates empirically that we should not look to measurement outcomes to give us direct information about state, propensity, capacity, ability, or *counterfactual facts*. From fact to modality, only the most meager inferences are allowed (p. 125, italics mine).

It may be worth noting, however, that in his argument van Fraassen ignores the role of the locality condition in the derivation leading to Bell's inequality. As we remember from chapter 1, Bell's argument in its original version relied on the assumption that the values which objectively characterize one system cannot be changed by a distant, space-like measurement performed on the other system. Now, in van Fraassen's counterfactual version of Bell's theorem counterfactuals of the form $M(\sigma_i) \;\Box\!\!\to\; \sigma_i = a$ replace the assumption of the existence of the possessed values. This means that we have to make sure that a new, counterfactual version of the locality assumption is applicable here, too. Later on, we will analyze some arguments in support of the view that the locality principle does not necessarily licenses the assumption that counterfactuals pertaining to a distant space-time region should remain unchanged while the local region undergoes changes. So it is possible at least in principle that even with the Counterfactual Definiteness Bell's inequality can be avoided. This issue will be extensively analyzed in chapter 6.

There is no question, however, that the Law of Conditional Excluded Middle had better be abandoned in the logic of counterfactuals. One more argument against it comes from the fact that with this law holding true there is no way to distinguish between two types of counterfactuals: "would" counterfactuals and "might" (or "could") counterfactuals. In natural language we distinguish between "categorical" counterfactuals: "If I jumped from the thirtieth floor on a concrete pavement, I would kill myself", from weaker assertions of the sort: "If I jumped from the second floor, I *might* break my leg" (but it's not necessarily true that I definitely *would* break my leg). The most natural way to define the "might" counterfactual is in terms of the "would" counterfactual: the statement about the possibility of breaking my leg is equivalent to saying that it is not the case that if I jumped from the second floor, I *would not* break my leg.[7] Symbolically, this may be written as follows:

$$P \lozenge\!\!\rightarrow Q =^{df} \sim\!(P \,\square\!\!\rightarrow \sim\!Q),$$

where $P \lozenge\!\!\rightarrow Q$ stands for "If it were the case that $P$, then it *might* be the case that $Q$". But when (CEM) is true, the left-hand side formula becomes equivalent to $P \,\square\!\!\rightarrow Q$, and hence the difference between the "might" and "would" counterfactuals collapses. In order to keep this distinction, we should find an alternative semantics for the counterfactual in which the law of Conditional Excluded Middle would not hold. And this task has been accomplished within Lewis's possible worlds semantics.[8]

## 2.2  LEWIS'S COUNTERFACTUAL SEMANTICS

Lewis's groundbreaking book *Counterfactuals* (1973) has become the primary reference point for all subsequent analyses of the counterfactual conditional. The scope and depth of the discussion of various formal and informal aspects of the counterfactual semantics presented there was unprecedented in the literature of the time. Lewis drew significantly on Stalnaker's approach; in particular, he adopted the idea of comparing possible worlds with respect to their similarity to the actual world, and the idea that only those worlds that are in some sense closest to the actual one should be taken into account when evaluating a counterfactual. In spite of these similarities, there are important differences between these approaches. Lewis's analysis can be seen as more general than Stalnaker's, as it implies (but it is not implied by) the latter as a special case.

Lewis's starting point for building the formal semantics for counterfactuals is the standard assumption that for any world $w$ in which a

---

[7]  For a discussion and subsequent rejection of some other possible methods of defining the "might" counterfactual, see (Lewis 1973, pp. 80-81).

[8]  However, it has to be added that Stalnaker vigorously defends his position regarding the validity of CEM in (1978). He argues, on the basis of an apparent analogy with the "will" conditionals, that in natural language there is no quantifier scope ambiguity that would differentiate between counterfactuals $\exists x \,(P \,\square\!\!\rightarrow Qx)$ and $P \,\square\!\!\rightarrow \exists x \, Qx$. For an extensive analysis of Stalnaker's defense see (Bennett 2003, pp. 185-193).

counterfactual conditional is to be evaluated (this world is usually referred to as the "actual world"), there is a set $S_w$ of possible worlds *accessible* from $w$ (Lewis calls this set "a sphere of accessibility"). Further particulars of this semantic structure can be presented in different but equivalent ways. Lewis's primary method of presentation adopted in (1973) employs the concept of a *centered system of spheres*, but we will follow an alternative approach given with the help of the comparative similarity relation between possible worlds (p. 48). The reason for this is, firstly, that this approach has become standard in most applications of Lewis's semantics to the quantum-mechanical phenomena, and, secondly, that it lends itself naturally to a particular generalization which later will be shown to be necessary. The symbolic representation of the similarity relation will be as follows:

$$w' \leq_w w''$$

which will be read as "the world $w'$ is at least as similar to the world $w$ as the world $w''$ is". The relation $\leq_w$ is assumed to be a weak linear ordering of the worlds in $S_w$, with $w$ being strictly minimal. This is to say that the following conditions are supposed to hold:

(2.1)  *Transitivity.* For all worlds $w'$, $w''$ and $w'''$ in $S_w$, if $w' \leq_w w''$ and $w'' \leq_w w'''$, then $w' \leq_w w'''$.

(2.2)  *Strong connectedness.* For all worlds $w'$, $w''$ in $S_w$, $w' \leq_w w''$ or $w'' \leq_w w'$.

(2.3)  *Minimality.* For all worlds $w'$ in $S_w$, if $w' \neq w$, then $w \leq_w w'$, and it is not the case that $w' \leq_w w$.[9]

It is important to notice that the formal system introduced above permits "ties" between possible worlds, i.e. there can be different worlds $w'$, $w''$ such that $w' \leq_w w''$ and $w'' \leq_w w'$ (we will symbolize this situation as $w' \cong_w w''$ and will read this as "$w'$ and $w''$ are equally similar to the world $w$"). This will ensure that the law of Conditional Excluded Middle is not valid. First, however, we have to present the formal truth condition for the counterfactual. (We will assume, as it is standardly done, that for every statement $P$ formulated in our language, and for every possible world $w'$, $P$

---

[9]  The condition expressed in the consequent of this implication can be shortened to $w <_w w'$.

is true at $w'$ or $\sim P$ is true at $w'$. Statement "$P$ is true at $w'''$" will often be shortened to "$w'$ is a $P$-world".)

(L)     $P \; \square\rightarrow Q$ is non-vacuously true at $w$ iff there is a $P$-world $w'$ in which $Q$ is true, and there is no $P$-world $w''$ such that $w'' \leq_w w'$ and $\sim Q$ is true in $w''$.

The counterfactual $P \; \square\rightarrow Q$ is called vacuously true if there is no accessible world $w'$ in which $P$ is true. This stipulation can be seen as equivalent to the assumption that all material implications with false antecedents are vacuously true; except, now, the condition is obviously that the antecedent has to be *necessarily* false for the vacuity clause to apply.[10]

The truth condition (L) can be stated equivalently in many ways (the equivalence being secured by the set of assumptions (2.1)-(2.3)), for example as

(L')     $P \; \square\rightarrow Q$ is non-vacuously true at $w$ iff there is a $P$-world $w'$ in which $Q$ is true, and for every $P$-world $w''$, if $\sim Q$ is true in $w''$, then $w' \leq_w w''$ and it is not the case that $w'' \leq_w w'$.

No matter which verbal representation we choose, it should be clear that the intuition behind Lewis's truth condition is unambiguous: in order for the counterfactual conditional $P \; \square\rightarrow Q$ to be true, the set of $P$-worlds ordered linearly by $\leq_w$ should be such that starting with a certain world, all the worlds lying "lower" with respect to $\leq_w$ are, without exception, $Q$-worlds. This stands in contrast to Stalnaker's simpler account, according to which the truth of $P \; \square\rightarrow Q$ is decided in exactly one, "hand-picked" possible world, which is supposed to be *the* closest of all $P$-worlds. But Lewis's semantics does not assume that such a minimal $P$-world exists, let alone that it is unique. In Lewis's terminology, the assumption that there will be $P$-worlds which are closest to $w$ is called the Limit Assumption, and it can be presented as follows:

---

[10]    Standard modal operators "it is necessary that $P$" and "it is possible that $P$" can be easily introduced into Lewis's semantics with the help of the customary conditions "$P$ is true in all accessible worlds" and "$P$ is true in some accessible worlds" respectively.

(LA)     For all antecedents $P$, there is a possible $P$-world $w'$ such that for all $P$-worlds $w''$, $w' \leq_w w''$.

Lewis points out that this assumption is not always reasonable. It is conceivable that there may be antecedents $P$ for which a set of $P$-worlds has no minimal element with respect to $\leq_w$. As an example he considers the statement "This line is more than an inch long", where it is assumed that in the actual world the line is exactly one inch long. Now it can be argued that there is a continuum of possible $P$-worlds numbered by the length of the line, and that the closer to one inch the line is, the more similar to the actual one the appropriate world is. From this it easily follows that there will be no most similar $P$-world, because $P$-worlds will be approaching the actual one infinitesimally close, without actually reaching it.

When the Limit Assumption is accepted, the truth-conditions (L) can be expressed in a simpler and more appealing way as follows:

($L_{LA}$)     $P \;\square\!\!\rightarrow Q$ is non-vacuously true at $w$ iff $Q$ is true in all $P$-worlds closest to $w$.

In most cases, when Lewis's semantics of the counterfactual is applied, this is actually the truth condition that is implicitly or explicitly adopted.

However, it has to be noted that adding the Limit Assumption to Lewis's semantics still does not produce Stalnaker's version of counterfactual logic. (LA) does not imply that there will be *exactly one* $P$-world which is most similar to the actual one. It is still possible that there may be two or more "tied" worlds that are closest. And this fact is of crucial importance to the question of what logical laws should be accepted as valid for counterfactual conditionals. The law of conditional excluded middle (CEM) is invalid even with the Limit Assumption, for there may be two worlds closest to the actual word and such that in one of them $Q$ is true, whereas in the other the opposite ($\sim Q$) holds. As a consequence, Lewis's logic permits that there may be statements $P$ and $Q$ such that none of the counterfactuals $P \;\square\!\!\rightarrow Q$ and $P \;\square\!\!\rightarrow \sim Q$ will come out true, which opens the door to the definition of a non-trivial "might" counterfactual, not equivalent to the "would" counterfactual.[11]

---

[11]  Another consequence of this stipulation is that the negation of a counterfactual statement is not the same as a counterfactual with the negated consequent. To illustrate this with our previous example: when I negate the statement that if I jumped

Also, the problem which previously arose in the context of the quantum measurement is resolved. The truth of the Definite Response principle (DR) now does not imply the unreasonably strong Counterfactual Definiteness (CD). To see this, it suffices to imagine that there are exactly $n$ possible $M(A)$-worlds equally similar to the actual one and such that in each of them a different admissible value $a_i$ is revealed. Because of this assumption, in every such world the disjunction $A = a_1 \vee \ldots \vee A = a_n$ will be true, and hence, according to the truth conditions given by (L), the counterfactual (DR) will come out true. Yet the counterfactual (CD) requires, in order to be true, that a particular value $a_i$ is revealed in *all* possible $M(A)$-worlds which are closest to the actual one, and this by assumption is not the case.

### 2.2.1 True-antecedent counterfactuals

A common feature that is shared by both Lewis's and Stalnaker's approaches is their method of analyzing a particular, non-standard kind of counterfactual—counterfactuals with true antecedents. It is obvious that counterfactuals whose antecedents are true are in a sense pragmatically unacceptable. We have mentioned before that when we use the subjunctive mode, it presupposes that whatever condition we assume, it is not satisfied in actuality. Hence a sentence starting for example with the clause "If the Earth was round..." would be seen as defective. This, however, does not mean that a formal analysis cannot assign certain truth values to such pragmatically deficient statements. The case of the material implication creates a powerful precedence. Even though uttering certain material conditionals seems to be "out of place", it is customary to assign to them particular truth values as prescribed in the truth table, and to argue that there are certain pragmatic rules of use, over and above the truth conditions, which explain why we feel uncomfortable when asserting such defective conditionals.[12] Hence, it should not come as a surprise that the formal analysis of the counterfactual will attach truth values to counterfactuals with true antecedents. The question is, however, how to do this. When should such a deficient counterfactual be seen as true, and when should it be seen as false? As Lewis observed (1973, p. 27), our linguistic intuitions are not entirely reliable in this case, for we will always see true-

---

from the second floor, I would break my leg, I don't mean that if I jumped from the second floor, I would definitely not break my leg. I still *might* break it.

[12] The most famous account of such pragmatic rules is given in the form of Grice's conversational implicatures.

antecedent counterfactuals as defective, and this judgment will override any possible true/false distinction that may be made. One possibility for making a judgment regarding the truth value of such counterfactuals may be to consider situations in which a counterfactual had initially been uttered under the impression that its antecedent was false, but subsequently this impression turned out to be unsubstantiated. But, first, let us analyze how Lewis's formal system resolves this issue.

Because of the assumption of minimality (2.3), valuations of true-antecedent counterfactuals are done solely within the actual world. When there is no world closer to the actual one than the actual one itself, the truth value of a counterfactual $P \ \square \rightarrow Q$, where $P$ is true in $w$, will depend only on the value of $Q$ in the same actual world $w$. This means that when $Q$ is true in $w$, the counterfactual will be true, and when $Q$ is false, the counterfactual will be false as well. Summing it up, we can say that in the case of true antecedents, the counterfactual conditional reduces to the material conditional. This fact can also be stated with the help of two rules of inference which are valid within Lewis's logic:

$$\frac{P, Q}{P \ \square \rightarrow Q} \qquad\qquad \frac{P, \sim Q}{\sim(P \ \square \rightarrow Q)}$$

The second of the above rules seems to be acceptable. To reject the counterfactual "If John had talked to Mary yesterday, she wouldn't have left him" it seems sufficient that we observe that, actually, John *did* talk to Mary, but it didn't help and they did break apart. It would be very odd indeed if we held that a counterfactual is true even after somebody had told us that its antecedent, but not its consequent, had actually been realized. However, the first of the above rules leads to "paradoxical" consequences. According to it, all facts that take place in the actual world are counterfactually connected with one another. But this seems to go against our intuitions regarding the proper usage of the counterfactual conditional, quite independently of the issue of the truth of the antecedent.

Let us consider the following example, illustrating the oddity of this solution. Suppose that somebody says "I'll never believe that if George performed the magical ritual, his neighbor's house would be set ablaze", and that somebody else replies "Well, you'd better believe it, for George did perform the ritual a minute ago, and look—there is a fire in his neighbor's house". I think it reasonable to respond to this that the fire co-occurring with the ritual could still have been a coincidence, and that these two separate facts do not support the initial counterfactual, unless we give evidence that the fire had no other plausible causes but George's ritual. The basis for the initial rejection of the counterfactual was skepticism about the existence of a causal connection between the two facts in question, and their mere co-occurrence does not dispel this skepticism. This example—if accurate—shows that Lewis's own method of testing valuations of counterfactuals with true antecedents gives us a reason for being suspicious about his semantic proposal.

To be fair, we have to admit that Lewis is aware of the controversial character of his solution, and he even considers weakening his semantics in a way that could avoid the above consequence (1973, pp. 29-31). An obvious way to do this is to abandon the minimality assumption and to replace it with a weaker minimality, stating that the actual world is at least as close to itself as any other world, but permitting ties between the actual world and other possible worlds:

(2.3′)   *Weak minimality.* For all worlds $w'$ in $S_w$, $w \leq_w w'$

With (2.3′) replacing (2.3) it is now possible to maintain that a counterfactual $P \; \square\!\!\rightarrow Q$ can be false in spite of $P$ and $Q$ being true in the actual world. This will happen if there is a possible world $w'$ for which $w' \cong_w w$ holds, and such that $Q$ is false in $w'$. However, this way of weakening Lewis's original semantics can be opposed on the grounds of fundamental intuitions regarding the notion of similarity (closeness) between possible worlds. It may be claimed that one of the main reasons for introducing ties between possible worlds with respect to their similarity to the actual one is the intuition that one difference between a world $w'$ and $w$ can be entirely "compensated" by another difference between $w''$ and $w$. For example, the difference between Verdi being French and being Italian is arguably seen as "equal" to the difference between Bizet being Italian and being French. But when it comes to comparing a given possible world with the actual one, there is nothing to compensate with: on the one hand we have some difference, albeit a tiny one, and on the other hand there is no difference. To uphold Lewis's correction we would have to assume that our similarity relation is "coarse grained", and that it does not recognize divergences that fall below certain threshold. This surely can be done, but whether it is a reasonable option remains an open question.

Opposition to Lewis's original treatment of true-antecedent counterfactuals (we shall subsequently call them, following Griffiths (1999), "null counterfactuals") is quite common among theoreticians trying to apply counterfactual semantics to quantum-mechanical phenomena. One additional reason for rejecting the view that the truth of a null counterfactual depends solely on the value of its consequent in the actual world may be given. There is a strong intuition that points to a particular interpretation of tensed counterfactuals (counterfactuals in which the antecedent refers to an event well localized in time): in order to assess a counterfactual $P \ \square\rightarrow Q$ we should imagine a possible world which is identical with the actual one up to the moment of the occurrence of $P$, and then follows the usual evolution as determined by the actual laws of nature. Under such an interpretation it becomes a non-trivial question to ask "What would the world look like if I went back in time and did exactly the same thing I actually did?". If we assume that strict determinism holds in the actual world, then whatever happened in the actual world would happen again if the initial conditions were the same. But this assessment is invalid in an indeterministic world, and in particular in the quantum world (according to the standard, Copenhagen interpretation, of course). Suppose that in the actual world a measurement of an observable $A$ for a system which hadn't been prepared in an eigenstate for $A$ was made, and that it revealed one of its admissible values $a$. How should we, then, evaluate the null counterfactual "If the observable $A$ had been measured, the revealed outcome would have been $a$"? According to the above interpretation, we should imagine the actual world running its course "once again", so that upon reaching the point of the $A$-measurement all the results remain possible, and nothing can guarantee that the result will be $a$.[13]

According to Lewis's weakened system, in order for the above null counterfactual to be rendered false, all worlds with different outcomes of

---

[13] The objection can be raised that the phrases "going back in time" or "the world running its course again" seem to suggest that what we actually consider here are not null counterfactuals, but legitimate false-antecedent counterfactuals in which it is assumed, contrary to our knowledge, that such actions like time travel are possible. But I think that we have to treat expressions like the ones above as figures of speech only, and not literally. The role of these expressions is only to stress that in order to evaluate a particular counterfactual we have to "build" an appropriate possible world in which the antecedent is true and which satisfies some additional restrictions, like the ones mentioned in the main text. The point being made here is that it is possible that the world built in such a way will not be identical with the actual one.

the $A$-measurement should be seen as "equisimilar" with the actual world. This means that we should recognize certain facts as not salient for the similarity relation $\leq_w$. If we want to avoid treating all null counterfactuals as material conditionals, we have to accept that similarity between possible worlds cannot rely solely on an indiscriminate maximization of the number of particular events that are identical with those in the actual world, no matter whether they are past, present or future with regard to the antecedent-event. This is the case, because otherwise we would always judge worlds which repeat the actual outcome of a quantum measurement as closer to the actual one, contrary to the above-mentioned intuition. But this conceptual difficulty clearly shows that Lewis's formal counterfactual semantics is empty unless clear guidelines regarding the proper interpretation of the similarity relation are provided. The next section of this chapter will sketch the well-known method of interpreting the similarity relation that has been proposed by Lewis.[14]

## 2.3 RELATIVE SIMILARITY BETWEEN POSSIBLE WORLDS

Philosophers often complain that there are few terms more vague than the term "similarity". What does it mean that an object is similar to another? The standard response to this question is that two objects are similar if they have at least one common property. But it is always possible to find something that two objects have in common, no matter how unlike each other they are, making the similarity relation trivial. It seems much more precise, then, to speak about the degree of similarity, or a comparative similarity, rather than about absolute similarity. For example, we would intuitively agree that Venus is more similar to the Earth than is Jupiter, and that a triangle is more similar to a rectangle than to a circle. However, one can still complain that such judgments are intelligible only when we agree what aspect of similarity we are interested in. It can be argued, for instance, that Jupiter is more similar to the Earth than Venus with respect to the property of having natural satellites, for Venus has none, and both Jupiter and the

---

[14] J. Bennett has put forward an interesting proposal (he calls it, very aptly, "Home from Abroad"), according to which, in the case both $P$ and $Q$ are true in the actual world, counterfactual $P \,\square\!\!\rightarrow Q$ should be rendered true if it remains true in the closest non-$P$-worlds (Bennett 2003, p. 241). This solution ensures that the counterfactual "If I measured $A$, the result would be $a$" could be false even if in reality $A$ has been measured and outcome $a$ obtained, provided that the closeness criterion is insensitive to the actually obtained but indeterministic outcome (for the discussion of this problem see sec. 3.3).

Earth have some. And, when we move to the problem of how to compare possible worlds with respect to their similarity to the actual world, things get even worse. There are innumerable ways to select different aspects of such complicated structures as possible worlds, and to feed them into the criterion of relative similarity. And each such method will in turn result in different evaluations of common-sense counterfactual statements.

To illustrate strong dependence of truth-values of counterfactuals on the accepted standards of the relation of similarity, we can use one of the most famous examples known from the literature (see Fine 1975). Suppose that a "doomsday" machine has been created: an electronic switch connected to all existing nuclear missile launch pads, able to send all the warheads onto their targets, and that a person in command considers pressing its main button. Fortunately for the unsuspecting world, the person finally decides not to press the button, but a question remains what would happen, had the button been pressed. Our immediate response would be: the world in its known form would cease to exist. However, it can be argued that the analysis based on the comparative similarity between possible worlds yields an entirely different valuation of this counterfactual. To see this, let us imagine two possible worlds: one in which, according to our predictions, the button's pressing causes a total annihilation of all life on Earth; and the other in which there is a small malfunction in the mechanism of the doomsday machine, and the world is spared the terrible end. Now, it seems natural to agree that the latter world is quite like the actual one—except the incident with pressing the button everything in it remains more or less the same as in our world. On the other hand, the world in which a nuclear holocaust takes place would certainly be very different from the world in which we live. But if we agree with this assessment, it follows that for every nuclear holocaust world there will be a world which is more similar to the actual one and in which the holocaust does not occur, which means that according to Lewis's truth conditions (L) the counterfactual "If the button had been pressed, there would have been a nuclear holocaust" comes out false, contrary to our intuitions (other, quite entertaining examples illustrating the same problem can be found in Bennett 2003, p. 196).

This objection (known as "the future similarity objection") to Lewis's initial counterfactual semantics prompted him to address the issue of formulating some definite criteria of comparative similarity between possible worlds. Lewis points out emphatically that not all properties of possible worlds should enter the similarity relation with positive weight. Rather, we should create a hierarchy of aspects under which we decide to compare possible worlds with one another in the context of evaluating counterfactuals similar to the one given above. One aspect of the similarity relation that Lewis selects is the comparison with respect to spatiotemporal regions which contain *exactly the same* individual facts. If we compare two possible worlds with respect to their similarity to the actual one, and if it turns out that one of them differs from the actual world in area $\Gamma$ only whereas the differences in individual fact between the other one and the actual world are contained in a different area $\Delta$, and when we make sure that $\Gamma$ is greater than $\Delta$,[15] then we should agree that, all other things being equal, the second world is more similar to the actual one than is the first one.

But Lewis insists that we should also take into account another aspect of similarity, separate from the matching the individual facts. He assumes that there may be possible worlds in which not only individual facts, but also the laws of nature could be different from the facts and laws that exist in the actual world. In other words, Lewis admits that some possible worlds may contain "miracles", i.e. events which from the perspective of the actual world are unlawful. The reason why Lewis thinks it necessary to introduce the controversial notion of "miracle" into his description of possible worlds is as follows. First of all, his semantic analysis of the counterfactual conditional is carried out under the assumption of strict determinism, according to which a complete description of the world at any moment uniquely determines its future and past evolution. From this assumption it obviously follows that if two worlds that obey the same set of laws as the actual one differ from each other at a given moment $t$, they'll also diverge from each other at *every* moment other than $t$. So, in particular, when we consider a contrary-to-facts assumption $P$ which refers to an event taking place at $t$, then the only possible $P$-worlds in which the same laws as in the actual one hold will be the worlds which have both a future *and a past* of $t$ different than the actual ones. But this last conclusion (especially its italicized part) leads to a clash with another firm conviction held by Lewis, namely that counterfactuals used in everyday life are typically time-asymmetric: they almost always point into the future, and almost never point into the past.

---

[15] Note that there may be different senses of what it means for an area to be greater than another. One possible interpretation of this notion is in terms of their measurable sizes, but there is another, which employs only a set-theoretical notion of inclusion (an area $\Gamma$ is greater than an area $\Delta$ iff $\Delta$ is included in $\Gamma$, but is not identical to $\Gamma$). These two notions obviously do not coincide (for example there may be two areas both of an infinite size such that one is properly included in the other.)

The last remark requires some clarification. What is claimed here is that, typically, we treat the past as being *counterfactually locked*, and the future as being *counterfactually open.* For example, considering an action that might have been taken at a moment *t*, we hardly ever derive from this that events *before t* would have been different, but we typically say that some events *after t* would have been definitely different as a result of this action. To use Lewis's terminology, we may say that *back-tracking* counterfactuals are typically prohibited in the ordinary discourse. And yet, if we accept strict deterministic laws, then arguably there are plenty of true back-tracking counterfactuals, because of the adjustments that have to be made both in the past and the future every time we insert a contrary-to-facts event into a possible world. To avoid this, Lewis not only accepts that there may be possible worlds in which "miracles" (law-breaking events) occur, but also admits that some of these worlds may, in fact, be closer to the actual one than the worlds which are perfectly lawful, but instead contain a lot of differences in individual fact.

### 2.3.1   Lewis's similarity ranking

This intuition calls for a sophisticated set of criteria for evaluating similarity between possible worlds. As our discussion suggests, Lewis has to consider two factors: differences in particular facts and differences in laws. The key point in Lewis's proposal is that these two factors are not meant to be weighed directly against each other; rather they create a hierarchy of comparisons in which a particular level is taken into account only if the preceding one does not yield a definite answer to the query. Lewis presents his informal ranking of respects of similarity as follows:

(S1)   It is of the first importance to avoid big, widespread, diverse violations of law.

(S2)   It is of the second importance to maximize the spatio-temporal region throughout which perfect match of particular fact prevails.

(S3)   It is of the third importance to avoid even small, localized, simple violations of law.

(S4)   It is of little or no importance to secure approximate similarity of particular fact. (Lewis 1986a, pp. 47-48).

The above criteria work as follows. In order to compare a world $w_1$ with another world $w_2$ with respect to their closeness to the actual world $w_0$, we have to use the criterion (S1) first. If it gives an unambiguous answer, i.e.

if violations of laws in one of our worlds (for example in $w_1$) are much more widespread than in the other one ($w_2$), then the procedure ends here with the conclusion that $w_2$ is closer to $w_0$ than $w_1$, *regardless* of what the criteria (S2)-(S4) would yield. But if (S1) does not give a definite answer (i.e. if the big violations of laws in $w_1$ and $w_2$ are the same), then criterion (S2) has to be considered, and the procedure is repeated until a verdict can be reached.

The fact that criteria (S1)-(S4) use very vague terms, like "big", "widespread", "small", "localized", "approximate" may be seen as a serious disadvantage for Lewis's proposal; a disadvantage that in the eyes of many logically-oriented readers can even disqualify the entire conception. Yet Lewis points out that our intuitions regarding the truth-value of counterfactuals are vague, too, and that a "formal" reconstruction should reflect this linguistic fact. So there is no denying that sometimes criteria (S1)-(S4) will not yield an unambiguous answer as to whether particular worlds are more or less similar to the actual one, and this in turn will lead to the inability to decide whether a particular counterfactual is true or not. However, according to Lewis this is to be expected, as counterfactuals are vague in the first place. There is obviously a tendency in formal logic to resolve the vagueness of natural expressions in one precise and conventional way (for example in the case of material implication), but Lewis definitely does not want to follow this path. This obviously does not exclude the possibility that in particular, well-defined contexts (for example in the context of quantum-mechanical phenomena) the vagueness of criteria (S1)-(S4) may be eliminated or at least seriously minimized.

We can now see that the criteria (S1)-(S4), when applied properly, produce the correct valuation for the "nuclear holocaust" counterfactual. To remind ourselves: in the example the actual world is supposed to contain a doomsday machine, but its button is not pressed, and the nuclear conflict does not ensue. But we can consider possible worlds in which it is true that someone pressed the button. Among the great number of such worlds (some radically different from the actual world—imagine for instance a perfectly possible world in which the warheads are full of confetti) we can distinguish a couple of "finalists" in our similarity contest—worlds that have the greatest odds of being selected as most similar to the actual world. The contest will be decided among these few worlds. In one of these possible worlds (let's call it $w_1$) there will be no law violation, and hence, due to the assumption of determinism, $w_1$ will differ from $w_0$ in the entire stretch of time from the past to the future. But we can imagine another possible world exactly as ours up to the point right before the pressing of the button, but where a miracle occurs causing some person to press the button. What will happen next, depends on several assumptions. First, we can imagine a situation in which another small miracle occurs a second later preventing the electric signal from reaching the missiles, and thereby thwarting the realization of the doomsday plan. Let us call this world $w_2$. And finally, there will be the "nuclear holocaust" world $w_3$ in which everything goes according to plan, and the world vanishes in a cloud of nuclear explosions.

If the analysis were to yield the expected results, the world $w_3$ had better be the closest to $w_0$ of all the worlds considered. Let us first compare $w_3$ with $w_1$. Although $w_1$ contains no miracles, and $w_3$ does contain one, it may be argued that the miracle in $w_3$ is small and localized, rather than big and widespread. Lewis conjectures that for the button to be pressed, it is sufficient that a couple of neurons in the operator's brain fire slightly differently than they should given the deterministic evolution of the world. If we agree with that, we'll see that the first criterion (S1) does not differentiate between the worlds in question, so the second criterion has to be considered. But surely $w_1$'s area of divergence in individual facts is bigger than the area of divergence in $w_3$, for the former contains the entire stretch of time, whereas the latter only the period of time after the pressing of the button. Hence $w_3$ is closer to $w_0$ than $w_1$.

Let us now compare $w_3$ with $w_2$. Here Lewis's main argument is that although in $w_2$ the holocaust is avoided, and a qualitative similarity between $w_2$ and $w_0$ is achieved, still there are some differences between $w_2$ and $w_0$ in the future run of events. Although the signal didn't reach the launching silos, still in $w_2$ there are some consequences of the fact that the button was pressed, which are nonexistent in $w_0$. These consequences include the memories of the operator of the doomsday machine, the light rays carrying his picture while pressing the button, the amount of heat created by the pressing, and so on. Although a superficial similarity between $w_2$ and $w_0$ has been achieved, this doesn't matter, as the approximate match of particular facts is the least important criterion (point (S4) above). And, strictly speaking, criteria (S1) and (S2) do not decide which one of the two worlds $w_2$ and $w_3$ wins the contest. Criterion (S1) is not applicable, for there is no big, widespread violation of laws in any of the worlds $w_2$, $w_3$. And criterion (S2) does not single out any of these worlds, either, for we have just argued that in both of them the areas of divergence in terms of particular facts contain the entire future following the button being pressed, although admittedly the divergence in $w_2$ is qualitatively much less conspicuous than in $w_3$. Hence the job of differentiating between $w_2$ and $w_3$ goes to criterion (S3) which speaks about small, "contained" miracles. And because world $w_2$ contains two such small miracles, and $w_3$ only one, the winner is $w_3$.

In world $w_2$ some, but not all, of the consequences of the counterfactual action have been erased by an appropriately selected miracle. However, one may ask whether it wouldn't be possible to introduce more miracles in order to erase *all* of the causal consequences of the button being pressed, and therefore to ensure a perfect "convergence" with the actual world. The aim here, of course, is to create a world such that criterion (S2) would select it as being closer to $w_0$ than the nuclear holocaust world $w_3$. Hence, it looks like a new world has entered the competition—a world $w_4$ in which a perfect "cover-up" job has been made. Fortunately for Lewis, it can be argued that this world does not pose a serious threat for $w_3$, because the number of miracles needed to erase all the causal consequences of a particular event far exceeds the limit of what we can call a small miracle. Lewis argues convincingly that the full cover-up requires a big miracle, and this fact ensures that $w_3$ is more similar to $w_0$ than is $w_4$ on the basis of criterion (S1).

Provided that there are no other possible worlds which could win the competition with $w_3$, it looks like Lewis's intricate method of assessing comparative similarity between worlds solves the future similarity objection. It also produces the required result regarding time asymmetry of counterfactuals. The fact that there are many more true counterfactuals with the consequent-event transpiring later than the antecedent-event, than there are counterfactuals with the consequent referring to the past events is explained by the postulated asymmetry of miracles. It takes one small miracle to create a world which shares its past with the actual world but diverges in the future; it takes many correlated miracles to ensure a perfect convergence of a possible world whose initial history differs from that of the actual one. Ultimately, this asymmetry comes from the asymmetry of overdetermination: typically events have few pre-determinants (causes) in their past, but many post-determinants (effects) in the future.[16]

---

[16] Some authors disagree with the asymmetry of miracles thesis, though. One of the most vocal critics of this thesis is Bennett (1984, 2003). Recently A. Elga (2001) argues that statistical mechanics allows for the existence of possible worlds which diverge from the actual one in the past while converging with it in the future, and such that they arguably contain only a small miracle ensuring the convergence. Another recent criticism of Lewis's asymmetry of miracles can be found in (Field,

As it may be expected, Lewis's informal criteria of similarity (S1)-(S4) have been the subject of a number of different criticisms. Some authors complain generally that the criteria proposed by Lewis explain our intuitive and off-hand assessments of counterfactuals with the help of an unnecessarily oversophisticated strategy (Horwich 1987, pp. 172-173). Others attack them by pointing out that they do not work exactly as they should under the assumption of indeterminism (Percival 1999; Noordhof 2000). In the Postscripts to his article "Counterfactual Dependence and Time's Arrow" (1986a) Lewis considers the question of how to modify criteria (S1)-(S4) in order to make them applicable in the case when the actual world is not deterministic. Obviously, in this case miracles are not necessary in order to ensure a divergence from the temporal evolution of the actual world. If chance events are sufficiently abundant, then any divergence from the actual world can be accounted for as a result of such an event. However, there is the danger that chance events can be used not only to ensure divergence, but also to secure perfect convergence to the actual world. If the convergence can be achieved without introducing any real miracle, then the converging worlds will always be deemed closer to the actual world, according to criterion (S2), and, hence, the nuclear holocaust counterfactual will never come out true (in fact, any counterfactual whose consequent refers to a future event not occurring in the actual world will be rendered false). Lewis is aware of this problem, and he proposes to introduce the notion of a quasi-miracle, which should replace "ordinary" big miracles. A quasi-miracle is an extraordinary coincidence of many, otherwise perfectly lawful chance events. From this definition it follows that there can't be *small* quasi-miracles—a single chance event is just a commonplace occurrence in an indeterministic world.

Accordingly, the four criteria applicable in the deterministic case will reduce to three criteria that can be employed in the indeterministic case, with big miracles mentioned in (S1) being replaced by quasi-miracles, and criterion (S3) being eliminated altogether. However, the lack of small quasi-miracles contains the seed of destruction for Lewis's conception. As Percival (1999) points out, once we have eliminated small miracles altogether, we can achieve an *approximate* match between the actual world and a possible world at no cost at all. Recall from our previous example that when we compared possible world $w_3$ with the approximate match world $w_2$, the reason why we voted for $w_3$ as being more similar to $w_0$ was

---

2003, pp. 453-459). I am not going to discuss this in detail, as the problem of the asymmetry of miracles is tangential to our main considerations.

that in $w_3$ there is only one small miracle, whereas in $w_2$ there are two, and avoiding small miracles is more important than securing an approximate match. But once criterion (S3) disappears, as it does in the indeterministic case, the only applicable condition is (S4), which still favors the approximate match. Moreover, even if we eliminated (S4) completely, as some of Lewis's remarks may suggest ("approximate convergence counts for little *or nothing*"), still this would not produce the correct valuation for the counterfactual "If the button had been pressed, then there would have been a nuclear holocaust". The best we can achieve when comparing $w_3$ with $w_2$ is to render them equidistant from $w_0$, but since only in $w_3$ the consequent of the above counterfactual is true, according to (L) the counterfactual cannot be true. In order to secure the right valuation of the counterfactual, we have to make sure that $w_3$ is the closest among all the contenders, and this apparently cannot be done in the modified Lewis's system.

### 2.3.2 Similarity ranking and the EPR correlations

The problem sketched above is unquestionably a serious one, especially for those who want to employ Lewis's semantics in the context of quantum mechanics—the most serious scientific theory that seems to accept that the world is indeterministic. There have been some attempts to rectify Lewis's approach by introducing a new criterion of similarity based on the probability of chancy events occurring in a particular world (Nordhoof 2000, Percival 1999). However, rather than evaluating these attempts, I would like to formulate yet another objection to Lewis's similarity ranking that comes from quantum mechanics. The following objection is derived not from the indeterminism of the quantum world, but rather from another of its non-classical features, namely its (apparent) non-locality. In particular, I suggest that we consider a common EPR situation with two spin-½ particles (e.g. electrons) prepared in the singlet state, in which the total spin equals 0.

As we already noted in chapter 1, because of the principle of the conservation of angular momentum, the total spin of these electrons cannot change, as long as the particles are isolated from external influences. Hence, if the actually performed measurement of the $x$ spin component of the left-hand side particle L yields value $\sigma_x^L = +1$, the value of the same spin component of the right-hand side particle is bound to be $\sigma_x^R = -1$ (see Fig. 2.1). This correlation is independent of the relative location of the particles, so we can assume that both measurements are space-like separated.

Let us now analyze the following counterfactual conditional:

(2.4)  $\sigma_x^L = -1 \ \Box\!\!\rightarrow \sigma_x^R = +1$.

Intuitively, this counterfactual expresses our belief that if the result of one of the measurements was different, the distant outcome would have to change too in order to keep the total spin unchanged, thereby rendering (2.4) true. However, it can be argued that Lewis's complex set of criteria (S1)-(S4) gives the opposite answer. In order to see this, we have to consider two possible worlds $w_1$ and $w_2$ such that in both of them the outcome of the left-hand side measurement is $\sigma_x^L = -1$. Their main difference is that in $w_1$ the law of the conservation of angular momentum is upheld exactly as in $w_0$, and hence the outcome of the other measurement is $\sigma_x^R = +1$. However, in $w_2$ a temporary suspension of the law occurs, allowing for the other outcome to remain unchanged: $\sigma_x^R = -1$. Now the issue of what the logical value of the analyzed counterfactual is boils down to the question which of the worlds $w_1$ and $w_2$ should be seen as closer to $w_0$. If $w_1$ is more similar to $w_0$ than $w_2$ is, then (2.4) comes out true as predicted. But if $w_2$ is equally or more similar to $w_0$ than $w_1$ is, the value of the counterfactual is "false".

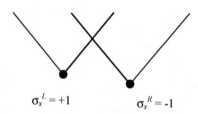

$\sigma_x^L = +1$          $\sigma_x^R = -1$

Figure 2.1 The actual world $w_0$

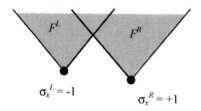

perfect match

Figure 2.2 Possible no-miracle world $w_1$

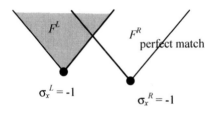

Figure 2.3 Possible miracle world $w_2$

It is not difficult to see, however, that Lewis's criteria seem to favor $w_2$ over $w_1$. First of all, it may be argued that in none of these worlds is there a big, widespread violation of laws, mentioned in criterion (S1). The violation of law that is allowed to happen in $w_2$ is quite well located and limited, so it may arguably count as a "small miracle" in Lewis's terminology, and hence can be taken into account no sooner than in the third step. But before that criterion can be applied there comes condition (S2), which demands that the world in which the region of perfect match in terms of particular facts is bigger should be counted as more similar. But as it is clearly depicted on Fig. 2.2 and 2.3, world $w_2$ has a significantly smaller region of divergence of particular facts in comparison with $w_1$. World $w_1$ differs from $w_0$ in causal consequences of the outcome of the left-hand side measurement, and the right-hand side measurement alike. These causal consequences include electromagnetic radiation spreading from the locations of the experiments and carrying the information about the outcomes, the records written on a computer's disk, the experimenters' memories, etc.[17] In world $w_2$ these diverging causal consequences are constrained to the future light cone of the left-hand side measurement only, so the exact match in this part of $F^R$ which is disjoint from $F^L$ (note that $F^R - F^L$ is potentially infinite) is bought at the price of one small miracle. And, according to Lewis's conditions, this trade-off brings a net profit. Thus, $w_2$ is more similar to $w_0$ than $w_1$, and counterfactual (2.4) becomes false, in spite of our strong intuition to the contrary.

### 2.3.3. Time-asymmetry of counterfactuals and the role of miracles

Sure enough, there may be several ways of getting around this particular difficulty that the non-local lawful correlations of quantum-mechanics pose for Lewis's approach. It could be argued, for example, (without real chances for success, in my opinion) that the miracle required in order to cut the non-local connection is a big and widespread one. Although the singlet-state particles can be, in principle, located at a considerable distance from one another, this in my view does not constitute an excuse to call the violation of the conservation of spin in this case "a widespread miracle". Also, one may suggest that counterfactual (2.4) is expected to be false, if one assumes that the real source of the correlation between outcomes revealed for the electrons is an event in their common past typically referred to as "the common cause". But the success of this solution is contingent upon the acceptability of the common cause hypothesis, and as it is well known the common cause hypothesis is extremely unlikely to be true.

A more serious attempt to overcome the above obstacle calls for a more substantial change in the approach to counterfactual semantics. Lewis himself considered an alternative to his preferred analysis, referring to it as "the asymmetry-by-fiat approach" (1986a, p. 39). Rather than applying the complex set of guidelines (S1)-(S4), we could do as follows. When evaluating counterfactual (2.4), let us consider a possible world which is exactly as $w_0$ up to the moment directly preceding the measurement of $\sigma_x^L$, at which point a small miracle occurs permitting the outcome of the measurement to be $\sigma_x^L = -1$. The miracle is assumed to be "minimal" required to do the job with no unnecessary divergences from the actual world being

---

[17] It is irrelevant whether we agree that these differences will be slowly fading away with time, or that they may accumulate over time to produce situations much different qualitatively from those in the actual world. After all, according to Lewis an approximate match between a possible world and the actual one is the weakest criterion of all four.

permitted. Finally, after the measurement the world evolves according to the usual laws, with no miracles whatsoever. If the consequent of the analyzed counterfactual turns out to be true in all such worlds, the entire counterfactual comes out true; if not—the counterfactual is false.

This method would obviously yield the required value for (2.4). The alteration of the outcome of the $\sigma_x^R$-measurement would come out as a result of keeping standard laws, including the principle of the conservation of angular momentum. A similar strategy has been already adopted almost unanimously by the authors working with quantum counterfactuals (Redhead 1987, Clifton *et al* 1990, Bedford & Stapp 1995, Finkelstein 1998, 1999). In order to make it relativistically invariant, some of these authors interpret the phrase "up to the moment preceding the measurement" as denoting the past light cone with its apex in close proximity of the $\sigma_x^L$-measurement (we will talk about this issue later).

However, Lewis raises two powerful arguments against the above solution. Firstly, it arbitrarily renders all backtracking counterfactuals false. And although Lewis is definitely not a fan of backtracking counterfactuals, he would like to leave open the *possibility* that some of them may actually be true (1986a, p. 40). After all, the fact that we don't typically encounter cases when the past depends counterfactually on the future is supposed to be a contingent feature of our world; in an alternative world this might be different. Secondly, the proposed analysis has a limited scope of applicability, as it is applicable only to counterfactuals with antecedents referring to spatiotemporally localized events. This objection can be, to a certain extent, dealt with, as it appears that the "asymmetry by fiat" solution is amenable to some generalizations, either with the help of a specially prepared overall similarity relation (Finkelstein 1999, Bigaj 2004) or on a case-by-case basis (again, we will take up this issue later in the book).

As for the first objection, it may be alleviated, if not eliminated, with the help of a slight modification of the proposed "asymmetry by fiat" solution. The modification in question aims at eliminating miracles altogether from possible worlds. One should first ask what do we need miracles for in this approach to counterfactuals. The original motivation behind the introduction of law-breaking events in some of the possible worlds was to allow for the existence of worlds which share with the actual one the entire past up until the occurrence of a counterfactually supposed event, *under the assumption of determinism*. But now the situation has changed—we can talk freely about events that are not nomologically connected with the past, and hence their occurrence can be considered without adjusting the past, and without introducing any violation of the existing laws. This means that at least part of Lewis's original worries is taken care of—as long as the considered counterfactual event is chance, there will be no true back-tracking counterfactuals with their antecedent referring to that event. On the other hand, some events still permit back-tracking counterfactuals; namely those that participate in causal or any other nomologically connected chains of events starting in their past.[18]

However, Lewis would probably complain that this solution gives us too many back-tracking counterfactuals—after all, even in an indeterministic quantum world there are still sufficiently many causal links to create a problematically big number of true counterfactuals leading from the present to the past. But then the question is: what is the primary source of our suspicion towards back-tracking counterfactuals? What is so wrong with saying that if the Earth followed a different orbit around the Sun, the cloud of dust from which the solar system was created would have had a slightly different shape or rotational speed, or mass distribution? After all, this looks like a perfectly valid scientific conjecture.[19] I think that the explanation for our unquestionable reluctance to accept backtracking

---

[18] Limited backtracking in an indeterministic universe is also accepted in the modification of Lewis's semantics of counterfactuals put forward by S. McCall (1984). His main idea is to replace Lewis's "otherworldly" possible worlds with possible worlds understood as "alternative histories" of the actual world, where the sole criterion of similarity relies on the length of the "shared pasts" of appropriate worlds. We will use this intuition later, adopting it to the case of relativistically invariant theories. Similarly, backtracking is allowed in Bennett's conception of "forks", where a fork indicates a moment in which a possible world diverges from the actual one (Bennett 2003, pp. 202-221 and pp. 276-278).

[19] Someone might object to this statement on the basis of the fact that a different orbit of the Earth could be the result of many different causes—for example the fact that some stray comet from outside the solar system passed by and caused the disturbance. Be that as it may, it still seems reasonable to expect that if the Earth's orbit were different now, this would be a result of some past event, so at least the general backtracking counterfactual "If the Earth followed a different path now, the world would have been different before that" is true. On the other hand, according to Lewis's approach the following, highly suspicious counterfactual is always true: "If things were different right now, this would be a result of a miracle". But it goes against our fundamental linguistic intuitions—even under the assumption of strict determinism—to admit that every divergence from the world as we know it requires a law-breaking event. And besides, this example shows that Lewis's approach does not completely eliminate backtracking counterfactuals, as in the case of the last counterfactual the consequent event takes place earlier than the antecedent event (see a similar argument in Field 2003, p. 455).

counterfactuals stems from the fact that we don't think it appropriate to suspect that there could be *causal links* leading from the present to the past. And the statement "If the present were different, the past would have been different" suggests that it is possible to "create" a change in the past by appropriately modifying some present states of affairs. Yet this suggestion is in my opinion misleading. It derives from the underlying assumption that the counterfactual change in the present state of affair can be effected "at will" by an agent acting at the present moment. But this is true for chance events only. Events which belong to chains of deterministically connected occurrences cannot be brought about at a given moment—we would have to go back in time and change the initial conditions in order to create circumstances appropriate for their occurrence.

Hence, my (somewhat tentative) suggestion is that we should disconnect the notion of counterfactual dependence from the notion of causal relation—contrary to what Lewis famously argues for in (1986b). More precisely, I would agree with Lewis that counterfactual dependence *restricted* to chance events indeed implies the existence of the causal relation. But this is not the case with deterministic events. If you have two events $E_1$ and $E_2$ where $E_1$ is determined by its past, and such that if $E_1$ didn't occur, $E_2$ would not occur either, this dependence by itself does not guarantee that $E_1$ is causally related to $E_2$. Some additional conditions have to be satisfied in order for $E_1$ to be a cause of $E_2$. Speaking loosely, the counterfactual dependence between $E_1$ and $E_2$ has to be relatively insensitive to the way $E_1$ is brought about, even in possible worlds which are not the closest $E_1$-worlds. For example, we believe that my (possible, not actual) striking the match is a cause for its subsequent lighting, because the effect can be brought into existence no matter whether the match was struck by my hand, or by somebody else's hand, or by an artificial arm, no matter whether I wanted to light a cigarette, or burn down a house, etc. On the other hand, we suspect that there is no causal correlation between the change of the Earth's orbit and the initial state of the proto-solar cloud of dust, because there are many conceivable ways of creating this change today which don't have to be accompanied by the adjustment in the initial conditions of the cloud. Once again, the reason for this seems to lie in the *de facto* asymmetry of overdetermination that Lewis postulates: it is much easier to "cut off" a nomological connection of an event with its predeterminants than with its post-determinants.

An advantage of the proposed simplification of Lewis's criteria of similarity (beside one obvious advantage—that it is a *simplification*) is that we get rid of the troublesome notion of "miracle". It is characteristic that no theoreticians who try to apply counterfactual semantics to foundational problems of quantum mechanics ever speak about law-violating possible worlds (see for instance remarks about Lewis's notion of "miracles" in Bedford & Stapp 1995, p. 140). It looks like they accept unanimously that the notion of "possibility" in this context should be understood as "physical possibility" and not "logical possibility". In contrast, Lewis wants to keep his analysis general enough to be able to consider *counter-legal* rather than counter-factual conditionals of the sort "If gravity went by the inverse cube of distance..." (1986a, p. 40). Fair enough, but it seems that by ensuring that this can be done in his semantics, Lewis actually limits its generality, for it turns out to be unable to capture the use of counterfactuals in the contexts in which they are explicitly restricted to physical possibilities. The reason for this is that in Lewis's approach—as we indicated earlier when discussing criteria (S1)-(S4)—some worlds which diverge from the actual one with respect to actual laws have to be seen as more similar to the actual one than some worlds which are in perfect agreement with respect to laws, but instead differ in respect to individual fact.[20] But the consequence of this assumption is that we cannot introduce into Lewis's formal semantics a limited accessibility relation which would pick out only those possible worlds that obey the same laws of nature than the actual world, and therefore would be a semantic counterpart of the physical possibility. In other words, I claim that there is no way in Lewis's approach to give an interpretation of the modal operator of possibility $\Diamond$ under which it would represent "physical possibility". On Lewis's account, law-breaking possible worlds are enmeshed with law-abiding ones, and there is no easy way to disentangle them in order to keep separate two intuitions regarding the notion of possibility: physical and logical.

To sum up: the alternative method of evaluating counterfactual conditionals that is being proposed here is based on only a single criterion of similarity between possible worlds, namely on the spatiotemporal measure of differences in individual facts. Speaking simply, when evaluating a counterfactual $P \; \Box\!\!\rightarrow Q$ we should take into account those $P$-worlds which differ least radically from the actual world with respect to individual facts. When $P$ denotes a chance event (meaning that it is not determined by its *past*), this method reduces to Lewis's, as well as to the asymmetry-by-fiat

---

[20] However, this was necessary to make sure that the valuation of perfectly ordinary *counter-factual*, and not *counter-legal*, statements will be as predicted in natural language.

approach, for in this case there is no need to speak about miracles, and the simplest way to ensure the minimal degree of divergence in particular facts is to assume that up to the moment $P$ occurred the world was exactly as ours. But when $P$ is determined by its past, the main difference between criteria (S1)-(S4) and the approach proposed here lies in the fact that according to the latter we have to consider the possible world which differs from the actual one even *before P* happened. Perhaps it is worth noting that this divergence does not have to stretch infinitely far in the past—in an indeterministic world it is always possible that the causal chain of events leading to the occurrence of $P$ had its origin in other chance events.

## 2.4 CONCLUSIONS

In the chapter we have laid down the foundations for the semantic analysis of counterfactual conditionals that may be later used in the context of quantum measurements. The cornerstone of this analysis is the assumption that the semantics for quantum counterfactuals should be given with the help of the notion of possible worlds and the relation of comparative similarity (closeness) to the actual world. The formal structure in which the truth conditions for the counterfactual are given ought to allow for a violation of the law of conditional excluded middle, and this requirement is satisfied in Lewis's semantics as opposed to Stalnaker's. The truth conditions given by Lewis with the help of formula (L), or equivalent formulas, are commonly accepted as standard in most counterfactual analyses of quantum phenomena. Because in the majority of cases that are considered in the quantum context the Limit Assumption seems to be satisfied, the appropriate truth conditions assume the simple form of ($L_{LA}$), according to which a counterfactual is true if its consequent is true in all antecedent-worlds that are closest to the actual one.

The first problem occurs in the context of the analysis of true-antecedent counterfactuals, or, as we call them, null counterfactuals. According to Lewis's standard formalization, null counterfactuals are equivalent to material conditionals, but this consequence contradicts some intuitions regarding counterfactuals whose antecedents refer to actual measurement events in case the system is not in an eigenstate for the measured observable. One way to avoid this problem is to modify the condition of minimality of the actual world, and to replace it with weaker minimality. Another possible solution can be such that the minimality condition is retained, but instead an alteration in the truth conditions is made, excluding the actual world from the set of worlds relevant to the valuation of the counterfactual. With the Limit Assumption satisfied, those modified truth conditions can be expressed as stating that for a true counterfactual the consequent should be true in all antecedent-worlds closest, but not identical, to the actual world. However, whether any of the above modifications can produce false counterfactuals with both antecedent and consequent true, depends on the details of the similarity relation between possible worlds. In particular, it has been argued that in order to do this job, the similarity relation should not take into account the identity with respect to truly chance (indeterministic) events that take place in the future of the antecedent-event.

Other than the minimality condition, another formal condition imposed on the similarity relation can be seen as also requiring some modifications. This is the strong connectedness requirement, which alleges that any two possible worlds are comparable with one another, i.e. that they are either equally similar to the actual one, or that one of them is more similar than the other. Yet there are some arguments that there may be possible worlds for which the similarity relation does not decide whether they are equally similar or not, and therefore the relation of similarity should be assumed to be a partial ordering only, rather than a linear one. It may seem at first that in every case when such an "incomparability" situation arises we can arbitrarily decide that the worlds in question are just equally similar (if we cannot decide which of two paintings we like more, why shouldn't we say that we like them the same?), but it appears that there may be situations in which such a solution would lead to an inconsistency. Imagine for example that we have two possible worlds $w_1$ and $w_2$ such that $w_1$ is strictly more similar to the actual one than $w_2$, but we also have good reasons to believe that neither $w_1$ nor $w_2$ can be compared to another possible world $w_3$. In such a case we cannot arbitrarily assume that $w_3$ is equisimilar to $w_1$ and $w_2$, for this would imply that $w_1$ is equisimilar to $w_2$, contrary to our assumption. An example suggesting that such a situation can indeed occur will be given in sec. 5.2. There we will also consider what alterations of the truth conditions for the counterfactual are required when the ordering of possible worlds by the similarity relation is assumed to be only partial.

The most controversial aspect of the possible world semantics for the counterfactual is the informal analysis of the similarity relation between possible worlds. Lewis favors an intricate way of comparing possible worlds, which takes into account both differences in individual facts and differences in laws, and which also differentiates between "big" and "small" violations of laws and divergences in particular facts. In contrast, it has been argued in this chapter that so-called miracles (violations of laws that hold in the actual world) should be avoided lest some counterfactuals describing apparent non-local correlations in quantum mechanics receive the wrong valuations. The most promising way of deciding which worlds are more similar to the actual one is in terms of differences in individual facts (and the size of the spatiotemporal regions containing those facts). However, no particular method of comparing these differences has been proposed yet. We will later see that a decision regarding which events are salient with respect to the similarity relation, and how to compare spatio-temporal regions containing those events, has to be made based on the analysis of the individual cases in which the quantum counterfactuals are evaluated. Consequently, rather than prematurely proposing an arbitrary criterion of similarity, we will move on to counterfactual reinterpretations of basic quantum phenomena and facts, including Bell's theorem, as proposed by some prominent authors. One of our goals will be to extract from these considerations a workable semantics of quantum counterfactuals.

# Chapter 3

# A COUNTERFACTUAL VERSION OF BELL'S THEOREM AND ITS CRITICISM

Groundbreaking theoretical achievements in science and mathematics often begin with surprisingly weak assumptions, and lead to unexpectedly strong conclusions. The highest acclamation is usually won by the theorems that establish much while assuming very little. For example, Gödel's famous incompleteness theorem received high praise partly because it was based on a meager set of initial premises: all you have to do is to assume that your theory can encompass standard arithmetic in order to show that there will be a statement such that neither it nor its negation can be proven within the theory. A somewhat similar feature is displayed by Bell's theorem. What is astounding about it is that a contradiction with quantum-mechanical statistics can be achieved at such a low cost. Without any particular, low-level assumptions, and without any reference to specific physical theories, it is possible to derive Bell's inequality from two general presuppositions regarding basic ontological features of the world. However, some theoreticians strive for more. They would like to eliminate one of the initial assumptions of the original Bell theorem while still being able to derive the same contradiction. The assumption that they think can be eliminated is realism regarding the possessed values. If they are right then starting just with the locality assumption we would be able to achieve the same result that had been achieved in the original Bell result.

In chapter 1 we already touched upon some of the possible methods of strengthening Bell's theorem in that way. Bell himself proposed a way of deriving his inequality from the factorization condition, which may be seen as representing an intuition bordering on locality. However, as we have argued, it is not clear what exactly is represented by the factorization condition. Hence, there is still a need to find some other route to Bell's inequality, if one wants to show that it is locality which is responsible for a clash with quantum-mechanical predictions. In this chapter we will analyze one of the first attempts to strengthen Bell's theorem using counterfactual conditionals, due to Henry Stapp and Philippe Eberhard.

## 3.1 COUNTERFACTUAL STRENGTHENING OF BELL'S THEOREM—A FIRST APPROXIMATION

The experimental set-up which we are going to work with will be similar to the one we considered in the exposition of the generalized Bell theorem in sec. 1.4. We consider a system consisting of two particles and two spatially separated measuring devices, each of which can be set up in one of two possible ways (the derivation given below is modeled on Redhead 1987, pp. 82-85). The first (left-hand side) apparatus can measure either an observable $A^1$ or an incompatible observable $A^2$, and the second (right-hand side) can measure $B^1$ or $B^2$. Each of the observables $A^1$, $A^2$, $B^1$, $B^2$ in turn can assume one of two values +1 or −1 (the typical illustration is provided, of course, by two fermions in the singlet spin state). As before, we will symbolize outcomes of particular experiments with the help of lower-case letters: $a^1$, $b^2$, etc. Obviously, there are four possible joint settings for the entire system, depending on the measured observables chosen on both sides: $(A^1, B^1)$, $(A^1, B^2)$, $(A^2, B^1)$ and $(A^2, B^2)$. However, for a given pair of particles only one joint setting can be selected.

Suppose right now—as was done in the original Bell theorem—that in spite of the fact that we can select only one setting out of four, the outcomes of measurements in all possible experimental settings are already determined before the choice of measurement is made. This supposition is usually associated with the realist stance, as was portrayed in chapter 1. It amounts to the thesis that all physical properties of quantum systems are actually well defined, although—for one reason or another—we can not know them all. In other words, we will accept as our working hypothesis the claim that for a given $n^{\text{th}}$ pair of particle in a sequence (1, ..., N) each setting $(A^i, B^j)$ is associated with its own unique response in the form of two definite outcomes $(a_n^{ij}, b_n^{ij})$.[1] This means that for each pair it is meaningful to define the following parameter:

$$(3.1) \quad \gamma_n = a_n^{11} b_n^{11} + a_n^{12} b_n^{12} + a_n^{21} b_n^{21} - a_n^{22} b_n^{22}.$$

From this it obviously follows that the mean value of $\gamma_n$ calculated over all pairs 1, ..., N will be given by

---

[1]　The double superscript $ij$ indicates that a particular value is to be revealed in the context of the double measurement $A^i$ and $B^j$. Later, we will address the issue of dropping the superscript referring to the distant measurement setting.

$$\langle \gamma_n \rangle = \langle a_n^{11} b_n^{11} \rangle + \langle a_n^{12} b_n^{12} \rangle + \langle a_n^{21} b_n^{21} \rangle - \langle a_n^{22} b_n^{22} \rangle,$$

where

$$\langle a_n^{ij} b_n^{ij} \rangle = \frac{1}{N} \sum_{k=1}^{N} a_k^{ij} b_k^{ij}$$

The mean values $\langle a_n^{ij} b_n^{ij} \rangle$ are also referred to as the correlation coefficients $C(A^i, B^j)$ between the outcomes of two experiments. It is important to know that although quantum-mechanical formalism cannot for obvious reasons calculate the individual values $a_n^{ij}, b_n^{ij}$, correlation coefficients $C(A^i, B^j)$ are computable within the standard statistical quantum mechanical algorithm, given the initial state of the system of both particles. This should be clear once we recall that a complete state description in quantum mechanics actually consists of the probability values for all possible results of experiments. Hence, although the exact value of the parameter $\gamma_n$ cannot be calculated within quantum mechanics, its mean value can be. Moreover, the values of the correlation coefficients $C(A^i, B^j)$ can be empirically measurable under certain conditions. Even though it is not possible to determine all of them directly from the defining formula, for this would require that we perform mutually exclusive measurements at the same time, we can still estimate each value $\langle a_n^{ij} b_n^{ij} \rangle$ by appropriately subdividing the entire ensemble of $N$ systems of particles into four groups, each group undergoing a particular type of measurement. Hence we can empirically calculate the value of $\frac{1}{n_1} \sum_{k=1}^{n_1} a_k^{ij} b_k^{ij}$ for $n_1 < N$, and argue that it should asymptotically approach the required value. The crucial assumption here is, of course, that the subensemble of $n_1$ particles was selected purely randomly, without any built-in bias.

The assumption of the determinedness of outcomes for all possible experimental settings was required in order to define the function $\gamma_n$. But we need one more assumption to finally derive a consequence that contradicts quantum-mechanical predictions. As we might expect, this will again be the infamous locality principle, this time in the disguise of the so-called "Matching Condition". This, essentially, is the condition stating that the predetermined outcome for a particular observable will remain the same, no matter what setting was selected for the other particle. As we recall, our notation allows for the possibility that, for example, value $a^{11}$ obtained as a result of the measurement of observable $A^1$ while the other particle underwent the measurement of $B^1$ may be different from the outcome $a^{12}$ for the same observable but with the distant setting changed to $B^2$. However, this would amount to saying that by changing the distant setting we could force the first particle to "jump" from one definite value of observable $A^1$ to the other, and which would constitute an example of non-local influence of the sort we called earlier "a Bell non-locality". Therefore, it stands to reason that we should impose the following restrictions on the predetermined outcomes:

(MC)     $a^{11} = a^{12}$ and $a^{21} = a^{22}$
         $b^{11} = b^{21}$ and $b^{12} = b^{22}$

With this assumption in hand, we can now erase the second superscript in all $A$-outcomes, and the first superscript in $B$-outcomes. Hence, our $\gamma_n$ parameter can now be presented as the combination

$$a_n^1 b_n^1 + a_n^1 b_n^2 + a_n^2 b_n^1 - a_n^2 b_n^2$$

However, we can then transform this algebraic expression into the following:

$$a_n^1(b_n^1 + b_n^2) + a_n^2(b_n^1 - b_n^2).$$

Remembering that all parameters in this formula can take only values 1 or −1 we immediately notice that one of the two expressions in parentheses will have to yield the value zero, whereas the other one will give 2 or −2. Consequently, the value of the entire parameter $\gamma_n$ can be only either 2 or −2. But this implies that the mean value of $\gamma_n$ has to be a number between −2 and 2. That way we have finally arrived at the inequality already known from chapter 1:

(CHSH)     $|\langle a_n^1 b_n^1 \rangle + \langle a_n^1 b_n^2 \rangle + \langle a_n^2 b_n^1 \rangle - \langle a_n^2 b_n^2 \rangle| \leq 2$

As we remember, the above inequality is clearly violated with some combinations of measured observables $A^1$, $A^2$, $B^1$, $B^2$. If the system consisting of two spin-1/2 particles has been prepared in the initial singlet state given by the superposition

$$\Psi = \frac{1}{\sqrt{2}}(|+1\rangle|-1\rangle - |-1\rangle|+1\rangle),$$

where $|+1\rangle$ ($|-1\rangle$) symbolizes the state of the particle in which its spin along a given direction equals $+1$ ($-1$), then the calculated correlation coefficients are $C(A^i, B^j) = -\cos\theta_{ij}$, where $\theta_{ij}$ is the angle between the direction in which spin $A^i$ is measured and the direction selected for the measurement of $B^j$. It is now a matter of simple calculation to show that when we choose the directions that define $A^1$ and $A^2$ separated by the angle 60° and ensure the same angle separates $B^1$ and $B^2$, while making the directions $A^1$ and $B^1$ identical (the directions of measurements of $A^2$ and $B^2$ are separated by 120°), then the calculated mean value $\langle\gamma_n\rangle$ will equal $-2.5$, which disagrees unambiguously with inequality (CHSH). Hence, if we want to save the quantum-mechanical formalism, we have to reject one of the two crucial premises leading to (CHSH). But first we have to make sure that both of them were really necessary in order to get the inequality.

It seems that assumption (MC) is indeed indispensable for the entire derivation. If we didn't have it, we wouldn't be able to put an upper limit on the expectation value of the parameter $\gamma_n$ appropriate for our purposes. In fact, according to the equation (3.1), $\gamma_n$ could reach as high a value as 4, which is well above all the quantum-mechanical estimations on the mean $\langle\gamma_n\rangle$. However, one may wonder if the definition of $\gamma_n$ really requires a realist assumption regarding the existence of predetermined values for measured observables. In fact, some theoreticians claim that it doesn't. For example H. Stapp and P. Eberhard maintain that it is meaningful to interpret outcomes $a_n^{ij}, b_n^{ij}$ in equation (3.1) not as predetermined results, but rather as *hypothetical* results of possible measurements. Here is how they explain this approach:

> If one is willing to accept that the three alternative experiments that could have been performed, but were not, would have had certain definite results if they had been performed, then the $n$'s can be defined to be the results that those experiments would have if they had been performed (Stapp 1971, p. 1306).
> (...) if the experimenters had actually adjusted the mechanical devices to give the alternative experimental setup, then these alternative experiments would have had certain definite results (Stapp 1971, p. 1307).

(...) it makes sense to consider the different results of a future experiment for different settings of the knobs *a* and *b*, although only one setting, at most, will actually be chosen for the actual experiment (Eberhard 1977, pp. 76-77).

The above quotations suggest that Stapp and Eberhard endorse the view according to which considering the possible results of the alternative measurements doesn't commit us to the realist position regarding the possessed values. In fact, they claim that their counterfactual version of Bell's theorem shows that locality is incompatible even with the standard, or "minimalist" interpretation of quantum mechanics. By eliminating the assumption of realism (or "hidden-variable" hypothesis) from the derivation of inequality (CHSH) they purport to have shown that the only assumption which has to be abandoned is the Matching Condition (MC), embodying the intuition of locality.[2] Hence, the strong version of non-locality has to be somehow accepted.

The counterfactual reinterpretation of Bell's theorem has been criticized by M. Redhead in his (1987) book. The main thrust of his criticism was directed against the accepted interpretation of the Matching Condition. He argues that (MC) actually contains more than only the intuition of locality—that a closer analysis of the counterfactual statements involved in the formulation of (MC) reveals that (MC) includes also a residual assumption of "determinism" (or, in our terminology, "realism of possessed values"). We will return to the analysis of this claim later, when we'll argue that it is based on some sort of semantic ambiguity regarding the proper interpretation of counterfactual conditionals. However, for now we will focus on the validity of the counterfactual interpretation of outcomes included in formula (3.1). How can we justify the claim that even though nothing in the entire physical situation determines the outcomes of unperformed possible experiments, yet it is legitimate to include these "outcomes" into the meaningful expression (3.1)? Undoubtedly, the main assumption which supposedly can guarantee this is the principle we called "the Definite Response principle" (DR), and which states that each *performed* measurement has a unique outcome. In other words, if we had measured spin along a given direction *d*, then (even though we haven't actually measured it) it would have revealed precisely one of two possible values: 1 or −1. Now, it may be tempting to "use" (hypothetically, of course) this unique value as a component in our definition of parameter $\gamma_n$. The Definite Response prin-

---

[2]    Eberhard in (1978) compares the Matching Condition with some other locality conditions, including the factorizability condition (F) that we know from chapter 1.

ciple holds for all settings of the spin-measuring device, so it may look like we are justified in considering the entire expression defining $\gamma_n$ (even though the value of this expression cannot be calculated for any concrete pair of particles).

## 3.2 CHSH INEQUALITY ACROSS POSSIBLE WORLDS

No matter how convincing the above argument is, it turns out to be based on certain illegitimate assumptions, and therefore has to be treated with great suspicion. There is no question that we should accept the Definite Response principle, but let's not forget that it speaks about what would have happened, had we decided to measure a particular observable, and not about what obtains in our actual world, in which a different observable was actually selected. The DR principle assures the uniqueness of the outcome under certain conditions, which are not actually satisfied, but we take this uniqueness for granted in our world, in which we define parameter $\gamma_n$. Why this step is illegitimate can perhaps be better understood when we present it in terms of possible worlds. The DR principle can be equivalently expressed by a sentence stating that in every possible world in which the measurement of a particular spin component $A$ is performed (where the possible world is also closest to the actual one, according to some predefined similarity relation), there is exactly one outcome $a$ of the measurement. However, as we explained in chapter 2, in Lewis-type semantics it is perfectly acceptable that there may be more than one possible world closest to the actual one. And if we adopt the minimalist interpretation of quantum mechanics (under which the revised version of Bell's theorem should supposedly proceed) then it should be pretty clear that possible worlds in which the measurement of $A$ has been performed, and which differ only in so far as the recorded value was $+1$ in the first world and $-1$ in the second, should be deemed equally similar to the actual one. Hence, although in each of these worlds $w_+$ and $w_-$ only one outcome obtains, from our perspective we still don't know which one we should include in the expression defining $\gamma_n$.[3]

---

[3] For example, Redhead in his exposition of the Stapp-Eberhard proof uses the following definition without any further comment, and therefore probably approvingly: "$a_n$ = response $A$-meter *would* show if experiment $I$ (...) were performed" (Redhead 1987, p. 91) Yet, in light of our analysis, the description on the right-hand side of the equation doesn't have any definite referent (there are two values which could be revealed, each in its own world of course, so it can not be

A similar point can be made with the help of the counterfactual connective. The principle (DR) amounts to the following counterfactual conditional:

(3.2)     $M(A) \; \Box\!\!\rightarrow (O(A) = +1 \; \underline{\vee} \; O(A) = -1)$

where $M(A)$ stands for "observable $A$ is measured", $\underline{\vee}$ is the exclusive disjunction, and $O(A)$ refers to the outcome of this measurement. However, the above formula is definitely not equivalent to, nor does it imply, the following disjunction:

(3.3)     $(M(A) \; \Box\!\!\rightarrow O(A) = +1) \; \underline{\vee} \; (M(A) \; \Box\!\!\rightarrow O(A) = -1)$

The latter disjunction would be true only if we assumed the law of conditional excluded middle (CEM), already discussed in chapter 2. But we argued there that a logic of counterfactuals which accepted this rule would be entirely inadequate for the purpose of describing quantum events, as we couldn't use counterfactual statements to, for example, express our belief that when (and only when) a system is in an eigenstate for $A$, there is a value $a$ of $A$ such that if $A$ were measured, $a$ would be revealed. So it is possible, and indeed very plausible, that neither of the disjuncts in (3.3) is true. But this means that we cannot use the expression "an outcome which would occur if the measurement was performed" as part of a meaningful formula, so the parameter defined in (3.1) remains without a proper counterfactual interpretation. It looks like the above attempt to counterfactually reinterpret Bell's theorem fails independently of whether the Matching Condition represents the proper locality assumption.

It appears, however, that it is possible to formulate a more sophisticated counterfactual version of Bell's theorem, which avoids the unjustified talk of "outcomes which would occur if the appropriate measurements were performed", and yet seemingly escapes the need to use any form of the realist assumption in order to derive some sort of contradiction with quantum predictions. The argument to this effect has been sketched in an extensive critical analysis by Clifton, Butterfield and Redhead (Clifton *et al.*, 1990),

---

said of either of them that it *would* definitely occur), and therefore doesn't provide parameter $a_n$ with any definitive meaning.

whom I will henceforth refer to as CBR.[4] The argument starts with the assumption that all $N$ measurements have been performed using a single selected setting, let's say $(A^1, B^1)$. This means that we are left with a list of $N$ pairs of outcomes received in the actual world:

$$\{(a_1^{11}, b_1^{11}), (a_2^{11}, b_2^{11}), ..., (a_N^{11}, b_N^{11})\}$$

Now, we have to consider different possible worlds. In particular, there will be three groups of possible worlds such that in each of them a different setting will have been selected: $(A^1, B^2)$, $(A^2, B^1)$ and $(A^2, B^2)$. Every possible world will obviously have its unique $N$-tuple of outcomes (according to the Definite Response principle). But now we can use the Matching Condition in order to argue that different worlds which share one particular setting should have exactly the same outcomes for the repeating observable even though the other setting is different. So, for example, the possible world in which $(A^1, B^2)$ was chosen, should have the same outcomes of the measurement of $A^1$ as the actual one $(A^1, B^1)$. This, once again, is argued for by reference to the locality intuition: the only difference between these worlds is the setting chosen for the distant measuring device, and this should not affect whatever happens with the first particle. If this supposition is right, we will have the following three possible worlds in addition to our actual one:

$$(A^1, B^2)\text{-world: } \{(a_1^{11}, b_1^{12}), (a_2^{11}, b_2^{12}), ..., (a_N^{11}, b_N^{12})\}$$
$$(A^2, B^1)\text{-world: } \{(a_1^{21}, b_1^{11}), (a_2^{21}, b_2^{11}), ..., (a_N^{21}, b_N^{11})\}$$
$$(A^2, B^2)\text{-world: } \{(a_1^{21}, b_1^{12}), (a_2^{21}, b_2^{12}), ..., (a_N^{21}, b_N^{12})\}$$

We can now define the parameter $\gamma_n$ not as characterizing a physical condition existing in the actual world, but rather as a function "across possible worlds". In spite of this new interpretation, the entire formal inference leading to (CHSH) is still valid—all the necessary mathematical prerequisites are met by the construction. However, we have to be careful to draw the right conclusion from the fact that the existence of the foregoing worlds leads to the Bell inequality. We know that the Bell inequality—in its particular form of (CHSH)—is incompatible with the quantum-mechanical

---

[4]    They call it "a quarter approach" (Clifton *et al.* 1990, p. 12). This argument is extracted from Stapp's comprehensive article (1985). See also an earlier attempt in (Stapp 1977).

statistics defined for a certain selection of observables. This shows that in our situation at least one of the four worlds has to violate quantum-mechanical statistics. In other words, at least one of the four $N$-tuples of outcomes disagrees with what is predicted by the probabilistic laws of quantum mechanics. For quite obvious reasons we would eliminate the actual world as a potential culprit—quantum-mechanical predictions regarding statistics of observed values have never been experimentally falsified. So we may conclude as a result of the above derivation that in at least one of the *possible* worlds the $N$-tuple of counterfactually obtained outcomes disagrees with the statistical distribution predicted by QM.

The question can be asked, however, if this consequence is really bad enough to warrant an unconditional rejection of the locality principle. After all, in some approaches it makes perfect sense to consider possible worlds in which some laws of nature are temporarily violated, or suspended (this is, as we remember, one of the main tenets of Lewis's similarity ranking). And, although we generally argued against such approaches in the previous chapter pointing out certain unwelcome consequences of admitting "law-breaking" worlds in the context of quantum-mechanical analysis, still some readers may remain unconvinced. However, I think it would be a desperate move to attempt to save the locality principle by postulating the existence of closest "law-breaking" possible worlds in which only a different setting was chosen, while admitting that the actual world conforms to the no-mological requirements of quantum theory. If we opted for this way out, we would have to admit that nature is conspiring to ensure that whatever measurement settings we select, we always end up with a "law-abiding" world, while some alternative settings would have consistently and mali-ciously led to the worlds disobeying quantum principles. For that reason, we believe that the consequence that some of the possible worlds with alternative measurement choices have to violate quantum statistics is almost as bad as the consequence that the actual world displays that sort of dis-crepancy.[5]

---

[5]  CBR actually consider another possibility, connected with the fact that quantum-mechanical laws are only probabilistic, and the occurrence of a sequence of events that doesn't follow the quantum statistics is not strictly speaking impossible, but merely extremely improbable. It may therefore happen, that although a particular world obeys quantum laws, yet by chance it displays certain statistics of outcomes not conforming to those laws (CBR call it a "ropey world"). However, in response to this objection they show that if we accept a reasonable restriction on the number of ropey words, still the Bell-like inequality will follow (Clifton *et al.* 1990, pp. 24-27).

This version of Bell's theorem is attacked by CBR in two steps. Firstly, following Redhead's line in his 1987 book they criticize the Matching Condition, arguing that it doesn't represent the proper formulation of the locality condition. And secondly, they spell out an objection (they call it "the broken square problem") which shows that even the full Matching Condition cannot justify one crucial step in the inference leading to the conclusion that there exist three possible worlds which, together with the actual world, create a quarter satisfying the CHSH inequality. In what follows we will reject their first argument, but the second one will be reaffirmed. We will also use this opportunity to learn valuable lessons about the semantics of the quantum counterfactual conditional, which will be developed subsequently and refined in later parts of the book.

Redhead started his critique of the Matching Condition by proposing its counterfactual account. Suppose that we consider the $n^{\text{th}}$ pair of particles, and that the actually performed measurements were $A^1$ and $B^1$ with the results $a_n^{11}, b_n^{11}$. Now let us consider counterfactually what would have happened, had we decided to measure $B^2$ rather than $B^1$. According to the intuition behind the Matching Condition, this change should not affect the spatially separated measurement $A^1$ and its outcome, hence the following counterfactual should hold in the actual world $w_0$:

(3.4)     $M(B^2) \ \Box\!\!\rightarrow O(A^1) = a_n^{11}$

Statement (3.4) is supposed to guarantee that the value of $a_n^{12}$ (the outcome of measurement $A^1$ obtained in the world in which $M(B^2)$ is performed) will be equal to that of $a_n^{11}$, which licenses dropping the unnecessary superscripts. However, Redhead questions whether (3.4) correctly represents our locality intuition. Using certain "thought experiments", and appealing to some common intuitions he argues that (3.4) would hold only if the outcome of the measurement of $A^1$ were deterministic, i.e. nomically connected with the past state of the system. However, if—as it is assumed in the Copenhagen interpretation of quantum mechanics—outcome $a_n^{11}$ is not determined, then if we consider an alternative situation in which $B^2$ is chosen rather than $B^1$ and if we let the world run its course again, the alternative value $-a_n^{11}$ may be picked by nature, and hence (3.4) is not justified.

## 3.3 THE MATCHING CONDITION AND THE SEMANTICS OF SPATIOTEMPORAL COUNTERFACTUALS

The compactness of the above presentation gives no scope for a reasonable assessment of Redhead's conclusions. There are many issues entangled in this problem, including the issue of the spatiotemporal location of the event referred to in the consequent in relation to the event constituting the antecedent of the counterfactual (3.4).[6] We will start disentangling this web by considering the different spatiotemporal relations that can hold between those events, such that they are definable in the special theory of relativity. There are basically three possibilities that we need to take into account: the outcome of the $A^1$-measurement can be located in the absolute past of the $B^2$-measurement, in the absolute future, or it can be space-like separated from $B^2$. In the first case there should be no controversy: if the measurement of $A^1$ already revealed a particular outcome $a^{11}$ *before* the measurement of $B^1$, then by choosing an alternate setting $B^2$ we shouldn't be able to change this outcome. The past is *counterfactually locked*, meaning that if the present were different, the past would still remain the same. This assessment is independent of whether the past event in question is ontologically indeterministic, or deterministic. It is simply a consequence of our basic assumptions regarding the semantics of the tensed counterfactual. In conclusion, in this case statement (3.4) turns out to be true unconditionally.

When the event described in the consequent of (3.4) is located in the absolute future of the antecedent, things become quite different. Now it makes sense to consider an alternate outcome of the $A^1$-measurement under the supposition that $B^2$ was chosen instead of $B^1$. The counterfactual (3.4) invites us to consider an alternative history of the world in which at a certain spatiotemporal point a different selection has been made. Whatever

---

[6] Unfortunately, both semantic analyses of the counterfactual in (Redhead 1987) and (Clifton *et al.* 1990) are given in the non-relativistic setting, with the reference to the "absolute" time instants. In later publications Redhead corrected this drawback (Redhead, LaRivière 1997). Here we will be consistently using the relativistic framework to express relations between the consequent and the antecedent. Also, CBR in their discussion have proposed an alternative way of assessing the similarity between possible worlds and, therefore, evaluating counterfactuals like (3.4), which does not take into account relativistically invariant spatiotemporal relations, but rather distinguishes between various sorts of events (settings versus outcomes). Later in this chapter I will criticize that approach to the semantics of quantum counterfactuals.

happens in the future of this change depends on the causal laws that govern the evolution of the system. Hence, if we accept the possibility that the outcome of the later $A^1$-measurement is not causally determined by its past, then we should consider two alternative evolutions: one with the outcome of the $A^1$-measurement equal $a_n^{11}$, and the other with $-a_n^{11}$. Neither of these possible histories is preferable to the other, thereby rendering (3.4) false.

I admit that this conclusion may be seen by some as somewhat controversial. After all, the world in which the future result of the $A^1$-measurement is the same as in the actual world has a wider area of compatibility with the actual world than the alternative world, so why shouldn't we deem it closer than the alternative? This general semantic argument can be reinforced by another, taken from linguistic practice. It happens very often that upon learning an unfortunate outcome of a seemingly random course of events, we complain: if I'd earlier done this rather than that, I'd be better off right now. A typical example would be a gambler's grumble, when he loses a bet: "If I'd only put my bet on the number that actually won, I'd be a rich man now." There is no question that examples like this have a persuasiveness about them, although I personally tend to see them as cases of the general "gambler's fallacy" (if I'd made another bet, the entire random selection process would have started anew, and nothing would guarantee my success in that case, just as in the actual case).[7] However, the decisive argument against such an interpretation of counterfactuals in the context of quantum mechanics comes from an altogether different angle. As I already indicated in the previous chapter when analyzing null counterfactuals, if we decided to include future indeterministic events in the evaluation of tensed counterfactuals, then the entire business of the application of counterfactuals to quantum mechanics would be in serious troubles.

In particular, we would have to admit that for all experiments that have actually been performed, their outcomes had been counterfactually determined all along. That would have tremendously unintuitive consequences.

---

[7] It was Pavel Tichý who has used for the first time a similar example against Lewis's analysis of counterfactuals (1976). Bennett in turn has proposed to distinguish between future indeterministic events which are nevertheless causally related to the antecedent-event, and those that are not, suggesting that only the latter should count toward similarity (2003, pp. 234-237). As a result, "the gambler's counterfactual" would come out true, but the apparently similar one "If I rolled a die instead of Steve, the result would still be the same" would be false. A similar intuition regarding the gambler's counterfactual is expressed in (Müller 2002, p. 287). For a dissenting view see e.g. (Pagonis *et al.* 1996, p. 53, note 5).

For instance, let us imagine that an experimenter is spatially orienting her Stern-Gerlach device to measure spin of an oncoming electron in a particular direction. As a philosopher observing this preparation, I formulate the following counterfactual: there is a particular value (although I don't know it yet) such that if she measured spin in this direction, she would reveal it (of course, I mean the value that will be revealed later anyway by the measurement which its on its way). But now let us imagine that something turned up which at the last moment prevented the measurement from being carried out (there was a temporary power loss, or simply the experimenter changed her mind). Now I would have to correct my assessment: actually, I was wrong, there was no value which would appear, had the experiment been performed. But this means that ultimately the truth of my counterfactual—and, consequently, the truth about some dispositions of the system—depends on such accidental things as technical problems or the experimenter's whim. For that reason I will stand firm by my initial statement that future indeterministic events (such as outcomes of future measurements) should not be taken into account when evaluating tensed counterfactuals.[8]

---

[8]  We should mention, however, one approach to quantum counterfactuals that openly includes future results of measurements into the evaluation procedure. The notion of the so-called "time-symmetrized counterfactuals" has been advanced by L. Vaidman in support of the Time-Symmetrized Quantum Theory (originally proposed in Aharonov *et al.* 1964). The time-symmetrized formalism is based on the assumption that the quantum description of a system between two subsequent measurements at moments $t_1$ and $t_2$ should include not only the initial, preselected state $\psi_1$ but also the final, postselected state $\psi_2$ that the system ends up in after the second measurement. Aharonov, Bergman and Lebowitz derive a formula (the ABL rule) which allows them to calculate the probabilities of outcomes of an intermediate measurement that actually takes place between $t_1$ and $t_2$, given the states $\psi_1$ and $\psi_2$. Vaidman in a series of publications (Vaidman 1999a, 1999b, 1999c) defends the counterfactual interpretation of the ABL rule, according to which the rule gives the correct probabilities not only for the actually performed intermediate measurements, but also for all possible observables that may be selected for measurement between $t_1$ and $t_2$. In order to support this claim, he introduces the time-symmetric interpretation of counterfactuals, which prescribes that when considering a counterfactual intermediate measurement, we should keep fixed the results of measurements both at the past time $t_1$ and at the future time $t_2$. The detailed analysis of this proposal lies beyond the scope of our book. However, it is clear that Vaidman's conception faces serious difficulties. Vaidman himself admits that his method of evaluating counterfactuals sometimes leads to an impossibility. For instance, if the system undergoes three consecutive measurements of spin-components $\sigma_z$, $\sigma_x$, and $\sigma_z$ again, and if the result of the last measurement is differ-

This leaves the third and most controversial case. In that case we have to evaluate the counterfactual conditional (3.4) when the outcome of the $A^1$-measurement obtains in a spatiotemporal region which cannot be linked by means of any signal with the place of the selection of the $B$-measurement. If we consider an alternative selection $B^2$, it is not at all obvious that we should retain the actual outcome of the $A^1$-measurement, as if this outcome belonged to the already unchangeable past. On the other hand, however, it is not certain whether the fragment of space-time which is space-like separated from the location of the antecedent in (3.4) should be seen as part of an open future, where all possibilities are still unrealized. In the classical picture the situation looks much more clear. There the absolute surface of simultaneity cuts through the selection event of $B$-measurement. Whatever event lies on this surface, belongs to the absolute "present" with respect to the antecedent-event, and, therefore, has objective existence relative to the former event. Were we evaluating the counterfactual (3.4) in the classical situation, we should most probably treat the consequent the same way as when it belonged in the past, and should deem that the possible world in which $B^2$ is selected and the $A^1$-measurement has

---

ent from the outcome of the initial one (which is possible due to the intervening measurement of $\sigma_x$), then it is impossible to keep these two outcomes fixed and at the same time to assume counterfactually that the intermediately measured observable was $\sigma_z$ instead of $\sigma_x$ (Vaidman 1999a). Vaidman's tends to downplay this shortcoming by arguing that his method still works well in many different cases, but this can be doubted. An argument given in (Kastner 1999) shows that practically in each case when we consider two consecutive measurements of two spin-components along directions $a$ and $b$ on a big ensemble of particles, the distribution of possible outcomes of the last measurement as predicted by quantum mechanics will non-trivially depend on the selection of the intermediate direction $c$. In consequence, Vaidman has to accept (and he admits this openly; see Vaidman 1999b) that his rule of evaluating counterfactuals regarding the intermediate selection, which requires keeping all the future outcomes, and hence their distribution intact, leads to considering possible worlds that violate the statistical prediction of quantum mechanics (in Vaidman's terminology: extremely improbable worlds). And, finally, there is an argument advanced in (Sharp, Shanks 1993) and supported by Kastner, showing that when we calculate the total probability of a given outcome for the intermediate measurement on the basis of the ABL rule and its time-symmetrized counterfactual interpretation, the result will be inconsistent with standard, quantum mechanical calculations. Vaidman responds to this that when doing this calculation we should adjust the distribution of the outcomes of the final measurement so that it reflects the change in the intermediate measurement, but how this can be done without rejecting his strict rule of keeping all the future outcomes exactly as in the actual world, remains a mystery to me.

the same outcome as the actual outcome is the closest to the actual world. However, in the relativistic case the right way to proceed is not so clear. There are legitimate physical frames of reference in which the outcome of the $A^1$-measurement appears to precede temporarily the choice of the $B$-measurement, which suggests that the evaluation of (3.4) should follow the case of the consequent in the past. But there are equally legitimate frames of reference in which it is the opposite: the outcome of the $A^1$-measurement belongs to the future of the $B$-measurement. From this perspective whatever happens as a result of the $A$-measurement is not yet "decided" with respect to the $B$-measurement, so two possibilities remain open.

It seems that, in the absence of a decisive argument in favor of one of these options, we have to consider both of them equally acceptable. We can now clarify their implications. According to one approach, all events which are space-like separated from the counterfactually considered event (the antecedent-event) are treated as if they had already been brought into existence, analogously to the events from the absolute past. Hence, when evaluating a tensed counterfactual with the antecedent-event space-like separated from the consequent-event, we should, if possible, keep the consequent-event exactly the same as in the actual world, no matter if this event is deterministic or not. Therefore, we should accept (3.4) as true even though there is an alternative world in which the $A^1$-measurement yields the opposite value. However, we have to admit that this world is farther from the actual world than the former world is. The only situation in which we would be forced to admit the falsity of (3.4) is when there is no possible world with the $B^2$-measurement and the outcome of the $A^1$-measurement equaling $a_n^{11}$ at all. But this would be a case of non-locality: the performance of the $B^2$-measurement in the distance *forces* (through certain lawful correlations) the $A^1$-measurement to reveal the opposite value $-a_n^{11}$. In conclusion, according to the above semantics of the spatiotemporal counterfactual, statement (3.4) seems to be a proper instantiation of the general locality condition.

There is an alternative method of approaching this case, though. If we, following Redhead, analyze the case of space-like separation between the consequent-event and the antecedent-event in the same manner as the case of the consequent in the future, then the conclusions regarding counterfactual (3.4) will be quite different. For, in order to evaluate (3.4) we would have to consider a possible history of the world in which $B^2$ had already been selected, but the outcome of the distant $A^1$-measurement had not been revealed yet. Hence, two alternative ways the world might develop are on a par: one with the $A^1$-outcome equaling $a_n^{11}$, and the other with the opposite outcome $-a_n^{11}$. Consequently, sentence (3.4) would come out true only if the alternative way the world might develop were for some reason eliminated. But this amounts to saying that nature selects value $a_n^{11}$ as the result of the $A^1$-measurement, and hence is equivalent to the assumption of determinism. Redhead seems to be right then in his assessment that (3.4) encompasses more than the locality principle allows. The only problem, though, is that this assessment is contingent upon acceptance of the second method of evaluating space-time counterfactuals. As long as there is an alternative method, not leading to the above conclusion, Redhead's criticism of the Matching Condition seems to be inconclusive. Redhead would have to present strong arguments in favor of his version of spatiotemporal semantics for the counterfactual, much stronger than the arguments presented in his (1987) book and in (Clifton *et al.* 1990).[9]

From this moment on, we will be considering both interpretations of space-time counterfactuals as equally acceptable, and we will use them independently in our counterfactual analysis of quantum-mechanical phenomena. It can be noted that one aspect that distinguishes the first semantic approach from the second is the different underlying intuition regarding the shape of the "surface of the temporal growth of the universe" relative to a particular spatiotemporal point. Compatible with the first, Stapp-Eberhard approach, is the view that the alternative evolution of the universe which starts at the point of the selection of the $B$-measurement follows the hypersurface of the future light cone of this point, so that everything which occurs "below" that hypersurface has already come into existence. On the other hand, the Redhead-Clifton-Butterfield approach

---

[9]   A somewhat similar objection questioning the validity of Stapp's (1985) condition of locality has been raised by R.A. Guy and R.J. Deltete in (1988). They claim that since the outcomes obtained in both wings of the apparatus are assumed to be random, it cannot be guaranteed that under the alternative setting selected for one wing, the sequence of outcomes in the other wing remains the same as in the original setting. Stapp responded to this in (Stapp 1988a), correctly pointing out that his proof requires only that the sequence of outcomes *could* remain the same (meaning that there *is* a possible world with the outcomes of the unaltered measurement remaining the same). F. Fellows (1988), in turn, alleged that the fact that Stapp simultaneously uses outcomes for incompatible measurement settings in one formula indicates that he implicitly assumes realism of possessed values, to which Stapp once again replied (correctly, in my opinion) that theoretical considerations of *possible* outcomes in alternative settings are admissible even for the followers of Heisenberg and Bohr (Stapp 1988b).

seems to assume that the universe grows along the hypersurface of the past light cone of the $B$-measurement, so that everything that is space-like separated from this point does not have objective existence at the moment of the selection.[10] I don't see any argument which could decisively settle the issue of which approach is superior. The only possibility is that future analysis can reveal that one of the alternative semantics may, for that reason or another, be more appropriate for the task of describing quantum events.

However, we have to stress that even if we agreed with Redhead's critique of the Matching Condition in its counterfactual form, presented in (3.4), still this would not affect the alternative version of the Stapp-Eberhard proof, namely the version "across possible worlds". Let us see why this is the case. As we remember, all we have to show in order for the proof to go through is that there are three possible worlds with alternate choices of settings and such that the outcomes obtained for the same measurements match. So, for example, we need to make sure that there will be a possible $(A^1, B^2)$-world with the following sequence of outcomes:

$$\{(a_1^{11}, b_1^{12}), (a_2^{11}, b_2^{12}), ..., (a_n^{11}, b_n^{12})\},$$

where the results for the $A^1$-measurement are identical to those obtained in the actual $(A^1, B^1)$-world. But the existence of such a world is quite independent of whether we agree with Redhead's way of evaluating the counterfactual analogously to (3.4). In the case where we consider a sequence of measurements, and not one particular measurement, the counterfactual in question will have the following form:

$$(3.5) \qquad M(B^2) \;\square\!\!\rightarrow (O_1(A^1) = a_n^{11} \wedge O_2(A^1) = a_2^{11},..., \wedge O_N(A^1) = a_N^{11})^{11}$$

---

[10] This does not mean, however, that I am ascribing to these theoreticians the view that they accept the objective existence of the passage of time ("the temporal becoming"). The classical criticism of this notion is presented in (Williams 1967); see also a collection of essays in (Čapek 1976). We should not forget that within the special theory of relativity there is no way to introduce consistently the hypersurface separating the sphere of the determined past from the sphere of the open future. In particular, if we took any space-time point $p'$ which is "co-existing" with a given point $p$ according to any of the above intuitions (which lies on the surface of either the future or the past light cone), then $p'$'s own "surface of the temporal evolution" would be different from that of $p$.

[11] We assume, of course, that all outcomes obtained for the $A^1$-measurements are space-like separated from the location where the choice of $B^2$ is made. Note also

Now, Redhead can argue that this counterfactual should not be rendered true, because there will most certainly be alternative $(A^1, B^2)$-worlds with different combinations of $A^1$-outcomes, and they should be treated as equally close to the actual $(A^1, B^1)$-world as the one with repeated $A^1$-outcomes. However, he cannot deny that some world among the closest $(A^1, B^2)$-worlds *has* to have the $A^1$-outcomes exactly identical to those obtained in the actual world. If it were otherwise, then we would have a clear case of non-locality, for it would be true that if an alternative $B$-setting were selected, *some* of the $A^1$-outcomes would be different than in actuality. And the existence of a possible $(A^1, B^2)$-world with the same $A^1$-outcomes is all we need to take the first step in the "quarter approach" to (CHSH) inequality.

It is actually not a coincidence that we have here stumbled upon a condition requiring the existence of particular possible worlds, and such that it is closely linked with the intuition of locality. For it looks like it may be a good idea to propose a general locality principle which would avoid using the counterfactual connective and, thereby, escape the controversy surrounding the interpretation of spatiotemporal counterfactuals.[12] Such a locality condition can be formulated in terms of possible worlds and their spatiotemporal areas of matching. The locality condition, which we will call "semantic locality" (SLOC) can be expressed as follows:

(SLOC)   For every non-contradictory event $E$ there is a possible $E$-world such that it is identical with the actual one in the entire region outside the future light cone of $E$ (all events that are either absolutely earlier than $E$ or space-like separated from $E$ are identical with the actual ones)

We will carefully scrutinize the expression (SLOC) in chapter 6, where we will compare it with the more standard, counterfactual expressions of the locality condition. For now let us only note that (SLOC) is entirely sufficient to guarantee the existence of two out of the three possible worlds necessary in the "quarter approach" to the CHSH inequality. According to

---

that we make the assumption that the selection of the $B^2$-measurement is made once for all $N$ particles (it can be done by turning and fixing the knob of the Stern-Gerlach device to the appropriate position), and hence it can be seen as a single point-like event.

[12] Following Dickson (1994) we can call it a "locality condition without counterfactual commitments".

SLOC, there should be an $(A^1, B^2)$-world such that it keeps all the outcomes of the $A^1$-measurements the same as in the actual world (because by assumption all these outcomes are space-like separated from $M(B^2)$), and hence its sequence of outcomes can be presented as $\{(a_1^{11}, b_1^{12}), (a_2^{11}, b_2^{12}), ..., (a_N^{11}, b_N^{12})\}$. The same argument establishes that when we consider an alternative selection of the $A^2$-measurement while keeping $B^1$, there will be an $(A^2, B^1)$-world with outcomes $\{(a_1^{21}, b_1^{11}), (a_2^{21}, b_2^{11}), ..., (a_N^{21}, b_N^{11})\}$. But now the question is whether (SLOC) can legitimize the existence of the third world necessary for the derivation, i.e. the $(A^2, B^2)$-world with the sequence of outcomes numerically equal to $\{(a_1^{21}, b_1^{12}), (a_2^{21}, b_2^{12}), ..., (a_N^{21}, b_N^{12})\}$. This world, as we may notice, contains a sequence of outcomes such that each $A^2$-outcome is identical to the one obtained in the previously selected $(A^2, B^1)$-world, whereas its counterpart (the $B^2$-outcome) is taken from the $(A^1, B^2)$-world. The relations of identity between the outcomes in all of the different settings can be presented on the following diagram with the help of connecting curved lines.

$$(A^1, B^1) \quad (A^1, B^2) \quad (A^2, B^1) \quad (A^2, B^2)$$

$$(a^{11}, b^{11}) \quad (a^{12}, b^{12}) \quad (a^{21}, b^{21}) \quad (a^{22}, b^{22})$$

Now, we have to notice that (SLOC), and the locality intuition behind it, can only guarantee that there will be *two* possible $(A^2, B^2)$-worlds: one obtained by considering the $(A^1, B^2)$-world and changing counterfactually $A^1$ for $A^2$, and the other reached from the $(A^2, B^1)$-world by switching counterfactually $B^1$ to $B^2$. That way we can arrive at two independent sequences of $(A^2, B^2)$-outcomes: $\{(a_1^{22}, b_1^{12}), (a_2^{22}, b_2^{12}), ..., (a_N^{22}, b_N^{12})\}$ and $\{(a_1^{21}, b_1^{22}), (a_2^{21}, b_2^{22}), ..., (a_N^{21}, b_N^{22})\}$, where $a_i^{22}$ and $b_i^{22}$ are unspecified results obtained in the counterfactually changed measurements. But we cannot guarantee that $a_i^{22} = a_i^{21}$ or $b_i^{22} = b_i^{12}$, at least not on the basis of (SLOC), or the Matching Condition in the form of counterfactuals (3.5). It may happen by accident that, for example, the $B$-outcomes obtained in the second of the two $(A^2, B^2)$-worlds will coincide with the sequence $b_1^{12}, b_2^{12}, ..., b_N^{12}$ taken from the $(A^1, B^2)$-worlds, but this need not be the case. The non-existence of the $(A^2, B^2)$-world containing the sequence of outcomes

$\{(a_1^{21}, b_1^{12}), (a_2^{21}, b_2^{12}), ..., (a_N^{21}, b_N^{12})\}$ does not seem to violate any locality condition one may invoke. That is precisely the objection CBR call "the broken square problem" (they depict the transitions from the actual world to all possible worlds in the form of a square whose vertices represent the worlds in question, and they claim that the last vertex will actually split into two vertices containing two different $(A^2, B^2)$-worlds—see Fig. 3.1). Based on our foregoing analysis, we have to admit that this objection is perfectly valid, and that it actually cuts off the possibility of proceeding with the proof to the final derivation of the (CHSH) inequality.[13]

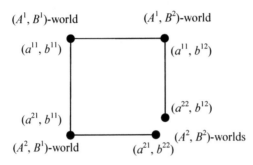

Figure 3.1 The broken square problem.

Actually, taking into account our earlier discussion on the consequences of the (CHSH) inequality, we can give a positive argument against the existence of a $(A^2, B^2)$-world which would "close" the broken square. The fact that (CHSH) is derivable from the assumption of its existence shows that such a world would violate quantum statistics. In other words, the sequence of outcomes $\{(a_1^{21}, b_1^{12}), (a_2^{21}, b_2^{12}), ..., (a_N^{21}, b_N^{12})\}$ necessarily does not conform to the statistical predictions of the quantum theory. No wonder, then, that without additional arguments we have no reason to assume

---

[13] Stapp's response to this argument given in (1990a) is, effectively, that in order to avoid the broken square problem his proof should be based on the assumption that is stronger than our Definite Response (DR) and yet weaker than the full-blown determinateness of results. Apart from my failure to comprehend what this assumption could look like, I would like to stress that in the possible-world framework we are using here there is no place for such a condition. Basically, we have two choices only: either to accept that for a given selection of measurement setting there are several possible worlds each containing different outcomes (which leads directly to the broken square), or to claim that there is only one, unique possible world (which is equivalent to realism of possessed values).

that such a possible world would exist. One conceivable general argument in favor of the existence of a unique $(A^2, B^2)$-world "reachable" from both the $(A^1, B^2)$ and $(A^2, B^1)$-worlds can be given in the form of the strong determinist thesis, stating that in all $(A^2, B^2)$-worlds which share with the actual world the joint absolute past of both measurements, the sequences of all outcomes are exactly the same (in other words, the outcomes of joint $(A^2, B^2)$-measurements are uniquely and unconditionally determined by their physical pasts).[14] Were that the case, then if we wanted to save the locality principle in the form of the condition (SLOC), we would obviously have to admit that this unique sequence of outcomes has to be identical to $\{(a_1^{21}, b_1^{12}), (a_2^{21}, b_2^{12}), ..., (a_N^{21}, b_N^{12})\}$. But this rescue of the proof is of no help for Stapp and Eberhard, because their goal was to proceed without any assumption that resembles the thesis of determinism, or realism of possessed values. By inserting the extra premise justifying the last step in the derivation of the (CHSH) inequality, we slipped back into the old version of Bell's result, showing that the locality principle plus determinism are incompatible with the quantum-mechanical predictions. But to achieve that

---

[14] CBR derive this sort of determinism from a broader principle they call "Montague-Earman determinism", which roughly states that if two possible worlds match with respect to all physical phenomena up to a certain point of time, they match everywhere (footnote 12, p. 23—note the non-relativistic way of expressing this condition). However, they notice that with this variant of determinism things are getting more complicated. We have to reconsider our way of evaluating counterfactual conditionals, such as for example the Matching Condition (3.4), because there will be no possible worlds with exactly the same absolute past of the antecedent-event as the actual world. For example, in order to construct a possible $(A^2, B^2)$-world, we have to "adjust" events located in the past of the choice of the alternative measurements, which causally lead to that new choice. A new possible method of evaluating counterfactuals can stipulate that we should take into account only those possible antecedent-worlds which minimize necessary adjustments in the antecedent's past. But now it is theoretically possible that we can again end up with two such "minimal" $(A^2, B^2)$-worlds, one obtained from the $(A^1, B^2)$-world by considering an alternative $A^2$-measurement, and the other reached from the $(A^2, B^1)$-world. The difference between these worlds can come from the fact that the causal antecedents of an alternative measurement choice, stretching infinitely into the past, may subluminally affect the absolute past of the other measurement. Hence, if the above two worlds differ from one another with respect to the total past of $(A^2, B^2)$-measurements, there is no immediate reason to claim that their respective outcomes will remain the same. It seems, therefore, that we need an additional assumption to the effect that the processes leading to the measurement choices $A$ and $B$ are causally separated from one another.

result we didn't need the entire battery of counterfactual semantics—we have known all along that that was the case.

## 3.4 ALTERNATIVE SEMANTICS OF QUANTUM COUNTERFACTUALS

The main tenet of CBR's analysis seems to be right—Stapp-Eberhard's argument does fail to establish that the quantum-mechanical formalism by itself requires that there be superluminal connections between the choice of measurement setting and the outcomes revealed in the distant part of the system. However, as we have pointed out, CBR's paper also contains some controversial claims, which under close scrutiny appear to be unwarranted. One of them is the proposal of a particular method of judging the similarity relation between possible worlds, which relates to the issue of the semantics of quantum counterfactuals. Already earlier we suggested one possible way of interpreting the Clifton-Butterfield-Redhead approach to the truth-conditions for counterfactuals. That interpretation was defined entirely with the help of absolute spatiotemporal relations between the antecedent-event and the consequent-event. It basically reduces to the requirement that when comparing possible worlds with respect to their similarity to the actual one, we should disregard all the events which are located outside the past light-cone of the antecedent-event, and are not causally connected with this region. But some of CBR's remarks explicitly suggest a different approach, in which not the spatiotemporal location, but the "physical nature" of an event should determine whether to take it into account when comparing possible worlds. As we are on the quest to find a semantics of counterfactuals best suited for the purpose of describing quantum entangled systems, we are obliged to take a closer look at this proposal. First of all, they distinguish (quite typically, one must admit) between two types of events: meter settings and meter responses. And the main claim is that the responses should not count towards similarity when evaluating counterfactuals, whereas the meter settings should.

We can clarify this statement by the use of an example. Let us use counterfactual (3.4), which can be read as follows: it is true in the actual $(A^1, B^1)$-world that if the $B^2$-measurement had been selected, the result of the $A^1$-measurement would have remained the same. Now, in order to evaluate this counterfactual according to the Lewis semantics we have to consider all $M(B^2)$-worlds which are closest to the actual world, and check whether the consequent holds in all of them. According to the analyzed proposal, none of the outcomes $a_n^{11}, b_n^{11}$ should count toward similarity, i.e. all $M(B^2)$-worlds with the outcomes $(a_n^{11}, b_n^{11})$, $(-a_n^{11}, b_n^{11})$, $(a_n^{11}, -b_n^{11})$ and $(-a_n^{11}, -b_n^{11})$ should be treated as equally similar to the actual one. On the other hand, it makes a difference whether in a $M(B^2)$-world the second measurement is performed, as in the actual world, in the $A^1$-setting, or in some other setting. In agreement with CBR's suggestions, only the first world can be seen as the closest to the actual world.

CBR give some general arguments in support of their method of assessing similarity between possible worlds. Without those arguments the method might be seen as having been adopted *ad hoc* for the mere purpose of defeating Stapp's proof. Firstly, they say that the outcome of the counterfactually unchanged measurement (i.e. the $A^1$-measurement in our case) cannot be salient with respect to the similarity relation, because if it were, the counterfactual (3.4) representing the locality condition would come out true by *fiat*. In other words, the truth of the locality condition would be guaranteed by nothing more than terminological stipulations, and hence would acquire the status of an analytic statement. And yet we would like to see the locality condition as saying something non-trivial about the world, something that could be false, even if it is actually believed to be true. In response to this argument, we have to admit first that the truth of (3.4) indeed should not be a consequence of terminological conventions, especially when we entertain the possibility (which is actually the ultimate conclusion of the Stapp-Eberhard proof) that (3.4) may be violated. However CBR are wrong to maintain that when we take the outcome of the counterfactually unchanged experiment as relevant for the purpose of comparing possible worlds, (3.4) will necessarily come out true. We have already indicated that if we elect to treat the possible $(A^1, B^2)$-world in which the outcome of the $A^1$-measurement is $a^{11}$ as closer to the actual world than the world with the alternative outcome $-a^{11}$, then the only way to make (3.4) false is to accept that the former possible world does not in fact exist.[15] In other words, by admitting non-local influences we decide that the laws of nature prevent the existence of a possible world in which the measurements of $A^1$ and $B^2$ are performed, and $A^1$ reveals the outcome identical to the actual one $a^{11}$. And this is perfectly understandable—after

---

[15] Obviously, in this case the counterfactual "$M(B^2) \ \square\!\!\rightarrow O(A^1) = -a^{11}$" would become true, which, incidentally, agrees with CBR's interpretation of the nonlocal influences, based on Lewis's notion of counterfactual dependence (see later in this section).

all, one of the typical ways of interpreting the causal relation between events $C$ and $E$ is to say that the laws of nature prohibit a situation in which $C$ occurs, while $E$ fails to occur (see also the response to CBR's argument in Bedford and Stapp 1995, pp. 146-147). The moral from this case is that we should keep in mind that there are actually two factors which determine the truth of counterfactual conditionals: the similarity relation imposed on the set of possible worlds, and the set of possible worlds itself. Even if the first factor seems to be decided by way of stipulation, the second one may yet contain factual elements, independent of our terminological decisions, and related only to the nomological structure of the world.

CBR also believe that the outcome of the counterfactually changed measurement should not be included in the similarity relation. I agree with that assessment, for the quite obvious reason that this outcome is *always* located in the absolute future of the antecedent-event, and hence should be disregarded based on our previous arguments. However, as we've seen CBR's approach changes when it comes to the measurement settings. Here they strongly advocate the view according to which meter settings *should* be salient with respect to the similarity relation. They offer basically two arguments in favor of this view, both of them quite puzzling. One of them, the positive argument, refers to their other controversial contention regarding the evaluation of the counterfactual, which I will not analyze here. The other, negative argument, derives an allegedly unacceptable consequence from the contrary premise—that meter settings do not count toward similarity. CBR first remark that, if the settings were irrelevant for similarity, then we would have no reason to maintain that the counterfactual "If one meter had been set differently, the other one would have remained the same" should be true. They further argue that this contention leads to the unacceptable conclusion that one meter's setting depends causally upon the setting of the other (according to Lewis's counterfactual explication of causal dependence), when we assume deterministic fixing of meter settings. Since they offer no details how to derive this surprising consequence, we must do so ourselves.

It is best to start by clarifying what we mean by saying that "settings do not count towards similarity". One conceivable interpretation would be that if we have two possible worlds which differ with respect to meter settings and are otherwise identical, then they should be treated as equally similar to the actual one. According to this interpretation, a possible world with settings $(A^1, B^2)$ and one with settings $(A^2, B^2)$ would be judged to be equally similar to the actual $(A^1, B^1)$-world, provided that different settings are the only deviations among these three worlds. As a consequence, the counterfactual $M(B^2)$ $\square\rightarrow$ $M(A^1)$ would indeed come out false, as predicted. However, when we assume deterministic fixing of settings, this conclusion does not necessarily follow from the adopted reading of the similarity rule considered by CBR. For in that case there would be no possible worlds which would differ *only* with respect to their meter settings—each alteration of a meter setting would have to be accompanied by a change of its causal antecedents, stretching into the past. Hence possible $(A^1, B^2)$-worlds would differ from the actual world with respect to a chain of causal antecedents of $B^2$, and possible $(A^2, B^2)$-worlds additionally with respect to causal antecedents of $A^2$, which undermines the argument that some of them should be seen as equally similar. The only way to secure the above conclusion regarding the counterfactual $M(B^2)$ $\square\rightarrow$ $M(A^1)$ in this case is to alter the intended meaning of the phrase "settings do not count toward similarity" and to stipulate that two possible worlds with different meter settings, and which otherwise depart in the least necessary degree from the actual world, should be still judged as equisimilar. Under this stipulation we can be sure now that there will be two $(A^1, B^2)$- and $(A^2, B^2)$-worlds equally close to the actual one, and that the conditional $M(B^2)$ $\square\rightarrow$ $M(A^1)$ will remain false.

However, there is still no obvious transition from this to the alleged conclusion regarding the causal dependence between meter settings. According to Lewis's approach, adopted by CBR, two events $c$ and $e$ are causally dependent, if the following counterfactuals are true: $O(c)$ $\square\rightarrow$ $O(e)$ and $\sim O(c)$ $\square\rightarrow$ $\sim O(e)$.[16] In our case the second counterfactual, $\sim M(B^2)$ $\square\rightarrow$ $\sim M(A^2)$, is trivially true, because the antecedent and the consequent are both true in the actual world. On the other hand, the truth of the first counterfactual $M(B^2)$ $\square\rightarrow$ $M(A^2)$ does not follow from the fact that $M(B^2)$ $\square\rightarrow$ $M(A^1)$ (and, hence $M(B^2)$ $\square\rightarrow$ $\sim M(A^2)$) is false. Even more, it is precisely the similarity criterion adopted that actually makes the counterfactual $M(B^2)$ $\square\rightarrow$ $M(A^2)$ false, showing that contrary to what CBR claim the two meter settings are not causally dependent. CBR could try to make a case for themselves by arguing that one of the "complementary" counterfactuals $M(B^2)$ $\square\rightarrow$ $M(A^2)$ or $M(B^2)$ $\square\rightarrow$ $\sim M(A^2)$ should nevertheless be true, and if it is not the latter, then it should be the former. However, this move, although vaguely evocative of the principle of determinism, would obviously disagree with their assumption that settings don't count toward

---

[16]    $O(e)$ means "event $e$ occurs".

similarity. All in all, it looks like their argument fails to establish that an unacceptable consequence would follow from the assumption that meter settings should not be salient with regard to similarity.

Obviously, our situation would be a bit more complicated if we allowed counterfactual altering of distant setting, for we would have to be careful in expressing the locality idea that changing the setting $B^1$ for $B^2$ should not affect the outcome of the $A$-measurement. As CBR point out, if there are two equisimilar $B^2$-worlds such that in one of them $A^1$ is selected, whereas in the other $A^2$ is measured, then there is no reason to believe that in all of these worlds the numerical value of the outcome would be the same as in the actual one. But, in this case, the simple remedy is to express the locality condition with the help of a counterfactual with a double antecedent: if we measured $B^2$ rather than $B^1$, *and* if we kept the same measurement $A^1$ as in actuality, then the outcome of the $A$-measurement would remain the same.

Our critical analysis revealed that the rules prescribed by CBR in order to determine the similarity relation between possible worlds cannot be supported by strong arguments. The different roles supposedly played by outcomes and meter settings in judging similarity remain without proper justification, and this gives rise to a suspicion that they were *ad hoc*. In contrast, our earlier proposal regarding the semantics of spatiotemporal quantum counterfactuals looks more uniform and simple. In the absence of a decisive argument to the contrary, I believe that what makes an event salient for the similarity relation is not its type (whether it is a setting selection or an outcome), but rather its location relative to the counterfactually altered event. An actually received outcome of the $A$-measurement, and an actually chosen setting *are* salient for similarity, if they occur in the absolute past of the $B$-measurement selection. On the other hand, they are not salient if they happen in the absolute future, *unless* they are causally connected with the absolute past of the antecedent-event. The case when they are space-like separated from the antecedent-event is, as we remember, most controversial, but we should at least be consistent and uniformly decide that either they are both salient or they are not. This solution avoids all the dangers CBR mention in their analysis: it does not render the counterfactual (3.4) true by *fiat*, and it also does not lead to any unintuitive consequences regarding causal dependence between meter settings.

## 3.5 LOCALITY AND "MIGHT" COUNTERFACTUALS

In response to Redhead's earlier (1987) criticism, Stapp has reformulated and substantially amended his proof of the strengthened version of Bell's theorem in (Stapp 1989). He presented his new argument in a semi-formalized way, using counterfactual statements which prescribe what *could* rather than *would* have happened under particular circumstances. CBR devoted an entire section of their (1990) analysis to the formalization and subsequent repudiation of this new counterfactual theorem. In what follows we will critically assess their efforts, along with another critical exposition of Stapp's proof given by M. Dickson in (1994). Basically, we will argue that this new counterfactual argument of Stapp is a weaker version of the quarter approach which we analyzed earlier, and that it suffers from the same shortcomings as the former did. However, as usual, we will use the opportunity afforded by Stapp's derivations to strengthen our grasp on quantum counterfactuals (this time of the "might" sort).

The starting point of this new derivation is the verbalization of two properties that are alleged to follow directly from a general locality principle. We shall present them in the formal language which uses the might counterfactual connective "$\Diamond\!\!\rightarrow$" (see Stapp 1989, p. 167; Clifton *et* al. 1990, p. 43).

$$(A.1) \quad \exists x_1 \, [((M(A^1) \wedge M(B^1)) \, \Diamond\!\!\rightarrow O(A^1) = x_1) \wedge \\ ((M(A^1) \wedge M(B^2)) \, \Diamond\!\!\rightarrow O(A^1) = x_1)]$$

$$(A.2) \quad \exists x_2 \, [((M(A^2) \wedge M(B^1)) \, \Diamond\!\!\rightarrow O(A^2) = x_2) \wedge \\ ((M(A^2) \wedge M(B^2)) \, \Diamond\!\!\rightarrow O(A^2) = x_2)]$$

In other words, the (A.1) principle claims that there is a value $x_1$ (not necessarily unique, of course) such that it *could* be produced as the outcome of the $A^1$-measurement when either $B^1$ or $B^2$ is chosen for the measurement in the right-hand side of the system. The (A.2) principle asserts the same property with regards to the $A^2$-measurement. Similarly, we can formulate analogous principles (B.1) and (B.2) referring to possible results of $B^1$ and $B^2$ measurements:

$$(B.1) \quad \exists y_1 \, [((M(A^1) \wedge M(B^1)) \, \Diamond\!\!\rightarrow O(B^1) = y_1) \wedge \\ ((M(A^2) \wedge M(B^1)) \, \Diamond\!\!\rightarrow O(B^1) = y_1)]$$

$$(B.2) \quad \exists y_2 \, [((M(A^1) \wedge M(B^2)) \, \Diamond\!\!\rightarrow O(B^2) = y_2) \wedge \\ ((M(A^2) \wedge M(B^2)) \, \Diamond\!\!\rightarrow O(B^2) = y_2)]$$

The principles (A.1) and (A.2) look quite innocuous, especially when we take into account that the might counterfactual is rather weak, and that no uniqueness of value $x_1$ is claimed. However, we should be able to give some sort of justification for them. As we have noted, Stapp maintains that they are derivable from his general principle of locality. However, his own exposition of this locality principle is very confusing and obscure. We will not attempt to sort out the possible interpretations of Stapp's (1989) locality principle (but see Dickson 1994, pp. 801-804, for an extensive analysis). Instead, we will try to give an independent justification of (A.1)-(A.2) based on our earlier condition (SLOC) and some auxiliary assumptions. First of all, it should be recalled that the standard truth conditions for the might counterfactual are such that the statement $P \lozenge\!\!\rightarrow Q$ is pronounced (non-vacuously) true at a given world $w$ if there is at least one possible $P$-world closest to $w$ in which $Q$ holds. The preliminary step which we have to make in order to evaluate (A.1) is to decide precisely *in which world* this counterfactual is supposed to hold. Let us provisionally accept that the intended "actual" world $w_0$ is the world in which no measurement is performed. Hence we have to consider the set of possible $(A^1, B^1)$-worlds closest to $w_0$, as well as the set of $(A^1, B^2)$-worlds closest to $w_0$. First let us notice that the truth of the following statement is a straightforward consequence of the Definite Response principle:

(A.0)    $\exists x_1 [(M(A^1) \wedge M(B^1)) \lozenge\!\!\rightarrow O(A^1) = x_1]$

It is obvious that in every possible $(A^1, B^1)$-world closest to $w_0$ the $A^1$-measurement has to have a unique value. But then the question is whether for some possible value $x_1$ appearing in one of these worlds we can find a possible $(A^1, B^2)$-world *closest to $w_0$* with the same outcome $x_1$ of the $A^1$-measurement. In order to argue for this, we must turn to the locality principle in the form of the (SLOC) condition. Observe first that $(A^1, B^1)$- and $(A^1, B^2)$-worlds differ principally at one spatiotemporal point—the point at which the $B$-measurement is selected. According to the (SLOC) principle, for any given $(A^1, B^2)$-world with the outcome $x_1$ for $A^1$, there will be a possible $(A^1, B^2)$-world (let's call it $w(A^1, B^2, x_1)$) that has an identical spatiotemporal region outside the future-light cone of $B^2$, which, therefore, retains the same outcome $x_1$ for $A^1$. The only thing we have to show right now is that this world, whose existence is guaranteed by (SLOC), will be the closest possible world to $w_0$. In order to argue for that, it will be convenient to consider two cases.

In the first case we assume that measurement selections are truly inde-terministic, i.e. no adjustment of the past is necessary when we consider an alternative world in which a different selection has been made. In that case, the joint past for both measurements selections in all possible $(A^1, B^1)$-worlds and $(A^1, B^2)$-worlds closest to $w_0$ will be identical to that in the ac-tual world. Whether their regions outside of the joint future of the measurements will all have to be the same as that in the actual world de-pends on the particular method of evaluating similarity between possible worlds we discussed earlier. However, independently of this choice, we can note that the world $w(A^1, B^2, x_1)$ whose existence we have already es-tablished, will by construction share with the actual world the entire joint past of $A^1$ and $B^2$-measurements. If we opt for the less stringent criterion of similarity, according to which we have to keep only the events from the absolute past of the antecedent-events, then this is all that is required for this world to be counted among the closest with respect to $w_0$ (granted, of course, that this world obeys the laws of nature, which is our underlying assumption). If, on the other hand, we prefer to heed Stapp's advice and include the events space-like separated from the antecedent-event in the similarity criterion, then our initial $(A^1, B^1)$-world with the $A^1$-outcome equal $x_1$ will obviously have to conform to the actual one within the entire region outside the future light cones of both measurements, and the same area of conformity will be transferred to $w(A^1, B^2, x_1)$, therefore it will be once again closest to $w_0$. All in all, under both readings of spatiotemporal counterfactuals the world $w(A^1, B^2, x_1)$ turns out to be one of the closest to $w_0$, so we have established the truth of (A.1) in the case of indeterministic measurement selections.

In the deterministic case the situation is more subtle. In this case even the closest possible $(A^1, B^1)$- and $(A^1, B^2)$-worlds will obviously depart from the actual one with regard to the joint past of the measurement selec-tions. The only thing we can do is make sure that the departure from $w_0$ stretching as it does into the infinitely distant past is the smallest possible. So, the closest possible $P$-world will be a world which differs from the ac-tual world in the area of $P$'s absolute past only as much as it is absolutely necessary to ensure $P$'s lawful occurrence. This calls for an additional as-sumption that had already appeared during our previous analysis; namely the assumption that the deterministic processes that lead to appropriate measurement choices are causally independent from each other.[17] Given this, we can infer that when we start with a particular $(A^1, B^1, x_1)$-world $w_{11}$, and consider a possible $(A^1, B^2)$-world $w_{12}$ which departs least radically from $w_{11}$, the chain of causal antecedents leading to $A^1$ will be the same in both $w_{11}$ and $w_{12}$. Again, using the semantic condition of locality we can argue that $w_{12}$ will retain the same $A^1$-outcome $x_1$, and from the assumption of the independence of the causal antecedents of $A^1$ and $B^2$ we can derive that $w_{12}$ has to be one of the closest possible $(A^1, B^2)$-worlds with regard to $w_0$, which ends the proof of (A.1).[18] Incidentally, it turns out that we've proven a slightly stronger statement than (A.1), to the effect that *whatever* possible result $x_1$ of the $A^1$-measurement in the $(A^1, B^1)$ setting we take, this result *might* also occur in the $(A^1, B^2)$-setting:

(A.1′)  $\forall x_1 [((M(A^1) \wedge M(B^1)) \diamondsuit\rightarrow O(A^1) = x_1) \Rightarrow$
$((M(A^1) \wedge M(B^2)) \diamondsuit\rightarrow O(A^1) = x_1)]$

Obviously (A.1′) with (A.0) imply (A.1), and this is what we wanted to accomplish.

Principle (A.1) would be even easier to justify if we interpreted both counterfactuals as true not in one actual world $w_0$, but in different worlds. For example, CBR suggest that the only way of interpreting (A.1) which assures its truth is when the first counterfactual $(M(A^1) \wedge M(B^1)) \diamondsuit\rightarrow O(A^1)$ $= x_1$ is assumed to be true in a $(A^1, B^2, x_1)$-world, and the second counterfactual $(M(A^1) \wedge M(B^2)) \diamondsuit\rightarrow O(A^1) = x_1$ is symmetrically true in a $(A^1, B^1, x_1)$-world. Under that interpretation, (A.1) follows almost trivially from (SLOC), with no need of an additional independence assumption in the case of determinism. However, CBR claim that (A.1) in its stronger version relativized to $w_0$ doesn't follow from their counterfactual formulation of the locality condition, given with the help of Lewis's notion of causal dependency. I will postpone a detailed analysis of CBR's locality condition

---

[17]  Basically, this means that in all closest $A^1$-worlds, no matter what the other measurement is, the causal antecedents leading to $A^1$ are the same. Se also footnote 14 above.

[18]  It may be claimed that the entire deterministic case should be dismissed, based on the fact that Stapp is not allowed to make any reference to the assumption of determinism in his proof. But I think that this objection is incorrect. Firstly, Stapp can neither assume, nor deny determinism, so his proof should work in both situations. And secondly, it is possible (however unlikely) that outcomes of quantum measurements are indeterministic, whereas measurement settings are determined by their pasts.

until chapter 6, where it will be showed that it is essentially equivalent to (SLOC) under certain reasonable restrictions. The reason CBR failed to derive (A.1) from their locality condition is, I think, that they didn't add the assumption of the independence of the causal antecedents of the alternative measurement selections. Without this premise there would, indeed, be no reason to claim that a possible $(A^1, B^2)$-world in which $O(A^1) = x_1$ will be closest to $w_0$.

The four counterfactual principles (A.1)-(A.2) and (B.1)-(B.2) used by Stapp can be presented in the form of statements regarding the existence of the particular eight possible worlds. For example (A.1) is equivalent to the statement that there is a possible $(A^1, B^1)$-world closest to $w_0$ in which the outcomes are $(x_1, y_{11})$, and that there is a possible $(A^1, B^2)$-world closest to $w_0$ in which the outcomes are $(x_1, y_{12})$, where $y_{11}$ and $y_{12}$ are just some unspecified values which could be revealed by $B^1$ and $B^2$ measurements. Considering again worlds where a series of $N$ measurements is performed, we can present the eight possible worlds whose existence is guaranteed by (A.1)-(A.2), (B.1)-(B.2) with the help of the following outcome sequences (this time superscripts denote the number of a particular measurement in a series):

1. $(A^1, B^1)$-worlds
$$\{(x_1^1, y_{11}^1), (x_1^2, y_{11}^2), \ldots, (x_1^N, y_{11}^N)\}$$
$$\{(x_{11}^1, y_1^1), (x_{11}^2, y_1^2), \ldots, (x_{11}^N, y_1^N)\}$$

2. $(A^1, B^2)$-worlds
$$\{(x_1^1, y_{12}^1), (x_1^2, y_{12}^2), \ldots, (x_1^N, y_{12}^N)\}$$
$$\{(x_{12}^1, y_2^1), (x_{12}^2, y_2^2), \ldots, (x_{12}^N, y_2^N)\}$$

3. $(A^2, B^1)$-worlds
$$\{(x_2^1, y_{21}^1), (x_2^2, y_{21}^2), \ldots, (x_2^N, y_{21}^N)\}$$
$$\{(x_{21}^1, y_1^1), (x_{21}^2, y_1^2), \ldots, (x_{21}^N, y_1^N)\}$$

4. $(A^2, B^2)$-worlds
$$\{(x_2^1, y_{22}^1), (x_2^2, y_{22}^2), \ldots, (x_2^N, y_{22}^N)\}$$
$$\{(x_{22}^1, y_2^1), (x_{22}^2, y_2^2), \ldots, (x_{22}^N, y_2^N)\}$$

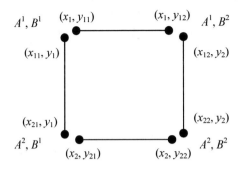

Figure 3.2. A new broken square

For instance, the existence of the first $(A^1, B^1)$-world and the first $(A^1, B^2)$-world on the list with the same $A^1$-outcomes is guaranteed by the principle (A.1), and the existence of the second $(A^1, B^1)$-world and the second $(A^2, B^1)$-world is a consequence of (B.1). But now a quick glance at the above list reveals that the collection of possible worlds we have obtained is even further from the required quarter of worlds than was the case with the original quartet approach. To put it differently—the quarter approach based on the matching condition failed because we had obtained five rather than four possible worlds, and there was no way to show that the two $(A^2, B^2)$-worlds were actually the same world, other than by appealing to determinism. Here we have an even worse situation: our square is broken not at one vertex, but at all four vertices, as Fig. 3.2 shows. We could attempt to eliminate unnecessary worlds by considering only a single vertex with a given set of responses and proceeding to the other ones (using the matching condition), but proceeding in that fashion we would actually end up with a broken square at the vertex located diagonally from the initial one.

So it seems that there is no strategy available to Stapp such that he could derive from his (A.1)-(A.2) (B.1)-(B2) principles the statement to the effect that there are four possible worlds whose outcomes satisfy the CHSH inequality. Despite this, let us continue analyzing his "might" counterfactual derivation, to see exactly where it goes wrong. The critical step Stapp makes is that from the conjunction of "amplified" conditions (A) and (B) to a particular might counterfactual which he labels (C). The formal reconstruction of this step (we will abbreviate the statement "$A^i$ and $B^j$ are measured" as $M_{ij}$, and we will symbolize the joint outcome of this measurement by $O_{ij}$) is:

137

(A+B)     $\exists x_1, x_2, y_{11}, y_{12}, y_{21}, y_{22} \; \exists y_1, y_2, x_{11}, x_{12}, x_{21}, x_{22}$
$\{ [M_{11} \diamond\!\!\rightarrow O_{11} = (x_1, y_{11})] \land$
$[M_{12} \diamond\!\!\rightarrow O_{12} = (x_1, y_{12})] \land$
$[M_{21} \diamond\!\!\rightarrow O_{21} = (x_2, y_{21})] \land$
$[M_{22} \diamond\!\!\rightarrow O_{22} = (x_2, y_{22})] \land$
$[M_{11} \diamond\!\!\rightarrow O_{11} = (x_{11}, y_1)] \land$
$[M_{12} \diamond\!\!\rightarrow O_{12} = (x_{12}, y_1)] \land$
$[M_{21} \diamond\!\!\rightarrow O_{21} = (x_{21}, y_2)] \land$
$[M_{22} \diamond\!\!\rightarrow O_{22} = (x_{22}, y_2)] \}$

(C)     $\exists x_1, x_2, y_{11}, y_{12}, y_{21}, y_{22} \; \exists y_1, y_2, x_{11}, x_{12}, x_{21}, x_{22}$
$\{ [M_{11} \diamond\!\!\rightarrow (O_{11} = (x_1, y_{11}) \land O_{11} = (x_{11}, y_1))] \land$
$[M_{12} \diamond\!\!\rightarrow (O_{12} = (x_1, y_{12}) \land O_{12} = (x_{12}, y_1))] \land$
$[M_{21} \diamond\!\!\rightarrow (O_{21} = (x_2, y_{21}) \land O_{21} = (x_{21}, y_2))] \land$
$[M_{22} \diamond\!\!\rightarrow (O_{22} = (x_2, y_{22}) \land O_{22} = (x_{22}, y_2))] \}$

(A+B) obviously expresses the same condition as the statement considered above that concerns the existence of eight possible worlds. It differs from (A) and (B) only in that it explicitly mentions the outcomes for both measurements and gives them a convenient symbolization. On the other hand, in formula (C) the consequents of the might counterfactuals with the same antecedents are combined together. In other words, rather than separately asserting the existence of two possibilities under, let say, the assumption $M_{11}$, it states that these possibilities will occur simultaneously, in the *one* possible world (of course under this condition it'll hold that $x_1 = x_{11}$ and $y_1 = y_{11}$ because of the principle of the Definite Response, so the outcome of the measurement will ultimately be $(x_1, y_1)$). But this move cannot be licensed by any principle of modal logic. Obviously, there is no logical entailment leading from $(P \diamond\!\!\rightarrow Q) \land (P \diamond\!\!\rightarrow R)$ to $P \diamond\!\!\rightarrow (Q \land R)$. Under the counterfactual assumption that Bizet and Verdi were compatriots, it might have been that they were both French and it might have been that they were Italian, but they couldn't have been French and Italian at the same time. Hence some extralogical justification of the transition from (A+B) to (C) is required.

Stapp does give a justification of his move, once again relying on the Definite Response principle, but his justification is most certainly misguided. He says "if $(M(A^i), M(B^j))$ is performed then some single pair $(x, y)$ must appear. If several conditions are imposed on this pair $(x, y)$, then they are imposed upon a single pair $(x, y)$; this single pair cannot be two different pairs." (Stapp 1989, pp. 169-170). In this way he would like to argue that the double appearance of, for instance, the antecedent $M_{11}$ in (A+B) refers actually to one and the same possible measuring procedure, and therefore to one unique pair of outcomes. But this surely is not the way the might counterfactual works. If we consider a contrary-to-fact assumption $M_{11}$, then we have to admit that there may be many ways in which this measurement can produce definite outcomes. Each of these ways leads to such an outcome, but when we consider these outcomes "across" all possibilities, they differ from one another. Characteristically, Stapp's argumentation would work, but only under the presupposition of determinism (see the same assessment in Clifton et al. 1990, p. 49). Once again, if in all possible $M_{11}$-worlds closest to $w_0$ the outcomes are the same, the property (C) has to hold. But this amendment doesn't promote Stapp's goal of deriving a contradiction from the locality assumption only. It looks like his attempt to counterfactually strengthen Bell's theorem fails once and for all.

Dickson (1994, pp. 808-810) gives a similar appraisal of Stapp's derivation. His analysis deserves mentioning here, because it is given in a language which doesn't use any counterfactuals at all (a language without "counterfactual commitments"). In Dickson's interpretation, the logical fallacy associated with the step from (A+B) to (C) becomes a fallacy in the probability calculus, which claims that if $P(A|C) > 0$ and $P(B|C) > 0$, then $P(A \wedge B| C) > 0$ (obviously the phrase "it could be that $X$" is interpreted here as "the probability of $X$ is greater than 0"). He then adds that the only way to argue for the conclusion of this fallacious derivation is to assume that for a given measurement-event there is only one possible result. Once again, Dickson claims, this doesn't follow from the Definite Response principle because, for example, values $x_1$ and $x_{11}$ are defined in different measurement contexts—$x_1$ is defined as a possible result of both $(A^1, B^1)$ and $(A^1, B^2)$-measurements, whereas $x_{11}$ is only a possible result of $(A^1, B^1)$. Given these constraints, $x_1$ and $x_{11}$ may turn out to be different, because a particular result of the $B^2$-measurement can "force" $x_1$ (through the principle of the conservation of spin) to assume only one of two available values, if directions in which $B^2$ and $A^1$ are measured are chosen parallel to each other. And such a restriction may not be imposed on the pair $(A^1, B^1)$, with the result that all values of $x_{11}$ remain possible. This clearly shows that $x_1$ and $x_{11}$ have different meanings and cannot be treated as one and the same possible outcome.

The result to be drawn from this chapter is that the attempt to prove non-locality of quantum mechanics using Bell's original two-particle and two-observable experimental set-up with the help of counterfactual conditionals fails. It appears that it is possible for the locality assumption to be preserved without any conflict with quantum-mechanical statistics resulting in the actual world, nor in any possible world. If Stapp wants to pursue his goal, he has to look somewhere else. And sure enough, this is exactly what he has done. In the next chapter we will scrutinize two new attempts to produce counterfactual proofs of the non-locality of quantum mechanics; one using the GHZ example, and one referring to the Hardy case.

# Chapter 4

# THE GHZ AND HARDY THEOREMS COUNTERFACTUALLY STRENGTHENED—WHAT WENT WRONG?

J ohn Bell's 1964 theorem opened up an entirely new chapter in the history of quantum mechanics. It established rigorously that statistical predictions of quantum mechanics cannot be faithfully reproduced within a deterministic hidden-variable theory that obey some reasonable constraints of locality. In addition to that, Bell's theorem has shown that it is in principle possible to put to the experimental test some of the high-level theoretical assumptions (one may even be tempted to call them "metaphysical" assumptions) that underlie such a hidden-variable theory. As we have already indicated, Bell's inequality—whether in its original 1964 form, or as presented in Wigner's popular exposition, or in the CHSH version—consists of elements that are in principle measurable. It is then feasible to design an experiment which would aim at confirming or disconfirming this inequality, and thereby provide a decisive test for the combined assumption of realism of possessed values and locality.[1]

Quite independently of the issue of experimental verification, one may ask whether the phenomenon discovered by Bell is unique or ubiquitous. If the possibility of deriving a contradiction with the formalism of quantum mechanics was restricted to the experimental situation considered by Bell, then apart from our increased admiration of the genius that let Bell discover this unique case, we could come to the conclusion that there may be something peculiar about this situation, as opposed to any other quantum setting, that is responsible for the inferred contradiction. And indeed such voices have been raised, pointing out for example that Bell's theorem has

---

[1] The most publicized of these experiments is the one performed by A. Aspect and others (Aspect *et al.*, 1982). A survey of all major experimental tests of Bell's inequality up to the year 1985 can be found in (Redhead 1987, pp. 107-113). One of the most recent experiments reconstructing the EPR correlations is presented in (Tittel *et al.* 1998).

to assume the existence of perfect correlations between outcomes obtained in separate wings of the measuring device, which is hardly a realistic assumption.[2] Others complain that Bell's inequalities are statistical only, and hence they admit the possibility that an agreement between quantum mechanics and realism plus locality may be restored within the margin of statistical error.[3] There are also suggestions that the peculiarity of Bell's theorem is connected with the notion of spin and spin's "non-classical" character. Regardless of the legitimacy of these misgivings, the question whether it is possible to extend Bell-like results seems to be important, both scientifically and philosophically.

It turns out that Bell's phenomena are by no means restricted to perfectly correlated EPR systems of two spin-½ particles; nor are they expressible in terms of statistical inequalities only. In 1989 D.M. Greenberger, M.A. Horne and A. Zeilinger (later joined by A. Shimony) formulated a new Bell-like theorem in which the contradiction with quantum mechanics was established not by deriving an inequality that violates statistical predictions of quantum mechanics, but rather by showing that certain algebraic constraints on the outcomes of measurements implied by the quantum-mechanical formalism cannot be jointly satisfied under the assumption of realism and locality (the details will be given below). The GHZ theorem, as it is now commonly referred to, does not use two EPR particles, but three or four, depending on its version. Interestingly, the three-particle version of the GHZ theorem dispenses with the notion of spin, considering instead an entangled state of the particles with respect to the directions of their propagation.

Another recent Bell-like theorem without inequalities is due to L. Hardy (1992). Once again, predictions regarding the joint probabilities of several outcomes are derived from the quantum-mechanical description of the state in which the system (this time consisting of two particles) is supposed to be prepared. It can easily be verified (especially in the simplified version of the argument presented by Mermin in 1998) that these predictions lead to a mathematical impossibility when it is assumed that all parameters in question have their objective values predetermined, and that no measurement

---

[2]  This worry was to a certain extent addressed by Bell himself in his generalized theorem (see sec. 1.4).

[3]  The issue of how the imperfections of measurements can affect the conclusions of Bell's theorem is considered in (Busch 2002).

on either particle can affect the existing value of a parameter of the other particle.[4]

Both GHZ and Hardy theorems serve as starting points for Stapp's most recent attempts to prove counterfactually the non-locality of quantum mechanics. Just as in the CHSH case of Bell's theorem that we analyzed in chapter 3, Stapp's method consists of replacing the realist assumption with the counterfactually defined locality assumption and some additional rules purportedly warranted by the semantics of the counterfactual conditional. The counterfactual strengthening of the GHZ theorem was first proposed informally in (Stapp 1990), and then rigorously formalized in (Bedford & Stapp 1995). The counterfactual proof of non-locality based on the Hardy case was given in (Stapp 1997), and later refined and explained in numerous polemics, replies and articles, to which references will be given later in this chapter. The main goal of this chapter is to subject these two proofs to a careful scrutiny. The overall result of our analysis will be that Stapp's formal derivations fall short of establishing their intended conclusions.

## 4.1 THE GHZ CASE

### 4.1.1. Initial assumptions

We will start our discussion by presenting the rudimentary assumptions of the GHZ experimental situation in its version with three particles. In their 1990 paper Greenberger, Horne, Shimony and Zeilinger presented the following *gedanken* experiment. Suppose that a stationary source emits three identical particles. By the principle of momentum conservation, the particles have to be emitted at an angular separation of 120°. However, we assume that any given triplet of created particles can be emitted in any direction with equal probability. Now, let us imagine that the source of particles is surrounded by a set of six apertures, three of which—$a$, $b$, $c$—are separated by 120°, as are the remaining three—$a'$, $b'$, $c'$ (the first triplet of apertures being set off from the second by some constant value—see Fig. 4.1). In this setting the particles emerging from the apertures will be in a state of superposition of two pure states: the state associated with passing through the first triplet of apertures, and the state representing passing through the second triplet. Formally this state can be presented as follows (the normalization constant is omitted):

---

[4] An excellent exposition of various Bell-like theorems can be found in (Placek 1997) and (Placek 2000a, chapter 5).

$$\Psi = |a\rangle_1 \, |b\rangle_2 \, |c\rangle_3 + |a'\rangle_1 \, |b'\rangle_2 \, |c'\rangle_3$$

where $|x\rangle_i$ represents the state in which the $i$th particle passes through aperture $x$.

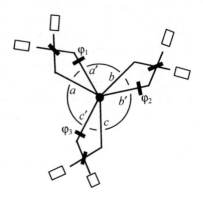

Figure 4.1 The schema of the GHZ experiment

Further away from the apertures, the beams of particles emerging from $a$ and $a'$ (as well as from $b$, $b'$ and $c$, $c'$) will be "crossed" using beam splitters, to allow interference to occur. Finally, two detectors will register whether the particle emerged from the direction of aperture $a$ or $a'$ (and similarly for $b$, $b'$ and $c$, $c'$). In order to introduce a parameter analogous to the direction of spin in the standard Bell theorem, one of each pair of interfering beams is allowed to pass through a so-called phase plate. The role of this plate is to shift the phase of the wave function for one beam by a fixed angle $\varphi_i$ without affecting the physical state of this beam, but changing the interference pattern with the other beam.

Using standard quantum-mechanical algorithms, it is now possible to calculate, for a given combination of phase shifts $\varphi_1$, $\varphi_2$, $\varphi_3$, the probabilities of registering particles in each of the six detectors. Assuming conventionally that in each pair of detectors one detector registers outcome +1 and the other −1, we can calculate the expectation value of the product of three outcomes. The formula which is derivable from the quantum-mechanical formalism is the following:

$$E(\varphi_1, \varphi_2, \varphi_3) = \sin(\varphi_1 + \varphi_2 + \varphi_3)$$

Now let us define the following observables. Let $X_1$, $X_2$ and $X_3$ represent measurements done on three pairs of beams when the phase shift is set to 90°, and let $Y_1$, $Y_2$ and $Y_3$ stand for measurements with the phase shift fixed at 0°. It can be quickly verified, on the basis of the equation above, that there will be some strict correlations between the outcomes of so defined observables. For instance, when three measurements $X_1$, $X_2$ and $X_3$ are performed simultaneously, the expectation value of the product of their outcomes equals $\sin 270° = -1$, and when the combination $X_1$, $Y_2$ and $Y_3$ is selected, the expectation value is $\sin 90° = +1$.[5] These predictions can be summarized in terms of the following strict implications (lower-case letters $x_i\, y_j$ stand for outcomes of appropriate measurements):

(GHZ1)     $X_1X_2X_3 \Rightarrow x_1x_2x_3 = -1$
(GHZ2)     $X_1Y_2Y_3 \Rightarrow x_1y_2y_3 = +1$
(GHZ3)     $Y_1X_2Y_3 \Rightarrow y_1x_2y_3 = +1$
(GHZ4)     $Y_1Y_2X_3 \Rightarrow y_1y_2x_3 = +1$

It is important to stress that these correlations occur even if the measurements are space-like separated from each other, so that no known physical interaction can take place between all particles.

Now, it is quite obvious that the above predictions lead to a contradiction when we assume that each observable in question has an objective value independently of the measurement revealing it and independently of the other two measurements—in other words, that all numbers $x_i$ and $y_i$ have determinate values. To prove this, it suffices to multiply all sides of the equations (GHZ1–4). On the right-hand side we will obtain the product $-1$, but on the left-hand side each particular value will be squared, so that their total product must equal 1.

Here we have repeated the usual Bell result that realism plus locality is incompatible with the standard QM formalism. Yet Stapp claims that with the help of this GHZ example we can prove even more: without assuming realism, only using counterfactual reasoning about possible experiments, and assuming some version of locality, he wants to show that a contradiction can be derived from (GHZ1–4). His proof of this contradiction, both in

---

5    Note that if the expectation value $E(X_1X_2X_3)$ of the product of three outcomes $x_1x_2x_3$ equals $-1$, then the product of individual outcomes is bound to be $-1$ in every single experimental run (if $x_1x_2x_3$ had a non-zero chance to become $+1$, the expectation value would be greater than $-1$). An analogous argument applies when the expectation value equals $+1$.

the earlier and in the refined version, actually consists of a quite complicated and not necessarily intuitive chain of derivations.[6] But we can make it a bit more accessible by pointing out that this proof basically mimics one of several alternative methods for deriving a contradiction in the easier case of realism. However, that method is not the particular simple one we have just presented. The reasoning sketched above obviously requires multiplication of six different results of experiments performed in mutually incompatible settings, and we cannot hope to reproduce this in counterfactual reasoning. We should rather find a way of proceeding such that at each step only a minimal number of different values is invoked. The way to do this is as follows.

We start with the assumptions (GHZ1) and (GHZ2), noting the following implication:

$$(4.1) \qquad x_2 x_3 = -p \Rightarrow y_2 y_3 = p$$

This implication goes through, because we assume the existence of the objective value of $x_1$ (from (GHZ1) we infer that $x_1 = p$, and this value, when fed into (GHZ2), gives us the consequent of (4.1)—note that we use the fact that $p$ can take only values $+1$ or $-1$). In the same way we can proceed from (GHZ3) and (GHZ4):

$$(4.2) \qquad y_2 x_3 = q \Rightarrow x_2 y_3 = q$$

And now suppose that the three observables $X_2$, $X_3$ and $Y_2$ take the following values: $x_2 = m$, $x_3 = n$, and $y_2 = r$. Then by (4.1) we have $y_2 y_3 = -mn$, and hence

$$(4.3) \qquad x_2 = m \land x_3 = n \land y_2 = r \Rightarrow y_3 = -mnr$$

---

[6] Although the proof that will be subsequently analyzed has been presented in a joint publication by Bedford and Stapp (1995), I will continue referring to it as "Stapp's proof" for short. Earlier Stapp used the GHZ example in yet another attempt to demonstrate the non-locality of quantum mechanics (1993) that is analogous to his older derivation (1971). Although I have no room here to explain this in detail, the 1993 proof is basically guilty of the same sort of error as the "quarter approach" analyzed in chapter 3, except that in this case it is the "broken triangle" rather than "broken square" problem that is responsible for the failure of the derivation.

But from (4.2), which is true for all $q$, we can obviously infer that $x_2 y_3 = rn$, which means, given (4.3), that $x_2 = -m$. Here we have ended up with a contradiction: from the assumption that $x_2 = m$ we have derived that $x_2 = -m$.

We can now hope to find counterfactual representations for each step in this reasoning, replacing objective values with outcomes of counterfactually considered measurements. For example step (4.1) could be presented as follows: if we measured $X_2$, $X_3$, and obtained $x_2 x_3 = p$, then, had we chosen $Y_2 Y_3$ instead of $X_2 X_3$, we would have obtained $y_2 y_3 = -p$. As it will soon appear, arguing for the validity of these counterfactual transitions is a tricky undertaking.

Stapp must obviously rely on some assumptions. His main premise is the assumption of locality, interpreted with the help of counterfactual conditionals in exactly the same way as he did it in the context of his first counterfactual proof (see chapter 3). In addition Stapp works with an entire battery of valid patterns of inference in the Lewis counterfactual calculus, whose validity Bedford and Stapp establish scrupulously in (1995). The third component of Stapp's auxiliary premises consists of two patterns of inference, which, though not generally valid in the Lewis calculus, are claimed to be valid in the particular context of the GHZ example. The first rule is called "Elimination of Eliminated Conditions" (note the tautological character of this nomenclature); the second has no name, but it can be called "Addition of Irrelevant Conditions". I will formulate them later, when they are needed. Not surprisingly, upon examination it will appear that one of them is essentially responsible for the failure of the entire reasoning.

## 4.1.2. First steps of the proof

The first step in the proof aims at showing the validity of the counterfactual analogue of the thesis (4.1):

$$(4.4) \qquad X_2 X_3 \wedge x_2 x_3 = -p \Rightarrow (Y_2 Y_3 \; \Box \!\!\to y_2 y_3 = p)$$

It appears that this is not such an easy task. First, we will have, following Stapp, to appeal to the locality assumption:

$$(\mathrm{LOC}) \qquad X_1 X_2 X_3 \wedge x_1 = p \Rightarrow (X_1 Y_2 Y_3 \; \Box \!\!\to x_1 = p)$$

Meaning that, if we obtain the result $x_1 = p$, while choosing for the other two particles measurements $X_2$ and $X_3$, then this result should be valid even if we counterfactually chose $Y_2$ and $Y_3$. Now, when we appeal to the predictions (GHZ1) and (GHZ2), we can easily convince ourselves that the following must hold:

(4.5)     $X_1X_2X_3 \wedge x_2x_3 = -p \Rightarrow (X_1Y_2Y_3 \; \square\!\!\rightarrow y_2y_3 = p)$

But (4.5) still falls short of the needed (4.4). In (4.5) the counterfactual derivation from $x_2x_3 = -p$ to $y_2y_3$ goes through only in virtue of the measurement $X_1$ being an "intermediate" element. But we need something stronger: no matter what measurement is performed on particle 1, as long as $x_2x_3 = -p$, the results of the would-be measurements $Y_2$ and $Y_3$ must obey the equation $y_2y_3 = p$. Obviously this transition looks quite suspicious— under the assumption of indeterminism implications (GHZ1–4) are typically interpreted as referring to the performed measurements and their outcomes only, so making the derivation from $x_2x_3 = -p$ to $y_2y_3 = p$ when the first measurement is $Y_1$ not $X_1$ requires some additional justification. In order to make his case, Stapp tries the following counterfactual strategy: suppose that the actual measurement performed on particle 1 is $Y_1$. In virtue of the locality assumption we can argue for the following:

(LOC′)  $Y_1X_2X_3 \wedge x_2x_3 = -p \Rightarrow (X_1X_2X_3 \; \square\!\!\rightarrow x_2x_3 = -p)$

Now we can proceed using the previously proven (4.5), and replacing the consequent of the counterfactual by the consequent of (4.5) (this move is in agreement with Lewis's rules of inference):

(4.6)     $Y_1X_2X_3 \wedge x_2x_3 = -p \Rightarrow (X_1X_2X_3 \; \square\!\!\rightarrow (X_1Y_2Y_3 \; \square\!\!\rightarrow y_2y_3 = p))$.

In order to return to the situation when $Y_1Y_2Y_3$ are performed, we can still appeal to the locality condition, arguing that the equation $y_2y_3 = p$ should remain intact. Hence we obtain the following chain of "nested" counterfactuals:

(4.7)     $Y_1X_2X_3 \wedge x_2x_3 = -p \Rightarrow (X_1X_2X_3 \; \square\!\!\rightarrow (X_1Y_2Y_3 \; \square\!\!\rightarrow$
          $(Y_1Y_2Y_3 \; \square\!\!\rightarrow y_2y_3 = p)))$.

We can see that the first and the last elements of this chain are exactly the ones we need to get, if we want to obtain a version of (4.5) with the measurement $Y_1$ replacing $X_1$. But how to get rid of the intermediate elements (intermediate counterfactual situations)? Here Stapp appeals to the previously announced principle of the "Elimination of Eliminated Conditions". Essentially, he claims that each counterfactual supposition in (4.7) annuls the preceding one, so we are finally left with the last only. This may look convincing at first sight, but let us look closer. First, consider the implication (4.6) and ask if we are allowed to cross out from it the counterfactual condition $X_1X_2X_3$. This might seem difficult to answer, because nested counterfactuals are quite unintuitive (they require us to imagine a possible situation, in which we consider another possible situation, in which we consider yet another possible situation…). But we can first try to restate (4.6) in terms of possible worlds, keeping in mind the ordinary truth-conditions for counterfactuals as imposed by Lewis (see sec. 2.2).

Let $w_0$ be the actual world, i.e. the world in which $Y_1X_2X_3$ are performed and the product $x_2x_3$ equals $-p$. Let $w_1$ represent the world closest to the actual, in which $X_1X_2X_3$ are performed. This is the world in which $x_2x_3$ still equals $-p$ (by the locality assumption), and therefore, by (GHZ1), $x_1 = p$. Now, in order for (4.6) to be true, the counterfactual $X_1Y_2Y_3 \; \square\rightarrow y_2y_3 = p$ must be true at $w_1$. This, on the other hand, means that when we take the world $w_2$ closest to $w_1$ in which $X_1Y_2Y_3$ holds, then in this world the consequent $y_2y_3 = p$ should hold. Because $w_2$ is closest to $w_1$, $x_1$ should arguably be the same as at $w_1$, therefore at $w_2$ $x_1 = p$ and by (GHZ2) we have $y_2y_3 = p$. In that way we can argue that (4.6) is indeed true, if we assume the ordinary truth-conditions for counterfactuals, together with some reasonable rules for comparing similarity between possible worlds. But in order to consider our main question whether it is legitimate to cross out the intermediate counterfactual condition from (4.6), we have to proceed slightly more formally. This requires some preparatory steps explained in the next section, after which we will return to the assessment of Stapp's "crossing-out" strategy.

### 4.1.3. A semantic model for the GHZ counterfactuals
Stapp's entire argument relies on the standard Lewis truth-conditions of counterfactuals and on some implicit rules of comparative similarity between possible worlds. Therefore, we can now formally construct a semantic model, consisting of a set of possible worlds and of some rules

defining the relation of comparative similarity between these worlds. These rules will be incomplete, for reason which will become clear soon, but sufficient for the valuations of all of Stapp's transformations. Let us first start with the definition of the set of possible worlds. In our case of the GHZ example a given possible world is fully defined by specifying three measurements and their results. Therefore, we will formally represent a possible world by a sextuple $\langle Z_1, Z_2, Z_3, z_1, z_2, z_3 \rangle$, where $Z_i = X_i$ or $Y_i$ and $z_i = +1$ or $-1$. In general, the experimental situation allows for $2^6 = 64$ different possible worlds, but because of the restrictions (GHZ1–4) we, in fact, have 16 worlds fewer, the final number of possible worlds being 48.

Now we have to introduce some rules of comparative similarity, with the intention of preserving Stapp's intuitions—in particular his locality assumptions. Let $w_0 = \langle Z_1^0, Z_2^0, Z_3^0, z_1^0, z_2^0, z_3^0 \rangle$ be the actual world, and let $w_1 = \langle Z_1^1, Z_2^1, Z_3^1, z_1^1, z_2^1, z_3^1 \rangle$ and $w_2 = \langle Z_1^2, Z_2^2, Z_3^2, z_1^2, z_2^2, z_3^2 \rangle$ be two possible worlds. In comparing $w_1$ and $w_2$ with respect to their closeness to $w_0$, we should take into account both the measurements performed and the results obtained. Let us define $\Xi^{1,0} = \{Z_i : Z_i^1 = Z_i^0\}$, i.e. $\Xi^{1,0}$ is a set of measurements performed in the world $w_1$, which are the same as in the actual one. Analogously, $\Xi^{2,0} = \{Z_i : Z_i^2 = Z_i^0\}$. The first partial rule of comparative similarity, compatible with Stapp's remarks, will be the following:

(CS1)    If the number of elements in $\Xi^{1,0}$ is no less than the number of elements in $\Xi^{2,0}$, then $w_1 <_0 w_2$ iff the number of measurements in $\Xi^{1,0}$ with the same result as in $w_0$ is greater than the number of measurements in $\Xi^{2,0}$ with the same results as in $w_0$.

The expression "$w_1 <_0 w_2$" is the shorthand for "$w_1$ is closer to $w_0$ than $w_2$". The rule (CS1) says that the number of the measurements with the same results as in the actual world counts towards similarity, provided that the number of repeated measurements is not decreased. (CS1) already implies Stapp's version of the locality assumption, because according to it we should always judge as closer to reality the world in which the result of an unchanged measurement is the same, even if the other measurements had been chosen different.[7] One more consequence of (CS1) is that the results

---

[7] Strictly speaking, (CS1) implies Stapp's locality under the assumption that *there is* a possible world with a different local measurement and unchanged distant measurements and outcomes. See later discussion in sec. 4.1.6.

of counterfactually altered measurements do not count towards similarity, which seems reasonable.

The second rule shows that in some cases the mere difference in number of the same measurements as in the actual world can count towards similarity.

(CS2)    If the number of measurements in $\Xi^{1,0}$ with the same result as in $w_0$ is no less than the number of measurements in $\Xi^{2,0}$ with the same result as in $w_0$, then $w_1 <_0 w_2$ iff the number of elements in $\Xi^{1,0}$ is greater than the number of elements in $\Xi^{2,0}$.

(CS2) implies another version of the locality assumption; namely that when we change some measurement settings, the remaining settings should be unchanged.

Let me point out that both rules (CS1) and (CS2) are not sufficient to determine in each case whether one world is closer to the actual than the other. Namely, the rules presented don't decide what is more important for comparative similarity: the number of repeated results, or the number of repeated measurements. For example, when the actual world is the following: $w_0 = \langle X_1, X_2, X_3, -1, -1, -1 \rangle$, our rules of comparative similarity cannot help in assessing which world is closer to $w_0$: $w_1 = \langle X_1, X_2, Y_3, +1, +1, -1 \rangle$, or $w_2 = \langle Y_1, Y_2, X_3, +1, -1, -1 \rangle$. In $w_1$ two of three measurements are the same as in $w_0$, but none of them with the same result; in $w_2$ the number of repeated measurements is lesser, namely one, but the result of this repeated measurement is the same as in $w_0$. But (CS1) and (CS2) are completely sufficient to evaluate the entire reasoning presented by Stapp.[8]

### 4.1.4. Elimination of Eliminated Conditions

Because our universe consists of finitely many possible worlds, we can use the following, simpler version of Lewis's original truth conditions for counterfactuals (see sec. 2.2):

($L_{LA}$)    Counterfactual $P \,\square\!\!\rightarrow Q$ is true at the world $w_0$ iff $Q$ is true in all $P$-worlds closest to $w_0$.

---

[8]    One way to deal with this situation is to admit that some possible worlds are not comparable with one another at all. As a consequence, the relation of comparative similarity would be no longer a linear ordering, only a partial ordering. See sec. 5.2 for a more extensive discussion.

Let us apply the above semantic model to reassess the validity of the statement (4.6). The strict implication is true if its consequent is true in all possible worlds that fulfill the antecedent. In other words: the counterfactual $X_1X_2X_3 \ \Box\rightarrow (X_1Y_2Y_3 \ \Box\rightarrow y_2y_3 = p)$ must be true in all of the following worlds: $\langle Y_1, X_2, X_3, \_, p, -p\rangle, \langle Y_1, X_2, X_3, \_, -p, p\rangle$, where "_" stands for any possible result. That means, according to rule (CS1), that in every world of the type $\langle X_1, X_2, X_3, \_, p, -p\rangle$ or $\langle X_1, X_2, X_3, \_, -p, p\rangle$, the sentence $(X_1Y_2Y_3 \ \Box\rightarrow y_2y_3 = p)$ must hold. But, because of the quantum-mechanical prediction (GHZ1), the blank in the result of the $X_2$-measurement should be replaced by $p$. Therefore, again according to (CS1), the closest $X_1Y_2Y_3$-worlds to these worlds are the following: $\langle X_1, Y_2, Y_3, p, \_, \_\rangle$. But using once more the quantum-mechanical prediction (GHZ2) we see that the product of the two blanks must equal $p$, and, therefore, the validity of (4.6) is proven.

But what about the validity of (4.6) with $X_1X_2X_3$ crossed out? Let us write it down:

(4.8)    $Y_1X_2X_3 \wedge x_2x_3 = -p \Rightarrow (X_1Y_2Y_3 \ \Box\rightarrow y_2y_3 = p)$

Now the truth-conditions imply the following: if (4.8) were to be true, $y_2y_3 = p$ must hold at all the worlds $\langle X_1, Y_2, Y_3, \_, \_, \_\rangle$ which are closest to some of the worlds $\langle Y_1, X_2, X_3, \_, -p, p\rangle$ or $\langle Y_1, X_2, X_3, \_, p, -p\rangle$. But because no measurement in the former is the same as in the latter, we can impose no condition on what the results of the measurements $X_1Y_2Y_3$ should be in $\langle X_1, Y_2, Y_3, \_, \_, \_\rangle$ that are closest to some "actual" world. Therefore, there will be such worlds in which $y_2y_3$ will not be equal to $p$ (for example $\langle X_1, Y_2, Y_3, -p, +1, -p\rangle$), and, hence, counterfactual (4.8) will come out false. The transition from (4.6) to (4.8) is definitely not validated by the rules (CS1–2) of comparative similarity between possible worlds.

The immediate conclusion from this is that the rule of the "Elimination of Eliminated Conditions" cannot be taken for granted. We have to look for some additional justification for it. Bedford and Stapp formulate their rule (EEC) in the following way: if $M_1$, $M_2$ and $M_3$ are three alternative triplets of measurements, $o$ is a possible outcome of $M_1$ and $P(o)$ is a proposition that "depends on $o$ but makes no reference to the part of $M_2$ that is asserted *not to occur* by the condition $M_3$" (p. 147; I slightly changed the symbols used), then the following pattern of inference is valid:

(EEC)    If $M_1 \Rightarrow (M_2 \ \Box\rightarrow (M_3 \ \Box\rightarrow P(o)))$, then $M_1 \Rightarrow (M_3 \ \Box\rightarrow P(o))$

The condition of $P$ being "dependent" on the outcome $o$ of $M_1$ is a little mysterious to me, particularly when we take into account that in the application of (EEC) to (4.6) sentence $P$ speaks about outcomes $y_2$ and $y_3$, whereas measurement $M_1$ includes alternative observables $X_2$ and $X_3$, but I think that the most important part of Stapp's antecedent conditions for (EEC) is the one that prevents $P$ from referring to the part of intermediate measurement $M_2$ that is "annulled" by $M_3$. This restriction does indeed give some credence to otherwise unreasonable rule (EEC). For it may be argued that in this case the truth of the double counterfactual $M_2 \ \square \rightarrow (M_3 \ \square \rightarrow P(o))$ is guaranteed by the facts of the matter that occur in the $M_3$-world only, and not by whatever we assume to happen in the preceding $M_2$-world. Hence one may be tempted to infer from this that the counterfactual $M_3 \ \square \rightarrow P(o)$ should hold true as well.

But this would be a mistake. Although $P$ does not explicitly refer to any condition in the counterfactual antecedent $M_2$ that would not be introduced by the supposition of $M_3$, still its truth may depend on some residual facts from the $M_2$-world that got transferred to the $M_3$-world by virtue of the assumption of the closeness of the latter to the former. And this is precisely what happens in case of statement (4.6). Sentence $y_2 y_3 = p$ holds true in the relevant $X_1 Y_2 Y_3$-world only because this world is assumed to be closest to the $X_1 X_2 X_3$-world in which the outcome of the counterfactually unchanged measurement $X_1$ equals $p$. Hence we have a situation in which our sentence does not refer to the assumption that $X_2 X_3$ were measured (this assumption is "eliminated" by the counterfactual supposition $M_3$), and yet its truth still depends on a fact that is assumed to occur in the $M_2$-world. Thus we cannot agree with Stapp's pronouncement that "the effect of the intermediate counter-factual conditional $M_2$ is completely eliminated by the subsequent countermanding condition $M_3$" (p. 148). Similarly, we cannot accept another general method of "justifying" EEC that Stapp offers in his other publications (1994a, 1994b) which basically reduces to showing that EEC is logically *compatible* with Lewis's rules of counterfactual logic. But this is a very weak method of defending EEC. EEC is obviously a contingent statement—in some physical situations, as we will show below, it may indeed be true. The only trouble is that its truth in these situations can be guaranteed by nothing shorter of the assumption of realism, and this isn't something Stapp should be happy to accede to.[9]

---

[9]   A similar to mine assessment of the rule EEC is presented in (Dickson & Clifton 1994) which contains an extensive polemic with yet another Stapp's proof that relies on EEC (Stapp 1992, 1994a). Dickson and Clifton nicely summarize the way

As we have noted, in the conditional (4.6) the element which guarantees the truth of the last consequent is the result of the measurement $X_1$ obtained in the $X_1X_2X_3$-world. Based on this observation it can be conjectured that in claiming the validity of the move from (4.6) to (4.8), Stapp implicitly assumes the objective reality of the value $x_1$, in spite of the fact that no measurement was performed to reveal this value. Indeed, if we assumed that all $X_1$-worlds have the form $\langle X_1, \_, \_, x_1, \_, \_ \rangle$ with the fixed outcome $x_1$, then it would be easy to show that (4.8) has to be true whenever (4.6) is true. For in this case all the $X_1Y_2Y_3$-worlds in which sentence $y_2y_3 = p$ must be true in order for (4.8) to be true would, by virtue of having the outcome of $X_1$ fixed, be precisely those worlds that are closest to the $X_1X_2X_3$-world with $x_1 = p$ being the only available outcome for $X_1$. This observation can serve as a possible hypothesis for explaining why Stapp was able to derive a contradiction from the locality assumption and quantum-mechanical predictions: he apparently included some residual form of reality assumption, at least with respect to the non-measured observable $X_1$. But Stapp is not allowed to help himself to these sorts of assumptions if he wants to show conclusively that it is locality alone which contradicts quantum theory.

### 4.1.5. Deriving the contradiction

If we agree with the above criticism of the (EEC) principle, then we have to admit that an important transition in Stapp's proof of non-locality is not justified, making the entire argument invalid. Having achieved this conclusion, we might stop here, but in order to make our evaluation of the whole reasoning complete, we should ask if this is the only flaw in Stapp's proof. So let us grant Stapp the transition from (4.7) to the final counterfactual without intermediate conditions:

$$(4.9) \qquad Y_1X_2X_3 \wedge x_2x_3 = -p \Rightarrow (Y_1Y_2Y_3 \; \Box\!\!\rightarrow y_2y_3 = p).$$

---

nested counterfactuals work by pointing out that the antecedent of EEC "does *not* consist of the repeated replacement of one condition of another. [...] It proceeds, rather, by piling new conditions on to the old ones" (p. 4254). In a last-ditch attempt to save his EEC, Stapp adopts a very peculiar restriction on the comparative closeness between possible worlds which reduces this qualitative relation to only two cases: either the distance between any two worlds is zero, or infinity (1994b, p. 4260). While indeed EEC follows from this assumption easily, resting EEC on the claim that is much more controversial than Stapp's controversial principle itself seems to help his cause very little.

Having derived (purportedly) sentence (4.9), Stapp then combines it together with (4.5) in order to obtain the required version of the implication (4.1), namely

$$(4.4) \quad X_2X_3 \wedge x_2x_3 = -p \Rightarrow (Y_2Y_3 \; \Box \rightarrow y_2y_3 = p)$$

I admit that this move is valid, given that we accept yet another instance of the locality principle, this time referring only to the choice of measurements (this principle is guaranteed by the rule (CS2)):

$$(\text{LOC}'') \quad X_1X_2X_3 \wedge x_2x_3 = -p \Rightarrow (Y_2Y_3 \; \Box \rightarrow X_1)$$
$$Y_1X_2X_3 \wedge y_2y_3 = p \Rightarrow (Y_2Y_3 \; \Box \rightarrow Y_1)$$

Using (LOC″) we can eliminate the reference to the measurement $X_1$ (or $Y_1$) from the consequent of the counterfactual in (4.5) (or (4.9)). For example, we can argue for the validity of the following:

$$(4.9') \quad Y_1X_2X_3 \wedge x_2x_3 = -p \Rightarrow (Y_2Y_3 \; \Box \rightarrow y_2y_3 = p),$$

because, according to (LOC″), in the $Y_2Y_3$-world closest to the actual, $Y_1$ must hold, and therefore from (4.9) we know that $y_2y_3 = p$ must hold as well. In that way we can obtain both strict implications in (4.9′) and similarly constructed (4.5′) with the same consequent, and appealing to standard rules of logic (under the assumption that the disjunction $X_1 \vee Y_1$ holds) we finally get (4.4).

Stapp uses analogous transformations to get from (GHZ3) and (GHZ4) to the counterfactual version of step (4.2):

$$(4.10) \quad Y_2X_3 \wedge y_2x_3 = q \Rightarrow X_2Y_3 \; \Box \rightarrow x_2y_3 = q$$

Not surprisingly, this transformation is guilty of the same unjustified application of the (EEC) principle as in the case of (4.4). This time, the missing element which could make the transition valid is the assumption of the reality of the objective value for $Y_1$. Summing up, we can say that Stapp is able to obtain his intermediate conclusions (4.4) and (4.10) only if he assumes the objective reality of values of two incompatible observables $X_1$ and $Y_1$ characterizing the first particle. Logically, this result constitutes a strengthening of the original GHZ theorem, which proceeded under the assumption of full-fledged realism, ascribing definite values to *all* observables in question. Stapp's corrected argument can be seen as establishing that the contradiction between quantum mechanics and the locality assumption can be derived under the weaker assumption that only *some* observables have their values predetermined. However, the physical significance of this strengthening is minimal. Although we may dub the assumption of realism limited to the first particle "partial realism" as opposed to "full realism" regarding the three particles, it is unclear what would explain the existence of such a strange asymmetry regarding the existence of predefined parameters between the first particle and the remaining two. For Stapp's result to be of any significance, it would have to eliminate all residual realist assumptions regarding the outcomes of measurements.

For the sake of completeness, let us briefly present the final steps of the argument. As the first step on the path to obtain a counterfactual counterpart of (4.3), from (4.4) one can derive:

$$(4.11) \quad X_2 \wedge x_2 = m \wedge X_3 \wedge x_3 = n \Rightarrow (Y_2Y_3 \ \Box\rightarrow y_2y_3 = -mn)$$

In order to get the equation $y_3 = -mnr$ figuring in (4.3), we must assume counterfactually that the result of the measurement of $Y_2$ was $y_2 = r$. Stapp inserts this supposition between the strict implication and the counterfactual conditional, in the form of yet another counterfactual:

$$(4.12) \quad X_2 \wedge x_2 = m \wedge X_3 \wedge x_3 = n \Rightarrow (Y_2 \wedge y_2 = r \wedge X_3 \ \Box\rightarrow (Y_2Y_3 \ \Box\rightarrow y_3 = -mnr))$$

The step from (4.11) to (4.12) is justified by the second pattern of inference, which we have dubbed "the Principle of Addition of Irrelevant Conditions" (AIC). It basically claims that when (4.11) is true, the following must be also true:

$$(4.13) \quad X_2 \wedge x_2 = m \wedge X_3 \wedge x_3 = n \Rightarrow (Y_2X_3 \ \Box\rightarrow (Y_2Y_3 \ \Box\rightarrow y_2y_3 = -mn))$$

The transition from (4.13) to (4.12) is just a matter of using some unquestionable logical rules together with simple algebra, although its proper formalization can be tedious. On the other hand, the validity of (AIC) is a more controversial issue, especially when we take into account that Lewis's logic of counterfactuals generally does not allow for "insertions" of intermediate counterfactual conditions. However, the validity of the transition from (4.11) to (4.13) can be verified with the help of the previously introduced semantic model, thanks to the logical strength of (4.11).

By rules of logic and algebra (4.13) and (4.10) lead to the following chain of counterfactuals:

$$(4.14) \quad X_2 \wedge x_2 = m \wedge X_3 \Rightarrow (Y_2X_3 \; \Box\!\to (Y_2Y_3 \; \Box\!\to (X_2Y_3 \; \Box\!\to x_2 = -m)))$$

The last step is to eliminate the intermediate conditions in order to arrive at the following formula:

$$(4.15) \quad X_2 \wedge x_2 = m \wedge X_3 \Rightarrow (X_2Y_3 \; \Box\!\to x_2 = -m)$$

(4.15) contradicts our initial assumption of locality, which entails that changing counterfactually observable $X_3$ for $Y_3$ should not change the result obtained in the measurement of $X_2$. The validity of the transition from (4.14) to (4.15) is again claimed to be secured by (EEC). We already know that the rule (EEC) is generally invalid, but it can be established that in this case the truth of (4.14) does indeed guarantee the truth of (4.15). Using the criteria of similarity (CS1) and (CS2) we can show that for (4.14) to be true the sentence $X_2Y_3 \; \Box\!\to x_2 = -m$ has to be true in all $Y_2Y_3$-worlds with no exception, which justifies crossing out the first intermediate condition $Y_2X_3$, and leads to:

$$(4.16) \quad X_2 \wedge x_2 = m \wedge X_3 \Rightarrow (Y_2Y_3 \; \Box\!\to (X_2Y_3 \; \Box\!\to x_2 = -m))).$$

Again, the truth conditions for (4.16) plus the rules of comparative similarity imply that for (4.16) to be true, sentence $x_2 = -m$ would have to be true in all $X_2Y_3$-worlds. Therefore, we can finally obtain (4.15) as our ultimate result.

### 4.1.6. Can the proof be rectified?

The conclusion of our current analysis is that Stapp's counterfactual proof of the non-locality of quantum mechanics in the GHZ case contains a fatal flaw. Still, this negative result does not exclude the possibility that there may be other ways of proving the same theorem. Obviously, showing that one particular way of deriving a conjecture $C$ is invalid does not by itself prove that $C$ is false. I would like to argue, however, that we are in a position to give a negative answer to the general question whether a proof of a contradiction between the locality assumption and quantum-mechanical predictions regarding the GHZ case is actually attainable. More specifically, I shall show that the locality condition, as assumed by Stapp, is consistent with predictions (GHZ1–4), by explicitly constructing a semantic model which satisfies both requirements. As is well known from elementary logic, if a pair of statements can be jointly satisfied in a particular model, then they cannot be contradictory.

Actually, the required semantic model has been already presented in subsection 4.1.3. It consists of sextuples $\langle Z_1, Z_2, Z_3, z_1, z_2, z_3 \rangle$ representing possible worlds with particular measurement selections and particular outcomes. In order to make predictions (GHZ1–4) valid in our model, we eliminate the worlds which do not satisfy the conditions expressed in their consequents, as explained in subsection 4.1.3. Then we introduce two rules (CS1) and (CS2) of comparative similarity between possible worlds. As we already argued, these rules are meant to guarantee that Stapp's locality conditions will be satisfied. The rules are constructed in such a way that if we start with the actual world $\langle Z_1, Z_2, Z_3, z_1, z_2, z_3 \rangle$, and consider possible worlds in which one or two measurements $Z_i$, $Z_j$ are changed, then we have to pronounce as the closest to $\langle Z_1, Z_2, Z_3, z_1, z_2, z_3 \rangle$ those worlds in which the remaining measurements are the same, and their outcomes are unchanged.

Strictly speaking, there is the possibility that (CS1) and (CS2) might not warrant the ordering of possible worlds that is required for the locality assumption to be satisfied. If for a given actual world *there were no possible worlds* in which one or two measurements were different and yet the remaining ones had the same outcomes (for example because such worlds would violate GHZ1–4), then obviously the closest possible worlds would have different outcomes of repeated measurements, and the locality assumption would be violated. A straightforward situation in which this is the case is when we adopt the realist assumption, according to which for every selection of measurements $Z_1$, $Z_2$, $Z_3$ there is only one admissible combination of outcomes. For, as we know from section 4.1.1, there is no way to satisfy all the conditions (GHZ1–4) while associating with each separate measurement $Z_i$ its unique outcome independent of the other two measurements, so it is necessary to admit that a particular measurement $Z_i$ will have outcome $+1$ when measured together with some observables $Z_j$ and $Z_k$, and outcome $-1$ when measured along with different observables $Z_j'$ and $Z_k'$. But this is precisely the situation in which even rules (CS1) and (CS2) cannot guarantee that the locality assumption will be satisfied (for a given world there is no possible world with the same outcomes of repeated measurements).[10]

Thus, in order to prove the existence of a semantic model satisfying both the locality condition and (GHZ1–4) we have to show that for each possible world $\langle Z_1, Z_2, Z_3, z_1, z_2, z_3 \rangle$ and each selection of changed measurements there is a possible world in which the remaining measurement has the same outcome as before. To do this, let us first observe that for every combination of measurements and outcomes $\langle Z_1, Z_2, Z_3, z_1, z_2, z_3 \rangle$ that violates one of the rules (QM1–4) (let us call this combination "excluded"), the alteration of any outcome $z_i$ produces a non-excluded combination (an existing possible world). With this in mind, we can now use the following procedure, which for every possible world together with a set of replacement measurements will construct a possible world whose unaltered (distant) measurements will have their outcomes unchanged. First, construct a combination in which the required measurements are replaced by new ones, and which has exactly the same numerical values for all three outcomes as the initial world. If this combination does not violate any of the conditions (GHZ1–4), then we have the required world. But if the obtained combination happens to be excluded, then we should replace the outcome of one of the counterfactually changed measurements with the opposite one. That way we have arrived at a combination which no longer violates (GHZ1–4), and in which the outcomes of counterfactually unchanged measurements are still the same as in the initial world. Hence we have constructed a world which shows that the locality assumption will be obeyed. This result, I believe, finally seals the fate of Bedford and Stapp's attempted proof of the non-locality of quantum mechanics.

---

[10] Another case in which the locality requirement cannot be satisfied is when we assume that the outcomes of measurements $X_1$ and $Y_1$ are fixed in all settings. To see why, let us assume that these fixed values are $x_1 = +1$ and $y_1 = -1$, and let us consider the world $\langle Y_1, X_2, X_3, -1, +1, +1 \rangle$. It is straightforward to notice that there exists no world in which $Y_1$ is replaced by $X_1$, the remaining measurements have unchanged outcomes, and the condition (QM1) is satisfied. This observation confirms what we have already learned from our previous analysis: that Stapp's derivation of an inconsistency works under the assumption of "partial realism" with respect to the first particle.

## 4.2 THE HARDY CASE

### 4.2.1. Physical background

The Hardy example describes a situation similar to that used in Bell's original argument. As in Bell's theorem, the experimental situation contains two particles: $L$ and $R$, and, for each of them, we consider two incompatible observables: $L1$, $L2$ and $R1$, $R2$. Moreover, we assume that each observable has two possible values + or − (we can think of these observables as spin-½ components). The crucial difference between the Hardy case and the EPR-Bell case lies in the initial quantum state $\Psi$ in which the two particles are prepared. Rather than being the spherically symmetric singlet spin state, the initial state of the particles is given as follows:

$$\Psi = |L1+\rangle\,|R1-\rangle \, - \langle L2- |\, L1+\rangle \, \langle R2+ |\, R1-\rangle \, |L2-\rangle \, |R2+\rangle$$

where each vector given in the formula above is a normalized eigenvector corresponding to a particular eigenvalue for a given observable (for instance, vector $|R2+\rangle$ describes the state of the right-hand particle in which observable $R2$ has value +). It can be easily verified that the following orthogonality relations hold for state $\Psi$ defined above:

$$\langle L1-, R2- |\, \Psi\rangle = 0$$
$$\langle L2-, R2+ |\, \Psi\rangle = 0$$
$$\langle L2+, R1+ |\, \Psi\rangle = 0$$

For example, the second orthogonality relation can be established as follows:

$$\langle L2-, R2+ |\, \Psi\rangle = \langle L2- |\, L1+\rangle \, \langle R2+ |\, R1-\rangle \, - $$
$$\langle L2- |L2-\rangle \, \langle R2+ |R2+\rangle \, \langle L2- |\, L1+\rangle \, \langle R2+ |\, R1-\rangle$$

and, because of normalization, the products $\langle L2- |L2-\rangle$ and $\langle R2+ |R2+\rangle$ equal 1, so the entire formula yields 0. In establishing the first and the third relation we use the fact that eigenvectors corresponding to different values of the same observable are always orthogonal.

The above orthogonality relations imply that the probabilities of obtaining the following combinations of outcomes: $(L1-, R2-)$, $(L2-, R2+)$ and $(L2+, R1+)$ equal zero. Hence, we can conclude that quantum mechanics predicts that the following strict implications have to be true when the particles are prepared in the Hardy state:

(H1)     $(L1 \wedge R2) \Rightarrow (L1- \supset R2+)$

(H2)     $(L2 \wedge R2) \Rightarrow (R2+ \supset L2+)$

(H3)     $(L2 \wedge R1) \Rightarrow (L2+ \supset R1-)$ [11]

For example (H1) predicts that when a measurement of $L1$ reveals value "$-$", then if we measure $R2$, the result is bound to be "$+$". However, once again the mathematical form of state $\Psi$ implies that both combinations $(L1-, R1-)$ and $(L1-, R1+)$ have non-zero probability of occurring. This means that when the measurement and the outcome on the left-hand side particle is $L1-$, we cannot foretell with certainty the outcome of the measurement of $R1$. This consequence of quantum-mechanical formalism can be written down as follows:

(H4)     $\sim[(L1 \wedge R1) \Rightarrow (L1- \supset R1-)]$

A convenient and illuminating method of picturing predictions (H1)–(H4) is to use a diagram (Fig. 4.2). The Hardy example can be used to repeat the Bell result, i.e. to show that quantum mechanical predictions together with the assumptions of realism and locality lead to a contradiction. An obvious advantage of the Hardy case compared to the standard Bell theorem is that the derived contradiction affects not the statistical predictions, but, rather, the "deterministic" (perfect) correlations between the outcomes (similarly as in the GHZ case). Consequently, the derivation is much simpler and accessible even for readers not advanced mathematically. If we assume that every observable involved in the experiment has its own predetermined value which is faithfully presented each time an appropriate measurement is conducted (realism), and if this value does not in any way depend on the selection of a distant measurement (locality), then the contradiction is indeed straightforward to obtain. First, we have to pick

---

[11] These predictions are often loosely presented without the antecedents stating which observables were selected for measurements (see Mermin 1998). However, strictly speaking this is incorrect. Statement $L1-$, for example, does not imply $R2+$, for it cannot be guaranteed that observable $R2$ was selected for measurement. Note that if we presented predictions (H1)–(H4) without appropriate antecedents, then they would already logically imply a contradiction. In our interpretation however (H1)–(H4) are not contradictory, for the antecedents are mutually inconsistent.

a pair of particles for which the result of the measurement of $L1$ is "−". On the assumption that the value for observable $R2$ exists, and using (H1) we predict that this value, even though not necessarily revealed in the actual measurement, has to be "+". In a similar way, appealing to (H2), we can argue that the hidden value for observable $L2$ must be "+", which in turn leads via (H3) to the conclusion that $R1$ has to have value "−". But this obviously contradicts the quantum-mechanical prediction (H4), which implies that there is a non-zero probability of obtaining the opposite result "+". Moreover, every experiment in which the joint outcome is $(L1-, R2+)$ shows that realism together with locality (plus predictions (H1)–(H3)) lead to a clash with experience, as well.

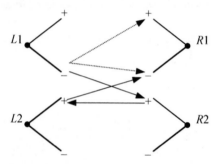

Figure 4.2 Quantum-mechanical predictions concerning the Hardy experiment. Solid arrows indicate conditional probabilities equal 1, dotted arrows indicate probabilities between 0 and 1. For example, the arrow leading from the result "−" of the experiment $L1$ to the result "+" of the experiment $R2$ shows that when $L1$ is performed and the result obtained is "−", the result of $R2$ must be "+". Dotted arrows leading from $L1-$ to $R1-$ and $R1+$ indicate that when $L1$ gives "−", both results of the measurement $R1$ have non-zero probability.

The Hardy case seems to be particularly suited to a counterfactual reformulation of the derivation that uses the realist premise. Each implication in (H1)–(H3) holds in a setting that differs from the previous setting with respect to just a single measured observable, so it is at least *prima facie* plausible that we could emulate the hidden-variable reasoning using a skillfully chosen chain of counterfactual statements. This is precisely the strategy employed by Stapp in his (1997) article. However, before we embark on a detailed exegesis of Stapp's last proof of the non-locality of quantum mechanics, let me mention another possible way of achieving his intended goal that uses the crucial assumption (EEC) that we discussed earlier.

### 4.2.2. The Hardy case and EEC

We have already learned that the most important premise of all Stapp's proofs is undoubtedly the locality assumption. The Hardy case is no exception. Here Stapp uses a version of the locality condition that is already familiar, as well as two new versions. The familiar version asserts that in a possible world in which a new measurement is selected, all outcomes pertaining to regions space-like separated from the location of this measurement should remain unchanged. In particular, if we imagine that in the actual world $L1$ and $R2$ have been selected for measurements, and that the result of measuring $R2$ is "+", this result should be the same in a world in which $L2$ rather than $L1$ has been chosen. This can be written as follows (other instances of the same principle will be analogous):

(LOC1) $(L1 \land R2+) \Rightarrow (L2 \; \Box\!\!\rightarrow R2+)$

In one of his earlier publications (1992, pp. 6866-6867) Stapp attempted to derive from the locality assumption a contradiction with quantum-mechanical predictions with the help of the previously analyzed rule EEC. Although his original proof does not explicitly use counterfactual conditionals, it can easily be transformed into a counterfactual derivation. On the basis of the quantum-mechanical predictions (H1)–(H3) and appropriate locality conditions (LOC1) it can be argued that the following counterfactuals should hold true:

(4.17)  $(L1- \land R2) \Rightarrow [(L2 \land R2) \; \Box\!\!\rightarrow (L2+ \land R2)]$
(by (H1), (H2), and (LOC1))

(4.18)  $(L2+ \land R2) \Rightarrow [(L2 \land R1) \; \Box\!\!\rightarrow (L2 \land R1-)]$
(by (H3) and (LOC1))

(4.19)  $(L2 \land R1-) \Rightarrow [(L1 \land R1) \; \Box\!\!\rightarrow R1-]$
(by locality (LOC1) alone)

Combining these three we obtain[12]

---

[12] Using the logical rule which validates the transition from $P \; \Box\!\!\rightarrow Q$ and $Q \Rightarrow R$ to $P \; \Box\!\!\rightarrow R$.

(4.20)   $(L1- \wedge R2) \Rightarrow ((L2 \wedge R2) \square\rightarrow ((L2 \wedge R1) \square\rightarrow$
$((L1 \wedge R1) \square\rightarrow R1-)))$

By appealing to (EEC) we could get rid of the intermediate counterfactual antecedents (after all, statement "$L1-$" does not refer to any fact introduced by these antecedents), thus being left with

(4.21)   $(L1- \wedge R2) \Rightarrow ((L1 \wedge R1) \square\rightarrow R1-)$

Statement (4.21) asserts that in the situation in which $L1$ and $R2$ are measured, and the outcome of the first measurement is "$-$", it is true that if we had chosen $R1$ rather than $R2$, the outcome of this measurement would necessarily be "$-$". This assertion looks as if it was inconsistent with the quantum-mechanical prediction (H4), but we have to be careful not to jump to conclusions. (H4) implies only that *there is* a possible world in which $L1$ and $R1$ are selected, and in which the outcomes are $L1-$ and $R1+$. However, the truth conditions for (4.21) do not require that $R1-$ be true in all $L1$-and-$R1$-worlds; it is only required that $R1-$ is true in those $L1$-and-$R1$-worlds which are *closest* to the actual one (with the actual world being any world in which $L1-$ and $R2$ hold). To argue that (4.21) is indeed inconsistent with (H4) we need some additional premise. But we will return to this issue later.

Nevertheless (4.21) comes sufficiently close for Stapp to being incompatible with (H4) to put his objective within reach. The only problem is to validate the crucial transition from (4.20) to (4.21). It appeals to the Elimination of Eliminated Conditions principle, which we have argued to be faulty in the previously considered case using the GHZ example. So unfortunately this easy way of deriving contradiction from just (LOC1) plus quantum-mechanical predictions (H1)-(H4) cannot be seen as airtight. It is symptomatic that in his later publications regarding the Hardy case Stapp did not try to repeat the strategy applied in (1993). Instead, he followed an alternative route which does not rely on any assumptions extraneous to Lewis's logic of counterfactuals. This route, as I mentioned above, involves two new locality conditions, one of which drew especially extensive criticism. Below we will lay out the fundamentals of Stapp's most recent derivation.

*4.2.3. Stapp's 1997 proof*

The subsequent method of presenting Stapp's Hardy-case proof from his (1997) paper will take into account some critical remarks formulated by Shimony and Stein in (2003), where they correctly identified a minor oversight in Stapp's logical derivation. The oversight consists in a misinterpretation of "nested" strict conditionals of the form $p \Rightarrow (q \Rightarrow r)$. Stapp apparently treats this formula as being logically equivalent to $(p \wedge q) \Rightarrow r$, whereas, according to the standard semantics for the strict conditional "$\Rightarrow$", the former statement is much stronger than the latter. In fact, the truth of the statement $p \Rightarrow (q \Rightarrow r)$ implies, surprisingly, that the strict implication $q \Rightarrow r$ will be true *unconditionally*, provided that $p$ is *possible*, i.e. true in some possible world. It can be easily checked that the correct equivalent of $(p \wedge q) \Rightarrow r$ is $p \Rightarrow (q \supset r)$, where the horseshoe "$\supset$" stands for the material implication.[13]

The first step of Stapp's corrected derivation will appeal to the previously mentioned locality principle:[14]

(LOC1) $(L2+ \wedge R2) \Rightarrow [R1 \; \square \rightarrow (L2+ \wedge R1)]$

The next step draws on predictions (H2) and (H3), which, when applied to (LOC1), yield

(4.22) $(L2 \wedge R2+) \Rightarrow [R1 \; \square \rightarrow (L2 \wedge R1-)]$

By logic alone we can get from (4.22) to the following statement

(4.23) $L2 \Rightarrow [R2+ \supset (R1 \; \square \rightarrow R1-)]$

---

[13] In (2001b) Stapp acknowledged his mistake and presented a corrected variant of his 1997 derivation. This logical error was also noted by T. Placek in (2000b, p. 161)

[14] This version of locality condition is precisely the same that was used in Stapp's earlier derivation under the name of the Matching Condition. Note that, as Redhead and the others pointed out, under one particular semantics for counterfactuals (LOC1) requires the assumption of determinism of outcomes to be valid. However, as we noted earlier (sec. 3.3), there is an alternative semantics of counterfactuals, of which more comes later, which makes (LOC1) a legitimate expression of locality. Placek in his (2000b) argues, in turn, that (LOC1) is not a correct representation of locality in the framework of Stochastic Outcomes in Branching Space-Time (SOBST). This may indicate that his interpretation of counterfactuals within SOBST comes closer to Redhead's than to Stapp's.

At this point Stapp introduces into the proof a second version of the locality condition (LOC2). Generally speaking, this condition is the rule of inference that permits the following transition:

(LOC2) If $Li \Rightarrow B(R)$ is true, then $Lj \Rightarrow B(R)$ is true,

where $Li$ and $Lj$ denote alternative selections of measurements in the left-hand side region, and $B(R)$ is a statement all of whose components refer to some *observable* phenomena in the right-hand side system that is assumed to be space-like separated from the left-hand side system. The validity of this rule became the most hotly debated topic in all subsequent polemics with Stapp's attempted proof. I defer a proper discussion of this issue for a later time, and will for continue with the presentation of the original derivation. The rule of derivation (LOC2) permits the inference of the following statement from (4.23) (note that the formula in brackets satisfies the conditions imposed on $B(R)$ in our formulation of (LOC2)):

(4.24) $\qquad L1 \Rightarrow [R2+ \supset (R1 \ \square \rightarrow R1-)]$

Using prediction (H1) this time, and applying again some uncontroversial rules of logic, we can arrive at the already familiar formula labeled earlier as (4.21):

(4.21) $\qquad (L1- \wedge R2) \Rightarrow ((L1 \wedge R1) \ \square \rightarrow R1-)$

To prove the fact that (4.21) (or rather its equivalent) leads to an inconsistency with (H4), Stapp employs one more "locality" principle (LOC3).[15] However, he uses an incorrect modal version of the quantum-mechanical prediction regarding the relation between the outcome $L1-$ and the outcomes of the measurement of $R1$, which makes the entire analysis go in the wrong direction. Stapp's version of (H4) is given with the help of the for-

---

[15] Shimony and Stein (2003, p. 505) point out that Stapp's formulation of (LOC3) contains the same sort of error we mentioned earlier, regarding nested strict conditionals (and counterfactual conditionals). I am not going to analyze the exact form and validity of (LOC3), since, as I explain in the main text, it has no use in the corrected version of Stapp's proof. Moreover, Stapp in his later versions of the 1997 proof does not make any use of (LOC3), contenting himself with a direct demonstration of the failure of (LOC2) in the Hardy case (Stapp 2001a, 2001b, 2004).

mula $L1 \Rightarrow [R1 \Rightarrow \sim(L1- \Rightarrow R1-)]$. Even if we fix the mistake of nested strict conditionals, of which we talked earlier, the rectified formula $L1 \Rightarrow [R1 \supset \sim(L1- \Rightarrow R1-)]$ still does not have the meaning intended by Stapp. As Shimony and Stein put it in their extensive analysis (2003), statements including negations of strict conditionals are "ludicrously weak". Indeed, because of the semantic peculiarities of the strict conditional, the last formula is true iff the strict conditional $L1- \Rightarrow R1-$ is false in *every possible world.*[16] This means only that there is a world in which $L1-$ holds, but $R1-$ does not (for example, because no measurement is performed on the right-hand side particle, or because the selected measurement was $R2$). Hence, Stapp's formula cannot ensure that if $L1-$ occurs and if $R1$ is selected, both outcomes of $R1$ are possible.

Rescuing Stapp's formula by substituting "$\supset$" for the second occurrence of "$\Rightarrow$" makes things even worse. Because $\sim(L1- \supset R1-)$ is logically equivalent to $L1- \land \sim R1-$, the expression $L1 \Rightarrow [R1 \supset \sim(L1- \supset R1-)]$ would imply that in all worlds in which $L1$ and $R1$ are selected, the outcome of the first measurement is always "$-$", and the second "$+$", which is obviously preposterous. In my opinion the only way to properly express the quantum-mechanical prediction regarding the lack of a perfect correlation between outcomes of the measurements $L1$ and $R1$ is with the help of the previously announced modal formula (H4) or its equivalents. According to the standard truth conditions for the strict conditional, (H4) is true iff there is a possible world in which the measurements $L1$ and $R1$ are performed, and in which the first outcome is $L1-$, but the second is not $R1-$ (hence is $R1+$). This is, I believe, a reasonable way to express the fact that $L1-$ cannot guarantee that the outcome of $R1$ will definitely be "$-$".

But now the issue of how to prove that (H4) contradicts (4.21) arises. It appears that formally proving incompatibility between (H4) and (4.21) encounters some difficulties. We could, for example, by appeal to (LOC1) and some simple logic, transform (4.21) into the following formula:

$$(4.25) \qquad (L1- \land R2) \Rightarrow [(L1 \land R1) \; \Box \rightarrow (L1- \supset R1-)]$$

If the expression in brackets contained the strict conditional, not the counterfactual, it would be identical to (H4) without the negation. In that

---

[16]  Shimony and Stein explained this surprising consequence by pointing out that if a strict conditional is true (false) at a given possible world, it has to be true (false) at all possible worlds. This is correct, given the assumption that every world has the same set of accessible worlds as any other world.

situation we could draw the conclusion that in order to maintain (H4) without contradiction we would have to assume that the combination $L1-$ and $R2$ is impossible, which is obviously unacceptable, and thereby Stapp's goal would be achieved. However, counterfactual conditional $A \;\Box\!\!\to B$ is logically weaker from strict conditional $A \Rightarrow B$, as the latter implies, but is not implied by, the former. Hence it is *logically* possible that $(L1 \wedge R1) \Rightarrow (L1- \supset R1-)$ is false, and yet $(L1 \wedge R1) \;\Box\!\!\to (L1- \supset R1-)$ is true (in a certain class of possible worlds, defined by the antecedent of (4.25)).

I can think of a simple argument that shows the incompatibility of (4.25) and (H4), but it is an informal semantic argument—and not a syntactic derivation. For that reason I don't think that it would satisfy the high standards of precision adopted by Stapp in his (1997), since he definitely strives for a thorough formalization of his proof.[17] The argument I have in mind uses the standard truth-conditions for counterfactuals, as formulated in previous sections, and accepts some "reasonable" constraints on the relation of similarity between possible worlds, similar in spirit to those presented earlier with the GHZ example. The Lewis truth conditions for the counterfactuals imply that for (4.25) to be true, statement $L1- \supset R1-$ has to hold in all possible $L1$ and $R1$-worlds which are *closest* to some $L1-$ and $R2$ world. And now it can be argued that the only constraint that the condition of closeness puts upon those worlds is that the result of the $L1$ measurement be "$-$"[18] (as the second chosen observable is different from the observable selected in the actual world, its outcome should not be salient for the similarity issue). If we agree with that, then we have to accept that the truth of (4.25) implies that $L1- \supset R1-$ is true in *all* possible worlds in which $L1-$ and $R1$ hold. But this plainly contradicts (H4), for it states that there is a world in which $L1-$ and $R1$ hold, but $R1-$ does not.

Whether this informal reasoning could be accepted as a supplement to Stapp's original derivation, I don't know. Still, I think it would be unfair to mount a case against Stapp on the basis of the fact that we cannot give a rigorous representation of an otherwise reasonable inference. Personally, I am convinced that (4.25) does lead to a serious clash with the quantum-mechanical predictions. The trouble is, however, that the derivation for (4.25) is afflicted with problems no less severe than those we have identified in the counterfactual version of both the Bell theorem and the GHZ theorem. As virtually all commentators of Stapp's 1997 proof unanimously

---

[17] Although in his latest paper (2004) Stapp gave up the ambitious task of formalizing the proof, instead using informal derivations given in natural language.

[18] This is obviously a semantic counterpart of the locality assumption (LOC1).

declare, the most dubious transition in it is the one leading from (4.21) to (4.25) and involving the locality assumption (LOC2). The subsequent subsection will be devoted to the evaluation of this move.

### 4.2.4. Locality condition LOC2

Before we start evaluating various possible attacks on the locality condition (LOC2) and the move from (4.23) to (4.24), let us distinguish between good and bad ways of criticizing this crucial point of Stapp's derivation. To begin with, it would do the critic no good to focus exclusively on the validity of the transition from (4.23) to (4.24). If someone merely questioned the validity of this move, or the validity of the general principle (LOC2) in the context of the Hardy example, Stapp would be more than happy to admit (as he actually did – see his 1998, p.925) that this is precisely the conclusion of the entire argument. His argument is a *reductio ad absurdum* for the thesis that quantum-mechanical phenomena obey the locality principle. We assume locality in one form or another, and we derive a contradiction, which later serves as a proof that one of our assumption is wrong. And Stapp is clear on the fact that in his opinion it is the condition (LOC2) which is responsible for the incompatibility with the quantum-mechanical predictions, so no wonder that at the end of the day (LOC2) turns out to be invalid.[19]

A more promising strategy would be not to challenge the mere validity, but the *prima facie* validity of (LOC2). If (LOC2) turned out to be unreasonable or ill-conceived at the outset, then Stapp's entire argument would be just beating a dead horse. Moreover, if (LOC2) cannot be given a *prima facie* legitimization, then it can hardly serve as a possible expression of our pre-theoretical intuitions regarding the notion of locality. After all, locality *does* look like a reasonable thing to assume. This brings us to the second conceivable strategy of attack on (LOC2)—it can be argued that the assumed validity of the move from (4.23) to (4.24) actually has very little to do with the issue of the nonexistence of any sort of "action at a distance". For example, if one could convincingly show that (LOC2) requires more than just the idea of the non-existence of interactions violating special relativity—for example that it requires some residual presumption of realism of properties—then one would demonstrate that Stapp's argument misses the point.

---

[19] Once again, in his latest papers (2001b, 2004) Stapp has abandoned the strategy of using *reductio ad absurdum*, replacing it with a direct derivation of the negation of (LOC2).

David Mermin's in-depth response to Stapp's 1997 proof (Mermin 1998) can be interpreted as following both of the available strategies (which are obviously closely connected).[20] Mermin focuses on the semantic analysis of the consequent of both conditionals (4.23) and (4.24), which can be expressed in words as follows:

(SR)    If experiment $R2$ was performed in region $R$, and the outcome "+" appeared, then if, instead, $R1$ had been selected, the outcome "–" would have been recorded in $R$

Statement (SR) looks as if it refers to the state of affairs localized in region $R$ only, and hence, according to the pre-theoretical locality intuition, its truth value should not depend on what transpires in a space-like separated region $L$ (in Stapp's wording, adopted by Mermin: it should not be the case that (SR) depends on the choice of measurement which in some legitimate Lorentz frame of reference occurs later than the state described in (SR)). However, Mermin notes that the fact that (SR) contains a counterfactual statement changes radically our off-hand assessment about the location of the referent of (SR). Mermin accepts explicitly that "a counterfactual [...] only has *meaning*, according to our criterion, as an inference from actual results of actual experiments in combination with theoretical principles." (Mermin 1998; p. 922). This interpretation of the counterfactual implies that formula (SR) in the context of statement (4.24) (when $L1$ rather than $L2$ is chosen to be performed on the left system) is meaningless, as we are not able to make an inference from the counterfactual supposition $R1$ to the statement about its outcome with the help of the available facts regarding results of actual experiments. Consequently, the general rule (LOC2) loses its initial plausibility, since it (apparently) overlooks the fact that the very meaning of some statements pertaining to one region can be dependent on outcomes obtained in a faraway region.

Mermin draws an interesting analogy between his proposed solution of Stapp's "paradox" and Bohr's famous reply to the EPR argument (Bohr 1935). The central point of Bohr's response to Einstein consists of a distinction between "mechanical disturbances" and "an influence on the very conditions which define the possible types of predictions regarding the future behavior of the system". Bohr maintains that what Einstein calls "non-locality" (or "spooky action at a distance") is actually the fact that the selection of the measurement of one observable rather than another changes

---

[20]    Another critic of Stapp's 1997 proof is W. Unruh (1999, 2002).

not the physical situation in a distant system, but our ability to speak meaningfully about some parameters characterizing this system. Mermin supports this assessment with his analysis of counterfactuals in quantum mechanics, which implies that some counterfactual statements about possible experiments on one system can indeed lose their meaning depending on the choice of what to measure on the other system. But this does not entail that there is any sort of "mechanical disturbance" caused by one system on the other one, and hence (LOC2) does not properly embody our intuitions regarding the notion of locality.

However, Mermin's interpretation of the meaningfulness conditions of counterfactuals is non-standard, and Stapp does not endorse it in his approach. As Stapp points out in his response (1998), statement (SR) is perfectly intelligible to us no matter what measurement is undertaken in region $L$. As we know from chapter 2, the meaning of counterfactuals is given in terms of possible worlds and the relation of comparative similarity between them. If there is no way to derive the consequent of a given counterfactual from its antecedent on the basis of the laws of nature and known facts about the actual world, this by itself does not imply that the counterfactual is meaningless, but only that it is false.[21] Consequently, Mermin's argument can be repudiated on the basis of the fact that the meaning of (SR) does not presuppose that a distant measurement of $L2$ has been performed.

Still, counterfactual conditional statements are semantically peculiar. Even if the meaningfulness of (SR) does not depend on distant facts of the matter, it is possible that its *truth-conditions* implicitly include facts spacelike separated from $R$. If this were the case, i.e. if (SR) in spite of its "surface" form depended semantically on some facts from distant space-time regions, then there would be no reason to believe in the *prima facie* validity of (LOC2), and (LOC2) would cease to be a reasonable candidate for an enunciation of the general locality condition. To illustrate this with the help of a simple example: we know that Oedipus's killing his father makes Jocasta instantly a widow, but we don't treat this as a case of a non-local influence. The reason for this is that the statement "Jocasta is a widow"—although on the surface making reference only to Jocasta and her properties—in fact derives its truth from a physical fact about another person,

---

[21] Obviously, the falsity of the counterfactual $P \;\Box\!\!\rightarrow Q$ is understood in such a way that it does not imply the truth of $P \;\Box\!\!\rightarrow \sim\!Q$ (thanks to the violation of the conditional excluded middle—see chapter 2). Hence, the falsity of (SR) does not imply that if $R1$ were performed, the outcome "+" would be obtained.

Jocasta's husband Laius. Similarly, if the truth-conditions for the statement (SR) turned out to contain reference to distant facts, then we would not expect that (SR) would retain its truth-value under different suppositions pertaining to those facts. Hence, (LOC2) would not be a legitimate articulation of the view that denies the existence of action at a distance.

Showing that (SR) indeed is not limited to facts of the matter contained in $R$ is precisely the route taken by Shimony and Stein in their critique of Stapp (Simony, Stein 2001, 2003). Their case against Stapp rests on the observation that the Lewis-like truth-conditions for the counterfactual $R1$ $\square\rightarrow R1-$ figuring in (SR) *explicitly* mention regions other than $R$. More specifically, Shimony and Stein adopt the following semantic interpretation of the foregoing conditional: $R1$ $\square\rightarrow R1-$ is true iff $R1-$ is true in all $R1$-worlds which are identical with the actual one everywhere outside the future light cone of region $R$.[22] This formulation clearly makes reference to the entire exterior of the future light cone of $R$, and hence to regions space-like separated from $R$. For Shimony and Stapp this fact undermines the *prima facie* appeal that Stapp's principle might otherwise have had.

However, things are not that simple. The truth-conditions mention regions space-like separated from $R$, but does merely mentioning them make the counterfactual *de facto* dependent on the states of affairs taking place in these regions? This may be questionable. As we know, commonplace non-quantum counterfactuals can be interpreted as following the same semantics as the statement under investigation, and yet they do not display any sort of dependence on distant facts. For instance, the statement "If this glass pane were hit by a metal hammer, it would shatter" is true regardless of the conditions that might occur in space-like separated regions. The reason for this is that, although in order to evaluate the counterfactual about the glass pane we have to consider possible worlds with fixed events in the

---

[22] In his reply to Shimony and Stein, Stapp makes it clear that their Lorentz-invariant interpretation of the counterfactual is not exactly identical with his own (Stapp 2001a, pp. 855, 856). He seems to follow the idea of choosing an arbitrary hypersurface of simultaneity, relative to which the right measurement happens later than the left measurement. Then he assumes that in order to evaluate the counterfactual $R1$ $\square\rightarrow R1-$ we have to keep every event that happens earlier than $R1$ exactly as in reality, which guarantees that the result of the left measurement will be unchanged. I think that this proposal is an unnecessary weakening of Shimony and Stein's interpretation, as it undermines any initial appeal the transition from (4.23) to (4.24) might have had. If the selection of the left measurement takes place earlier than the right measurement, then we should not wonder that a change in region $L$ can affect physical situation that happens *later* in $R$.

entire exterior of the forward light cone of the hitting event, still the events space-like separated from it have no bearing on the truth of the consequent. In all possible worlds that share with the actual world the absolute past of the hitting event (the backward light cone) the outcome is always the same: the glass pane is shattered.

### 4.2.5. Possible justifications of LOC2

The reason why the counterfactual in (SR) displays the *de facto* dependence on distant events is because the existence of "non-local" correlations between outcomes of measurements was assumed at the outset, as given in (H1)-(H3). So, a defender of Stapp's position might point out that it is precisely non-locality which is responsible for the failure of the transition from (4.23) to (4.24). Shimony and Stein show that the semantics they accept for the counterfactual makes it *possible* for statement $R1 \; \square \rightarrow R1-$ to derive its truth conditions from facts about space-like separated regions, but that by itself does not guarantee that this sort of dependence *will* occur.[23] The truth conditions put forward by them can be just as well presented as *prohibiting* any sort of dependence of the counterfactual on the absolute future of the antecedent-event (the interior of the future light cone), but not as unconditionally *affirming* the existence of a dependence on the regions space-like separated from the antecedent-event. A factual premise (in the form of the quantum-mechanical predictions (H1)-(H3), for instance) has to be added in order to achieve the intended non-local dependence.[24]

---

[23] Stapp had probably something similar in mind when he wrote "Shimony and Stein based their challenge on the fact that the statement SR has a certain potential *implicit* reference to region $L$ built into it" (2001, p. 857) —note the word "potential" in his statement. Following this line of thought we might add that in order to turn this potential reference into an actual one, we have to accept some sort of *de facto* non-locality.

[24] We already know from the discussion of Redhead's criticism of Stapp's earlier proof (chapter 3) that it is possible to propose an alternative interpretation of the counterfactual which would cut off any possibility of "non-local" influence on its truth-value, regardless of the *de facto* existence of superluminal causal interactions. Rather than selecting the exterior of the future-light cone of the antecedent-event, we could pick the interior and the surface of its past-light cone as the region which is supposed to be fixed. In other words, statement $R1 \; \square \rightarrow R1-$ would be true iff $R1-$ were true in all $R1$-worlds which are identical with the actual one inside the past light cone of the region $R$. In such a case no lawful change in space-like separated region $L$ can influence the truth value of the counterfactual, and the principle (LOC2) comes out valid by *fiat*. Needless to say, its validity would have very little

We can fill out the somewhat sketchy argument by pointing out that there is a contingent principle (a principle that does not follow from the arbitrary semantics for the counterfactual alone) which can be seen as a legitimate instance of the locality condition and which, together with Shimony and Stein's truth conditions for the counterfactual, implies (LOC2). The above-mentioned principle can be explicated as follows: suppose that we consider a true counterfactual $P \,\square\!\!\rightarrow Q$ such that $P$ and $Q$ refer to events localized in the same region $R$ of spacetime. According to the previously mentioned truth-conditions, $Q$ has to be true in all possible worlds which are identical with the actual one everywhere outside the future light cone of $R$. But, special relativity demands that all causally efficient factors relevant to the occurrence of $Q$ should be included within the past light cone of $R$ (otherwise, as Stapp points out, there would be a legitimate Lorentz frame in which a cause would occur later than its effect). Hence $Q$ should remain true in all possible worlds which share with the actual one only part of the exterior of the future light cone of $R$; namely $R$'s past light cone (in other words, whatever happens in the area outside both light cones should be irrelevant to the occurrence of $Q$). This can be summarized in the following locality condition:

(LOC\*)   If $Q$ is true in all $P$-worlds which are identical to the actual world everywhere outside the future light cone of region $R$ in which both $P$ and $Q$ happen, then $Q$ remains true in all $P$-worlds which share with the actual world the past light cone of $R$, but possibly differ from it outside both light cones.

Now we can apply (LOC\*) to the Hardy case in order to show that it does validate the transition from (4.23) to (4.24). Statement (4.23) asserts that in all actual worlds in which $R2$ is measured and the result is "+", and in which $L2$ is chosen for measurement in the left-hand side system (and, therefore, its outcome must be "+" as well, because of (H2)), the counterfactual $R1 \,\square\!\!\rightarrow R1-$ is true. This translates, according to the adopted truth conditions for the counterfactual, into the statement that $R1-$ is true in all possible worlds in which $R1$ is selected in region $R$, but $L2+$ remains true in region $L$. As we know, prediction (H3) supports this statement.

---

to do with the issue of locality, but would rather be a consequence of our arbitrary decision regarding what we treat as salient for the similarity relation. More on that will follow in chapters 5 and 6.

At this point, however, we can appeal to (LOC*), which ensures that $R1-$ should also remain true in all possible worlds whose area of exact match with the actual world is limited to the past light cone of $R$ only. Hence, in particular, (LOC*) guarantees that $R1-$ should be true in all worlds in which $L2$ is replaced by $L1$, as the left-hand side region is not included in the past light cone of $R$. But this means that (4.24) comes out true, as it states that $R1-$ is true in all possible worlds in which $R2$ is replaced by $R1$, while the distant measurement is $L1$.

In conclusion, it seems that—contrary to Shimony and Stein—Stapp's (LOC2) is indeed derivable from *some sort* of general locality principle rooted in special theory of relativity. Thus the violation of (LOC2) in the Hardy case shows that (LOC*) has to be abandoned, too. However, it is too early to pronounce Stapp's victory. Remember that his main goal is to show that according to standard quantum mechanics *a free choice of measurement* in one system can affect observable phenomena outside the future light cone of that system (in other words that quantum mechanics violates parameter independence). But the violation of (LOC*) in the Hardy case hardly proves that. The quantum-mechanical predictions show that the observable phenomenon $R1-$ (the outcome of a particular measurement) depends on facts that obtain in a space-like separated region $L$, but these facts include *the outcome* of the measurement, as well as the measurement itself. In particular, if in a possible world in which $R1$ is performed and $L1+$ obtains in region $L$ (as a remnant of the actual world) we changed the result "+" of the $L1$-measurement to "–" while keeping the measurement selection intact (this can be done, because $R2+$ is no longer true in region $R$), the change would affect the observable phenomenon $R1-$.

In fact, we knew even without Stapp's sophisticated derivation that (LOC*) is violated in the standard, anti-realistic interpretation of quantum mechanics. To see this, it suffices to invoke the ordinary singlet spin state of two particles. If in the actual world we select one particular direction in which spin on the left system is going to be measured, and if the result is, let's say, "up", then in all possible worlds in which the right system undergoes the measurement of spin in the same direction, and which shares with the actual world the entire exterior of the future light cone of the right system, the outcome is determined to be "down". But obviously this results is not guaranteed to occur in all worlds in which only the past light cone is "transferred" from the actual world (we assume, of course, that the outcome obtained on the left-hand side is not determined by the past state of the system). The breaking of (LOC*) in this case is due to non-local correlations known as "outcome dependence" (see sec. 1.5). But Stapp's goal, again, is to prove that it is *parameter dependence* which is inevitable in quantum mechanics, and this goal has not been achieved.

### 4.2.6. Einstein's criterion of reality

From what we have said it should be clear why Stapp is so keen to treat (LOC2) as an independent locality principle in its own right, and not as a mere consequence of (LOC*) or any other general condition. This is because only the form of (LOC2) (or, strictly speaking, its application to the transition from (4.23) to (4.24)) seems to suggest that it is a free choice of measurement, and not the outcome obtained, which induces a physical change in a distant system. But the only reasonable way to argue in favor of the *prima facie* plausibility of (LOC2) is to show that there is *a physical property* which corresponds to the nested conditional (SR), and which is located *entirely* in region $R$.[25] And, as Shimony and Stein underscore, this requires additional arguments, which are missing from Stapp's presentation.[26] The statement $R2+ \supset (R1 \ \square\!\!\rightarrow R1-)$ is semantically quite convoluted, and it is not at all clear that it represents a well-defined and unique physical property that can characterize the right-hand side system $R$. To begin with, let us notice that (SR) is logically equivalent to the following disjunction: $\sim\!R2+ \vee (R1 \ \square\!\!\rightarrow R1-)$. Yet it is a highly controversial

---

[25] Stapp feels that he needs the assumption of the existence of the objective localized property corresponding to SR in order to give the transition from (4.23) to (4.24) an appearance of plausibility. Throughout his writings he intersperses metaphysically laden phrases like "the property specified by SR", "a constraint on what appears to observers in $R$" (1998, p. 925), "the existence of a definite theoretical connection between the outcomes" (2001, p. 855).

[26] It should be mentioned, however, that in his (2001b, p. 9) Stapp made some remarks which may be interpreted as intending to convince the reader that SR genuinely refers to a physical state located in $R$. Namely, he stated that the truth value of SR is defined in terms of the truth values of all the elementary propositions $R2$, $R2+$, $R1$, and $R1-$, even specifying that SR is false iff the truth values for the remaining propositions are, respectively, "true", "true", "true", and "false". But this assessment is misleading. Counterfactual conditionals are non-truth functional statements, meaning that their truth value cannot be determined on the basis of the truth values of their components *in the actual world*. The values which Stapp presented are indeed sufficient and necessary for SR to be false, but only if they are assigned in special worlds: for $R2$ and $R2+$ in the actual world, and for $R1$ together with $R1-$ in a possible world preselected according to the previously accepted semantics. Thus, it cannot be maintained that SR represents a state of affairs which is an algebraic combinations of the referents of its components *in the actual world*.

matter whether a disjunction of two arbitrary properties (assuming for a moment that both disjuncts indeed represent some legitimate properties of the physical system in $R$) always forms a new genuine property, too. Moreover, it can be observed that if the purported property corresponding to (SR) existed, then it would have to characterize the right-hand side particles each time the measurement of $R2$ is *not* performed, independently of any other characteristics that the system may possess. But, how are we to imagine an objective property of a physical system which is in such a strange way dependent on the experimenter's free choice?

Still it is the status of the second disjunct and its referent that is undoubtedly the most contentious. It is by no means clear that in the actual world there is a property, or state of affairs, localized in the right region $R$, which constitutes the truth-maker for the counterfactual $R1 \ \square\!\rightarrow R1-$. As Shimony and Stein observe, the counterfactual is a proposition about classes of possible worlds, and not about what happens in the actual world only. To assume that there is a matter of fact in the actual world whose existence is necessary and sufficient for the truth of the above counterfactual requires at least some extra premise. Shimony and Stein even suggest what such an additional premise might look like. It would have to be a counterfactual equivalent of Einstein's famous criterion of reality: "If, without in any way disturbing a system, we can predict with certainty (...) the value of a physical quantity, then there exists an *element of physical reality* corresponding to this physical quantity" (italics mine). Applied to our case, Einstein's criterion could go something like that:

(ER)    If we can infer the truth of the counterfactual $R1 \ \square\!\rightarrow R1-$ without actually disturbing the physical system $R$, then there exists in $R$ an element of physical reality (an objective property of the system) corresponding to this counterfactual.

With this assumption at hand, it is at least reasonable to maintain that (SR) indeed represents a legitimate physical property in $R$, and that this property can be forced to disappear by switching the left-hand side measurement from $L2$ to $L1$, thus violating the intuitive principle of locality.

However, in spite of its intuitive appeal, Einstein's criterion of reality turns out to be a very strong contention, too strong to be easily accepted as a lemma in Stapp's argument. Not only does it supply us with the crucial element that makes the transition from (4.23) to (4.24) look like a legitimate application of the locality condition but, by itself, guarantees the validity of this step without any need to appeal to (LOC2). In fact, it can be shown that with (ER) and (LOC1) the statement (SR) turns out to be true regardless of any assumption about the measurement selection performed in the region $L$. Hence, rather than giving *prima facie* plausibility to the "locality" principle (LOC2), (ER) simply makes it redundant, as it alone is capable of deriving a contradiction from the quantum-mechanical predictions and the so far unquestioned locality condition (LOC1).

Following Shimony and Stein's approach (2001, p. 850), we can show that this is the case, i.e. that Stapp's proof can be completed with the help of (LOC1) and (ER) only. Let us start with the assumption that in the actual world the measurements of $L1$ and $R1$ have been performed, and that the outcome of the first one was $L1-$. Our goal will be to prove that the outcome of the second measurement *has* to be $R1-$, which obviously contradicts (H4). The first step is to notice that in the actual world the counterfactual $R2 \ \square\rightarrow\ R2+$ has to be true (on the basis of (H1) and (LOC1)). Now, using (ER) we can infer the existence of an element of physical reality $\rho$ in region $R$, equivalent to this counterfactual. The existence of $\rho$ can be next used to deduce the truth of yet another counterfactual, this time $L2 \ \square\rightarrow\ L2+$. Without (ER) or any other assumption of realism we wouldn't be able to do it, unless we knew that on the right-hand side $R2$ was chosen and the outcome was $R2+$.

But we can now reason as follows. Consider a possible world $w_{L2}$ in which $L2$ rather than $L1$ is selected, and which is identical to the actual world outside the future light cone of $L$. In such a world $\rho$ has to hold as well, *as in the actual world it was part of a physical characteristic of region* $R$, *located outside the future light cone of* $L$. And although we cannot apply quantum-mechanical prediction (H2) directly to $\rho$ in order to deduce that the outcome $L2+$ has to occur in $w_{L2}$, we can do it indirectly, by supposing that $L2-$ occurred and deriving a contradiction from this assumption. Suppose, then, that in $w_{L2}$ the outcome $L2-$ has been actually recorded. But, since in $w_{L2}$ the counterfactual $R2 \ \square\rightarrow\ R2+$ (equivalent to $\rho$) is still true, it means that there will be yet another possible world $w_{L2R2}$ in which $R2+$ is true, but the result of $L2$ is still "$-$"(this world retains the same exterior of the future light cone of $R$ as $w_{L2}$). However, such a world is impossible in light of (H2)—every world in which $R2+$ and $L2$ hold has to have outcome $L2+$. Hence, we have demonstrated that in the actual world the counterfactual $L2 \ \square\rightarrow\ L2+$ has to be true, and by (ER) this leads to yet another existential statement about an element of physical reality, this time in $L$ (let us call it $\lambda$).

At this point we have almost completed our task. In order to prove that in the actual world the result of the measurement of $R1$ must be "$-$", we have to basically repeat the above indirect reasoning. Let us then suppose that $R1+$ is actually true. Because $L2 \; \Box\!\!\rightarrow L2+$ has been proven to be true in the actual world, there has to be a possible $L2$-world which is identical to the actual world everywhere outside $L$'s future light cone and in which $L2+$ is true. But in this world $R1+$ would still be true (by (LOC1)!), and once again this would lead to a logical conflict with the quantum-mechanical predictions, this time with (H3). Consequently, the $R1$'s outcome in the actual world can be no other than "$-$". We have succeeded in showing that (ER) plus (LOC1) lead to a conclusion which is incompatible with quantum-mechanical predictions. But, observe that on the way to this conclusion we have not used any form of the locality assumption other than (LOC1). No suspicion-raising locality (LOC2) was necessary. I believe that this shows that it is the failure of (ER) rather than any of the locality conditions which is ultimately responsible for the derived inconsistency. But if (ER) fails in quantum mechanics, then it cannot lend any credence to the otherwise dubious (LOC2). It turns out that in quantum mechanics counterfactual statements regarding possible outcomes of unperformed experiments are not reducible to objective properties which should be kept the same as in the actual world during valuations of other counterfactuals. In other words, there are no facts of the matter responsible for the truth of counterfactuals of the same sort as $R2 \; \Box\!\!\rightarrow R2+$ and such that their existence or non-existence enters into the meaning of the phrase "possible worlds closest to the actual world".

The importance of this conclusion cannot, in my opinion, be overestimated. The Hardy example shows that Einstein's criterion of physical reality cannot be maintained together with yet another of his cherished intuitions—the locality condition. This is a true strengthening of Bell's original theorem, for in the latter theorem it was realism of possessed values (the hidden variable hypothesis) which together with locality lead to a conflict with quantum-mechanical statistical predictions. And Einstein's criterion of reality is definitely much weaker than the full-blown realism of possessed values.[27] The (deterministic) hidden variable hypothesis conjectures that for every meaningful parameter that may characterize a physical

---

[27] If Einstein's criterion *were* equivalent to the assumption of realism, then obviously the entire EPR argument would make no sense at all, for it would assume at the outset the thing that it wanted to prove (i.e. the incompleteness of quantum mechanics).

system there is an objective property of this system which determines the result of the possible measurement of this parameter. In contrast, Einstein's criterion asserts that the existence of such a property is guaranteed only if we can make an independent inference which reveals the exact value of the would-be measurement. This looks like a legitimate way to justify the existence of objective physical properties even in the quantum world that defies common sense, and no wonder that it was rarely attacked by even the most ardent proponents of the anti-metaphysical approach to physics, such as Bohr himself. And yet it turns out that such an intuitive principle has no place in the bizarre quantum world.[28]

### 4.2.7. Compatibility of LOC1 and quantum precepts
Of course, as in the original Bell theorem, there is always a possibility of retaining Einstein's criterion at the price of sacrificing the locality principle (LOC1). I am not denying this. However, I would like to point out that there can be no easy victory for somebody who would like to follow this line of defense. What I have in mind is that it is possible to show that (LOC1) is by itself unable to produce any consequences contradicting quantum-mechanical predictions in the Hardy case (in other words, that (LOC1) is consistent with those predictions). This by no means proves that (LOC1) is true, for many statements compatible with quantum-mechanical predictions are obviously false. Yet, at the same time the result I am talking about logically permits the view I described earlier, according to which it is the failure of the criterion (ER), rather than that of the rudimentary locality principle (LOC1), which is responsible for the incompatibility with quantum theory. In the absence of any arguments to the contrary, I decide to subscribe to this view.

Now let me sketch the details of the argument showing the compatibility of (LOC1) and the quantum predictions regarding the Hardy case. I shall show that there exists a semantic model consisting of possible worlds in which the following statements are jointly true: the quantum-mechanical predictions derived from the Hardy state, the assumption that the experimenters have free will, and the locality assumption (SLOC) regarding

---

[28] One passage in A. Fine's excellent essay on the historical development of quantum mechanics (1986, pp. 62-63) suggests that Einstein might not have been so convinced about the validity of "his" criterion of reality, after all. Fine points out that nowhere outside the famous (1935) article did Einstein formulate a similar principle. Fine even seems to toy with the idea that the insertion of this principle into (1935) may have been due to the other co-authors (in particular, Boris Podolsky).

alternative choices of experiments. This will obviously mean that the statements in questions are consistent, for inconsistent statements cannot be simultaneously true.

Let us symbolize possible worlds relevant to the Hardy case with the help of the following pairs: ⟨the left-hand side experiment and its result; the right-hand side experiment and its result⟩. Without quantum-mechanical restrictions there would obviously be 16 different possible worlds of that sort. However, because of those restrictions only some of them are possible. The table below contains all the possible worlds which are admissible by the quantum-mechanical predictions derived from the Hardy state.

| | | | |
|---|---|---|---|
| ⟨$L1+$; $R1+$⟩ | ⟨$L1+$; $R2+$⟩ | | ⟨$L2+$; $R2+$⟩ |
| ⟨$L1+$; $R1-$⟩ | ⟨$L1+$; $R2-$⟩ | ⟨$L2+$; $R1-$⟩ | |
| ⟨$L1-$; $R1+$⟩ | ⟨$L1-$; $R2+$⟩ | ⟨$L2-$; $R1+$⟩ | ⟨$L2-$; $R2+$⟩ |
| ⟨$L1-$; $R1-$⟩ | | ⟨$L2-$; $R1-$⟩ | ⟨$L2-$; $R2-$⟩ |

Tab. 4.1. Possible worlds in the Hardy case

Empty cells indicate worlds eliminated by quantum predictions (i.e. combinations whose probability of occurrence equals zero). We assume that all the differences between the worlds presented above are confined to the set-theoretical sum of two future light-cones: one with its apex in region $L$ and the other in $R$. If it is necessary, we may add to the list of worlds above the "null" world ⟨0; 0⟩, in which no experiments are performed. Now, it should be clear that in a semantic model prepared in this way all the required statements are true. The free choice assumption is satisfied, because no matter what world on the list we consider (including the null world), we can always find another possible world with any alternative measurement selection we desire (so it is always true that an experimenter could have chosen an alternative measurement setting). The truth of the quantum predictions is ensured by construction, but if necessary, we can prove it directly. For example, in order to show the truth of the prediction given by the strict conditional $L2+ \Rightarrow (R1 \supset R1-)$ equivalent to (H3), we have to check that in all $L2+$-worlds (given in the third column, second row, and the fourth column, first row) the material implication $R1 \supset R1-$ is true.

Finally, the locality assumption (LOC1). Restricted to the choice of experiments, it ensures that for a given possible world there is a world in which an alternative measurement selection is made, even while everything pertaining to the distant system remains unchanged, including the outcome of the distant experiment. This means that for a given pair $\langle Lab; Rcd \rangle$ there have to be pairs $\langle La'b'; Rcd \rangle$ and $\langle Lab; Rc'd' \rangle$ with $a \neq a'$ and $c \neq c'$ (the first one representing a world with a different experiment in $L$ and an unchanged situation in $R$, the second the opposite). I leave it to the reader as a simple exercise to check, with the help of the table above, that this is indeed the case. Let us consider only one example: the world $\langle L2+; R1- \rangle$. The worlds of the first type we can find in the first column, second and fourth row; the second-type world is present only in the last column, first row.

This argument shows once and for all that in order to derive a contradiction with the quantum mechanical precepts, the locality assumption (LOC1) has to be strengthened by an additional premise. As we have learned, this additional premise may be Einstein's counterfactual criterion of reality (ER), or the rule of inference labeled (LOC2). But Stapp failed to give an airtight argument showing that there is a legitimate version of the locality condition which can do the job. In particular, the logical form of (LOC2) does not by itself suffice to convince us that it represents the proper intuition of locality, as suggested by the restriction of special relativity placed on the transfer of information between space-like separated regions.

### 4.2.8. Conclusions

The 1997 argument employing the Hardy case is thus far the closest we have been able to get to a successful counterfactual strengthening of the Bell theorem, in which the assumption of realism is replaced by the locality condition supplemented with the modal logic of counterfactuals. The argument avoids the formal and conceptual flaws of its predecessors (i.e. of counterfactual versions of the Bell theorem and the GHZ theorem), but it is unclear whether its ultimate conclusion can be interpreted as stating that there exists a non-local link between an act of selecting a particular observable on the one system, and a *physical situation* pertaining to the other system. What Stapp's proof does unquestionably show is that there exists a complex statement connecting in a non-truth-functional way propositions pertaining to one physical region, whose truth depends non-trivially on the choice of experiment in a space-like separated region. But we cannot agree with Stapp's optimistic pronouncement that this conclusion establishes the violation of the general locality principle, understood as prohibiting a physical situation being affected from a distance. The missing link in

Stapp's argument is the issue of whether the statement in question really refers to a physical state of affairs localized in one wing of the experimental set-up. In the light of the arguments presented above, this contention seems to be doubtful.

However, one more general conclusion should be drawn from our lengthy analysis of Stapp's three counterfactual proofs. Although Stapp made a substantial effort to present his derivations in a formalized and precise way, similar to that used in mathematical logic, still two crucial elements of his arguments are treated with insufficient care. One of these elements is the meaning, or more precisely the truth condition, that is associated with the counterfactual connective used by Stapp. Mere reference to Lewis's formal theory of counterfactuals is not enough, for we already know that we need informal criteria of similarity between possible worlds in order to apply counterfactual statements to particular quantum-mechanical cases. The second problem haunting Stapp's arguments (with probably even more devastating consequences) is the lack of a single, un-ambiguous and precise formulation of the locality condition, which would be accepted in advance and kept fixed throughout the entire derivation. As we have seen, rather than consequently adopting one such condition, Stapp helps himself to various more or less intuitive assumptions bordering on "locality", whose status is far from clear. It is understandable, then, that before embarking on a program of the counterfactual reinterpretation of quantum-mechanical "paradoxes" we should finish the task of constructing a satisfactory semantics for "quantum counterfactuals" that we began in chapter 2.

# Chapter 5

# TWO INTERPRETATIONS OF SPATIO-TEMPORAL COUNTERFACTUALS

One general (and straightforward) observation which can be made based on chapters 3 and 4 is that there is more than one way to employ Lewis's semantic framework for counterfactual conditionals in the analysis of quantum entangled states. The main reason is that, as we indicated at the end of chapter 2, there may be various ways to define the similarity relation between possible worlds, and this relation is indispensable for the evaluation of counterfactual statements. To characterize the relation of similarity it is necessary to decide which facts from the actual world are salient with respect to the affinity of possible worlds with it, and which are not. We have already reiterated (and this assessment is unanimously, if mostly tacitly, accepted by all who make use of Lewis's semantics in quantum mechanics) that in the context of the quantum-mechanical phenomena there is no room for law-breaking possible worlds; therefore Lewis's requirement that the number of unlawful events ("miracles") be minimized cannot act as a criterion of similarity between possible worlds. Only singular, individual and contingent facts can set one possible world apart from another, and only such facts can be taken into account when comparing possible worlds with respect to their affinity with the actual world. But it has already been argued that not all facts taking place in the actual world should count towards similarity. It is imperative, then, to make clear how to tell apart those facts that count from those that do not.

## 5.1 "ASYMMETRY BY FIAT" SOLUTION REVIVED

It seems evident that two dominant intuitions regarding the evaluation of quantum counterfactuals have emerged from the extensive discussion in the two previous chapters. However, it will be much more convenient to describe them in terms of extensions to one of Lewis's alternative approaches to counterfactuals rather than in terms of the similarity relation. As we recall (sec. 2.3.3), Lewis indicates that the problem with the temporal asymmetry of counterfactuals can find its solution not only within his favorite semantics, but also within the approach he calls "asymmetry by fiat". According to this approach, in order to consider what would have happened in a situation in which a contrary-to-fact event had taken place at time $t$, we should imagine the world which is exactly as ours up to moment $t$, in which this new event occurs, and which evolves according to the usual laws of nature.[1] Not surprisingly, the above-sketched intuition leads to the following, partial truth-condition for the counterfactual:

(5.1)    If $P$ describes an event occurring at $t$, then $P \,\square\!\!\rightarrow Q$ is true iff $Q$ is true in every possible world $w$ such that $w$ is identical with the actual one at all times earlier than $t$, $w$ evolves according to the ordinary laws of nature, and $P$ is true in $w$.

One of the manifest defects of this formulation is that, for obvious reasons, it is not relativistically invariant. The phrase "at all times earlier than $t$" has no unambiguous meaning within the relativistic theory of time (you might ask: earlier with respect to which inertial frame of reference?). This fact stems from the impossibility of defining the absolute notion of simultaneity. Considering a spatiotemporal point-event $e$ which exists at time $t$, we will obtain different answers to the question "What events are simultaneous with $e$?" depending on the selected frame of reference. And the same applies to the definition of the set of events which are earlier than $e$: given different frames of reference this set will contain different events.

There are two basic, relativistically invariant interpretations of the phrase "events earlier than a given event $e$". We can consider two light cones originating at the location of $e$: one spreading into the future (forward, or future light cone), and the other one spreading into the past (backward, or past light cone). As the past of $e$ we can now select either all events located outside the forward light cone, or all events from the inside of the backward light cone.[2] These choices can also be presented with an explicit reference to inertial frames of reference. In the first case the past of

---

[1]    It should be stressed, however, that some authors question the assumed asymmetry of counterfactual dependence. For example H. Price, who defends the idea of backward causation, argues that when evaluating counterfactuals we should hold fixed not the past of the antecedent-event, but rather what is *epistemologically accessible* to us (see Price 1996, pp. 169-170, 178-179).

[2]    It is a matter of choice whether to include or exclude the surface of the light cones in the respective "pasts" of $e$. We will follow the convention according to which, in the first case, the surface of the forward light cone is excluded from the past, but in the second case the surface of the backward light cone is included in it.

*e* contains all events that are earlier than *e* in *some* frame of reference; in the second case the past of *e* is limited to events that are earlier than *e* in *all* frames of reference.

To each of these interpretations corresponds a slightly different, relativistically invariant reading of counterfactuals, and the two readings may be presented as follows:

(C1)     If *P* denotes a point-like event, then $P \; \square \rightarrow Q$ is true iff *Q* is true in all possible worlds which are exactly like the actual world in the entire region outside the forward light cone of the event described by *P*.

(C2)     If *P* denotes a point-like event, then $P \; \square \rightarrow Q$ is true iff *Q* is true in all possible worlds which are exactly like the actual world in the entire region inside the backward light cone of the event described by *P*.

We should immediately recognize (C1) as the truth condition adopted by Shimony and Stein in their interpretation of Stapp's proof of non-locality (see sec. 4.2.4). Although Stapp himself expressed some reservations towards this reading of his intended meaning of the counterfactual, I shall continue associating (C1) with his name. On the other hand, (C2) seems to fit best the position taken by Redhead and the others in their extensive criticism of Stapp's earliest attempt to prove non-locality of quantum mechanics, and in particular of his Matching Condition (see sec. 3.3). Redhead insists, for example, that if we counterfactually consider an alternative measurement selection at a given location, we cannot assume that the outcome of a distant (i.e. space-like separated) measurement will remain the same as in the actual world, unless this outcome is predetermined by the common past of the system. This is consistent with the assumption that the only region of space-time whose physical "contents" is transferred from the actual world is the backward light cone of the counterfactual event.

It needs to be underscored that both truth-conditions (C1) and (C2) have to be restricted to a special type of antecedent-events. For instance, (C1) stipulates that the truth of the counterfactual depends on whether its consequent holds in the antecedent-worlds that share with the actual world the whole area outside the future light cone of the antecedent-event. But what if such worlds do not exist? According to our earlier stipulation, no law-breaking possible worlds are permitted. But it may happen that for a lawful occurrence of a given event it is necessary to adjust some of its predetermining factors, or even some events space-like separated from, and yet nomologically connected with it. In such a case the right-hand side of the equivalence in (C1) becomes meaningless, and does not offer any clue regarding the truth value of the evaluated counterfactual. It is, of course, always possible to introduce a "vacuity clause", similar to that suggested by Lewis, which would make all counterfactuals true in the case where there is no antecedent-world with the required matching area. But this move would have unacceptable consequences. For example, in the cases where a non-local, law-like connection exists between two space-like separated events, all counterfactuals whose antecedents state the occurrence of one of these events would become vacuously true regardless of their consequents. As a result, we wouldn't even be able to counterfactually express the idea of the existence of the non-local influence between two particular events, even though this was one of the main reasons for starting the semantic analysis of counterfactuals in the first place.

Given this problem, it seems best to explicitly limit the applicability of truth conditions (C1) and (C2) to a particular class of antecedent-events, which we will dub after J. Finkelstein "free-choice events". Later on we will consider some methods for extending the current semantic analysis to other types of antecedent-events. By a free-choice event we understand an event that is not causally, or in any other nomological way correlated with any fact located outside its absolute future (see Finkelstein 1999, p 294). As an example of such an event Finkelstein gives an experimenter's decision to select a particular setting of his measuring apparatus, which is supposedly independent of the earlier states of the system, and also should not affect (or be affected by) anything that transpires at space-like separated locations. The exact definition of free-choice events is as follows:

(FCE)    $E$ is a free-choice event iff there exists a possible $E$-world which agrees with the actual world everywhere outside the forward light cone of $E$.

Let us now compare the two notions of spatiotemporal counterfactuals introduced above.[3] The truth-conditions given by (C1) and (C2) agree when evaluating counterfactuals $P \ \Box\!\!\rightarrow Q$ for which the event described by $Q$

---

3    The reason for calling counterfactuals defined in (C1) and (C2) "spatiotemporal" is obvious: both truth-conditions are restricted to counterfactuals whose antecedents refer to spatiotemporally localized events only.

lies in the absolute past of $P$. If $Q$ is located in the backward light cone of $P$, then according to both (C1) and (C2) the counterfactual $P \,\square\!\!\rightarrow Q$ comes out true iff $Q$ is true in the actual world.

However, there are significant differences between (C1) and (C2) when the consequent $Q$ is assumed to refer to a location outside the absolute past of $P$. Let's first consider the region consisting of all events space-like separated from $P$ (the region outside both the backward and forward light cone of $P$). Take an event $Q$, space-like separated from $P$, and assume that $Q$ occurs in the actual world (see Fig. 5.1). Then, according to (C1) the sentence $P \,\square\!\!\rightarrow Q$ must be true, for in all possible worlds we keep everything outside the future light cone of $P$ fixed, and $Q$ belongs to this region. But the intuition expressed in (C2) can lead to a different answer. Everything depends on the nomological connections between $Q$ and the absolute past of $P$. If $Q$ is a necessary consequence of some of the events in the backward light cone of $P$, then it must occur in all possible worlds in question (once again we invoke the assumption that all possible worlds obey the actual laws of nature). But if $Q$ is not causally or in any other way determined by the past of $P$, there will be possible worlds exactly like ours with respect to the past of $P$, but in which $Q$ will not hold; and therefore the sentence $P \,\square\!\!\rightarrow Q$ will turn out false.

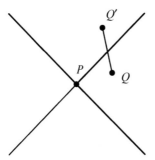

Figure 5.1 An example illustrating the differences in evaluating counterfactuals between (C1) and (C2). $Q$ is a free-choice event space-like separated from $P$, and $Q'$ lies in the absolute future of $P$ and is causally connected with $Q$.

The same difference concerns the future light cone of $P$. Let us assume that $Q'$ singles out an event from this region (see Fig. 5.1). If the consequent $Q'$ represents an event causally connected with $P$ or with any event absolutely preceding $P$, or if $Q'$ is a free-choice event, then both approaches will give exactly the same answer. However, there is the possibility that $Q'$ may be determined by some earlier free-choice event $Q$, space-like separated from $P$. In such a case, according to (C1), the event $Q$ should be kept fixed, and the counterfactual $P \;\square\!\!\rightarrow Q'$ will, therefore, be judged true. However, according to (C2) we can consider possible worlds other than those in which $Q$ takes place. Because $Q$ is an "indeterministic" event, there will be two possible worlds matching the actual one with respect to the absolute past of $P$, such that in one of them $Q$ will be present, and in the other it will be absent. As a result, the sentence $P \;\square\!\!\rightarrow Q'$ will be pronounced false.

The differences in truth-value attributions to counterfactuals between approaches (C1) and (C2) have a profound impact on the counterfactual exposition of the locality condition. Followers of (C1) will insist that a proper counterfactual intuition of locality requires that for all statements $P$ and $Q$ representing space-like separated events, if $Q$ is true in the actual world, the counterfactual $P \;\square\!\!\rightarrow Q$ should remain true. However, for a proponent of (C2) this condition demands too much. For the above counterfactual to be true, the event described by $Q$ has to be guaranteed to occur in all possible $P$-worlds which share with the actual world the absolute past of $P$, and this amounts to saying that $Q$ is causally determined by events in $P$'s past. Yet the locality condition should also work for indeterministic events, such as the outcomes of quantum measurements. Hence it is clear that the approach (C2) requires a different formulation of the locality condition. We will return to this problem in the next chapter.

## 5.2 GENERALIZATION OF (C1)

In this section we will take up the important and challenging task of generalizing both approaches (C1) and (C2) to cover a wider class of antecedents. The generalization I have in mind should take care of two problems, already indicated earlier. Firstly, it should enable us to assign truth-values to counterfactuals whose antecedents refer not only to events localized in one particular spatiotemporal point, but instead to states of affairs of more complex spatiotemporal locations, or even without proper location at all. Secondly, it ought to cover the antecedent-events that are not free-choice, i.e. events that are correlated with other events outside their future light cones. The second objective is of particularly great significance to the goal of making counterfactuals capable of expressing the concept of non-local influence. This is the case, because, due to the restriction of (C1) and (C2) to free-choice events, the truth conditions given there are not applicable when a non-local correlation between space-like separated events exists. To eliminate this undesirable situation, some way of generalizing the conditions (C1) and (C2) is necessary.

Fortunately, it appears that at least in the case of the interpretation given by (C1) the required generalization is relatively easy to obtain. I will follow the proposal put forward by Finkelstein in (1999) with some cosmetic changes that in my opinion help to better express his idea. Finkelstein noticed that we can introduce quite a straightforward similarity relation between possible worlds which, together with the appropriate Lewis-style truth conditions for counterfactuals will yield (C1) as a special case. This similarity relation can be defined as follows. First, for each possible world $w_j$ we define a set $D_j$ of *primary points of divergence (PPD)*, which are informally characterized as the earliest spatiotemporal points at which a difference between $w_j$ and the actual world occurs. A more formal definition looks like this:

(PPD)    A spatio-temporal point $p$ is a *primary point of divergence* for a given possible world $w_i$ iff $p$ is a point of divergence (i.e. there is an event $e$ such that $e$ is localized at $p$ and it takes place in $w_i$ but not in the actual world), and there are no other points of divergence in $w_i$ absolutely earlier than $p$.

Next, we consider the closure $\overline{D}_j$ of the set $D_j$ of points with respect to their absolute future, i.e. the set of all spatiotemporal points such that they are absolutely later than some primary point of divergence. Intuitively, $\overline{D}_j$ represents the entire region of all possible differences between the world $j$ and the actual one (see Fig. 5.2). Now the definition of the similarity relation can be easily presented as follows:

(SIM)    World $w_j$ is at least as similar to the actual world as $w_k$ iff $\overline{D}_j \subseteq \overline{D}_k$.[4]

---

[4]   This characteristic of the similarity relation comes very close to Stapp's proposal developed in (1994a, pp. 3183-3184). There Stapp suggested that the closeness between a possible world $w_j$ and the actual world $w$ be judged based on the set of all worlds that can lawfully evolve into both $w_j$ and $w$ (symbolized as $W(w_j, w)$). Stapp elects to call world $w_j$ closer to $w$ than $w_k$ if the union of the pasts of the worlds in $W(w_k, w)$ is properly included in the union of the pasts of the worlds in $W(w_j, w)$. Although Stapp does not make it precise what he means by "the past of a world",

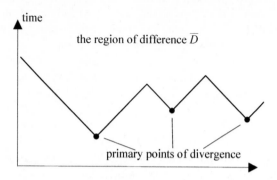

Figure 5.2 An example illustrating Finkelstein's criterion of comparative similarity between possible worlds.

It can be quickly checked that the above similarity relation reproduces (C1) as a special case, when antecedent $P$ refers to a localized free-choice event. For, in that case, the set $\overline{D}_j$ reduces to the future light cone of event $P$, and hence in evaluating the counterfactual $P \, \square\!\!\rightarrow Q$ we should take into account every possible world $w_k$ such that $\overline{D}_k = \overline{D}_j$. But this in turn means that we should keep everything which happens outside the future light cone of $P$ exactly the same as in the actual world, so (C1) follows readily. On the other hand, the truth conditions based on the proposed definition of the similarity relation give us the ability to evaluate counterfactuals not restricted to those mentioned in (C1). For example, we can easily handle cases where the antecedent $P$ is equivalent to a finite disjunction or conjunction of sentences $P_1$, $P_2$, ..., $P_n$, each of which picks one particular localized free-choice event. In both cases we should obviously consider all possible antecedent-worlds $w_j$ such that they are closest to the actual world according to the relation given in $\overline{D}_j \subseteq \overline{D}_k$. So, for instance, in the case of the disjunction $P_1 \vee P_2 \vee ... \vee P_n$ the closest antecedent-worlds will be identified with those which have only one primary point of divergence, being the location of such an event $P_i$ for which there is no other $P_j$ occurring in its absolute future (see Fig. 5.3). The number of the closest antecedent-

---

from his examples it is clear that the union of the pasts of the worlds in $W(w_j, w)$ is identical to the exterior of the closure of $D_j$, and therefore his condition becomes equivalent to (SIM).

worlds depends on how many absolutely latest $P_i$'s of this kind exist (where the number may vary from 1 to $n$, of course).[5]

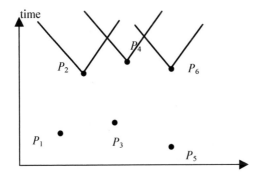

Figure 5.3 A possible space-time layout of six events referred to by the disjuncts in the antecedent of the counterfactual $(P_1 \vee P_2 \vee \ldots \vee P_6) \; \square\!\!\rightarrow Q$. In order to evaluate the counterfactual, we should consider three possible worlds $w_2$, $w_4$ and $w_6$, with their PPD's located at $P_2$, $P_4$ and $P_6$ respectively.

---

[5] Incidentally, from this it follows immediately that those disjuncts $P_i$ whose referents are absolutely earlier than referents of some other disjuncts are totally irrelevant for the evaluation of the entire counterfactuals (they can be dropped from the antecedent of the counterfactual without affecting its truth-value). This feature is in general agreement with a consequence of Lewis's semantics, according to which if we consider a counterfactual $(P_1 \vee P_2) \; \square\!\!\rightarrow Q$ for which some $P_1$-worlds are closer to the actual world than all $P_2$-worlds, then the counterfactual becomes simply equivalent to $P_1 \; \square\!\!\rightarrow Q$. We should add that some authors see this consequence of Lewis's logic as highly unintuitive (compare a convincing counterexample in Nute 1975, p. 776). D. Nute in (1975) develops an alternative logic of counterfactuals in which the formula $[(P \vee Q) \; \square\!\!\rightarrow R] \supset (P \; \square\!\!\rightarrow R)$ is adopted as one of the axioms (and one of Lewis's axioms is eliminated in order to avoid trivializing the logic). Consequently, the counterfactual $(P \vee Q) \; \square\!\!\rightarrow R$ becomes equivalent to $(P \; \square\!\!\rightarrow R) \wedge (Q \; \square\!\!\rightarrow R)$. For an argument against accepting this equivalence see (Lewis 1977). J. Bennett (2003, pp. 168-171) defends Lewis's position by pointing out that although conditionals with disjunctive antecedents are not logically equivalent to the conjunction of conditionals, they are pragmatically treated as such (in the sense of Gricean conversational implicatures).

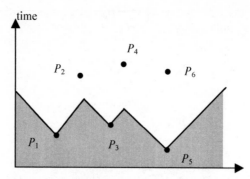

Figure 5.4 The single possible world in which the evaluation of the counterfactual $(P_1 \wedge P_2 \wedge \dots \wedge P_6) \,\square\!\!\rightarrow Q$ should be made. The grayed area indicates perfect match with the actual world.

For a conjunction $P_1 \wedge P_2 \wedge \dots \wedge P_n$ there is only one (up to the irrelevant differences in the future) possible world we need to consider. It is the world $w_k$ for which $D_k$ includes all spatiotemporal points referred to by those among the conjuncts $P_1$, $P_2$, ..., $P_n$ for which no remaining conjunct-event is absolutely *earlier* than they are. $\overline{D}_k$ will obviously contain all the other points identified by the remaining conjuncts (see Fig. 5.4). It is now also possible to obtain the required extension for cases where $P$ describes an event which is not free-choice. For example, when there is a strict correlation between $P$ and another event $R$ space-like separated from $P$ such that $R$ occurs each time $P$ is present, we should consider possible worlds which have not one, but two primary points of divergence, these being the points at which $P$ and $R$ transpire.

It seems that, with the help of a specifically designed similarity relation, we have succeeded in reducing truth condition (C1) to a special case of Lewis's general truth conditions for counterfactuals. However, there is still one formal difficulty that needs to be resolved. As it was explained in chapter 2, Lewis's semantics works under certain assumptions regarding the similarity relation, one of them being that this relation forms a linear ordering of possible worlds. This means that the similarity relation is assumed to meet the strong connectedness condition, which prescribes that every two possible worlds are comparable with one another: either one of the possible worlds is more similar to the actual world, or they are equisimilar. But a quick look at the relation defined in (SIM) reveals that it is not strongly connected: there are possible worlds $w_j$ and $w_k$ such that neither

$w_j \lesssim_i w_k$, nor $w_k \lesssim_i w_j$. The obvious example of such a situation is when worlds $w_j$ and $w_k$ both have only one primary point of divergence, and these points are mutually space-like separated. In that case sets $\overline{D}_j$ and $\overline{D}_k$ overlap, hence neither $\overline{D}_j \subseteq \overline{D}_k$ nor $\overline{D}_k \subseteq \overline{D}_j$ holds.

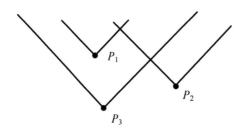

Figure 5.5 An example illustrating the non-connectedness of the relation (SIM).

It is not an option to try to achieve connectedness by "brute force", i.e. by introducing a new and broader equisimilarity relation "$\approx$" which would cover all the cases in which neither $\overline{D}_j \subseteq \overline{D}_k$ nor $\overline{D}_k \subseteq \overline{D}_j$ is true. For such a relation would obviously fail to satisfy transitivity, as the example depicted in Fig. 5.5 shows. Here each of the points $P_1$, $P_2$ and $P_3$ is a sole PPD for respective worlds $w_1$, $w_2$ and $w_3$, and from the diagram we clearly see that $w_1 \approx w_2$ and $w_2 \approx w_3$, but $w_1 < w_3$. Hence we have to accept the non-linearity of the relation SIM as a fact. But what are the consequences of this deviation from Lewis's standard semantics for counterfactuals? The main problem that we face right now is that the truth conditions (L) and (L') presented in sec. 2.2 (and claimed there to be equivalent) no longer work under the assumption that possible worlds are only partially ordered by the relation of relative similarity. What this means is that (L) and (L') produce unintuitive, and clearly unacceptable valuations for counterfactuals in case the similarity relation is only a partial ordering. To show that this is the case, let us consider some examples. Suppose that the partial ordering on a set of antecedent-worlds looks like the tree presented in Fig. 5.6, where worlds (represented by dots) lying lower on a given branch are assumed to be closer to the actual world. In this example it is easy to verify that according to definition (L) both counterfactuals $P \mathbin{\Box}\!\!\to Q$ and $P \mathbin{\Box}\!\!\to {\sim}Q$ will come out true. For example, $P \mathbin{\Box}\!\!\to Q$ is true, because there is a *P*-and-*Q*-world (any world on the left branch) such that no *P*-and-not-*Q*-world is closer to reality than it. But *P* □→ ~*Q* turns out to be true all the same, which is obviously an abnormality.

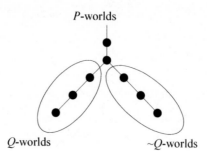

Figure 5.6 An example of the ordering of possible worlds which shows that the truth condition (L) does not work.

Truth-condition (L′), which was equivalent to (L) under the linearity assumption, but is no longer when ≤ is a partial ordering, produces other pathological valuations. Consider an ordering of *P*-worlds depicted in Fig. 5.7. In this situation it seems reasonable to expect that the counterfactual *P* □→ *Q* should turn out to be true. Intuitively, this follows from the fact that all the *P*-worlds closest to the actual world appear to be also *Q*-worlds. But according to (L′) this counterfactual is obviously false. Take for instance the *Q*-world at the bottom of the right branch. This world is not comparable to the ~*Q*-world that lies on the left branch, and therefore (L′) is not satisfied.

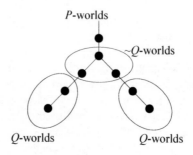

Figure 5.7 A counterexample for the truth condition (L′).

The way out of this difficulty is to propose yet another version of truth-conditions, which will not produce any troublesome valuations. As it may be easily verified, the following formulation can do this job relatively well.

(L″)     $P \,\Box\!\!\rightarrow Q$ is non-vacuously true iff for every $P$-world $w$ there is a $P$-world $w'$ such that $w'$ is also a $Q$-world, that $w' \leq w$, and that there is no $P$-world $w''$ in which $Q$ does not hold and $w'' \leq w'$.[6]

The slight awkwardness of (L″) is a small price to pay for its accurateness. (L″) makes sure that for a counterfactual to be true, its consequent has to be true in all "branches" containing antecedent-worlds that come as close as possible to the actual world. (L″) together with the definition (SIM) of comparable similarity creates a workable, Lewis-style semantics for space-time counterfactuals that produces intuition (C1) as its special case when the antecedent denotes a free-choice point-like event.[7]

## 5.3 TROUBLES WITH GENERALIZING (C2)

The next logical step of our analysis should be to produce an analogous generalization for counterfactuals interpreted as in (C2). However, this task encounters unexpected difficulties. One may think, by symmetry, that (C2) could be reproduced with the help of a modified similarity relation (SIM), where the maximization of the absolute joint past rather than the minimization of the absolute joint future of primary divergence points is a measure of similarity with the actual world. But this approach will not work. The proposed method of comparing possible worlds would obviously pronounce worlds with more than one primary point of divergence as *closer* to the actual world than a world with only one PPD. But this consequence is not acceptable. It appears that not every formally acceptable spatiotemporal relation between possible worlds  can serve as a potential relative similarity relation. We need to start our search for a similarity relation capable of reconstructing (C2) with a specification of certain minimal

---

[6]  This formulation can be shown to be equivalent to truth condition (O) given in (Lewis 1981, p. 230). Lewis formulates (O) as an adequate truth condition for counterfactuals in the case when neither linearity nor the limit assumption is satisfied.

[7]  The extension of the interpretation (C1) achieved with the help of the similarity relation (SIM) and the generalized truth condition (L″) will be henceforth referred to as (C1+).

requirements that every admissible similarity relation should satisfy. These requirements should not be too restrictive, in order not to imply that the only acceptable similarity relation is (SIM), yet they must not allow "pathological" similarity relations, which do not reflect any reasonable way of comparing possible worlds with respect to their closeness to the actual world. Here I propose the following constraints on $<$, which seem to be an acceptable weakening of criterion (SIM) of comparative similarity.

(S1)    For every $w_1$, $w_2$, if $D_1 = \{ p_1^1, \ldots p_1^n \}$ and $D_2 = \{ p_2^1, \ldots p_2^n \}$, and at least one of the points $p_1^1, \ldots p_1^n$ occurs absolutely later than its counterpart in $p_2^1, \ldots p_2^n$, whereas all the remaining points of divergence in $w_1$ are identical to those in $w_2$, then $w_1 < w_2$.

(S2)    If $w_1 < w_2$, then $\overline{D_1} \subset \overline{D_2}$ and $\overline{D_1} \neq \overline{D_2}$.

The first requirement expresses the straightforward intuition that when we consider a possible world $w_2$ which diverges from the actual world at certain primary points, and when we allow some of these points of divergence to occur a bit later, we will always end up with a world $w_1$ which is strictly more similar to the actual world. However, we must be careful not to take this intuition too far. We cannot allow those initial points of divergence to occur arbitrarily later, for it can turn out that our "deferred" possible world has a smaller number of primary points of divergence than the original one. This would mean that we ended up with Finkelstein's criterion of similarity (SIM), of which we know that it can't possibly produce intuition (C2). Therefore, it is important to stress that both worlds $w_1$ and $w_2$ in condition (S1) have the same number of primary points of divergence. We do not formulate any suggestions how to compare possible worlds $w_1$ and $w_2$ such that the region $\overline{D_1}$ is properly included in $\overline{D_2}$, but $w_1$ has a different number of primary points of divergence than $w_2$.

Requirement (S2) just gives a necessary condition for one world being strictly more similar to the actual world than another one. We assume that the proper inclusion of the region $\overline{D_1}$ in $\overline{D_2}$ is a necessary (but not sufficient) condition for world $w_1$ being strictly more similar to the actual one than the world $w_2$. Together, conditions (S1) and (S2) put a reasonable constraint on all similarity relations, which is obviously respected in case of (SIM), but which also gives hope that an alternative similarity comparison may exist which would do justice to the intuition (C2). In particular, (S1) and (S2) do not *prima facie* exclude the possibility that we may deem a world with two (or more) PPD's to be equisimilar to (or incomparable with) a world which has only one of these PPD's. This is crucial for the task of reconstructing interpretation (C2) of the counterfactual, for (C2) implies that antecedent-worlds relevant for the valuation of a counterfactual may differ from the actual world with respect to facts space-like separated from the antecedent-event, only if these facts are free-choice.

In spite of our effort, it turns out that the task of finding an appropriate similarity relation for the C2 interpretation of counterfactuals is impossible to complete. Below we will formulate and prove a theorem to this effect.

(Th 5.1)    There is no similarity relation $\leq$ between possible worlds satisfying conditions (S1)–(S2), such that together with truth condition (L″) it implies interpretation (C2) in the case of the antecedent denoting a free-choice point event.

We will prove the theorem by showing that the requirements (S1) and (S2) together imply that when we take $P$ and $Q$ as denoting space-like separated events, then when $Q$ is true in the actual world, the counterfactual $P \: \square\!\!\rightarrow Q$ must also be true. This means that no similarity relation obeying (S1) and (S2) can possibly produce (C2) as a special case, for (C2) implies that in some cases the counterfactual $P \: \square\!\!\rightarrow Q$ is false. Let us start the proof by presenting an equivalent version of the truth-condition (L″) for counterfactuals (the proof of its equivalence, being elementary, is omitted):

(L″)    $P \: \square\!\!\rightarrow Q$ is non-vacuously true iff for every $P$-and-not-$Q$-world $w$ there is a $P$-and-$Q$-world $w'$ such that $w' \leq w$, and there is no $P$-and-not-$Q$-world $w''$ that $w'' \leq w'$.

Assume that $P$ and $Q$ are space-like separated events, and that $Q$ does, but $P$ doesn't occur in the actual world. Let us, then, pick out any $P$-and-not-$Q$ world and call it $w_1$. Obviously, since neither $P$ nor $\sim Q$ occur in the actual world, the points of their occurrence $p(P)$ and $p(\sim Q)$ must belong to $\overline{D_1}$ (note that $p(\sim Q) = p(Q)$). We will restrict ourselves to the case where possible worlds have only finitely many points of divergence. Therefore, we can stipulate $D_1$ as being equal to $\{ p_1^1, \ldots p_1^n \}$. And now we will have to use the following lemma.

Lemma   For every set of primary points of divergence $D_1 = \{ p_1^1, \ldots p_1^n \}$ such that $p(P), p(Q) \in \overline{D_1}$ and $p(P)$ is space-like separated from $p(Q)$, there is a set of primary points of divergence $D_2 = \{ p_2^1, \ldots p_2^n \}$ such that

(a) for all $i$, $p_2^i = p_1^i$ or $p_2^i$ lies in the absolute future of $p_1^i$, and for some $i$ $p_2^i \neq p_1^i$,

(b) $p(P) \in \overline{D_2}$, but $p(Q) \notin \overline{D_2}$ [8]

This essentially means that we can find a world $w_2$ which is strictly closer to the actual one than $w_1$ ($w_2 < w_1$), and such that $P$ and $Q$ hold in it. Therefore the first part of the truth-condition (L″) is shown to have been satisfied: we have proved that for any $P$-and-not-$Q$-world $w_1$ there is a $P$-and-$Q$ world $w_2$ such that $w_2 < w_1$. The only thing we ought to do now is to show that there is no $P$-and-not-$Q$ world $w_3$ such that $w_3 \leq w_2$.

The situation described by $w_3 \leq w_2$ can be presented as the disjunction $w_3 < w_2$ or $w_3 \cong w_2$. The first case is impossible in the light of the condition (S2): obviously $\overline{D_3} \not\subset \overline{D_2}$, for $p(Q)$ belongs to the first and not to the second. Therefore the only possibility we have to consider is that $w_3 \cong w_2$. Suppose then that there is a $P$-and-not-$Q$-world $w_3$ which is as similar to the actual one as the $P$-and-$Q$-world $w_2$. It should be quite obvious that because of the continuity of space-time, we can always find another $P$-and-$Q$-world $w_2'$ which differs from $w_2$ only in so far as exactly one of its primary points of divergence $p_2^{i\prime}$ occurs absolutely a little *earlier* than its counterpart $p_2^i$ (consider the fact that the set $\overline{D_2}$ is a finite sum of future light cones such that $p(Q)$ lies outside it). Therefore, according to condition (S1), $w_2 < w_2'$. Together with our assumption that $w_3 \cong w_2$ it leads to the conclusion that $w_3 < w_2'$. But this last inequality is impossible due to condition (S2): world $w_3$ cannot be strictly more similar to the actual than $w_2'$, because $\overline{D_3}$ contains point $p(Q)$ which does not belong to $\overline{D'_2}$. Hence, there can be no $P$-and-not-$Q$-world which is equally similar to the actual one as $w_2$.

Incidentally, the above reasoning shows that an informal argument put forward by some authors (for example Redhead 1987; Clifton *et al.* 1990) in favor of the approach (C2), cannot be accepted. Redhead for instance argues that the counterfactual $P \;\square\!\rightarrow Q$, where $Q$ refers to a chance event

---

[8]   The proof of this lemma will be given shortly.

space-like separated from $P$, cannot be seen as true, because the closest possible world $w_{PQ}$ in which $P$ and $Q$ hold is arguably as close to the actual as any world $w_{P \sim Q}$ in which event $Q$ does not occur. However, since it is always possible to find two $P$-and-not-$Q$-worlds such that one is strictly more similar to the actual world than the other, this conjecture regarding the relation between worlds $w_{PQ}$ and $w_{P \sim Q}$ is incompatible with the minimal condition (S2) imposed on the relation of comparative similarity, and hence is not tenable. It appears that we cannot do justice to the intuition expressed in (C2) in such a straightforward way.

We will now prove the above-formulated lemma. Let us present set $D_1$ as the sum $D_Q \cup D_Q'$, where $D_Q$ consists of all and only points whose absolute future contains $p(Q)$, and $D_Q'$ is the complement of $D_Q$ to the entire $\overline{D_1}$. The non-emptiness of $D_Q$ is guaranteed by the assumption $p(Q) \in \overline{D_1}$, however it may be the case that $D_Q'$ is empty. Now we will consider two cases: case (1) in which there is a point $p_1^i \in D_Q'$ such that $p(P) \in F(p_1^i)$, and case (2) in which there is no such a point, and in which, therefore, there must be a point $p_1^i \in D_Q$ such that $p(P) \in F(p_1^i)$.[9] Let us first assume that (1) is the case. Denote by $F_Q$ the sum of all future light cones of points in $D_Q$, and by $F_Q'$ the appropriate sum for the set $D_Q'$. From the definition of $D_Q'$ it follows that $p(Q) \notin F_Q'$. Now define the following region $R = F(p(Q)) - F_Q'$ (see Fig. 5.8). This region is non-empty by the fact that $p(Q) \notin F_Q'$, and obviously it forms a connected, continuous set of space-time points (because it can be presented as a finite combination of sums and products of light cones). Moreover, $R \subset F(p_1^i)$ for all points $p_1^i \in D_Q$. Therefore, we can choose any finite set $S$ of mutually space-like separated points from $R$, and in particular $S$ can have the same cardinality as $D_Q$. From what was said above it follows that the set $S \cup D_Q'$ fulfills all requirements put on the set $D_2$ in the lemma. The condition (a) is met, because all points in set $S$ lie in the absolute future of all points from $D_Q$. Because $S$ was chosen from the region outside $F_Q'$, all points in $S$ are space-like separated from points in $D_Q'$, and so $S \cup D_Q'$ is a set of primary points of divergence. And, finally, (b) is satisfied by the construction of $S$ and by assumption (1).

---

[9]   By $F(p)$ I will denote the forward light cone of point $p$. Analogously, $B(p)$ will refer to the backward light cone of $p$, and both $NF(p)$ and $NB(p)$ will symbolize the surfaces of the forward and backward light cones respectively.

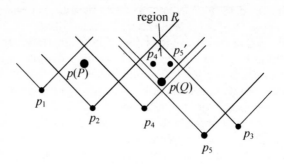

Fig. 5.8 An illustration of the proof of the lemma in case (1). $D_Q' = \{p_1, p_2, p_3\}$; $D_Q = \{p_4, p_5\}$; $S = \{p_4', p_5'\}$

Now let us move to case (2). In this case there is no point $p_1^i$ such that $p(P)$ belongs to its absolute future $F(p_1^i)$, but $p(Q)$ does not. Therefore, we cannot appeal directly to the above procedure of constructing set $D_2$, for $\overline{D_2}$ thus obtained would not include $p(P)$. However, we can adopt the following strategy. We can try to construct a set $D_1'$ such that it has all the elements of $D_1$ with one exception: instead of a particular point $p_1^i \in D_Q'$ such that $p(P)$ and $p(Q)$ are included in its absolute future $F(p_1^i)$, there is a point $p_1^{i}{}' \in D_1'$ such that $p_1^{i}{}' \in F(p_1^i)$, $p(P) \in F(p_1^{i}{}')$, but $p(Q) \notin F(p_1^{i}{}')$. If such a set $D_1'$ exists, then we can apply to it the procedure from case (1) and obtain the set $D_2 = S \cup D_B'$, fulfilling the condition of the lemma. So now we must prove that $D_1'$ always exists.

More specifically, we are going to show now that for any finite set $T$ of mutually space-like separated points $\{p_1, ..., p_k\}$ lying in the common absolute past of events $P$ and $Q$, there is a set $T' = \{p_1, ..., p_i', ..., p_k\}$ such that $p_i' \in F(p_i)$, $p(P) \in F(p_i')$, but $p(Q) \notin F(p_i')$, and $p_i'$ is space-like separated from all other points $p_j \in T'$. We will prove this by construction. Let us first consider for each point $p_i \in T$ a following set of points: $NF(p_i) \cap NB(Q)$. This set is an intersection of two light cones: the forward light cone coming from $p_i$, and the backward light cone with its apex at $p(Q)$ (see Fig. 5.9). Next we can consider only this fragment of the intersection which lies within the past light cone of $P$: $NF(p_i) \cap NB(Q) \cap B(P)$. And finally we can take any light ray $r$ coming from $p(Q)$ and going backward in time, and such that it intersects all regions $NF(p_i) \cap NB(Q) \cap B(P)$. It is a simple geometrical fact that such a ray will always exist, and moreover that it will intersect every region $NF(p_i) \cap NB(Q) \cap B(P)$ at exactly one point $q_i$. Now, from all points $q_i$ on the ray $r$ we should take this one which is the farthest from $Q$. However, it can happen that two or more points $q_i$ can coincide. But in this case we can appeal to the fact that the regions $NF(p_i) \cap NB(Q) \cap B(P)$ for different points $p_i$ can intersect only at a discrete numbers of points, so if it's necessary we can always find a ray $r'$ "infinitesimally" close to $r$ and such that it singles out the unique farthest point of intersection $q_i{}^*$.

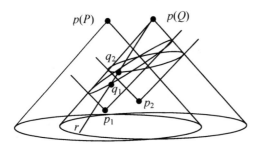

Figure 5.9 An illustration of the proof in case (2). In this example $T = \{p_1, p_2\}$ and $q_1$ is the farthest point $q_i{}^*$.

Let us observe that the point $q_i{}^*$ has "almost" all features we were looking for. Obviously, $q_i{}^* \in F(p_i)$ for some point $p_i$. Moreover, $q_i{}^*$ is space-like separated from all other points $p_j \neq p_i$. The fact that $q_i{}^*$ cannot lie in the absolute past of any point $p_j$ follows immediately from the fact that $q_i{}^* \in F(p_i)$ and from the assumption that all points in $T$ are space-like separated. But if $q_i{}^*$ were to be located in the absolute future of any point $p_j$ other than $p_i$, then the appropriate point $q_j$ of intersection of the future light cone of $p_j$ with the ray $r$ would have to lie at least as far from $Q$, and possibly farther, as $q_i{}^*$ itself, and this contradicts our initial supposition. Finally, $p(P) \in F(q_i{}^*)$ and $p(Q) \in NF(q_i{}^*)$, which means that $Q$ lies on the surface of the future light cone of $q_i{}^*$. For our purposes we need slightly more: we need $Q$ to be entirely outside the future light cone of $q_i{}^*$. But this can be achieved quite easily by an appropriate "infinitesimal" shift of point $q_i{}^*$, which doesn't change any of the previously mentioned features of $q_i{}^*$ except that it causes $Q$ to "fall out" of the future light cone of $q_i{}^*$.

The rest is just "mopping-up". We have started off with the set of points $D_1 = D_Q \cup D_Q{}'$, and we have been considering the case when $D_Q{}'$ contains no point whose absolute future includes $A$. Therefore, the subset $D_{PQ}$ of the set $D_Q$, consisting of all and only points which contain both $p(P)$ and $p(Q)$ in their absolute futures, must be non-empty. From the above result we know that $D_{PQ}$ can be replaced by a set $D_{PQ}{}'$ of mutually space-like separated points, which differs from the former only in that it contains one "deferred" point $q_i{}^*$ for which $p(P) \in F(q_i{}^*)$, but $p(Q) \notin F(q_i{}^*)$. The point $q_i{}^*$ must be obviously space-like separated from all points in $D_Q{}'$, because by the assumption no point from $D_Q{}'$ contains $p(P)$ in its absolute future. Also $q_i{}^*$ is space-like separated from points belonging to $D_B - D_{AB}$, for they don't lie in the absolute past of $A$, either. Hence, we have finally constructed the set $D_1{}'$ to which we can apply the argument from case (1), and therefore the entire proof is complete.

## 5.4 GENERALIZATION OF (C2) ACHIEVED—A STEP BEYOND LEWIS'S ORTHODOXY

The main conclusion from the above theorem is that we cannot hope for a generalization of the second alternative truth-condition (C2) along the same way we generalized the case (C1). Apparently there is no required similarity relation that could do the trick. Does that mean that the second proposed reading of relativistically invariant counterfactuals has to be abandoned? I am going to argue that it would be overly hasty to draw this conclusion. Although simply copying Lewis's similarity-based semantics cannot yield the required generalization of (C2), it is possible to produce an alternative to the Lewis truth-condition for counterfactuals which would make it possible to evaluate all counterfactual conditionals with no restriction on their antecedents, and which could be justifiably seen as an extension of (C2). The only constraint put on this proposal, which will be presented next, is that the Limit Assumption in the version appropriate for a non-linear ordering of possible worlds is assumed to be satisfied. More precisely, we will proceed under the assumption that the following condition is satisfied:

(LA′)    For all antecedents $P$ and for every $P$-world $w$, there is a $P$-world $w'$ such that $w' \leq w$ and there is no $P$-world $w''$ for which $w'' < w'$.

Let us now consider an arbitrary counterfactual $P \; \Box\!\!\rightarrow Q$. The proposed method for its evaluation will be given in several steps (the truth-conditions for counterfactuals resulting from this procedure will be later referred to as "C2+"). First we will select the set of possible worlds $\Pi$ which contains all the closest $P$-worlds according to the similarity relation SIM:

$w_i \in \Pi$ iff $w_i$ is a $P$-world and there is no $P$-world $w_j$ such that $w_j < w_i$.

Owing to (LA′), set $\Pi$ will always be non-empty, provided that there is at least one $P$-world (that $P$ is not impossible). Note that if we wanted to evaluate counterfactual $P \; \Box\!\!\rightarrow Q$ using the generalization of (C1), we would only have to verify if $Q$ is true in all the worlds from $\Pi$. But as we want to follow the intuition encapsulated in (C2), we need to introduce a new element to the procedure. Hence for each world $w_i \in \Pi$ we will consider its set of primary points of divergence $D_i$, and we will define the spatiotemporal area $\Gamma_i$:

$$\Gamma_i = \bigcup_{p \in D_i} B(p),$$

i.e. the sum of all backward light cones originating at points from $D_i$.

As the last step let us define for a given world $w_i$ a set of possible $P$-worlds $\Lambda_i$ such that each world in $\Lambda_i$ agrees with $w_i$ (*ergo* with the actual world) in the entire area of $\Gamma_i$, but possibly differs in all other regions (within the limits of the laws, of course). Hence, worlds in $\Lambda_i$ can have more primary points of divergence than $w_i$, if only the additional PPD's include indeterministic events, whose occurrence is neither excluded, nor implied by the laws of nature (worlds in $\Lambda_i$ can be informally called "extensions" of $w_i$). Having defined $\Lambda_i$ for every world $w_i$ belonging to $\Pi$ we can finally stipulate that the counterfactual $P \; \Box\!\!\rightarrow Q$ will be deemed true iff for all $w_i \in \Pi$ and all $w_j \in \Lambda_i$, $Q$ is true in $w_j$.

It should be quite clear that this evaluating method will reduce to (C2) in case $P$ refers to a free-choice point event. For in this case $\Pi$ contains all and only worlds which match the actual world everywhere outside $P$'s forward light cone, and the "extensions" of such worlds will be just the possible worlds with $P$'s backward light cone identical to that in the actual world. And yet the procedure is general enough to be applied to every imaginable antecedent, if only the Limit Assumption is satisfied. Later on we will show what the result of this procedure will be when applied to some typical cases of antecedents.

But before that, it may be instructive to see why the above-given procedure cannot be incorporated directly into the framework of Lewis's similarity-based semantics. After all, our method of evaluating a counterfactual $P \,\square\!\!\rightarrow Q$ reduces to the selection of the set of possible worlds $\bigcup \Lambda_i$ in which $Q$ has to be true. Wouldn't it be possible, then, to invent a similarity comparison which would prescribe for any antecedent $P$ that the $P$-worlds most similar to the actual one are precisely those within $\bigcup \Lambda_i$? However, the trouble is that such a comparison cannot be provided consistently and *independently* of a given antecedent. The cornerstone of Lewis's formal approach is that we have to put possible worlds in order according to a similarity ranking *before* we choose a particular antecedent. But it can be verified that the currently introduced evaluation method implies that the comparison between possible worlds is dependent on the exact form of the antecedent. There are situations in which a given world $w_i$ has to be seen as more similar to the actual world than world $w_j$ when evaluating a counterfactual with antecedent $P_1$, but it is not so when evaluating another counterfactual with a different antecedent $P_2$.

To give an example let us consider three contrary-to-fact statements $P_1$, $P_2$ and $P_3$, each of which describes one free-choice point-event. Moreover, let us assume that the event picked by $P_1$ is space-like separated from both events described by $P_2$ and $P_3$, but $P_2$ happens absolutely later than $P_3$. Now suppose that we are interested in evaluating counterfactual $(P_2 \vee P_3)$ $\square\!\!\rightarrow Q$. It can be easily checked that according to our procedure one of the worlds which is essential for the evaluation of this counterfactual is the world $w_{12}$ in which both $P_1$ and $P_2$ hold, but not $P_3$. On the other hand, the world $w_{13}$ in which $P_1$ and $P_3$ are true is not part of the evaluation procedure, as it can be introduced only as an "extension" of the world $w_3$, which is obviously less similar to the actual one than $w_2$ according to SIM. Hence it follows that for the purpose of evaluating the above counterfactual with a disjunctive antecedent, $w_{12}$ should be seen as closer to the actual world than $w_{13}$. But now consider the same evaluating procedure as applied to statement $P_1 \,\square\!\!\rightarrow Q$. Here both worlds $w_{12}$ and $w_{13}$ are proper "extensions" of world $w_1$, and as such should be part of the counterfactual's evaluation. It appears that, from the perspective of counterfactual $P_1 \,\square\!\!\rightarrow Q$, both worlds $w_{12}$ and $w_{13}$ are equisimilar. This situation is impossible to obtain in the Lewis-style semantics, for the relation between $w_{12}$ and $w_{13}$ should be independent of the statement we are evaluating. This example shows that the generalization of (C2) obtained in such a way does not contradict theorem (5.1) regarding the non-existence of an appropriate similarity relation. In order to achieve a generalization of (C2), we had to go beyond the limitations of Lewis's own counterfactual semantics.[10]

Let us now apply the method described earlier to some typical cases of counterfactuals which can occur within the context of quantum-mechanical considerations, and yet are outside the limited scope of the applicability of (C2). To begin with, suppose that we are interested in evaluating a counterfactual with an antecedent which is a finite conjunction of statements: $(P_1 \wedge P_2 \wedge ... \wedge P_n) \; \square \rightarrow Q$, where each of $P_i$ denotes one free-choice point-event. According to the procedure, we have to first identify the set of worlds $\Pi$ containing all antecedent-worlds that are closest to the actual world in the sense of similarity relation SIM. These worlds have already been described, during the discussion the Lewis-type extension of (C1), as the worlds whose primary points of divergence contain all and only points picked by those $P_i$'s whose backward light cones do not include any points selected by other conjuncts $P_j$. Now, according to the strategy that extends the intuition expressed in (C2), we should verify the truth of $Q$ in all possible antecedent-worlds which share with the actual world the sum of the backward light cones of these selected "earliest" points while possibly differing from it everywhere else (see Fig. 5.10). Similarly, in case of the disjunctive-antecedent counterfactuals of the form $(P_1 \vee P_2 \vee ... \vee P_n) \; \square \rightarrow Q$, we have already established that the similarity relation SIM pronounces as the closest antecedent-worlds all worlds which have a single point of divergence selected by a disjunct $P_j$ for which there is no other disjunct-selected point in its future. Consequently, the generalized (C2) approach will demand that for the counterfactual to be true, $Q$ should hold in every possible world which shares with the actual one the backward light cone of one of the "latest" disjunct-events (see Fig. 5.11). It hardly needs mentioning that the above-introduced procedure is applicable in cases of arbitrary

---

[10] J. Bennett in his (2003, p. 299) mentions the possibility of a semantics of counterfactuals that is based on an antecedent-relative similarity relation. However, he suggests that in such a case some legitimate principles of counterfactual logic may become invalid, such as Limited Transitivity: $P \; \square \rightarrow Q$ and $(P \wedge Q) \; \square \rightarrow R$, therefore $P \; \square \rightarrow R$. I believe that the restricted relativization of the similarity relation that is advocated here does not lead to such dramatic consequences, but I will not elaborate on that problem.

logical combinations of statements in the antecedent, not limited to con-junctions and disjunctions only. Once again, the key step is to identify the closest possible worlds (in the sense of SIM) which make the antecedent true, and then to basically replace these worlds with a broader category of worlds keeping only backward light cones of appropriate PPD-s the same as in the actual worlds.

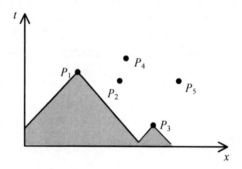

Figure 5.10 According to C2+ the evaluation of the counterfactual $(P_1 \wedge P_2 \wedge ... \wedge P_n)$ $\square \rightarrow Q$ has to be done in the possible world whose region of matching the actual world is restricted to the grayed area.

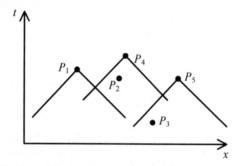

Figure 5.11 Three worlds in which the evaluation of the counterfactual $(P_1 \vee P_2 \vee ... \vee P_n)$ $\square \rightarrow Q$ should be done are: $w_1'$, $w_4'$ and $w_5'$, that agree with the actual world within the backward light cone of, respectively, $P_1$, $P_4$ and $P_5$.

The cases in which the antecedent is not a free-chance event present no greater challenge. In typical situations we will have certain law-like corre-lations between the antecedent-event $P$ and some events either space-like separated from it, or lying in its absolute past. Hence, we have to consider once again all possible antecedent-worlds which are permitted by the laws of nature, and which are closest to the actual world according to SIM, and then to "limit" their areas of matching to the past light cones of appropriate PPD-s. For instance, in the case of a perfect correlation between antecedent event $P_1$ and another event $P_2$ at a space-like separation (i.e. laws of nature demand that each time $P_1$ occurs, it is accompanied by the occurrence of $P_2$), the consequent $Q$ of the evaluated counterfactual $P_1 \; \Box\!\!\rightarrow Q$ has to be true in all $P_1$-and-$P_2$-worlds which share with the actual world the sum of both $P_1$ and $P_2$'s backward light cones. If, on the other hand, the laws of nature require adjustments to be made in the absolute past of $P_1$, then we can keep only the backward light cones of the earliest adjusted events exactly the same as in reality.

## 5.5 THE APPLICATION TO THE GHZ CASE

In this section we will apply both strategies (C1+) and (C2+) to the evaluation of some counterfactual statements describing correlations between outcomes of measurements in the three-particle variant of the GHZ case. We will treat this example as the "testing ground" for our freshly introduced evaluation methods, but also as a way of learning something about possible ontological interpretations of the correlations present in this physical situation. As we remember from the discussion in sec. 4.1, it is possible to select three observables $X_1$, $X_2$, $X_3$ pertaining to three different particles, such that the outcomes of measurements for these observables obey a simple condition $x_1 x_2 x_3 = -1$. Let us first suppose that the outcomes obtained in the actual world were, respectively, $x_1 = -1$, $x_2 = +1$, $x_3 = +1$. Our task will be to establish what would have happened, had the result of the $X_1$ measurement been +1 instead of −1. It is straightforward that some changes in the remaining outcomes are necessary, in order to satisfy the requirements of quantum-mechanical predictions. But what precisely these changes will be, depends on the relative locations of the three measurements in question, as well as on the adopted method of evaluating counterfactual conditionals. Below we shall examine several layouts in which the measurements may be spatiotemporally organized, examining each of them from both the (C1+) and (C2+) perspectives.

1. The first case considered will be one in which all three measurements are space-like separated (Fig. 5.12). We are interested in finding out the logical value for counterfactuals of the form

(*)        $x_1 = +1 \; \Box \rightarrow Q,$

where obviously the antecedent "$x_1 = +1$" refers to a localized event, but this event (an alternative outcome) is not free-choice, because of the above-mentioned correlations. The change in one outcome has to be accompanied by an appropriate change in the remaining outcomes to preserve the equation $x_1x_2x_3 = -1$. There are only two possible ways to save this equation when $x_1$ has been switched: either $x_2$, or $x_3$ has to switch its value (but not both). This means that we have to consider two possible worlds (more precisely, two *classes* of possible worlds) $w_{12}$ and $w_{13}$ such that the respective outcomes in these worlds are: $x_1 = +1$, $x_2 = -1$, $x_3 = +1$ and $x_1 = +1$, $x_2 = +1$, $x_3 = -1$. In the currently analyzed case when all three measurements are space-like separated, the closest antecedent-worlds (in the sense of the similarity relation SIM) will have two primary points of divergence: for $w_{12}$ it will be $D_{12} = \{p_1, p_2\}$, and for $w_{13}$ $D_{13} = \{p_1, p_3\}$. Obviously, neither $\overline{D_{12}} \subseteq \overline{D_{13}}$ nor $\overline{D_{13}} \subseteq \overline{D_{12}}$ is the case, so both worlds have to be considered when evaluating counterfactuals (*) according to method (C1+). It follows, then, that we cannot say for sure which of the observables $X_2$ and $X_3$ would have changed its value. All we can say is that the counterfactual $x_1 = +1 \; \Box \rightarrow (x_2 = -1 \lor x_3 = -1)$ has to be true, i.e. that one or the other outcome would have been altered. The same conclusion follows from (C2+). We have to consider all the worlds which retain either the backward light cones of $p_1$ and $p_2$, or of $p_1$ and $p_3$. Hence both scenarios are possible in the contrary-to-fact situation of altering the result of the $X_1$ measurement.

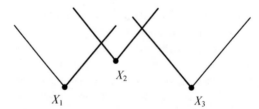

Figure 5.12

2. Let us assume that both measurements $X_2$ and $X_3$ occur in the absolute future of $X_1$ (Fig. 5.13). In this case both worlds $w_{12}$ and $w_{13}$ will have one and the same PPD: namely the locus of measurement $X_1$ (point $p_1$). As a consequence, no counterfactual that predicts which of the remaining outcomes will be changed comes out true. As before, only a disjunction can be counterfactually derived from the supposition $x_1 = +1$. The same holds true for the method (C2+), as can be easily verified.

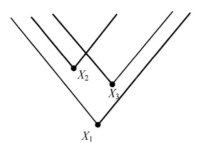

Figure 5.13

3. The case in which both measurements $X_2$ and $X_3$ are assumed to take place in the absolute past of the first measurement is an example of a situation in which, according to the adopted method of evaluating counterfactuals, it is necessary to counterfactually adjust some of the past—a move that would be frowned upon by orthodox Lewisians. However, we are left with no other option once we relegate miracles from the realm of possible worlds (see the discussion in chapter 2). This is not to say that we accept that the present actions can causally influence the past events. We opt for a separation of counterfactual dependence from causal dependence, admitting that in some cases the former leads to the latter, but in some other cases it does not.

When one of the past measurements $X_2$ and $X_3$ occurs unambiguously later than the other (Fig. 5.14), then the world in which this later measurement has the alternative outcome will depart less from the actual world (once again, according to SIM) than the world in which the other measurement switched its outcome. Consequently, under the counterfactual supposition that $x_1 = +1$ it would be true that one, but not the other, of the remaining outcomes must have been changed (this reflects a more general feature of our approach to counterfactuals, which allows for alterations in the past, but only those which are "minimal"). This holds true for both approaches (C1+) and (C2+). However, when there is no unambiguous time order between the two measurement-events (i.e. when $X_2$ and $X_3$ are space-like separated—see Fig. 5.15), only the "either..., or" clause is counterfactually derivable from "$x_1 = +1$". We can say that there are two, equally plausible ways to adjust the past events in order to ensure that the outcome of the first measurement is +1 rather than −1.

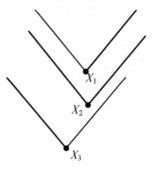

Figure 5.14

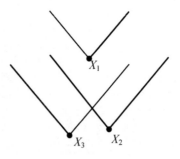

Figure 5.15

4. Let us now assume that one of the alternative measurements, for example $X_2$, takes place in the absolute future of $X_1$, whereas $X_3$ is space-like separated from $X_1$ (Fig. 5.16). Here world $w_{12}$ has exactly one PPD, namely $p_1$, whereas world $w_{13}$ has two: $\{p_1, p_3\}$. Because $\overline{D_{12}} \subseteq \overline{D_{13}}$, only world $w_{12}$ enters the competition. From this it follows that the counterfactual $x_1 = +1 \;\square\!\!\rightarrow x_2 = -1$, as well as the counterfactual $x_1 = +1 \;\square\!\!\rightarrow x_3 = +1$

both come out true. In other words, according to the analysis (C1+), the second outcome (that which happens in the absolute future of $X_1$) is bound to be switched when $x_1$ changes, but the third, space-like separated measurement will reveal the same value.

Note, however, that this time (C2+) will produce a different valuation. For now we have to consider all extensions of world $w_{12}$ with one primary point of divergence located in the locus of the $X_1$ measurement. In other words, the evaluation of all counterfactuals (*) will be done in worlds which share with the actual one the backward light cone of $p_1$. But among such worlds will be not only the worlds with the two other outcomes $x_2 = -1$ and $x_3 = +1$, but also the worlds with the other admissible combination: $x_2 = +1$ and $x_3 = -1$ (we assume, of course, that the result of the $X_3$ measurement is not causally determined by any event in the absolute past of $X_1$). Hence both counterfactuals $x_1 = +1 \ \square\!\!\rightarrow x_2 = -1$ and $x_1 = +1 \ \square\!\!\rightarrow x_3 = +1$ will be false, and only the disjunctive counterfactual $x_1 = +1 \ \square\!\!\rightarrow (x_2 = -1 \lor x_3 = -1)$ will remain true. Under the (C2+) reading of counterfactuals, we cannot say for sure that had the outcome of $X_1$ been changed, the outcome of the measurement occurring in the absolute future would have been changed, and the outcome of the space-like separated measurement would have remained the same. Either of the remaining measurements *might* change its outcome, but none can be said to change it for sure.

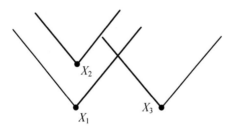

Figure 5.16

The observed discrepancy between the assessment based on (C1+) and that based on (C2+) calls for some investigation. We may ask which of the alternative valuations of counterfactuals (*) accords more closely with our pre-theoretical intuitions. On the surface it looks like (C1+) produces the answer to be expected.[11] The counterfactual dependence of $x_2$ on $x_1$ seems to be a consequence of the fact that in our spatiotemporal layout there is the possibility of a subluminal signal transfer between measurement $X_1$ and measurement $X_2$, and hence an ordinary causal link may exist between these two events. Thus if we knew nothing about the underlying mechanism of the GHZ correlation, our off-hand assessment would be that the change in the outcome of the $X_1$ measurement should be accompanied by an appropriate change in $X_2$'s outcome, but the third measurement should remain unchanged, as there is no way for a physical signal carrying the information about the result of $X_1$ to reach its location. But this argument assumes that the GHZ correlations can be explained with the help of ordinary, local physical interactions. And we know that this is not the case. The theoretically predicted correlations exist even if all three measurements are space-like separated, and subluminal interactions are, thereby, excluded. When we realize this, the initial plausibility of the (C1+) valuation begins to fade away. If we accept that particles partaking in the GHZ measurements can "coordinate" their respective outcomes without sending classical signals, why would this mechanism be prohibited in the case in which only one measurement is space-like separated from the initial one? To put it bluntly, it seems implausible that the non-local mechanism of correlating the outcomes in the GHZ situation, whatever it may be, transforms immediately into a local and causal one when there is the opportunity to do so. It would look like Nature decided to use non-locality only when it is absolutely necessary, but at the slightest opportunity it went back to the old ways.

It may be argued, then, that the valuation offered by (C2+) is in no worse position than that offered by (C1+), and maybe it is even more attractive, as it promotes a more uniform view of Nature's capabilities of "communicating" outcomes of quantum-mechanical measurements. However, it has to be emphasized that the difference in the truth-values of counterfactuals (∗) between the two approaches does not have any direct, empirically testable consequences. For obvious reasons we are unable to put sentences of the form $x_1 = +1 \;\square\!\!\rightarrow x_2 = -1$ to a direct experimental test. The truth of these statements reveals, so to speak, our ontological commitments regarding the ultimate structure of reality and the interdependencies among its elements. Hence we cannot hope for a quick defeat of one of the alternative approaches to counterfactual semantics,

---

[11]  This is the view that Finkelstein accepts without hesitation, when he openly praises (C1+) for implying such a valuation. See (Finkelstein 1999).

based on the result of some experimental investigations. If we want to choose between (C1+) and (C2+), we have to look at the broader picture (we will take up this issue in the next section).

5. The next situation analyzed in our example is when both measurements of $X_2$ and of $X_3$ are space-like separated from that of $X_1$, but there is an unambiguous temporal order between the former two—for instance, $X_2$ happens absolutely later than $X_3$ (Fig. 5.17) In this case both worlds $w_{12}$ and $w_{13}$ have two PPD-s, but because the locus of $X_2$ lies within the forward light cone of the locus of $X_3$, it follows that $\overline{D_{12}} \subseteq \overline{D_{13}}$. Consequently, method (C1+) prescribes that counterfactuals $x_1 = +1 \ \square\rightarrow x_2 = -1$ and $x_1 = +1 \ \square\rightarrow x_3 = +1$ should be ascribed the value of truth. According to the analysis (C2+), the evaluation of these counterfactuals has to be done in all possible worlds which have the absolute past of both $X_1$ and $X_3$ which is exactly the same as in the actual world, so the result of the $X_3$ measurement will be kept intact, which leads to the same truth-value ascription as in the C1+ case.

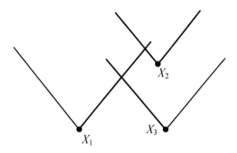

Figure 5.17

However, the resulting asymmetry between measurements of $X_2$ and $X_3$ may come as a surprise, and indeed this case looks like an anomaly. From the perspective of the antecedent-event, measurements $X_2$ and $X_3$ are both space-like separated, i.e. they belong neither to its absolute future, nor to its absolute past. Why, then, should it be the case that the (counterfactual) change in $X_1$'s outcome induces the change in one of the remaining measurements ($X_2$) only, and not in the other one ($X_3$)? One possible answer may be that $X_3$ belongs to the absolute past of $X_2$, and the past should be preserved (if possible) in our method of analyzing counterfactual situations. But this is the past relative to $X_2$, and not to $X_1$. And isn't it the case that only the past of the antecedent-event should be kept intact when evaluating a counterfactual?

One may reply that underlying the intuition (C1) is an implicit assumption that the sphere of the unchangeable "past" for a given contrary-to-fact event is comprised of its backward light cone *plus* the entire exterior of both backward and forward light cones (after all, this is the area which is supposed to be kept fixed according to (C1)). Hence, the case being considered may be claimed to be analogous to case (3) above, in which both $X_2$ and $X_3$ occurred inside the backward light cone of $X_1$. And we have remarked that in such a situation, when we are forced to make some corrections to the past, we should keep these corrections as minimal as possible. This can give some justification for keeping the outcome of $X_3$ intact, as it is revealed absolutely earlier than that of $X_2$. But even if we grant this, there is still no similar argument to justify the above valuations when adopting the competing strategy C2. It should be clear that according to C2, only the backward light cone of the antecedent-event counts as the immutable past; everything else can be altered, if such an alteration does not offend any law of nature. Thus there is no reason why under the extended strategy (C2+) the outcome of $X_3$ rather than $X_2$ might not be changed. We will leave this difficulty unresolved until after briefly considering the last possible spatiotemporal setup in the GHZ example.

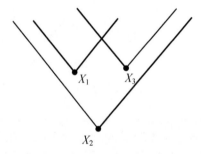

Figure 5.18

6. Suppose, finally, that the measurement of observable $X_2$ took place absolutely earlier than the measurement of $X_1$, but the measurement of $X_3$ was space-like separated from $X_1$. This case has to be divided further into two subcases. In one of them $X_2$ lies in the common past (the intersection of two backward light cones) of both $X_1$ and $X_3$ (Fig. 5.18) In this situation, according to our expectations world $w_{13}$ with two PPD-s becomes the clos-

est antecedent-world, and both methods of evaluation (C1+) and (C2+) predict that if $X_1$ switched its outcome, $X_2$ would remain intact, but $X_3$ would reveal the opposite result. However, things look quite different when we consider another possibility; namely that $X_2$, while remaining inside the backward light cone of $X_1$, is at space-like separation with $X_3$ (Fig. 5.19). In this setup both worlds $w_{12}$ and $w_{13}$ become incomparable with respect to the similarity relation SIM. Although $w_{12}$ has one PPD in the locus of $X_2$, and $w_{13}$ has two PPD-s in the loci of $X_1$ and $X_3$, it can be easily verified that neither $\overline{D_{12}} \subseteq \overline{D_{13}}$ nor $\overline{D_{13}} \subseteq \overline{D_{12}}$ holds. From this it follows that according to (C1+) both measurements $X_2$ and $X_3$ can change their outcomes under the counterfactual assumption that $x_1 = +1$, in spite of the fact that one of these measurements happens in the unambiguous past of $X_1$. And the procedure (C2+) does not change this assessment. But this, I believe, is not what we should expect. If $X_2$ is performed absolutely *before* $X_1$, and $X_3$ is space-like separated from $X_1$, then when we consider an alternative outcome of $X_1$ we should hold $X_2$'s outcome fixed regardless of the relative location of $X_2$ and $X_3$. Once again, at least from the perspective of the intuition underlying (C2), the counterfactual alteration of $X_3$'s outcome in order to preserve the quantum-mechanical requirements should take precedence over the change of $X_2$'s outcome. Hence, both cases 5 and 6 present a challenge, mostly to our proposed extension (C2+) of the intuition (C2), as their analysis according to (C2+) seemingly violates the basic intuitions that (C2) was supposed to preserve.

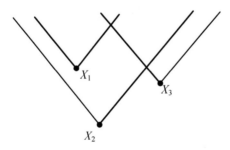

Figure 5.19

This challenge can be tackled in the following way. We noted in sec. 5.1 that both truth-conditions (C1) and (C2) have to be restricted to a certain class of antecedents, namely those that refer to free-choice point-events, because for events that are not free-choice there would not be a possible world which is required by the conditions expressed in (C1) and (C2) for the evaluation of the counterfactual. However, this is not exactly true. The restriction to free-choice antecedent-events is indeed necessary for (C1) to be applied, because (C1) requires the existence of at least one antecedent-world which is identical with the actual one everywhere outside the antecedent-event's forward light cone. However, (C2) will work for some non free-choice events, namely those whose occurrence is lawfully accompanied by some changes in the exterior of both forward and backward light cones, but not inside the backward light cone (in other words, for events which may display non-local correlations with distant events, but do not require any adjustments in their absolute past). Such events can be called "indeterministic". An event $E$ is considered indeterministic if there exists an $E$-world which shares with the actual world the whole backward-light cone of $E$ (from this definition it follows immediately that all free-choice events are indeterministic, but not the other way around). And now we can correct our proposed extension (C2+) of the truth-condition (C2). We can stipulate that if the antecedent of a counterfactual refers to an indeterministic event, then (C2) should be applied as it stands. Only in the situation in which the antecedent-event is not indeterministic, we should resort to method (C2+).

This correction immediately takes care of both cases 5 and 6. For in both situations presented there is a possible antecedent-world which shares with the actual world the backward light cone of $X_1$. Hence, rather than applying the whole procedure (C2+) "parasitic" upon the ordering of possible worlds according to SIM, we can resort to the simpler truth-condition (C2) and decide that the valuation of all counterfactuals (*) will be done in the possible worlds which keep the backward light cone of $X_1$ intact, and which satisfy all quantum-mechanical principles and predictions. As a consequence of that, in case 5 we should see worlds $w_{12}$ and $w_{13}$ as being on a par, which leads to the conclusion that it can't be said which of the measurements $X_2$ and $X_3$ would change its outcome for sure. As for case 6, the truth condition (C2) immediately implies that the measurement of $X_2$, being in the past of $X_1$, will remain unchanged, and instead the outcome of $X_3$ will be altered.

## 5.6  A COMPARISON OF THE TWO NOTIONS OF COUNTERFACTUALS

It looks like we are now suffering from an embarrassment of riches. We were searching for the interpretation of the counterfactual connective that could be successfully applied to the task of formalizing various inferences involving entangled quantum systems, and we have found two such interpretations, both seemingly well suited for the job. Wouldn't it be desirable, then, to be able to show that one of these approaches is for some reason superior to the other, and hence that ultimately there is only one unique way of interpreting quantum counterfactuals that should be recommended? But what kinds of arguments can be brought in to defeat one of the two available semantics for quantum counterfactuals? One possibility is to compare (C1) with (C2) on the basis of their formal properties only. For example, if it were true that (C1) is amenable to a suitable generalization that can cover all reasonable kinds of counterfactual conditionals, whereas for (C2) there is no uniform way of extending it beyond cases of counterfactuals with free-choice antecedents, then we would have a good argument in favor of (C1). And there even was a moment when it looked like this might have been the case, after we had proven the "no-go" theorem regarding the possibility of a generalization of truth condition (C2). However, sec. 5.4 provided us with an alternative: at the price of abandoning the requirement of independent ordering of possible worlds, we have produced a viable generalization of (C2) working in all cases which satisfy the Limit Assumption (practically all quantum-mechanical cases that we have considered so far seem to respect this restriction). Apart from those small and rather insignificant restrictions, both truth conditions (C1) and (C2) seem to be on an equal footing with respect to their formal features.

Another strategy of eliminating one of the two interpretations may be to test both of them in some unquestionable cases involving counterfactual conditionals, and to verify which one produces valuations that are expected, and which does not. However, finding such a testing ground in the realm of quantum-mechanical phenomena is not an easy task, because we cannot rely uncritically on our pretheoretical intuitions in the context of one of the most common-sense defying theories. A clear example of such a hard-to-decide case is supplied by the foregoing case of the GHZ correlations between outcomes of three separate measurements. As we remember, there are spatiotemporal arrangements of three experiments in which (C1+) produces different valuations from (C2+) regarding counterfactuals connecting outcomes obtained in different measurements. However, we pointed out that it is debatable which of these valuations should be seen as *prima facie* more plausible, so the issue between the two alternative approaches remains undecided.

Some of Stapp's remarks made on the occasion of his counterfactual proofs of non-locality can be interpreted as providing a different sort of argument in favor of the C1 approach to the semantics of quantum counterfactuals. The argument that can be extracted from these remarks goes as follows.[12] If you consider a contrary-to-fact event described by a statement $P$ (the antecedent of a given counterfactual), and if you take any event $Q$ space-like separated from $P$, then there exists a legitimate (Lorentz) frame of reference in which $Q$ occurs *earlier* than $P$. That implies, argues Stapp, that if $Q$ takes place in the actual world, it has to remain part of any $P$-world in which the counterfactual is to be evaluated, and hence $P \; \square \rightarrow Q$ should be rendered true. If it weren't the case, if the counterfactual $P \; \square \rightarrow Q$ were to be evaluated as false, then it would mean that the occurrence of $P$ would change or influence this part of space-time which, in some frame of reference, already belongs to the past of $P$. In other words, it would mean that there are "causal" influences leading (once again, in some frame of reference) from the present to the past. Because $Q$ was selected arbitrarily, it follows that all events space-like separated from $P$ should be kept fixed when evaluating a counterfactual with $P$ as its antecedent.

But is this argument sufficient to convince us that (C1) is to be preferred to its rival (C2)? This can be doubted, given the following counterargument. Stapp's strategy can be turned around in such a way as to favor (C2) rather than (C1). Suppose that $Q$ is a genuine indeterministic event (not determined by its past) that occurs in the actual world. Now let us select a frame of reference different from the one Stapp picks, in which $Q$ happens *later* than $P$ (because $P$ and $Q$ are space-like separated, there always will be such a frame). If, as truth condition (C1) prescribes, we

---

[12] My reconstruction of Stapp's possible argument for truth condition (C1) is based on fragments from his (1997, p.31) and (2001a, pp. 854-855). It needs to be stressed, though, that Stapp does not fully endorse (C1), but rather its non-invariant version with an arbitrary selected Lorentz frame of reference used as the basis for the distinction between past "fixed" events and future "open" events. However, as I pointed out earlier (section 4.2.4, note 22), the method of evaluation of spatiotemporal counterfactuals which Stapp "officially" subscribes to is not consistent with some assumptions of his 1997 proof, so I decided to follow Shimony and Stein in their reconstruction that uses (C1) as the foundation for Stapp's counterfactual derivation.

evaluated counterfactual $P \ \Box\!\!\rightarrow Q$ only in possible worlds with $Q$ fixed, then this would mean that $Q$ is an event that lies in the future of $P$ and whose occurrence is guaranteed under the counterfactual assumption that $P$. But doesn't this imply that $Q$ must be determined by its past, contrary to the assumption we've made? How else could we guarantee a certain occurrence of an event which does not yet exist (in a given legitimate frame of reference, of course)?

It looks like Stapp's argument is a double-edged sword, as it can be molded in order to support both (C1) and (C2). The reason for this lies in the arbitrariness of the selection of the reference frame. Nothing can prevent us from picking one frame in which $P$ is later than $Q$, and another frame in which the temporal order in which these two events occur is reversed. But this fact reminds us that we should be extremely careful when interpreting frame-dependent notions like "later in a frame", "earlier in a frame", etc. as denoting something "real". One of the lessons from the special theory of relativity is that only Lorentz-invariant notions (i.e. notions that do not depend on an arbitrarily selected Lorentz frame of reference) are physically meaningful, and therefore can be assumed to represent objective properties of the world. Hence it does not seem appropriate to conclude from the fact that one event occurs earlier than the other in *an arbitrarily selected* frame of reference that the former event has some sort of "objective reality" when the latter one occurs. Unfortunately, according to the special theory of relativity there is no absolute and unique way to divide the entirety of all events into the (already decided) past, the (happening) present and the (open) future with respect to a given event. If we need to make such a distinction, we can choose to restrict the past of a given event to its backward light cone (to events which precede the given event in *all* frames of reference), or to the exterior of its forward light cone (containing events that precede the selected one in *at least one* frame of reference). That way we can obtain either of the C2 and C1 interpretations of spatiotemporal counterfactuals. But is there any "relativistically invariant" argument that could decide which interpretation is better?

Once again, I think that we can argue equally successfully for either of them. Someone who prefers (C2) can point out that it seems to be perfectly legitimate to treat as the absolute past of an event $e$ only this part of spacetime from which a physical signal can reach $e$, or in other words, which can causally influence $e$. The remainder of spacetime should be seen as "open" with respect to $e$, because no physical information about states of affairs taking place in this area can possibly reach $e$ (according to Special

Relativity, at any rate). On the other hand, someone who favors (C1) can start with his definition of "future" regarding $e$: by the future of $e$ he may understand this part of spacetime which can be influenced by $e$ via a physical signal. If an event cannot be in principle affected by $e$, it should be treated as already "given", and hence belonging to $e$'s past. Both arguments seem to me equally convincing (or equally unconvincing, if you like), and I see no reason other than individual taste to prefer one to the other.[13]

But maybe we have given up the hope of deciding between (C1) and (C2) in the context of quantum-mechanical phenomena too early. Let us first notice that one obvious difference between counterfactuals interpreted along the lines of (C1) and (C2) is that the latter is relatively "insensitive" to what transpires in regions space-like separated from the location of the antecedent-event. This has the following, surprising, consequence: if we consider a system consisting of two EPR particles with spin, and if the measurement of the $x$-component of spin on the left-hand-side particle reveals one value, let's say "up", then according to truth condition (C2), we cannot derive from this the conclusion that, had the $x$-component of spin of the other particle been measured, it would have revealed the opposite value "down". This is the case, because from the perspective of the counterfactual measurement, the left-hand-side outcome hasn't occurred yet. The distant measurement still belongs to the open future, and it can reveal one of two possible values. Hence the local measurement can yield one of two possible outcomes, too.

It seems that this may be the case we have been looking for. After all, doesn't it follow from the quantum-mechanical formalism that the probability of recording the outcome "down" in the right-hand side of the

---

[13] Yet another argument in favor of (C2) can be found in (Pagonis *et al.* 1996, p. 51). Pagonis, Redhead and La Rivière argue there that the only reason for keeping any spatiotemporal area fixed while evaluating a counterfactual is that events in this area cannot be influenced by the occurrence of the antecedent $P$ of that counterfactual. This assumption can justify why we should keep fixed the backward light cone of $P$, but when it comes to events space-like separated from $P$ fixing them amounts—according to PRL—to the supposition of locality. PRL are right that the truth condition (C1) can be used only when the locality condition is satisfied (when there is a possible $P$-world which differs from the actual world only within the confines of the forward light cone of $P$), but we have at our disposal the extension of (C1) in the form of (C1+) which is not limited to free-choice events, and hence does not require the asumption of locality. So their argument falls short of delivering a decisive blow to the interpretation (C1+) of counterfactuals.

apparatus, given the outcome "up" in the left-hand side, equals 1? This conclusion is clearly consistent with the valuation received on the basis of (C1), according to which the counterfactual

$$(5.2) \qquad M(\sigma_x^R) \; \square \!\rightarrow O(\sigma_x^R) = -1$$

is true whenever $O(\sigma_x^L) = +1$ in the space-like separated region (where as usual $M(X)$ stands for "$X$ was measured", and $O(X)$ for the outcome of the measurement). Hence, one can argue that (C2) has to be rejected, as it produces a consequence that is apparently inconsistent with the quantum-mechanical predictions regarding the probabilities of joint outcomes in the EPR case.

But is this "inconsistency" real, or only a result of our incorrect interpretation of otherwise consistent formulas? Let us look again at the counterfactual $M(\sigma_x^R) \; \square \!\rightarrow O(\sigma_x^R) = -1$. On the surface, it does not mention the outcome of the left-hand side experiment, so why should its value be consistent with the probability *conditional* on the left-hand side outcome? The answer is that the assumption about the outcome of the $\sigma_x^L$-measurement enters the evaluation of the counterfactual not via the counterfactual supposition, but via the assumed description of the actual world. Speaking precisely, it is not the counterfactual (5.2) alone, but rather the statement

$$(5.3) \qquad \text{"} M(\sigma_x^R) \; \square \!\rightarrow O(\sigma_x^R) = -1 \text{" is true at a world in which the outcome}$$
$$O(\sigma_x^L) \text{ equals } +1$$

which is supposed to be a counterfactual counterpart of the statement about the conditional probability

$$(5.4) \qquad P(O(\sigma_x^R) = -1 \mid O(\sigma_x^L) = +1) = 1.$$

Still, is it really the case that (5.3) holds iff (5.4) holds, in all possible experimental arrangements? What if the measurement on the left-hand side of the apparatus actually happened *unambiguously later* than the counterfactual measurement in (5.2)? In such a situation even an ardent proponent of (C1) has to acknowledge that (5.3) will not be true. The future outcomes of experiments cannot enter the evaluation procedure of quantum counterfactuals. However, the conditional probability given in (5.4) will remain true, regardless of the relative location of both measurements. The truth of (5.4) in this case implies, basically, that if we select *post factum* all the experimental runs in which the later measurement revealed +1, it will turn out that the earlier measurements consistently showed the opposite value: −1. Yet this does not mean that at the moment of the earlier measurement it was already *predetermined* that this outcome would be revealed. For all we know about the quantum-mechanical world, there were still two possible results of that experiment, and hence no quantum counterfactual predicting one of these results should come out true.

The case in which (5.3) and (5.4) are unquestionably equivalent is when the $\sigma_x^L$-measurement is assumed to precede temporarily (in the absolute sense) the $\sigma_x^R$-measurement. But the contentious case is, again, when both measurements are space-like separated. The person who prefers (C1) will include the outcome of the $\sigma_x^L$-measurement to the "already decided" part of spacetime, while the proponent of (C2) will insist that it should be seen as part of the still open future. Consequently, followers of (C2) will not agree that (5.3) represents a correct counterfactual counterpart of the conditional probability (5.4) in this case. In accordance with (C2), the only counterfactual way to represent (5.4) is to explicitly add the extra condition $O(\sigma_x^L) = +1$ to the antecedent of (5.2). Once we realize that this strategy is available to us, we should stop worrying about an apparent inconsistency between (C2) and quantum-mechanical predictions in the EPR case.

For now we have failed to produce an unassailable argument favoring one interpretation of the quantum counterfactual over the other. As a consequence, I believe that we should continue using both legitimate truth conditions (C1) and (C2) and their appropriate extensions (C1+) and (C2+) in our future analyses of quantum entanglement phenomena, at least until a new, more decisive argument emerges. The next issue that we will have to tackle head-on now is how these two alternative interpretations of counterfactuals affect the counterfactual reconstruction of the locality condition.

# Chapter 6

# LOCALITY EXPLAINED AND THE EPR-BELL THEOREMS RECONSIDERED

T his book's main question—Is quantum mechanics non-local?—still looms large. But now we at least know that there can be no hope for a simple and unqualified "yes" or "no" answer to this riddle. There is such an enormous variety of interpretations of what constitutes a violation of the locality intuition, not to mention miscellaneous "degrees of severity" of these violations, that it would be utterly hopeless to expect a quick, once-and-for-all resolution to this problem. Yet we have made some progress. Along the quest to find the best counterfactual formulation of the condition of locality we have uncovered two possible interpretations of counterfactual conditionals which seem to be appropriate for describing quantum-mechanical phenomena that are in the center of our analysis. We should now take an important step forward and utilize these alternative interpretations to propose a precise formulation of the locality condition that could serve as a tenable explication for various intuitions associated with this notion. As we have already seen throughout this book, philosophers of physics and physicists alike often content themselves with pretty nebulous characterizations of the locality condition, of which the following are a representative sample:

> An event cannot be *influenced* by events in space-like separated regions. In particular, the outcome obtained in a measurement cannot be influenced by measurements performed in space-like separated regions; and analogously, possessed elements of physical reality referring to a system cannot be *changed* by actions taking place in space-like separated regions (Ghirardi & Grassi 1994).

> Since at the time of measurement the two systems no longer interact, no real change can take place in the second system in consequence of anything that may be done to the first system (Greenberger *et al.* 1990, p. 1132)

For many purposes these descriptions may be considered sufficient, but without a thorough investigation into the possible meanings associated with terms such as "influence", "changed by", "in consequence of", etc. we could hardly treat them as satisfactory from a philosophical point of view. Fortunately, we can avoid resting the notion of "locality" on such unstable grounds. Possible-world semantics offers us a powerful tool, with the help of which we can propose an elegant and conceptually uncontroversial explication of the notoriously obscure locality condition. We have already witnessed several examples of "locality-like conditions" formulated in terms of the counterfactual connective and used in various derivations of strengthened Bell's theorems. We will now try to extract from these proposals a general counterfactual locality condition.

## 6.1 TWO VARIANTS OF COUNTERFACTUAL LOCALITY

In Stapp's first attempt to counterfactually strengthen Bell's theorem the locality assumption takes on the form of the Matching Condition (see sec. 3.2). In the counterfactual reformulation it amounts to saying that if an alternative measurement setting were selected in one wing of the apparatus, the outcome obtained in the other, space-like separated wing would remain the same as in the actual world. Similar assumptions have also been made throughout Stapp's other derivations. In the GHZ case Stapp applies, for instance, the assumption (LOC) stating that with two out of three measurements counterfactually changed, the result of the unchanged, space-like separated measurement should remain the same (sec. 4.1.2). Finally, in his latest proof based on the Hardy example, Stapp once again introduces basically the same type of condition (LOC1) to assure the preservation of a distant measurement and its outcome under a counterfactual change of the "local" experiment (sec. 4.2.3). These examples should make it clear that the underlying general locality condition that Stapp adopts consistently in his writings can be presented in the following counterfactual form:

(L1)     For all $P$, $Q$, if $P$ and $Q$ describe events mutually space-like separated, then $Q \Rightarrow (P \:\square\!\!\rightarrow Q)$.[1]

---

[1]     It remains to be decided how we are to interpret the term "events" in the above formulations. Obvious examples of events are performed measurements and revealed outcomes, but the question may be asked whether semantic referents of more complex statements can count as events too. In particular, one may ask if a counterfactual statement, whose antecedent and consequent both refer to states of affairs pertaining to one location, defines an event which can enter the formula (L1). Our answer to this question is negative. The conceptual analysis done in sec. 4.2.6 shows clearly that the supposition that counterfactual statements represent objective physical events taking part in the actual world has to be regarded with

This can be expressed as follows: in all worlds in which $Q$ is true, it is also true that if any event $P$ pertaining neither to $Q$'s absolute future, nor to its absolute past, took place, then $Q$ would remain unchanged. Expression (L1) seems to be fairly intuitive and uncontroversial. Indeed, if we believe that no physical signal can connect space-like separated locations, we should exclude the possibility that the presence or absence of any event in a distant place could have an effect on the truth of a statement describing the local situation as it happens in the actual world. However, we have to ask what the intended meaning of the counterfactual connective used in (L1) is. Having two alternative ways, (C1) and (C2), of interpreting counterfactuals at our disposal, we ought to decide which one is more appropriate to be associated with the condition (L1).

It is quite straightforward to see that formula (L1) works well when coupled with the truth condition given in (C1), or rather in its extension (C1+). For, according to (C1+), (L1) is obviously satisfied when $P$ is assumed to be a free-choice event (FCE). This is so, because in this situation the closest possible $P$-world is the world which is exactly like the actual world outside $P$'s forward light cone, and hence $Q$ is true in this world. This consequence is to be expected—after all, free-choice events are events that by definition cannot participate in any sort of non-local interactions. However, when combined with the approach (C2) to counterfactuals, (L1) appears to imply more than the requirement of the nonexistence of the influence at a distance. Suppose, for example, that $Q$ denotes an event which is also an FCE, so that $Q$ is not determined by its absolute past. According to (C2), we have no right to claim that the counterfactual $P \: \square\!\!\rightarrow Q$ will be true given that $Q$ is true in the actual world, because $Q$ lies outside the backward light cone of $P$, and therefore cannot be taken for granted while counterfactually considering $A$. The backward light cone will be shared by possible worlds in which $Q$ transpires, and worlds in which $Q$ does not.

This means that when we are asserting the truth of $Q \Rightarrow (P \: \square\!\!\rightarrow Q)$ under the interpretation (C2), we are saying more than merely that $P$ cannot influence $Q$: we are assuming implicitly that $Q$ is determined by the absolute past of $A$ (or, even worse, that there is a non-local influence between $P$ and $Q$ which "keeps" $Q$ true in all relevant worlds). And this is devastating for the issues connected with Bell's theorem, for we should clearly sepa-

---

caution. To avoid possible misunderstandings, we will assume (unless stated otherwise) that letters $P$, $Q$ used in this and subsequent formulas can represent only "atomic" sentences of our formal language, and not compound statements.

rate two different problems: the problem of locality and the problem of determinism, or the hidden-variable hypothesis. Therefore, we must come up with another notion of locality, appropriate for the intuition (C2).

But this time such a notion of locality does not present itself easily. The best we can do is to turn to the main proponents of (C2)—i.e. R. Clifton, J. Butterfield, and M. Redhead (CBR)—who in their extensive analysis (Clifton *et al.* 1990) put forward a locality condition alternative to (L1). Their main idea was to ground the locality condition in Lewis's analysis of counterfactual (causal) dependence. According to Lewis's famous definition, an event $E$ is counterfactually dependent on $E'$, iff both counterfactuals $E' \; \Box \rightarrow E$ and $\sim E' \; \Box \rightarrow \sim E$ are true in the actual world (Lewis 1986b). CBR propose to use Lewis's notion in order to stipulate that the locality condition is satisfied when each of the two space-like separated events are counterfactually independent from each other. From this, and from Lewis's definition it follows that CBR's condition of locality may look like this:

(6.1)    For all $P$, $Q$, if $P$ and $Q$ describe events mutually space-like separated, then either $P \; \Box \rightarrow Q$ is false, or $\sim P \; \Box \rightarrow \sim Q$ is false.

Admittedly, (6.1) is not as clear and intuitively appealing as (L1), due to the presence of the disjunction of two negated counterfactuals. Let us then try to reformulate it somehow, in order to capture the essence of the condition expressed. First of all, let us consider separately cases in which, in the actual world, $P$ is true and cases in which $P$ is false. If $P$ is true in $w_0$, then the first counterfactual in (6.1) becomes a null counterfactual, i.e. a counterfactual with a true antecedent. For the sake of this analysis, let us adopt Lewis's way of interpreting null counterfactuals, namely as material implications (see sec. 2.2.1). Then, immediately, if $Q$ were false in $w_0$, the first counterfactual would be false and the entire locality condition would be satisfied. So suppose that $Q$ is true. In this case the first counterfactual becomes trivially true, and the only way to satisfy (6.1) would be to make sure that the second counterfactual is false. Analogous reasoning can show that when $P$ and $Q$ are false, the first counterfactual should turn out to be false. Hence, we can write the following, equivalent reformulation of (6.1):

(6.2)    For all $P$, $Q$, if $P$ and $Q$ describe events mutually space-like separated, then

(a) if $P$ and $Q$ are true in the actual world, then $\sim P \,\square\!\!\rightarrow\, \sim Q$ is false, and

(b) if $P$ and $Q$ are false in the actual world, then $P \,\square\!\!\rightarrow\, Q$ is false.

Actually, assuming that $P$ and $Q$ can have the form of negated atomic sentences, we can eliminate condition (a), for it would be contained in (b) by the stipulation that $P = \sim R$ and $Q = \sim S$, for some $R$ and $S$. This leads to the following simplification of formula (6.2):

(6.3)    For all $P$, $Q$, if $P$ and $Q$ describe events (or negations of events) mutually space-like separated, then $(\sim P \wedge \sim Q) \Rightarrow \sim( P \,\square\!\!\rightarrow\, Q)$

The meaning of this locality condition can be summarized by the following informal statement: a contrary-to-fact assumption of $P$ cannot "create" counterfactually any event $Q$ in the region distant from $P$ that wasn't already present in the actual world.

In spite of its intuitiveness, condition (6.3) has one flaw which will later turn out rather crucial, and which needs to be corrected right away. Let us observe that there might be cases which justifiably deserve the name of "non-local correlations" and which nonetheless satisfy (6.3). Consider, for example, the GHZ case of quantum entanglement that we have already exploited for our purposes several times. As we recall, it involves three spatially separated particles labeled 1, 2 and 3, and three measurements $X_1$, $X_2$ and $X_3$, each with two possible results 1 or $-1$. We stated in sec. 4.1.1 that the product of all three outcomes must give $-1$, as a consequence of the quantum-mechanical predictions. Suppose, then, that the actual results obtained are the following: for $X_1$: 1, for $X_2$: 1, and for $X_3$: $-1$. We can ask, what would have happened, if the outcome $x_1$ for the first particle had been $-1$ instead of 1 (we have already considered cases like this in sec. 5.5). In order to accommodate the above quantum-theoretical relation, exactly one of the other two results must be changed. But which one? On the basis of quantum-mechanical predictions we can say neither that in the counterfactual situation the result of $X_2$ measurement would be $-1$, nor that the result of $X_3$ would be 1. Therefore condition (6.3) is not directly violated. However, it is still true that under the counterfactual supposition that the outcome of the $X_1$-measurement was $-1$, it must be that either $X_2$ or $X_3$ would give a result different than actually obtained. And this clearly constitutes a case of non-local correlation, for both measurements $X_2$ and $X_3$ are space-like separated from $X_1$. In order to cope with cases like these, we have to introduce the following correction to (6.3), thereby arriving at the required alternative for (L1):

(L2)     For all $P$, $Q$, if $P$ describes a localized event (or a negation of an event) and $Q$ is equivalent to a disjunction of statements, each of which describes a single localized event (or a negation of an event), space-like separated from $P$, then $(\sim P \wedge \sim Q) \Rightarrow \sim (P \; \Box \rightarrow Q)$

The above correction takes care of the GHZ case, for now it is going to be classified as an example of the locality violation, because the counterfactual $x_1 = -1 \; \Box \rightarrow (x_2 = -1 \vee x_3 = +1)$ is obviously true, in spite of the fact that statements $P \equiv (x_1 = -1)$ and $Q \equiv (x_2 = -1 \vee x_3 = +1)$ clearly satisfy the antecedent conditions of the locality requirement (L2).

We can also verify that (L2) most likely represents the correct expression of the locality feature once the counterfactual connective is given the interpretation (C2). First of all, (L2) no longer erroneously implies (as was the case with (L1) under (C2)) that actual-world events space-like separated from $P$ are determined by $P$'s absolute past. For we can see now that if $Q$ is an indeterministic event occurring in the actual world, then according to (L2) the counterfactual $P \; \Box \rightarrow \sim Q$ has to be *false*.[2] And this is precisely what the truth condition (C2) prescribes: because of the indeterminacy assumption there will be two $P$-worlds sharing with the actual one the backward light cone of $P$, and such that in one of them $Q$ happens, and in the other it does not. So the above counterfactual turns out false. Therefore there is no logical conflict between (L2)+(C2) and the assumption that $Q$ is indeterministic.

What is more, (L2) is clearly satisfied when $P$ is assumed to be a free-choice event. If $P$ and $Q$ are false in the actual world, and therefore $\sim Q$ is obviously true, then there is a possible $P$-world in which $\sim Q$ happens and which is exactly identical with the actual one inside $P$'s backward light

---

[2]   Note that in the formula (L2) it is assumed that $Q$ is false in the actual world. This is why in the currently considered case where we suppose, in agreement with (L1), that $Q$ is true, we have to insert the negation before the consequent of the counterfactual in (L2).

cone.[3] This immediately makes the counterfactual $P \,\square\!\!\rightarrow Q$ false, precisely as predicted in (L2).

But now the question about the logical relation between both locality conditions (L1) and (L2) arises. On the surface they definitely look different[4], but we have to remember that in the two formulations symbol $\square\!\!\rightarrow$ is used in a slightly different sense. So it is possible that those differences effectively cancel each other out, and that ultimately (L1) and (L2) represent one and the same intuition concerning the notion of locality. In what follows I am going to show that this is indeed the case. I will prove the equivalence of (L1) and (L2) by way of showing that both statements are equivalent to yet another expression of the locality condition, which doesn't rely on the logical connective of counterfactual conditional at all, but instead speaks about the existence of a certain possible world. I shall call this version "the semantic condition of locality" (SLOC in short).

## 6.2 SEMANTIC CONDITION OF LOCALITY AND THE EQUIVALENCE THEOREM

We have, actually, already encountered the simple locality condition that we are going to invoke to prove the equivalence between (L1) and (L2). When analyzing the first of Stapp's derivations and its criticism by CBR, we noticed that part of their critique regarding the Matching Condition misses the point, for Stapp can base his derivation on a different, general locality condition that could hardly be questioned by any side of the dispute. This locality condition is precisely the one that we are going to scrutinize right now:

(SLOC)    For all point-events $P$ that are non-contradictory, there is a possible $P$-world $w$ such that $w$ is exactly the same as the actual world everywhere outside the future light cone of $P$.[5]

---

[3]   This is the world which shares with the actual one the entire outside of the forward light cone of $P$, and whose existence is guaranteed by the assumption that $P$ represents a FCE.

[4]   This "surface" difference is precisely the one stressed by CBR in (Clifton *et al.* 1990), who maintain that the formulation of the locality condition based on Lewis's notion of counterfactual dependence is superior to the one adopted by Stapp.

[5]   We have to mention here one important limitation of the applicability of this locality condition. As we remember, our analysis of counterfactuals allows for the possibility (and indeed sometimes requires) that some adjustments in the absolute

Let us call the world whose existence is asserted in (SLOC) "the least diverging $P$-world", and symbolize it by $w_P{}^*$. The meaning of the above formulation should be clear. It states that whatever counterfactual situation we are entertaining, it is admissible by the laws of nature that the part of spacetime which is physically "beyond reach" of this situation will remain intact. I would like to emphasize that it wouldn't be appropriate to claim in (SLOC) that *all* $P$-worlds should be the least diverging ones, for there can be factual chance events involved that might or might not occur under the counterfactual supposition of $P$. In order to satisfy our intuitions of locality, it is sufficient to assume that *there is* at least one least diverging $P$-world. Now, let us formulate and prove the following theorem:

(Th 6.1)  Condition (L1) together with the truth condition (C1+), and condition (L2) together with the truth condition (C2+), are equivalent to (SLOC) (and, consequently, they are equivalent to one another).

As usual, the proof will proceed under certain assumptions. The main premise adopted here will again be the Limit Assumption (LA′), as presented in sec. 5.4. One of the cases considered in the proof will require an assumption stronger than (LA′), but I will explain it in due course. In the first part of the proof we will attempt to prove the equivalence between

---

past of the antecedent-event should be made. If the antecedent $P$ describes a possible event that is a result of a deterministic process, then in order to consider a world in which $P$ occurs lawfully, we have to assume that appropriate changes took place in $P$'s past. Hence, in this case condition (SLOC) would be violated, for there would be no law-preserving world with the same outside of $P$'s forward light cone as the actual world, and yet no non-local interactions would necessarily emerge. For that reason we will restrict the use of (SLOC) to *indeterministic* events only, i.e. events for which there is a possible world sharing with the actual world their backward light cones (see sec. 5.5). The issue of how to generalize (SLOC) for other types of events will be addressed later in sec. 6.6. Note also that the same restrictions are implicitly imposed on the counterfactual reconstructions of the locality condition (L1) and (L2). For example, (L1) could be clearly violated by a case involving a common cause: if $P$ requires for its appearance an adjustment of a past event $R$ that in turn causes some actual $Q$ not to occur, then the counterfactual $P \,\square\!\!\rightarrow Q$ would come out false in spite of a perfectly local character of all interactions involved. This difficulty does not affect Stapp's derivations though, for he applies (L1) to counterfactual alterations of measurement selections only, and those events are commonly treated as indeterministic.

(L1) and (SLOC). As is commonly done, we will split this equivalence into two implications, showing their validity separately.

1. (SLOC) → (L1). Let us take two propositions $P$ and $Q$ describing space-like separated events, and assume that $Q$ is true in the actual world. According to (SLOC), there exists the least diverging $P$-world $w_P{}^*$, which is exactly the same as the actual world $w_0$ outside the future light cone of $P$, and hence $Q$ holds in $w_P{}^*$. But $w_P{}^*$ is obviously the closest possible world to the actual one among all $P$-worlds, according to the similarity relation (SIM). Hence the counterfactual $P \; \Box\!\!\rightarrow Q$ must be true, when the counterfactual connective is interpreted along with (C1+).

2. (L1) → (SLOC). By assumption the counterfactual $P \; \Box\!\!\rightarrow Q$ is true for every $Q$ such that $Q$ denotes an event space-like separated from $P$, and $Q$ is true in the actual world. Because we have restricted the applicability of (SLOC) and both (L1) and (L2) to indeterministic antecedent-events (cf. footnote 5), it follows that the counterfactual also remains true when $Q$ is taken from the backward light cone of $P$, and therefore the counterfactual must be true for all $Q$'s located outside $P$'s future light cone. Consider now the set of all possible $P$-worlds. This set is (partially) ordered by the relation of comparative similarity $\leq$, as defined in (SIM). The assumption (LA') entails that there must be a $P$-world $w'$ such that there is no other $P$-world $w$ for which $w < w'$. And obviously, if counterfactual $P \; \Box\!\!\rightarrow Q$ is to be true, $Q$ must be true in this world $w'$. Hence, all statements $Q$ describing events outside the forward light cone of $P$ and true in the actual world must be true in $w'$ as well. But this means that $w'$ is the least diverging $P$-world, and that shows the fulfillment of (SLOC).

One comment. From a formal point of view, the limit assumption was indispensable in the above derivation. For if it hadn't been true, (SLOC) could have been strictly speaking false in spite of (L1) being true. To see this, suppose, for example, that there is no least diverging $P$-world, but that for every single spatiotemporal point $\pi$ space-like separated from $P$ there is a possible $P$-world $w(P, \pi)$ with two initial points of divergence from the actual world: $P$ and $\pi$. It appears that with such a set of $P$-worlds all counterfactuals of the form $P \; \Box\!\!\rightarrow Q$, where $P$ is true in the actual world, turn out to be true according to (C1+). In essence, given any $Q$, for every $P$-world $w$ you can find a world $w'$ which is strictly closer to the actual one than $w$ is: $w' < w$, and in which $Q$ is true, as well as such that whatever world $w'' \leq w'$ we take, $Q$ remains true in $w''$. And yet those $P$-worlds have no lower limit with respect to $\leq$. However, the possibility of the existence of an uncountable set of such $P$-worlds, which would nevertheless lack the lower limit with respect to $<$, albeit mathematically conceivable, seems to be a little far-fetched. What physical reason could be given for the exclusion of the world $w_P{}^*$ in the situation in which worlds $w(P, \pi)$ approximate it infinitesimally closely? And besides, even if we continue to look suspiciously at the limit assumption, we could still derive from (L1) an "infinitesimal" version of (SLOC), stating roughly that in the limit $P$-worlds can approximate $w_P{}^*$ arbitrarily closely. For all practical purposes this condition is as good as the original (SLOC). Let us now move on to the proof of the equivalence between (L2) and (SLOC).

3. (SLOC) $\rightarrow$ (L2). Consider any $P$ and $Q$ such that they are both false in the actual world $w_0$, and $Q$ is equivalent to a (finite) disjunction of sentences describing events space-like separated from $P$. Locality condition (L2) states that in such a case counterfactual $P \; \square \rightarrow Q$ should be false. And that's exactly the case, which can be shown in the following way. Because of our assumptions, $Q$ is false in the least diverging $P$-world $w_P{}^*$ (whose existence is guaranteed by SLOC). But this means that there is a possible world which is exactly the same as the actual one within the past light cone of $P$, in which $P$ is true and yet $Q$ is false. This, according to (C2), implies that counterfactual $P \; \square \rightarrow Q$ is going to be false, which was to be proved. We have thus demonstrated that (SLOC) implies (L2) under the interpretation given in (C2).

4. (L2) $\rightarrow$ (SLOC). To prove this implication, we will need yet another assumption, this time the finiteness assumption, stating that for all antecedents $P$ there is only a finite number of $P$-worlds which agree with the actual one in the spatiotemporal region of $P$'s absolute past.[6] A discussion of this assumption will follow after the proof has been completed. Let us first assume that (SLOC) is violated, i.e. that for some $P$ there is no least diverging world $w_P{}^*$. This implies that for every possible $P$-world $w_P{}^i$ which keeps fixed the absolute past of $P$ there is an event $Q_i$ such that $Q_i$ is space-like separated from $P$, and $Q_i$ is true in the actual world $w_0$ but false in $w_P{}^i$. From the finiteness assumption it follows that there is a finite number of such $Q_i$-s, so we can consider the following disjunction: $\sim Q_1 \vee \sim Q_2 \vee \ldots \vee \sim Q_n$. This sentence is obviously false in $w_0$, but true in all $P$-worlds preserving the absolute past of $P$, and therefore the counterfactual $P \; \square \rightarrow (\sim Q_1 \vee \sim Q_2 \vee \ldots \vee \sim Q_n)$ must be true, according to the method of evaluation prescribed in (C2). But this contradicts (L2), therefore the proof of the

---

[6] From the finiteness assumption the limit assumption obviously follows.

implication (L2) $\rightarrow$ (SLOC) is complete. This also concludes the entire proof of the equivalence theorem.

It might be instructive to see that, in contrast to the above result, implication (6.3) $\rightarrow$ (SLOC) doesn't hold, which shows the real necessity of the correction we have included in (L2). According to (6.3), when space-like separated events $P$ and $\sim Q$ do not occur in the actual world, counterfactual $P \; \square\rightarrow \sim Q$ must be false as well, but this is true only for $Q$ describing a single spatiotemporally localized event. This implies that for every event $Q$ space-like separated from $P$ and occurring in the actual world, there must be a possible $P$-world with the same absolute past of $P$ as in the actual world and such that $Q$ holds in it. But this fact by no means guarantees that there is a *single* $P$-world in which all such $Q$-s hold, and therefore falls short of proving that the world $w_P{}^*$, described in (SLOC), exists.[7]

Let us now discuss the unquestionably weakest element in the proof of the equivalence between (L2) and (SLOC), which is the finiteness assumption. Although it may be papered over by reference to the "plausible" assumption that the physical universe is finite, and hence that there is only a finite number of actual states of affairs, it still leaves us with an unpleasant feeling of an *ad hoc* trick. After all, we have already considered a reasonable example of an infinite set of possible worlds $w(P, \pi)$, with two primary points of divergence. However, this "finiteness debacle" in my opinion does not show that the general locality condition (SLOC) is unjustified, but rather that even the corrected formula (L2) falls short of providing an ideal expression of our fundamental notion of locality.

(L2) requires that in order for a non-local influence to be present, we need a finite list of potential "effects" spatiotemporally separated from the cause $P$, and such that the occurrence of $P$ would imply that at least one of the events on the list should happen. And for all practical purposes that is true, as shown in the GHZ example where we had two potential effects brought about by a change in the one outcome, or in the original EPR case with its one-to-one apparently non-local correlation between outcomes. However, it is in principle conceivable that the occurrence of $P$ unfailingly makes some changes in a space-like separated region, but these possible changes are so diverse that they cannot be exhausted by a finite list of potential effects. This possible situation deserves the name of "non-local

---

[7] However, I feel it necessary to emphasize that the correction in (L2) has not been introduced *ad hoc* merely for the sake of proving the equivalence with (SLOC), for we have already presented independent arguments that the original form (6.3) does not fully capture the essence of the locality condition (see sec. 6.1).

influence", and yet cannot be accounted for by (L2), for we have no linguistic means of considering disjunctions of infinitely many statements, let alone uncountably many statements. As far as the main result presented here—namely the equivalence of (L1) and (L2)—is concerned we may say that it retains its validity, provided that the locality condition (L2) is used within its "scope of applicability". If in a certain situation (L1) happens to be false in spite of (L2) being true, due to the violation of the finiteness assumption, then in that situation (L2) ceases to be a proper verbalization of our intuition of locality.

## 6.3 THE COUNTERFACTUAL EPR ARGUMENT AT LAST

Finally, after long preparations, we can risk the announcement that our logical and conceptual tools are ready for a serious quantum application. We have at our disposal two working semantics of quantum counterfactuals, and we have rigorously formulated the locality condition which is appropriate for indeterministic contrary-to-fact events (such as measurement selections). Moreover, the proposed locality condition has an obvious advantage because of its independence from the adopted interpretation of counterfactuals. Condition (SLOC) does not use the counterfactual connective at all; instead it speaks about possible, law-obeying worlds and their spatiotemporal relation to the actual world. Hence, no matter which of the two available truth conditions (C1) or (C2) we will follow, we can safely adopt (SLOC) as our underlying assumption. The first testing ground for our logical apparatus will be provided by the ubiquitous EPR argument. Thus far we had to rely on the informal presentation of the argument given in sec. 1.2. Now, the time has come to carry out a serious overhaul of this argument. Surprisingly, this will reveal that there is still much left to say about the argument with the help of which Einstein tried to checkmate the quantum orthodoxy some seventy years ago.

### 6.3.1 Basic assumptions
The counterfactual reconstruction of the EPR argument proposed here will be modeled on the approach put forward by Ghirardi, Grassi (1994) and modified by Redhead, La Rivière (1997). One of their main motivations behind using the logic of counterfactuals was to make the original EPR relativistically valid. However, the necessity of resorting to counterfactual conditionals in making the EPR argument relativistically invariant was recently questioned by Abner Shimony (2001). Shimony basically claims,

contrary to Ghirardi, Grassi and Redhead, La Rivière, that it is possible to establish the validity of the relativistic EPR argument using "inductive logic" rather than counterfactual logic. My position on this issue differs slightly from both sides of the controversy. I think that the structure of the original, non-relativistic EPR argument, in spite of significant improvements which have been done to it by various commentators (among them, by Shimony himself), is still somewhat murky. Contributing to this situation is the lack of a clear-cut verbalization of the locality criterion, which enters the EPR derivation in many forms, very often unbeknownst to the person reconstructing it. There are also some additional presuppositions of a metaphysical character, which may be questioned by hard-nosed followers of the Copenhagen interpretation of quantum mechanics—and that obviously weakens the general appeal of the argument. A systematic formalization of the argument within a rigorous logical semantics could help to change this undesirable situation. In the interpretation I will propose I will argue—against Ghirardi, Grassi and with a stronger emphasis on the semantic of counterfactuals than that placed by Redhead and LaRivière in their response to the former analysis—that the EPR argument needs additional and questionable premises to reach its final conclusion. In consequence, I claim that if we don't accept these premises, then the thesis of the incompleteness of the standard quantum-mechanical formalism does not follow from Einstein's assumption of the non-existence of the influence that the selection of measurement can make on a distant quantum system. Whether this conclusion (if true) can secure "the peaceful coexistence" between standard quantum mechanics and the requirements of the special theory of relativity, remains to be seen. Actually, in sec. 6.6 it will be argued that some form of non-locality is indeed inevitable in the quantum-mechanical description of the EPR phenomena, but it is not the type of non-locality whose negation Einstein assumed in his original argument (EPR-nonlocality, in terminology introduced in sec. 1.2).

Let us start by restating some of the argument's basic assumptions. We will consider here a generic EPR case with two distant particles $L$ (left) and $R$ (right) prepared in the singlet spin state, and a pair of non-commuting observables (spin-components) for each of them: $X_L$, $Y_L$ and $X_R$, $Y_R$. Moreover, we assume that $X_L$ commutes with $X_R$ and $Y_L$ commutes with $Y_R$. The initial state $\Psi$ in which the particles are prepared is such that the probability of a joint occurrence of any two given results $x_L$, $x_R$ ($y_L$, $y_R$) equals either 0 or 1 (the case of perfect correlations). The original EPR argument was formulated in the non-relativistic setting, implicitly assuming the existence of a preferred frame of reference, and therefore the existence of an absolute time frame (see Einstein *et al.* 1935). The argument, as we recall from sec. 1.2, can be outlined as follows. Suppose that the measurement of $X_L$ was performed on $L$ at time $t$ giving a particular result $x_L$. Using the assumption of perfect correlations we can infer that at time $t$ particle $R$ has a determinate value of $X_R$ (let's call it $x_R$). By appealing to the locality principle, which roughly states that the measurement on $L$ cannot instantaneously change a physical state of $R$, and by the criterion of physical reality, it is argued that observable $X_R$ had to have its value determined even before time $t$. But this contradicts the initial assumption that before $t$ both particles had been jointly in state $\Psi$, different from an eigenstate for observable $X_R$, and therefore the incompleteness of the quantum-mechanical description follows.

We will consider separately two counterfactual reconstructions, based on the two notions of space-time counterfactuals introduced and analyzed above. In both reconstructions we will explicitly adopt the semantic formulation of the locality condition (SLOC), which has been shown to be equivalent to the versions (L1) and (L2) of counterfactual locality when each is coupled with the appropriate reading, (C1) or (C2) respectively, of counterfactual conditionals. And finally, we will stipulate, following the approach proposed in (Ghirardi, Grassi 1994, p. 404), that any property attribution statement (statement that attributes a definitive property to a system, even if the system is not subject to any measurement) should be interpreted counterfactually (we will call this interpretation Counterfactual Property Attribution, or CPA) as follows:

(CPA)  The statement "At $t$ an observable $A$ characterizing a quantum system $x$ possesses a definite value $a$" (symbolized as $P(A_x = a, t)$) is interpreted as synonymous with "If the measurement of $A$ were performed at $t$, the outcome would be $a$" (in symbols: $M(A_x, t) \,\square\!\!\rightarrow O(A_x, t) = a$).[8]

---

[8]  To be correct, we have to admit that Ghirardi and Grassi explicitly accept only the implication leading from the counterfactual $M(A_x, t) \,\square\!\!\rightarrow O(A_x, t) = a$ to the property attribution statement $P(A_x = a, t)$, although in the footnote on p. 404 they admit that the converse implication is justified by the principle of faithful measurement. In spite of this observation, further in their reconstruction of the EPR argument they continue to use property attribution statements as if they were irreducible to quantum counterfactuals. This fact, in my opinion, is responsible for their not noticing that the EPR argument contains a gap which may be exploited for the

Finally, in order to satisfy the condition of applicability of (SLOC) mentioned in footnote 5, we will explicitly assume that all measurement selections are indeterministic events, i.e. that for every event $M(A)$ there is a possible world in which $M(A)$ occurs and which matches the actual world within the entire backward light cone of $M(A)$. This condition is sometimes referred to as "the observer's free will" assumption, as it presupposes that the observer is able to select their measurement at will, without the necessity of "adjusting" facts from their past.

### 6.3.2. The EPR argument and (C1)

Let us start our reconstruction with the (C1) interpretation of counterfactuals, formally generalized using the similarity relation given by (SIM). In the simplest case, when $P$ represents a free-choice event, evaluation of the counterfactual $P \; \square \!\!\rightarrow Q$ reduces to the following procedure: we take all the possible worlds which are identical with the actual one everywhere outside the future light cone of $P$, and check whether $Q$ holds in all of them. In general, there might be no such world because of some non-local correlations between $P$ and some other event space-like separated from it. But if we assume (SLOC) then, because the existence of such a world is now guaranteed, it follows that this procedure is always executable. The first step of the EPR argument is as follows:

$$(6.4) \qquad [M(X_L, p) \wedge O(X_L, p) = a] \Rightarrow P(X_R = a', p')$$

where $p$ and $p'$ denote space-time locations space-like separated from each other. Using our rule of interpretation (CPA) we can reformulate (6.4) counterfactually, by replacing the property attribution statement with the appropriate counterfactual:

$$(6.5) \qquad [M(X_L, p) \wedge O(X_L, p) = a] \Rightarrow [M(X_R, p') \; \square \!\!\rightarrow O(X_R, p') = a']$$

In words, (6.5) says that if in the actual world the left-hand particle underwent the measurement of observable $X$ at $p$, and the result of this measurement was $a$, then if $X$ had been measured on the right-hand particle at $p'$, the result would have been $a'$. The question now is whether the truth of (6.5) can be guaranteed by the truth condition (C1) for counterfactuals

---

purpose of defending the completeness of quantum mechanics and the locality assumption, as we propose to do in the current reconstruction.

and by the assumption (SLOC). The truth condition dictates that the counterfactual $M(X_R, p') \ \square\!\!\rightarrow O(X_R, p') = a'$ is true when the consequent
$O(X_R, p') = a'$ is true in the possible world that is closest to the actual one
with respect to the similarity relation (SIM), and in which the antecedent
holds. According to (SLOC), there is a possible world $w(X_R)$ in which
$M(X_R, p')$ is true, and $w(X_R)$ is identical to the actual one everywhere outside the forward light cone of $p'$ (see Fig. 6.1 and 6.2), hence in $w(X_R)$ it
must be that $M(X_L, p) \wedge O(X_L, p) = a$, and moreover $w(X_R)$ is obviously the
closest possible world according to the criterion (SIM). Finally, appealing
to the quantum-mechanical predictions we can derive that at $w(X_R)$
$O(X_R, p') = a'$ must hold. Therefore, step (6.5) of the EPR argument has
been proven to be correct under the counterfactual interpretation (C1).

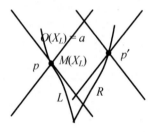

Figure 6.1 The actual world.

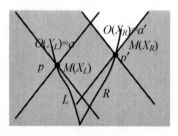

Figure 6.2 The possible world $w(X_R)$. Shaded area indicates the region shared with the
actual world.

It is interesting, however, to notice that—in contrast to the non-
relativistic and non-counterfactual version of EPR—the locality assump-

tion was already necessary in the derivation (the necessity of appealing to the locality condition in the derivation of (6.5) is also acknowledged by Ghirardi and Grassi in 1994, p. 409). In the version of the EPR argument which employs an absolute time frame it is quite obvious that the counterfactual $M(X_R, p') \; \Box\!\!\rightarrow \; O(X_R, p') = a'$ has to be evaluated in the world whose absolute past, as well as its distant present, is the same as in the actual one, and hence the outcome $O(X_L, p) = a$ is simply "given" in it. However, because by assumption $p$ and $p'$ are space-like separated, the existence of a possible world which retains the same outcome at $p$ has to be ensured independently. In other words, in order to argue that particle $R$ has the objective property expressed in $P(X_R = a')$, we have to assume that a measurement which would aim to reveal this property cannot change anything in system $L$, and thereby affect the derivation of the would-be outcome $O(X_R, p') = a'$ from the actual outcome $O(X_L, p) = a$. (Notice incidentally that this instance of the locality assumption refers, quite surprisingly, to the nonexistence of a non-local influence leading from the distant system to the local one, and not—as in the original EPR—from the local measurement to the distant one.)

In the original, non-relativistic EPR argument step (6.4) served as the basis for the subsequent derivation (with the help of the locality condition) of the conclusion that the property attribution statement $P(X_R = a')$ must have been true even before the time measurement $M(X_L)$ was made. But, now, we can't talk of the absolute time frame covering locations of both measurements. The closest we can get to the spirit of the original argument is to try to project the property attribution statement $P(X_R = a', p')$ into the common absolute past of $p$ and $p'$. In other words, we may want to reach the conclusion that the property of the right-hand side particle that we were able to derive from the outcome of the left-hand side measurement without physically interacting with the first particle was already present at the moment both particles were created. However, can this move be supported directly by the locality condition (SLOC) that we have adopted? When we consider a spatiotemporal point $p''$ on the world-line of particle $R$ lying in the absolute past of $p$, there is obviously no immediate reason to believe in the truth of the counterfactual $M(X_R, p'') \; \Box\!\!\rightarrow \; O(X_R, p'') = a'$, for in this case the spatiotemporal region which should be kept fixed in the evaluation of this counterfactual does not include point $p$, and therefore we cannot take the outcome of the measurement $M(X_L, p)$ for granted (this outcome belongs to the unambiguous future of $p''$). To put it differently: the assumption that the counterfactual $M(X_R, p'') \; \Box\rightarrow \; O(X_R, p'') = a'$ is false in no way contradicts the locality condition as given in (SLOC).

One may point out that in the original EPR argument it was the criterion of physical reality together with the locality assumption that was used to argue for tracking the property attribution $P(X_R = a')$ back to the unambiguous past of $p$ and $p'$. But appealing to the locality principle in such a way seems to be justifiable only when we talk about genuine physical states of affairs, or events.[9] If $P(X_R = a', p')$ denoted a genuine physical event taking place in $p'$, which should be taken into account when assessing the identity between space-time regions of possible worlds, then we could argue on the basis of (SLOC) that there is a possible world in which measurement $M(X_L, p)$ is not performed, but the fact expressed in $P(X_R = a', p')$ remains unchanged. This conclusion is not sufficient by itself to justify that the property attribution statement regarding the right-hand side particle should also be true in the common past (i.e. that $P(X_R = a', p'')$ is true), but we can appeal to a hard-to-question deterministic principle regarding the evolution of quantum states that are not subjected to measurement, from which it follows that quantum properties cannot come to exist "out of nowhere" without an external cause.[10] And since in the world in which there is no measurement $M(X_L, p)$, the property (if it *is* a genuine property) $P(X_R = a', p')$ would still be there, if we objected to the conclusion that $P(X_R = a', p'')$, we would have to admit that at some point between $p''$ and $p'$ the right-hand side particle underwent an inexplicable change in its quantum property.

As we can see, the required conclusion of the EPR argument can be reached when two additional presuppositions are accepted: the assumption that there are genuine physical facts of the matter located in the actual world that are semantic counterparts of true counterfactual conditionals of the form given in (CPA), and that the evolution of quantum-mechanical systems is deterministic when no measurement is involved. While I have no cause to question the second assumption, it looks to me that we have already said enough about the semantics of counterfactual statements (cf. sec. 4.2.6) to be very suspicious of the first one. After all, one of the main

---

[9] As we have stressed several times, we don't give our unconditional assent to the supposition that semantic referents of counterfactual statements are physical events taking place in the actual world. More on that will follow in sec. 6.4.

[10] This deterministic principle is a direct consequence of the Schrödinger equation governing the evolution of quantum systems not subject to measurements. As it is well known, the so-called unitary evolution is deterministic.

reasons for introducing the interpretive rule (CPA) was to free ourselves from the unwanted "metaphysical" baggage that the Einsteinian notion of "elements of reality" is burdened with. The statement $P(X_R = a', p')$ is to be interpreted not as an atomic sentence of our language, but just as an abbreviation for the compound sentence $M(X_R, p')\ \square\rightarrow O(X_R, p') = a'$. Based on the theoretically predicted and empirically confirmed correlations between observable outcomes of measurements in the EPR situation, and with the help of the locality assumption (SLOC), we can predict that the right-hand side particle has a *disposition* to reveal a particular value $a'$ upon measurement, given that the left-hand side measurement actually revealed the opposite value $a$. But does this entitle us to claim that this disposition has to be grounded in an objective property of the right-hand side particle? It seems to me that there is a consistent way of speaking about quantum phenomena which avoids this sort of metaphysical assumption (and which will be discussed later).[11]

But before we analyze deeper the nature of quantum dispositions, let us proceed with our unfinished counterfactual analysis of the EPR argument. Einstein, Podolsky and Rosen in their article consider an alternative way to derive the incompleteness thesis which is quite popular and needs to be looked into. Instead of tracing the "property" of the right-hand side particle back to the common past, they propose to consider an alternative measurement selection for the left-hand side particle. Under the counterfactual reconstruction, EPR reason as follows: if we consider a counterfactual situation in which $Y_L$ was measured instead of $X_L$, this change should not affect the property attribution of particle $R$. We can write this step formally as follows:

$$(6.6) \qquad [M(X_L, p) \wedge O(X_L, p) = a] \Rightarrow [M(Y_L, p)\ \square\rightarrow P(X_R = a', p')]$$

and using (CPA) we can rewrite it as:

$$(6.7) \qquad [M(X_L, p) \wedge O(X_L, p) = a] \Rightarrow \{M(Y_L, p)\ \square\rightarrow [M(X_R, p')\ \square\rightarrow O(X_R, p') = a']\}$$

---

[11] Shimony in (1986, pp. 153-154) expresses a similar opinion in this matter. He states explicitly that the certainty (probability equal 1) with which we know that the result of the right-hand side measurement would be $a'$ is not tantamount to the *actualization* of a spin-property of the particle. Shimony is of course aware of the fact that this position amounts to rejecting Einstein's criterion of reality, but does not hesitate to accept this consequence.

In terms of possible worlds, this multiple counterfactual statement can be read in the following manner. In order for (6.7) to be true, statement $M(X_R, p')$ $\square\rightarrow O(X_R, p') = a'$ has to hold in the class of possible worlds which are closest (in the sense of SIM) to the actual one and in which the measurement of $Y_L$ was performed. Let us call these worlds collectively $w(Y_L)$. Due to the locality assumption (SLOC), worlds $w(Y_L)$ look like this: they should be exactly the same as the actual world everywhere outside the future light cone of $p$, and at $p$ the measurement of $Y_L$ should take place (see Fig. 6.3). In order to evaluate counterfactual $M(X_R, p')$ $\square\rightarrow O(X_R, p')$ $= a'$ in one of $w(Y_L)$, we have to invoke yet another class of possible worlds, in which $M(X_R, p')$ takes place, and which are **closest to $w(Y_L)$** **(and not the actual world!).** (In order to distinguish these $X_R$-worlds from the worlds $w(X_R)$ depicted on Fig. 6.2, we will refer to the former as "$w(X_R, Y_L)$"). Again, thanks to (SLOC) those will be the worlds which share with the actual world the entire spacetime excluding two forward light cones: one with its apex at $p$ and the other at $p'$ (see Fig. 6.4). But what is more important is that in worlds $w(X_R, Y_L)$ the left particle $L$ does not undergo any measurement of $X_L$, and consequently no outcome of this measurement can be given at $p$, which cuts off the derivation leading in (6.7) to the conclusion that the outcome of the measurement of $X_R$ is $O(X_R, p') = a'$. It looks like we may safely (i.e. with no apparent violation of (SLOC) as applied to the acts of measurement selection) assume that in some of worlds $w(X_R, Y_L)$ the outcome of the $X_R$ measurement will be $a'$, but in some it will be $a$. Consequently, there is no guarantee that the counterfactual $M(X_R, p')$ $\square\rightarrow O(X_R, p') = a'$ has to hold in $w(Y_L)$, and therefore the entire multiple counterfactual (6.7) becomes unwarranted.[12] It appears that without additional assumptions the principle of locality (SLOC) used with respect to the measurement selections is not sufficient to derive any contradiction with standard quantum mechanics under the counterfactual interpretation of the EPR argument based on the reading (C1) of spatiotemporal counterfactuals.[13]

---

[12] Again, (6.7) would be legitimized if we assumed that there is an actual physical event corresponding to the whole true counterfactual $M(X_R, p')$ $\square\rightarrow O(X_R, p') = a'$ which should be kept intact in worlds $w(Y_L)$.

[13] This conclusion can be stated more formally as follows. We claim that it is possible to create a semantic model consisting of possible worlds, in which statement (6.7) comes out false, and yet it remains true that for every possible world $w$ and for any admissible measurement selection (including the null selection, i.e. no measurement performed) there is a world $w'$ in which this selection has been made and yet

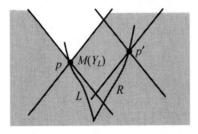

Figure 6.3 The possible world $w(Y_L)$.

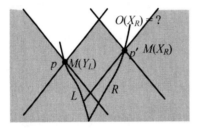

Figure 6.4 The possible world $w(X_R, Y_L)$.

$w'$ remains identical with $w$ at all places space-like separated from or absolutely earlier than the location of the measurement in question (in order to see this, it is sufficient to take the worlds we've introduced above and consider the possible alterations to the selected measurements). This result ensures that it is logically possible to maintain the locality condition (SLOC) limited to the measurement selections, without admitting that there are some true counterfactual property attributions not implied by the standard quantum-mechanical description of the state of both particles (the incompleteness thesis). However, this is not to say that the negation of (6.7) does not imply some other forms of SLOC-type non-locality, for instance referring to the outcome-events. Actually, as we will show later in sec. 6.6, the counterfactual EPR argument reconstructed under interpretation (C1) does indeed imply the violation of (SLOC) regarding the outcomes revealed. But this non-locality is of a different sort than EPR non-locality (regarding the measurement selections) that the original EPR argument was based upon.

### 6.3.3. The failure of the EPR argument under (C2)

The EPR argument using the second interpretation (C2) of counterfactuals fails even more spectacularly. It can be easily verified (see sec. 5.6) that when we interpret the counterfactual claim $M(X_R, p') \;\square\!\!\to\; O(X_R, p') = a'$ as stating that $O(X_R, p') = a'$ has to hold in all possible antecedent-worlds which are identical to the actual world only within the confinement of the backward light cone of $p'$, there is no reason to claim that (6.5) should be true. The locality condition (SLOC) assures us that there is a possible $M(X_R, p')$-world which shares with the actual one more than only the absolute past of $p'$; namely it shares the absolute past and the absolute "elsewhere". But the existence of such a world is not enough, for there still are possible worlds which can differ "elsewhere" with respect to some undetermined events while matching the absolute past of $p'$ with that in the actual world. And if we endorse the orthodox interpretation of quantum mechanics, according to which outcomes of measurements of a given observable are not determined by the physical state of a system unless this state is an eigenstate for that observable, then an obvious candidate for such an undetermined event would be the result of the measurement $M(X_L, p)$ on the left-hand side particle. So, since there is a possible $M(X_R, p')$-world in which the outcome of the left-hand side measurement is different from $a$, and this world retains the same absolute past of point $p'$ as the actual one (see Fig. 6.5), then, according to the truth condition given in (C2), the counterfactual $M(X_R, p') \;\square\!\!\to\; O(X_L, p) = a$ has to be false. And this in turn renders our counterfactual $M(X_R, p') \;\square\!\!\to\; O(X_R, p') = a'$ unjustified. If this analysis is correct, it appears that according to the second reading of counterfactuals we cannot even claim that when the outcome of the measurement of $X_L$ is known to be $a$, the property attribution for particle $R$ should be $P(X_R, p') = a'$, i.e. as inferred by ordinary rules of quantum mechanics.[14]

---

[14] This conclusion is in full agreement with the partial result of the counterfactual analysis of the relativistic EPR argument proposed by M. Redhead and P. La Rivère in (1997), which is a response to (Ghirardi, Grassi 1994). The authors implicitly assume the method of evaluating counterfactuals encapsulated in (C2) (see p. 212), and then conclude that in order to infer the value of the counterfactual measurement from the actual one, we would have to assume determinism of outcomes (stating that the value obtained in the actual experiment remains the same in all relevant possible worlds). While I agree with their general conclusion that the EPR argument allows for a "peaceful coexistence" between quantum mechanics and relativity, I think that in their attempt to improve Ghirardi and Grassi's deriva-

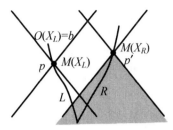

Figure 6.5 A possible world in which the outcome of the measurement of $X_L$ is different from $a$. Shaded area again indicates the region which remains as in the actual world.

The way the EPR argument is rebuffed under the interpretation (C2) of counterfactuals may seem to many readers too "cheap". The truth condition (C2) together with the interpretative rule (CPA) renders invalid all derivations that infer property attributions for some system from the outcome of the distant, and yet correlated system. But doesn't this fact violate basic quantum-mechanical predictions regarding the existence of (strict) correlations between outcomes of measurements in the EPR state? Fortunately, we have already addressed this worry in sec. 5.6, and we have argued there that no inconsistency with quantum-mechanical predictions arises when we adopt the (C2) reading of the counterfactual. The only thing the proponents of (C2) have to be careful about is not to attribute the failure of (6.5) to the violation of strict correlation between right- and left-hand side outcomes, but rather to the inappropriate counterfactual representation of this correlation. The correct counterfactual representation of strict correlations requires that the left-hand side outcome enter directly the antecedent of the counterfactual in (6.5), and not the antecedent of the strict conditional.

One lesson from this example is that the notion of "a quantum property", as explicated counterfactually in (CPA), clearly depends on the adopted semantic interpretation of counterfactual conditionals. From the perspective of (C2), in order to ascribe a definite quantum property to a system we have to be sure that a particular outcome will be consistently

---

tion, Redhead and La Rivère should point out that both interpretations rely on different readings of counterfactuals.

revealed in all backward light-cone sharing worlds, regardless of what transpires in space-like separated locations. This concept of quantum properties may be called "conservative", as it seems to presuppose that no fact located outside the absolute past of the measurement can have a direct influence on the outcome revealed. However, we have to note that even this conservative notion of quantum properties does not entirely exclude the possibility of influencing them "at a distance", as the following example shows. Suppose that the counterfactual $M(A) \ \square\rightarrow O(A) = a$ is true in the actual world according to (C2), which means that $O(A) = a$ holds in all worlds sharing with the actual world the absolute past of $M(A)$. Still, it is conceivable that there may be a possible event $X$ space-like separated from $M(A)$ whose occurrence unfailingly brings about some change in this part of the past of $M(A)$ which is space-like separated from $X$. In such a case it is possible that the counterfactual $M(A) \ \square\rightarrow O(A) = a'$ with a different value $a'$ will be true in the closest $X$-world $w(X)$, since in order to evaluate it we have to invoke the worlds which share the backward light cone of $M(A)$ not with the actual world, but with $w(X)$. Still, this influence requires an "intermediary" in the form of the non-locally induced change of the absolute past of the local measurement. On the other hand, the notion of property that is brought about by combining (CPA) with (C1) may be seen as more "liberal". It admits the possibility that property attributions of a given system may be *directly* derived from facts other than the past history of this system—in other words, that in spite of the absolute past of the measurement being intact, the outcome can be different than in the actual world. The only possibility that this interpretation excludes is that the property attribution at a given time be derived from events that occur unambiguously *later* than that time.

Another comment regarding the C2-based interpretation of the EPR argument needs to be made. As the argument apparently fails in its initial stage, we are not forced to abandon the assumption that there is a genuine physical state of affairs corresponding to the counterfactual in (CPA) in order to block the derivation of the incompleteness thesis. Hence it looks like the concept of quantum properties based on (C2) admits the possibility that they really are *genuine properties of the system*, and not only *dispositions* with no basis in categorical facts. Needless to say, the locality condition (SLOC) is too weak to guarantee the existence of such properties in the EPR situation. On the other hand, speaking about quantum properties and property attributions under interpretation (C1) looks like a mere *façon de parler* rather than literal speech. They are not so much properties of the system in their own right, as *dispositions* of the system to react in a certain way in certain conditions (those conditions include physical states of affairs in space-like separated regions of spacetime). But to better understand the difference between *categorical* and *dispositional* properties we have to stray from the main topic for a moment, and take up this important philosophical issue. [15]

## 6.4 QUANTUM DISPOSITIONS OR ELEMENTS OF REALITY?

Philosophers of science have long been interested in so-called dispositional properties (dispositions in short). Dispositions are typically informally characterized as properties whose existence manifests itself only in certain, precisely specified conditions. Classical examples of dispositions are water-solubility, fragility, or magnetism. To say of a sugar cube that it is soluble in water amounts to the statement that if we put it into chemically pure $H_2O$, it would dissolve. Similarly, it is common to characterize the property of being magnetized as the disposition of an object to attract things that are made of iron. But neither solubility, nor magnetism is manifest under "normal" conditions—we may be tempted to say that they are "latent" properties that are waiting for an occasion to reveal themselves. This feature sets them apart from categorical properties, such as size and shape, which are assumed to be actualized the whole time the object exists.

From the way in which we describe dispositional properties informally it should be quite clear that counterfactual conditionals can play a crucial role in their precise definitions. Early attempts to explicate the notion of

---

[15] Yet another counterfactual interpretation of the EPR argument and Bohr's response to it has been recently proposed in (Dickson 2002). Dickson bases his interpretation on the distinction between two types of the locality assumption (he calls them "non-disturbance principles"): a strong and a weak one. The strong locality claims that when we assume counterfactually that instead of observable $X$ an incompatible observable $Y$ was measured on particle $L$, the property attribution for particle $R$ should remain the same as when inferred from the result of the actual measurement of $X$ on $L$. On the other hand, the weak locality holds that the above counterfactual inference is valid only under the supposition that no measurement is performed on particle $L$. According to Dickson's interpretation, Bohr's response to the EPR amounts to the rejection of the strong locality, while retaining the weak one. The main problem I see with this interpretation is that even the weak locality leads ultimately to the incompleteness of quantum mechanics, contrary to Bohr. For the weak locality implies that there is a possible world in which the pair of EPR particles is not subject to any measurement, and yet one of these particles possesses a physical property not included in its standard quantum-mechanical description.

disposition relied on truth-functional logic and its only available conditional, i.e. material implication.[16] However, this method of characterizing dispositions leads either to the desperate conclusion that all objects which have never been immersed in water are *ipso facto* water-soluble, or to the no less desperate statement that water-solubility is definable only for objects which have been immersed in water, while for all remaining things the term "soluble" becomes meaningless. The non-truth-functional semantics of counterfactuals offers a much better tool to express the common intuition regarding dispositions. We can then stipulate generally that the statement "An object $x$ possesses a particular disposposition $D$" is shorthand for the counterfactual "If $x$ were in condition $C$, it would reveal a categorical property $P$".[17] Of course the meaningfulness of this counterfactual does not presuppose that $x$ actually *is* in condition $C$, nor does it follow that if the antecedent is not satisfied, the entire conditional becomes vacuously true.

One of the main problems that the theoreticians of dispositions consider is their relation to categorical properties. Is every disposition associated with, or based upon, a categorical property? Our scientific experience tells us that in many cases dispositional properties turn out to be grounded in more fundamental categorical properties of the object. For instance, both solubility and fragility are reducible to some structural features of the molecules that make up the substances such as sugar or glass. In fact, it is one of the main goals of science to find causal explanations for the apparent dispositions that physical objects display. If such explanation in terms of categorical properties is found, it may be concluded that the putative

---

[16] For a representative sample of this approach to dispositional terms see (Carnap 1936, 1937).

[17] Some philosophers object to defining dispositions with the help of counterfactual conditionals, though. The most ardent critic of the counterfactual explication of dispositions is C.B. Martin (see his 1994 paper). He points out that there may be situations in which the counterfactual supposedly defining a given disposition is made to be true, and yet the corresponding disposition is not present. Martin uses as an example the disposition of a "live" wire to trigger the flow of an electric current when touched by a (grounded) conductor, and then conceives an "electro-fink" device that makes an otherwise dead wire live the moment it is touched by a conductor. In this particular set-up the counterfactual "If I touched this wire with a conductor, electrical current would flow" is true, and yet the wire does not have the dispositional property of being live. An attempt to avoid similar problems was made by Lewis in (1997), but it was later criticized by A. Bird (1998). Lange suggests that we should add the clause "under standard conditions" to the antecedent of the counterfactual defining a given disposition (2002, pp. 72-73).

disposition is in fact "nothing more" than the appropriate combination of categorical properties. The mysterious "propensity" or "power" is replaced with a clear-cut property that may be investigated independently of whether the particular conditions associated with the disposition occur (for example, it is possible to verify that some alloy is fragile on the basis of the microscopic analysis of its molecular structure, without the need to subject it to an external force and to, subsequently, destroy it).

What does all this have to do with the criterion of reality that we are interested in? As was explained in the last section, it is sometimes possible to infer from the outcome of a measurement performed on one particle that a distant particle would reveal the correlated outcome, had it been subject to a measurement of the corresponding observable. In other words, we are able to infer a statement about a *disposition* to reveal precisely one outcome upon measurement. Einstein and his collaborators accepted without hesitation that this disposition has to be a manifestation of an underlying categorical property that the distant particle possesses, and to express this conviction they introduced their famous criterion of reality. The element of reality that supposedly underlies the inferred disposition is identified with the fact that the observable in question *possesses* the inferred value even if no measurement has been performed to reveal it. But in my analysis of EPR's argument I have questioned this particular assumption, pointing out that it is possible to interpret quantum property attributions purely in terms of counterfactual dispositions that have no basis in any categorical properties (see formula CPA above). Now the question is: can this view be upheld in light of the philosophical analysis of dispositional properties and their ontological relations with categorical properties?

If we were to accept the hypothesis formulated two paragraphs earlier that every disposition has to have its basis in a categorical property, then my way of dealing with the EPR argument would be in trouble. For then it would make perfect sense to expect that the categorical basis for the distant particle's disposition to reveal a precise outcome would remain unchanged even if I refrained from making the measurement that allowed me to infer this disposition in the first place, as long as my measurement had no chance of affecting the physical state of the distant particle. This stems from the fact that categorical properties of objects that belong to the "fixed" region of space-time have to be preserved when evaluating counterfactuals. But do we have conclusive reasons to believe that the reducibility thesis regarding dispositions has to be universally valid? After all, we can at best support it with an inductive argument from the past successes that science has had in finding categorical grounds for various dispositions. Is there any general argument which shows that this has to be always the case?

The following argument may be put forward. It may be suggested that we can conventionally identify each disposition with a categorical property of a given object. Such a proposal—that dispositions simply *are* categorical properties, but picked out in a special way—has been advanced by many authors.[18] On this account, the name "fragility" refers to whatever property causes an object to break when treated roughly. In the case of fragility in addition to that identification we are able to identify this property through an alternative means, by reference to the molecular features of the substance. But even if we didn't know that fragility reduces to some characteristics of the molecular structure, it would still be true that fragility is in fact some categorical property which we are able to identify only dispositionally. If we accepted this way of approaching the identity thesis regarding dispositional and categorical properties, it would clearly spell a disaster for our attempt to block the EPR argument by rejecting Einstein's criterion of reality.

Fortunately, there are some objections to this "terminological" way of identifying dispositions with their categorical basis. The most convincing argument—in my opinion—is presented in (Lange 2002, pp. 71, 77, 85). This argument turns on the fact that categorical bases for dispositions are supposed to causally explain the effects brought about by these dispositions. For instance, the categorical basis of fragility should act as a (partial) cause of the fact that a given fragile object broke after it had been dropped from the height of five feet onto a concrete floor. And yet if we identify the categorical basis of fragility with the counterfactual "If I dropped it, it would break", then it can be inferred by pure logic that if an object has this categorical property and is dropped, then (in the closest possible world) it has to break. In Lange's words, this implies that the purported cause is "too close" to the effect. The relation between cause and effect cannot be that of logical entailment; some laws of nature have to be involved. To explain the breaking of a fragile object given by pointing out that the object had the disposition to break under particular circumstances is for obvious reasons unsatisfactory. For in that way we could accomplish the task of "causal explanation" effortlessly in each case when a disposition is present.

---

[18] Compare (Quine 1974, p. 11; Mumford 1994, 1998); see also (Lange 2002, p. 75) for an analysis of this position.

Even if the task of proving generally that every disposition has to be associated with a corresponding categorical property is not within easy reach, still the particular case of quantum dispositions may admit some more specifically-oriented arguments. Dispositions defined in (CPA) reveal themselves under precisely defined circumstances, which we generally refer to as "measurements". And isn't it part of the meaning of the term "measurement" that which outcome is obtained in a measurement is supposed to give us an insight into the objective features of the object under investigation? To this one may reply that in quantum mechanics many seemingly unquestionable features of measurements (one may even be tempted to call them "definitional") had to be abandoned. One of these features is that if a properly conducted measurement reveals a given value for the selected observable, then this value (or a value sufficiently close to it, given that the measurement may introduce some classical disturbances) must have characterized the observable just before the measurement. The anti-realist interpretation of quantum mechanics rejects this view, replacing it with the much weaker condition that the value revealed must have had a non-zero probability of occurrence prior to the measurement. Still, even ardent proponents of quantum orthodoxy tend to accept that the truth of the counterfactual "If I measured $X$, then the result would be precisely $x$" shows that the system is in the eigenstate with respect to value $x$, and this in turn is interpreted as an objective, categorical property of the system.

I don't know if the controversy regarding the nature of quantum dispositions can be settled by speculating about the true meaning of the word "measurement" in quantum mechanics. However, it seems to me that the most promising way of to approach the problem is to look for more tangible arguments within quantum mechanics itself. And there we can find good reasons for questioning the existence of categorical properties that underlie quantum dispositions of the form (CPA). In sec. 4.2.6 we already saw an argument based on the Hardy example which shows that the joint assumption of the locality condition (LOC1) (which follows from (SLOC)) and Einstein's criterion of reality, which assumes that for a true counterfactual property attribution there is a categorical property causally responsible for it, leads to the conclusion that an outcome which is predicted to have a non-zero probability according to quantum mechanics is nevertheless impossible. I believe that this argument constitutes a true strengthening of Bell's theorem, where the realist assumption (the hidden variable hypothesis) is replaced by the seemingly weaker criterion of reality. And, as in Bell's original argument, we are free to save the locality condition and reject the existence of elements of reality corresponding to the counterfactuals derived on the basis of local measurements.

There is yet another quantum-mechanical argument worth mentioning here that shows the untenability of the reducibility thesis applied to quantum dispositions. R. Clifton, C. Pagonis and I. Pitowski (CPP, for short) in (Clifton *et al.* 1992) mount an extended attack on the EPR argument or, more specifically, on its premises of locality and of *the legitimacy to infer the existence of an element of reality.* As their second goal corresponds to ours, we will briefly sketch the way they achieve it. CPP consider three particles prepared in the GHZ state (see sec. 4.1.1 for the physical details) and flying away from each other. Their argument relies on the crucial premise that the truth of the counterfactual $M(A) \ \Box \rightarrow O(A) = a$ at time $t$ implies the existence of the element of reality $P(A=a, t)$ (formula (12) on p. 121 in Clifton *et al.* 1992). Next, they select three observers, each one moving next to one of the three particles, and they assume that the observers perform measurements of observables $X_i$ which result in outcomes $x_i$. CPP claim that the quantum-mechanical predictions regarding the GHZ (statements (GHZ2-4) in sec. 4.1.1) allow each observer to derive the conclusion that, had the other two observers measured $Y_j$ rather than $X_j$, the product of the outcomes would equal $x_i$. The conclusion derived by the first observer can thus be stated as:

(CPP) $\quad M(X_1, p_1) \Rightarrow [(M(Y_2, p'_2) \wedge M(Y_3, p'_3)) \ \Box \rightarrow y_2 y_3 = x_1]$

and similarly for the remaining two observers. It is assumed that all three spatiotemporal points of "counterfactual measurements" $p'_1, p'_2$, and $p'_3$ are absolutely earlier than the corresponding locations of the actual measurements $p_1, p_2$ and $p_3$, and that for every $p_i$ the counterfactual locations $p'_j$ and $p'_k$ are located later relative to the frame of reference associated with the $i^{th}$ observer.

From this and the criterion of reality formulated above CPP derive that each observer $i$ has to agree that at the region containing points $p'_j$ and $p'_k$ there exists the precise value for the observable that is defined as the product of $Y_j$ and $Y_k$. More specifically, the first observer infers that there exists the value of $Y_2 Y_3$ at $p'_2$ and $p'_3$, the second infers the value of $Y_1 Y_3$ at $p'_1$ and $p'_3$, and the third the value of $Y_1 Y_2$ at points $p'_1$ and $p'_2$. CPP then argue that points $p'_1, p'_2$, and $p'_3$ can be selected in such a way that they lie on one space-like hyperplane, so that it is possible to introduce a fourth observer for whom all these three values will exist simultaneously. But a quick algebraic argument shows that the assumption that $y_1y_2 = x_3$, $y_1y_3 = x_2$ and $y_2y_3 = x_1$ contradicts prediction GHZ1 (the product $x_1x_2x_3$ has to be $-1$, but it cannot, since it is equal to the product of three squared numbers).

In their discussion of the above result CPP point out that it is possible to avoid the ensuing contradiction by assuming that values for observables are defined not with respect to bounded space-time regions in which the measurements are performed, but with respect to entire hyperplanes of simultaneity (p. 126). Consequently, it is possible to maintain that an observable $A$ possesses value $a_1$ at point $p$ with respect to one hyperplane $H_1$, and a different value $a_2$ with respect to a different hyperplane $H_2$. But this method of rescuing Einstein's criterion of reality seems to me pretty desperate. After all, the counterfactual $M(A) \; \square\!\!\rightarrow O(A) = a$ does not contain any relativization to hyperplanes of simultaneity, unless we assume that the very notion of an observable requires such a relativization (but on what grounds?). It seems to me much more straightforward to accept that the contradiction is to be blamed upon the assumption that quantum dispositions to reveal particular values have to be grounded in categorical properties of systems. Seen from this perspective, CPP's results strengthen our criticism of the counterfactual version of Einstein's criterion of reality.[19]

## 6.5 BELL'S THEOREM WITH COUNTERFACTUAL HIDDEN VARIABLES

A substantial part of this book has been devoted to the assessment of Stapp's efforts to counterfactually strengthen Bell's theorem. As we re-

---

[19] C. Pagonis, M. Redhead and P. La Rivière criticize CPP's argument in (Pagonis *et al.* 1996), mainly on the basis of their observation that the counterfactual (CPP) requires two additional assumptions besides quantum-mechanical predictions: determinism and locality. I agree with the "locality" part of their thesis; indeed (CPP) could very well be false if we allowed for the fact that the counterfactual measurements of $Y_2$ and $Y_3$ influenced the result obtained in $X_1$. However, the suggestion that (CPP) contains a residual form of determinism comes from the fact that Pagonis, Redhead and La Rivière assume one of the possible interpretations of counterfactuals—namely (C2). If CPP decided to follow the (C1) interpretation, no assumption of determinism would be necessary to support (CPP). Consequently, I admit that CPP's result can be blocked by simply rejecting the locality condition (SLOC), but of course this is not an option for somebody who tries to find a loophole in quantum-mechanical theorems that would allow for a (limited) validity of locality.

member all too well, Stapp's main idea was to eliminate the assumption of realism altogether from the theorem, substituting in its place the locality condition in its appropriate counterfactual form. If we are right in our analysis, Stapp's program turns out to be overly ambitious. So far no uncontroversial counterfactual derivation of Bell's inequality without one or the other version of the hidden variable hypothesis has been presented. And there are even reasonably strong arguments, some of which were stated in chapter 4, that such a derivation is impossible. In this section we will pursue a much less ambitious task: rather than *strengthening* Bell's theorem in its standard form we will simply try to verify its validity under the counterfactual reconstruction (SLOC) of the locality condition. To put it differently, we will ask whether the general principle (SLOC) legitimizes the Bell-locality condition which, as we pointed out in sec. 1.4, is indispensable in the derivation of Bell's inequality. The crucial thing is of course that we do not reject the realist assumption ("hidden variables") in our counterfactual interpretation; the only deviation from the standard version of Bell's theorem is that we will take the liberty of interpreting this assumption in terms of counterfactual property attributions.[20]

---

[20] Brian Skyrms in (1981) proposed a different "counterfactual" reformulation of Bell's theorem. According to his analysis, the principle of counterfactual definiteness can be derived from the locality assumption and the perfect correlation assumption (which is a consequence of the conservation of spin), so there is no need to add an extra premise in the form of the counterfactual hidden variables hypothesis. If correct, his result would prove more or less what Stapp unsuccessfully tried to achieve: that (counterfactual) locality alone leads to a conflict with quantum-mechanical predictions. Unfortunately, there are in my opinion two serious problems with Skyrms's derivation. First, his argument has in fact very little to do with "counterfactuality". As Skyrms himself admits, the only accepted semantic characteristics of the conditionals used in the proof is that they obey the Modus Ponens rule. This may come as a surprise, for obeying Modus Ponens can hardly be regarded as a distinctive feature of the subjunctive conditional. Modus Ponens interpreted metalogically as the rule leading from "$A$ is true in $w$" and "$A \; \square \rightarrow B$ is true in $w$" to "$B$ is true in $w$" is of course valid in Lewis's logic, but its validity is somehow "vacuous", as in typical cases $A$ is obviously assumed to be false in the actual world. On the other hand, MP interpreted as the claim that from "$A \; \square \rightarrow B$ is true in $w$" and "$A$ is true in $w'$", "$B$ is true in $w'$" follows is clearly invalid. The second problem with Skyrms's derivation, limiting the novelty of his result, lies in its formulation of the locality condition, which unlike our (SLOC) relies on the probabilistic condition of independence of local outcomes from distant outcomes, and therefore can hardly be seen as an improvement on the generalized Bell theorem that uses the factorization condition as its initial premise.

To begin with, let us note that Bell's inequality is fully supported by (SLOC) when we interpret the hidden variable hypothesis as stating that every physical system possesses objective categorical properties which uniquely determine outcomes of all measurements involved. For in such a case these properties have to be "transferred" to the possible worlds that share with the actual world regions in which these properties are exemplified. So, if one of the two space-like separated particles prepared in the singlet spin state has a certain set of those properties in the actual world, the same properties will be present in the closest possible world in which the other particle undergoes any measurement (the existence of this world is of course guaranteed by SLOC). Consequently, no distant measurement can affect the objective properties possessed by the local particle, and any mathematical relation that the hidden variables obey will be satisfied by the outcomes revealed in joint measurements. Bell's inequality is then bound to be fulfilled by the values received in experiment. This result is quite independent of the semantics of counterfactuals that is adopted, as it appeals to the universal formulation of locality (SLOC) only.

However, it is by no means clear that Bell's theorem should hold when we interpret the realist assumption as the requirement that for every parameter in question an appropriate property ascription statement in the counterfactual form be true. This supposition is plainly weaker than the previous one, as it does not postulate that these counterfactual property attributions are grounded in some categorical properties of quantum systems. It only prescribes that for each observable $A$ pertaining to a physical system $x$ there is a value $a$ such that if the measurement of $A$ were performed on $x$, its outcome would be $a$. As explained in the previous section, counterfactuals of that sort are interpreted as representations of further unanalyzable primitive quantum dispositions, and not as indicators of deeper objective properties of quantum systems that we typically associate with statements "Measurable quantity $A$ of physical system $x$ possesses value $a$". Consequently, the truth of these counterfactuals is not automatically preserved in the possible worlds closest to the actual one. Now the question is, does such a weak counterfactual reinterpretation of the realist assumption suffice for deriving Bell's inequality, when coupled with the locality condition (SLOC)?

Let us clarify this question a bit using the CHSH version of Bell's theorem that we presented in sec. 3.1. This example involves two singlet-state particles and four selected observables (spin-components): $A^1$, $A^2$ characterizing one of the two particles, and $B^1$, $B^2$ pertaining to the other one. Let us suppose that in the actual world no measurement has been performed. However, according to our current version of the realist assumption, there are four values $a^1$, $a^2$, $b^1$, $b^2$ for which the following counterfactuals are true in the actual world:

(6.8)    $M(A^1) \; \square\!\!\rightarrow O(A^1) = a^1,$
         $M(A^2) \; \square\!\!\rightarrow O(A^2) = a^2,$
         $M(B^1) \; \square\!\!\rightarrow O(B^1) = b^1,$
         $M(B^2) \; \square\!\!\rightarrow O(B^2) = b^2.$

The joint existence of these four values implies, of course, that the following parameter can be meaningfully defined in the actual world:

$$\gamma = a^1 b^1 + a^1 b^2 + a^2 b^1 - a^2 b^2$$

Similarly, it makes sense to speak about the mean value of the parameter $\gamma$ calculated over a number of individual pairs each created independently in the actual world:

$$\langle \gamma_n \rangle = \langle a_n^1 b_n^1 \rangle + \langle a_n^1 b_n^2 \rangle + \langle a_n^2 b_n^1 \rangle - \langle a_n^2 b_n^2 \rangle$$

As we recall, a quick algebraic argument can convince us that when the values $a^i$ and $b^i$ are assumed to be either +1 or −1 the following inequality has to be obeyed (the details are given in sec. 3.1):

(CHSH)    $|\langle \gamma_n \rangle| \leq 2$

But in order to confront the CHSH inequality with quantum-mechanical predictions (as well as with experimental results) we have to show that the mean values $\langle a_n^i b_n^j \rangle$ that were defined in the world in which no actual measurement took place will be numerically equal to the expectation values of products of outcomes revealed in joint measurements. And this supposition would be substantiated, if we could establish that the outcomes $a^i$ and $b^j$ revealed in joint measurements $A^i$ and $B^j$ would be precisely the same as the values figuring in the counterfactuals (6.8) whose truth in the actual no-measurement world we have accepted as our initial premise. Some sort of locality assumption will surely be necessary to do the job, stating the independence of the local outcome of a distant measurement, but the crucial thing now is whether (SLOC) is strong enough to serve this purpose.

Expressing what has just been said in the counterfactual language, we may say that in order to prove Bell's theorem in the CHSH version we need to show that the following counterfactual will hold for all $i$ and $j$:

$$(6.9) \quad [M(A^i) \wedge M(B^j)] \ \Box\rightarrow O(A^i) = a^i$$

Once again, the truth of this counterfactual ensures that the measurement of a particular observable will reveal the same value as was predicted by counterfactuals (6.8) no matter what measurement is performed on the distant particle (by symmetry the same should hold for the outcomes of the $B$-measurements). Now let us consider the truth condition for the statement (6.9) according to the (C1+) method of evaluating counterfactuals. In order for (6.9) to be true, the consequent $O(A^i) = a^i$ has to hold in all possible antecedent-worlds which are identical with the actual world everywhere outside two forward light cones: one with its apex at the location of $M(A^i)$, and the other at the location of $M(B^j)$ (let's call these worlds $w(A^i, B^j)$). In order to prove that this is really the case, we may proceed as follows. From the initial assumption (6.8) regarding the truth of the counterfactual $M(A^i)$ $\Box\rightarrow O(A^i) = a^i$ in the actual world we can derive that $O(A^i) = a^i$ is true in all worlds $w(A^i)$ in which $M(A^i)$ is performed, and which differ from the actual world only within the confines of the forward light cone of $M(A^i)$. Applying the further assumption (SLOC) to one of these worlds $w(A^i)$, we can derive the existence of a world in which $M(B^j)$ is performed, and which is identical with $w(A^i)$ at all locations space-like separated from, or absolutely earlier than, $M(B^j)$. Putting all this together we can see that (SLOC) guarantees the existence of *at least one* world of the type $w(A^i, B^j)$ in which the outcome of the $A^i$-measurement is unchanged and equals $a^i$. But this is not enough for our purposes. As we stated before, we need to show that $O(A^i) = a^i$ holds in *all* worlds $w(A^i, B^j)$, and not only in *some* of them. Apparently, at this stage no contradiction with (SLOC) would arise from the supposition that in some worlds $w(A^i, B^j)$ the outcome of $M(A^i)$ equals $a^i$, and in some it equals the opposite. Hence, it looks like we have discovered a loophole in the counterfactual derivation of Bell's theorem, which may call into question its overall validity.

However, this loophole is actually very small, and can be closed relatively easily. Remember that our proof proceeds under the hypothesis that all available counterfactual property attributions for quantum systems are fully determined. So far we have applied this assumption to the physical situation in the actual world, in order to argue for the truth of the four counterfactuals in (6.8). But the counterfactual outcome definiteness, as we may call this premise, should presumably also hold in possible worlds, including the $M(B^j)$-worlds. This means that in every world in which the measurement of $B^j$ alone is performed, there still should be a unique value $\alpha$ (not necessarily equal to $a^i$) for which the counterfactual $M(A^i) \ \square\!\!\rightarrow O(A^i) = \alpha$ would be true at this world. Using this knowledge, we may now attempt to prove that in all worlds $w(A^i, B^j)$ the outcome of the $A^i$-measurement should be the same. Obviously, having already proven that in some of the worlds $w(A^i, B^j)$ the outcome $O(A^i)$ equals $a^i$, in this way we would quickly demonstrate that $O(A^i) = a^i$ in all worlds $w(A^i, B^j)$, thus achieving our goal of establishing the truth of (6.9).

Let us then suppose, contrary to our hypothesis, that there are two worlds $w_1(A^i, B^j)$ and $w_2(A^i, B^j)$ such that the outcome $O(A^i)$ equals $a_1$ in the first one, but $a_2$ in the second one, where $a_1 \neq a_2$ (see Fig. 6.6). We will now construct a particular $M(B^j)$-world in which no counterfactual of the form $M(A^1) \ \square\!\!\rightarrow O(A^1) = \alpha$ comes out true, thus violating our counterfactual hidden variable hypothesis. This $M(B^j)$-world, which we will call $w(B^j)$, will be identical to $w_1(A^i, B^j)$ everywhere outside the forward-light cone of $M(A^i)$, and there will be no $A^i$-measurement made in it (the existence of this world is again guaranteed by SLOC). From the construction of $w(B^j)$ it follows that the world $w_1(A^i, B^j)$ is one of the worlds in which the truth of the counterfactual $M(A^i) \ \square\!\!\rightarrow O(A^i) = \alpha$ should be evaluated. The only thing we need to do right now is to show that $w_2(A^i, B^j)$ is another world in which this counterfactual is to be evaluated. But there is a little snag here. Notice that worlds $w_1(A^i, B^j)$ and $w_2(A^i, B^j)$ possibly differ from one another in *both* forward light cones, including that of the $B^j$-measurement. As a consequence, $w(B^j)$ and $w_2(A^i, B^j)$ *may* differ from each other in the absolute future of $M(B^j)$, in which case $w_2(A^i, B^j)$ would not be relevant for the evaluation of the counterfactual $M(A^i) \ \square\!\!\rightarrow O(A^i) = \alpha$ at $w(B^j)$. But I would argue that on the basis of the world $w_2(A^i, B^j)$ we can construct yet another world $w_2{}^*(A^i, B^j)$ in which the outcome $O(A^i)$ would still be $a_2$, and which would share with $w_1(A^i, B^j)$ (and with $w(B^j)$) the absolute future of the $B^j$-measurement.

Notice first that the only differences between $M(B^j)$'s forward light cones in $w_1(A^i, B^j)$ and $w_2(A^i, B^j)$ can be with respect to the events that are not causally (deterministically) connected with anything outside these cones. In other words, the discrepancies between $w_1(A^i, B^j)$ and $w_2(A^i, B^j)$

are purely in regard to indeterministic, or chance events. Let us use the symbol $D_{12}$ to indicate the set of all events that are present in the forward light cone of $M(B^j)$ in world $w_2(A^i, B^j)$, but are absent in $w_1(A^i, B^j)$. Now let us consider the earliest event $E$ in $D_{12}$. According to (SLOC), there has to be the world in which $E$ does not occur, and which is otherwise identical to $w_2(A^i, B^j)$ outside its future light cone. Hence we have arrived at the world $w_2'(A^i, B^j)$ in which one of the diverging events of $w_2(A^i, B^j)$ has been eliminated. Repeating this procedure we will reach worlds $w_2''(A^i, B^j)$, $w_2'''(A^i, B^j)$, and so on, until in the limit we should reach the world $w_2^*(A^i, B^j)$ fully conforming with $w_1(A^i, B^j)$ within the whole forward light cone of $M(B^j)$. By construction, the world $w_2^*(A^i, B^j)$ participates in evaluating the counterfactual $M(A^1) \ \square\rightarrow O(A^1) = \alpha$ at $w(B^j)$, and since outcome $O(A^i)$ is different in it than in $w_1(A^i, B^j)$, the counterfactual comes out false for every value $\alpha$, which contradicts one of our assumptions.

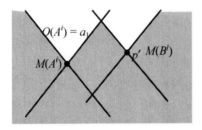

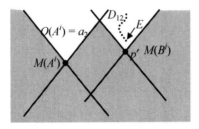

Figure 6.6 Two worlds $w_1(A^i, B^j)$ and $w_2(A^i, B^j)$ with two different outcomes of the $A^i$-measurement. The world $w(B^j)$ is constructed as being identical with $w_1(A^i, B^j)$ everywhere outside the forward light cone of $M(A^i)$, with $M(A^i)$ eliminated. Note that the interior of the forward light cone of $M(B^j)$ can happen to be different in world $w_1(A^i,$

$B^j$) than in $w_2(A^i, B^j)$. The set of points $D_{12}$ symbolize the events in $w_2(A^i, B^j)$ which are absent from $w_1(A^i, B^j)$

We should not try to conceal the fact that this procedure is executable only if certain mathematical conditions are satisfied, the most important of which is that the set $D_{12}$ be discreetly ordered. I don't think that this restriction dramatically diminishes the generality of the achieved result, for I am unable to conceive a reasonable example of a set of *independent* chance events that is temporally continuous, or even dense. I am, of course, willing to accept the existence of continuous chains of events causally connected with one another. But in such a situation the elimination of the first, "initial" cause takes care of the entire chain. If these loose remarks fail to convince the reader suspicious of some form of cheating (and rightly so), then I can do nothing better than propose yet another modification of the locality condition which could take care of this situation *en bloc*. The modified locality condition would assert that for any spatiotemporally extended and possibly complex state of affairs $S$, if the region where $S$ is located is entirely contained in a given forward light cone $F$, and if $S$ is causally independent of all events located in the intersection of $S$'s joint absolute past $B$ (understood as the sum of the backward light cones for all spatiotemporal points that $S$ occupies) and the exterior of $F$, then there exists a possible world in which $S$ does not occur, and yet the *entire* exterior of $F$ remains unchanged (see Fig. 6.7). This modified condition immediately warrants the existence of the world $w_2^*(A^i, B^j)$.

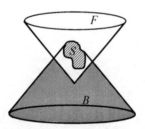

Figure 6.7 Modification of the locality condition (SLOC)

To sum up, the semantic locality condition (SLOC) seems to imply the validity of Bell-locality understood in a particular counterfactual way. The original Bell-locality asserted that an objective measurable property of a given system cannot change its value upon selecting a distant (space-like separated) measurement. In the currently proposed reinterpretation, counterfactual Bell-locality claims that if a counterfactual property attribution statement pertaining to one system is true for a given value, then a distant measurement cannot make this counterfactual statement true but for a different value. As we have just shown, this counterfactual locality condition is provable under the (C1) interpretation of counterfactual conditionals, and with the general semantic locality condition (SLOC) (or a proper extension thereof).

As we may expect, the semantic interpretation (C2) of counterfactuals makes it even easier to prove the counterfactual reconstruction of Bell's theorem. Counterfactual outcome definiteness, as assumed in (6.8), becomes a pretty strong statement under the (C2) reading. It amounts to the thesis that the outcome of a given measurement is bound to remain the same in all possible worlds which share with the actual one the absolute past of the measurement. Consequently, nothing that transpires in the space-like separated region of spacetime can directly affect this assessment. As we remarked in sec. 6.3.3., the only possible way to change at a distance the outcome that is counterfactually determined in the actual world is to affect non-locally the absolute past of the measurement. If this is prohibited by the locality assumption (SLOC), then the same outcome that is predicted to occur in the actual world according to (6.8) will be revealed in the world in which the measurement of $B^j$ is carried out on the other particle.

To present this result slightly more formally, we may note that in order to evaluate counterfactual (6.9) according to the procedure (C2+), we have to first select the closest $[M(A^i) \land M(B^j)]$-worlds with respect to the relation of similarity (SIM) and then extend the set of the closest worlds $\Pi$ by adding all the worlds that share with the $\Pi$ worlds the absolute pasts of their primary points of divergence. This procedure gets substantially simplified in the case when there exist $[M(A^i) \land M(B^j)]$-worlds which only differ from the actual world outside the two backward light cones—one with its apex at $M(A^i)$, and the other at $M(B^j)$—for now the evaluation of (6.9) can be done exclusively in these worlds. Indeed we can argue that such worlds have to exist, but surprisingly in order to do this we have to appeal to the locality assumption (SLOC). At first glance it may look as if the existence of the world with the pasts of $M(A^i)$ and $M(B^j)$ that are identical to those in the actual world should follow from the initial assumption regarding the indeterministic character of measurement selections (sec. 5.3.1). But this is not the case. The assumption that measurement selections are indeterministic entails only that there will be distinct $M(A^i)$-worlds and $M(B^j)$-worlds preserving the absolute pasts of each measurement separately. But it is generally possible that the occurrence of measurement $M(A^i)$ may non-locally affect this space-like separated part of space-time that happens to lie in the absolute past of $M(B^j)$ and *vice versa*. In order to exclude this possibility, we have to assume that for each measurement $M(A^i)$ and $M(B^j)$ there is a world that matches the actual world outside its forward light cone, and this is precisely the locality assumption (SLOC). With (SLOC) it can be easily verified that there is a $[M(A^i) \wedge M(B^j)]$-world that matches the actual world everywhere outside both forward light cones of the measurements, and that therefore there are possible $[M(A^i) \wedge M(B^j)]$-worlds that preserve both backward light cones of these measurements.

With this conclusion secured, it is straightforward to show that all the worlds in which the evaluation of (6.9) is to be made are *ipso facto* the worlds that keep the absolute past of $M(A^i)$ unchanged, and as such they enter the valuation of appropriate counterfactuals in (6.8). Thus from (6.8) it follows that in all these worlds the outcome will be $O(A^i) = a^i$, and the truth of counterfactual (6.9) follows immediately. We may remark that the locality condition (SLOC) played a more restricted role in the current derivation than in the derivation of Bell's inequality under the C1 semantics of counterfactuals, but its acceptance was necessary for the success of the proof nonetheless.

## 6.6. GENERALIZED LOCALITY CONDITION AND COUNTERFACTUAL OUTCOME-DEPENDENCE

So far it appears that the locality hypothesis emerged from our extended counterfactual analysis relatively undamaged. We have confirmed that Bell's theorem retains its validity under the reconstruction in which the standard realist assumption is replaced with the counterfactual definiteness principle. In consequence, we are faced with the old dilemma in a new guise: either abandon the locality assumption in the form of (SLOC), guaranteeing that a free act of measurement selection does not affect the physical situation that is space-like separated from this measurement, or give up the hypothesis that for every observable there is a true counterfactual predicting what the outcome of its measurement would be. As with the original Bell theorem, we are free to save locality at the expense of the counterfactual hidden variable hypothesis. But, in one respect, our situation has significantly improved. As we argued in sec. 6.3, the counterfactual version of the EPR argument does not hold up. We have rejected Einstein's bold attempt to derive the incompleteness thesis from his locality assumption only. If we are right, then it is possible to retain the locality condition (SLOC) regarding the measurement selection, and at the same time to maintain that when a quantum system is not in its eigenstate, no counterfactual property attribution about it is true. This means that when we choose the anti-realist horn of Bell's dilemma, no measurement-induced non-locality follows suit. EPR-nonlocality, purporting that a distant measurement selection can change the physical state of a local system from an "undefined" to a "definite" one, turns out to be an empty threat. If we accept that the only quantum statements that represent objective physical facts are selected measurements and *actually* revealed outcomes, and if we resist the temptation of interpreting counterfactuals that speak about would-be outcomes as if they referred to categorical properties of systems already present in the actual world, then Einstein's putative "non-locality" fails to contravene the locality condition (SLOC) as applied to measurement selections.

But does this mean that we have eliminated altogether any traces of non-local influences from quantum-mechanical description? It would be much too early to pronounce such a victory, for we haven't yet dealt with the other form of possible non-local interactions, known as outcome dependence. As we recall from our past discussions, the first apparently non-local feature of quantum entangled systems that meets a novice's eye is the correlation between the outcomes revealed in the separate wings of the measuring apparatus. Is this correlation a sign of a direct and superluminal connection between the two distant particles, or can it be explained by reference to a hidden common cause? Unfortunately, we are not ready yet for a serious consideration of this question, because our locality condition (SLOC) cannot be directly applied to outcome-events. As we have explained several times, (SLOC) represents a proper locality condition only if the event in question is an indeterministic one. For a non-actual deterministic event we cannot expect to find a possible, law-obeying world in which this event occurs, while its past remains intact. And yet, we should have the option of considering outcome-events to be classically determined by the initial (hidden) state of the system. Hence, we are in need of a more general locality condition which would overcome this limitation.

One possible verbalization of such a general locality condition may be based on the following consideration. Although for a deterministic contrary-to-fact event $E$ there is no possible world which would keep the entire spatiotemporal region outside its absolute future exactly as it is in the actual world, still the closest possible $E$-world should not contain any primary point of divergence (PPD) that is space-like separated from $E$. The mere fact that the closest $E$-world contains a diverging event $E'$ at a space-like separation from $E$ does not generally constitute a violation of locality, but if locality is to be preserved there must be another point of divergence in the absolute past of $E$ and $E'$ which acts as a common cause of both events. In short, $E'$ cannot be a PPD. The fact that in the above case the counterfactual $E \,\square\!\rightarrow E'$ comes out true does not indicate the existence of any suspicious action at a distance, but rather is a consequence of the common cause bringing about both events $E$ and $E'$. Thus, not surprisingly our proposal for the generalized locality condition will be as follows:

(GLOC)    For all non-contradictory point-events $E$ there is no possible $E$-world that contains a primary point of divergence (PPD) space-like separated from $E$, and such that of all $E$-worlds it is closest to the actual world according to relation SIM.[21]

The condition formulated in (GLOC) is less restrictive than that of (SLOC), as it allows for the situation in which the SIM-closest $E$-world is not the world that has only one PPD at $E$'s location, but instead all its PPD-s are contained in $E$'s absolute past. But it can be verified that

---

[21]    This formulation presupposes that the Limit Assumption (LA′) is satisfied, i.e. that *there are* closest possible $E$-worlds. It is possible to introduce a more general version of (GLOC) not limited by this condition, but it would have to be a bit cumbersome. In my earlier paper (Bigaj 2005, p. 153) I proposed a slightly different version of (GLOC), which excluded the existence of only those closest worlds which have more than one PPD and *for which* E *is one of their PPD's*. Yet this condition seems to me now a bit too weak. To see why let us consider the following example: suppose that in the actual world two space-like separated spin-measurements on two distant wings of the EPR apparatus have been performed in the same direction, and that a moment after completing one of the measurements the experimenter enters the lab and sees that the outcome is "up". Now let us consider a possible situation in which the statement "The experimenter sees the outcome "down"" is true, and let us assume that there is a world in which the pasts of both counterfactually altered experiments are the same as in actuality. It should be quite obvious that we have a case of non-locality here, and yet my 2005 condition is not directly violated, for there is no possible world in which the point where the experimenter sees the altered outcome is one of the PPD's (its PPD is at the location where the outcome was first registered, and not where it was later observed).

(SLOC) may be recovered as the special case of (GLOC) restricted to inde-terministic events. To prove this, let us suppose that $E$ is an indeterministic event, i.e. that there is an $E$-world $w_B(E)$ which is identical with the actual one within the backward light cone of $E$. Notice that in that case all the closest $E$-worlds have to be $w_B(E)$ worlds (no $E$-world $w(E)$ containing any diverging point within the backward-light cone of $E$ can be closer to the actual world than $w_B(E)$ according to SIM, for there will be a spatiotempo-ral region $R$ such that $R \subset \overline{D}_{w(E)}$ and $R \not\subset \overline{D}_{w_B(E)}$). But, of course, if we exclude by (GLOC) the possibility that there is the closest possible $E$-world with some PPD-s space-like separated from $E$, then the only closest possible $E$-world is the world which is identical with the actual one every-where outside $E$'s future light cone. Thus we have established that (GLOC) becomes equivalent to (SLOC) under the assumption that $E$ is indetermin-istic.

The main advantage of (GLOC) is that it is more universal than (SLOC). For instance, let us take a pair of EPR particles for which the same component of spin has been measured in both wings of the apparatus. As we know, the outcomes for the two particles have to be opposite. So, if we consider a possible world in which one of the actual outcomes has been changed, the other, space-like separated outcome has to change accord-ingly. But this fact by itself does not breach the locality condition (GLOC), although (SLOC) is certainly violated. Condition (GLOC) leaves us with an alternative: it is still possible that the closest world with the outcomes switched contains a PPD in the absolute past of both measurements. This unique primary point of divergence could, for instance, be the location at which both particles would have been equipped with a different set of hid-den variables that determines the alternative combination of measurement outcomes, and therefore accounts for the observable correlation without invoking any non-local interaction. But of course in order for this to hap-pen we have to make sure that this single-PPD world is the closest one, i.e. that there are no other admissible worlds in which both measurements changed their outcomes, and whose areas of divergence $\overline{D}$ are smaller. For instance, if it were confirmed that there is another possible world in which the outcomes are switched, and which is identical with the actual world everywhere outside the two forward light cones spreading from the loca-tions of the two measurements, then the locality condition (GLOC) would be immediately violated (this would be the world with one PPD space-like separated from $E$, and it would have to be closest to the actual world due to the principle of the conservation of spin).

267

But how can we decide whether there is a possible world with two correlated outcomes switched, but with the past of both measurements unchanged, without having a direct insight into the hidden initial state of the particles? It appears that the existence of a world of that sort follows as a corollary to the statement regarding the failure of the counterfactual EPR argument that we presented in sec. 6.3.2. There, in order to reject the counterfactual supposition

(6.7)     $[M(X_L, p) \wedge O(X_L, p) = a] \Rightarrow \{ M(Y_L, p) \ \Box\rightarrow [M(X_R, p') \ \Box\rightarrow$
          $O(X_R, p') = a']\}$,

according to which the counterfactual property attribution of the right-hand side system derived from the outcome of the actual $X_L$-measurement remains true even if this measurement is replaced with the alternative one $Y_L$, we invoked the possible world $w(Y_L, X_R, a)$ in which the outcome of the $X_R$-measurement equals $a$, and which is identical to the actual world everywhere outside the two forward light cones (it is one of the worlds depicted in Fig. 6.4). We also noted that the existence of this world does not in any way contradict the locality condition (SLOC) applied to measurement selections. But let us now look at this world from the perspective of the world $w(X_L, a, X_R, a')$, whose existence, guaranteed by (SLOC), makes counterfactual (6.5) true (Fig. 6.2). Seen from this perspective, the world $w(Y_L, X_R, a)$ is a world in which the outcome of $X_R$ was changed, and this change was accompanied by some change in the space-like separated location, while the absolute past of the $X_R$-measurement remained unaltered. Moreover, we know that there is no possible world in which the result of the $X_R$-measurement is the opposite of $a'$, and yet the area outside the forward light-cone of $X_R$ remains identical to that of $w(X_L, a, X_R, a')$ (this world would violate the perfect correlation assumption). From these two facts it follows that the condition expressed in (GLOC) is not satisfied.

It may be noted that the violation of locality which we have discovered here can be proved with the help of (SLOC) only, with no need of the generalized condition (GLOC). This is the case, because the existence of world $w(Y_L, X_R, a)$ entails that the outcome $O(X_R, p') = a'$ is an indeterministic event, as it can occur in a world that has the same past of the measurement as the world in which an alternative outcome has been recorded. Hence, (SLOC) *is* applicable to this case, and because there can be no $(O(X_R, p') = a)$-world which would be identical with the world $w(X_L, a, X_R, a')$ everywhere outside the forward light cone of $p'$, (SLOC) appears to be violated by an outcome-event.

Thus, the extended lesson from the counterfactual analysis of the EPR argument is as follows. Contrary to what Einstein and his collaborators have suggested, the assumption that all true counterfactual property attributions precisely reflect the quantum-mechanical state of the system as given in the state vector does not necessarily lead to parameter non-locality (the non-locality induced by the choice of measurement). However, it leads to a different version of non-locality, associated with the outcomes revealed. Speaking more accurately, the EPR argument offers us a choice: conditionally upon the acceptance of the (counterfactual) completeness of quantum mechanics we can either reject parameter locality and retain outcome locality, or we can retain parameter locality and reject outcome locality. We opt for the second solution, because, as it has been argued before, outcome non-locality seems to be the less offensive of the two to common sense and even to some interpretations of special relativity. All in all, we must admit that the existence of some form of non-local interactions is derivable from the assumption that quantum-mechanical description is complete.

An alternative way of presenting the foregoing result is that if we reject all considered types of non-locality (both measurement- and outcome-induced), we have to accept the counterfactual incompleteness of quantum mechanics. More specifically, from the assumption of full locality it is possible to derive the counterfactual statement (6.7), which entails that for every selected observable $X_R$ the counterfactuals of the form $M(X_R, p') \, \square \rightarrow O(X_R, p') = a'$ will be true in the possible world in which no $X_L$-measurement is performed on the distant particle, given that the $X_L$-measurement actually revealed the complementary value $a$. What is more, it can be easily verified that this consequence can be presented in a seemingly stronger manner, stating that in any no-measurement world every counterfactual $M(X_R, p') \, \square \rightarrow O(X_R, p') = x$ will be true for a particular value $x$. To see this, let us suppose that in the actual world $w_0$ two EPR particles have been created but no measurement has been done. We can now consider one of the closest worlds in which the $X$-measurement on the particle $L$ has been performed, i.e. the world $w$ which differs from the actual one only inside the forward-light cone of $M(X_L, p)$. Obviously, in this particular world the outcome of this measurement is unique, and hence we can call it $a$. According to (6.7), in all possible worlds in which an alternative measurement on $L$ has been made (including the trivial measurement represented by the identity operator, i.e. no measurement at all), and which are closest to $w$, the counterfactual $M(X_R, p') \,\square\!\!\rightarrow O(X_R, p') = a'$ comes out true. But plainly $w_0$ is one of the closest worlds to $w$, and hence the above counterfactual has to hold in it, which was to be demonstrated. It turns out, then, that the "uncompromising" locality assumption implies not only some form of incompleteness of quantum mechanics, but a full-blown counterfactual version of the hidden-variable theory.[22]

Finally, we can combine this conclusion with the lesson from Bell's theorem. As we have argued, its counterfactual version leads to the usual dilemma one of whose horns is the rejection of the (counterfactual) hidden variable theory, while the other horn is the rejection of the parameter locality. When coupled with the renewed EPR argument, Bell's theorem essentially steers us in the direction of the same sort of disjunction as in the case of the sole EPR argument (but this time, of course, the dilemma is not conditional upon the acceptance of the completeness of quantum mechanics): either the measurement-induced non-locality, or the outcome-induced non-locality has to be allowed. It is quite unlikely that a decisive argument for the stronger version of non-locality could turn up (taking into account Stapp's sustained but unsuccessful attempts), hence for the time being we are free to assume that the only type of non-locality present in quantum mechanics is the non-local influence exerted by the indeterministic and uncontrollable outcome selection that Nature makes when a quantum measurement is made.

---

[22] I would like to compare this result with the conclusion of a different EPR-like counterfactual argument which I formulated in (Bigaj 2005). There I was able to derive from the locality assumption (GLOC) the counterfactuals announcing the existence of definite outcomes for *joint* spin measurements carried out on both EPR particles in *the same direction*. While the existence of such true counterfactuals certainly proves the incompleteness of the standard formalism of quantum mechanics, surprisingly it does not lead to the full counterfactual hidden variable theory. I presented an argument in (2005) showing that in this situation it is still possible to maintain that measurements taken on each particle *separately* don't have their outcomes counterfactually determined, without violating (GLOC). Of course the key thing is not to assume that true counterfactuals about would-be outcomes are accompanied by categorical properties of the system which should be preserved in the closest possible worlds according to the semantics of counterfactuals.

# Chapter 7

# COMPARISONS AND CONCLUSIONS

A t the end of the book I will briefly review a few of the results that may have some element of novelty about them, and I will make some comparisons with the existing approaches for which I found no place in the main text. In the last chapter I proposed two ways of expressing the locality condition in the form of (SLOC) and (GLOC). The first one—the semantic locality condition—claims to reflect some common intuitions regarding the non-existence of causal influences between space-like separated events when the acting event is indeterministic, i.e. not causally conditioned by its absolute past. The requirement encapsulated in (SLOC) amounts to the stipulation that in order to preserve locality, no nomologically necessary consequences of a given event can occur in space-like separated regions. The generalized locality condition (GLOC), in turn, extends the domain of applicability of (SLOC) to all types of events, no matter whether they are indeterministic or causally connected with their past. Roughly speaking, (GLOC) excludes the possibility that the occurrence of a contrary-to-fact event $E$ could bring into existence a new fact space-like separated from $E$ and not affected causally by its absolute past (whose absolute past would be exactly the same as in the actual world).[1] While it can hardly be expected that these two conditions could exhaust all possible modes and ways of expressing our diverse intuitions associated with the notion of locality, I believe that they can cover the majority of cases considered in connection with quantum entangled systems.[2]

---

[1]  This interpretation of the generalized condition of locality seems to be akin to the necessary condition for the exclusion of superluminal influences that was proposed by Maudlin in (1994, p. 130). Maudlin's criterion of locality reads that "it *cannot* be the case for spacelike separated A and B that A would not have occurred had B not occurred *and everything in A's past light cone been the same*."

[2]  It may be asked whether my expressions (SLOC) and (GLOC) can cover the cases in which the non-local causal correlations are statistical only, and not deterministic. For it may be pointed out that sometimes the non-local influence originating in a given event $E$ results not in the definitive occurrence of a space-like separated event $E'$, but rather in lowering or raising the probability of the occurrence of $E'$ (see chapter 1 for some examples). In response to this I'd like to point out, first,

It should be stressed that the need to introduce condition (GLOC) as an extension of (SLOC) comes from our accepted way of analyzing counterfactual conditionals, clearly different from that of Lewis's. Within Lewis's original approach to counterfactual semantics, (SLOC) appears to be entirely sufficient, for Lewis's criteria of similarity, employing the notion of "miraculous events", ensure that in the preponderant number of cases there will be possible antecedent-worlds with the absolute past of the antecedent-event unchanged. Even when we consider a deterministic event $P$ whose *lawful* occurrence requires that the past be counterfactually altered, we are allowed to conceive a *law-breaking* world in which a small and temporary suspension of the laws occurs just before $P$, allowing for it to happen without any change in the past. And—as Lewis argues (see sec. 2.3)—in the majority of cases this world should be judged, according to his criteria, as being closer to the actual one than the no-miracle world whose area of divergence stretches into the past.

However, as we demonstrated in sec. 2.3.2, Lewis's multi-tiered set of similarity criteria clearly produces wrong valuations for the counterfactuals that connect space-like separated and yet nomologically correlated events in quantum mechanics. In consequence, it becomes impossible to express the locality condition in terms of the counterfactual connective (for example with the help of the formulas (L1) or (L2)—see sec. 6.1), as all counterfactuals linking space-like separated contrary-to-fact events would come out false by fiat. This may look like an easy victory for the defenders of the classical intuition of locality, but is in fact too easy a victory to be genuine. As should be pretty clear, even in the situation in which there exists a contrary-to-fact event $P$ such that all law-obeying possible $P$-worlds contain a new event $Q$, space-like separated from $P$, while being identical to the actual world in the joint absolute past of $P$ and $Q$, still Lewis's crite-

---

that if such a statistical correlation is to be seen as truly causal, and not merely a "side effect" of some hidden common cause, then the probabilities in question have to be interpreted objectively, as the measure of some "propensities" or "powers" of the remote system. But if that is the case, then probability ascriptions can enter the overall physical characterisation of spacetime regions, and as such will constitute part of the "matching" criterion between possible world and the actual world. Consequently, the world in which the occurrence of $E$ changes the objective probability of the occurrence of the space-like separated event $E'$ would diverge from the actual world in the area outside $E$'s forward light cone, and the violation of (SLOC) or (GLOC) would follow.

ria will prescribe that the counterfactual $P \;\Box\!\!\rightarrow Q$ is false.[3] For, as we have argued, the miracle-world in which $Q$ is allowed not to occur will be judged closer to the actual world than any of the law-obeying worlds with two points of divergence: $P$ and $Q$. And yet it seems pretty clear that this is a perfect case of a violation of the locality condition.

The reason why Lewis's similarity criterion does not work is that it is based on the pre-relativistic, classical intuitions of space-time. Classically, all causal consequences of a given contrary-to-fact event $P$ affect the same area of space-time that is already affected by the occurrence of $P$, namely the entire area located "above" the absolute hypersurface of simultaneity that cuts through the location of $P$ (the classical absolute future). Consequently, eliminating a single causal consequence of $P$ with the help of a tiny miracle cannot bring any net profit in the similarity comparison, as it will not diminish the area of the (potential) discrepancy between the possible world and the actual one. On the other hand, taking into account that in the relativistic approach space-like separated points have distinct futures (forward light cones) that only partially overlap, we can see that the world in which the nomological correlation between space-like separated events is cut by a miracle will have a lesser area of divergence of particular facts than the law-obeying world.

We should not forget, however, that there exists an alternative to Lewis's semantic analysis which, even though it makes some use of miracles, does so in a limited way that does not allow for the above-mentioned problem to arise. What I have in mind is one possible version of the approach called by Lewis "asymmetry by fiat", adjusted to the relativistic case. According to it, in order to consider a counterfactual $P \;\Box\!\!\rightarrow Q$ with $P$ denoting a deterministic event we have to invoke a possible world in which a miracle $M$ occurs right before $P$, so that the entire backward light cone of $P$ remains unchanged, and in which *no additional miracles are permitted* (everything else except $M$ occurs lawfully). If $Q$ is true in all such worlds, the counterfactual is rendered true; otherwise it is false. This interpretation does not imply that all counterfactuals connecting space-like separated events are false, and yet it does not require any extension of the locality condition in the form of (GLOC). For even deterministic contrary-to-fact events will have their absolute past guaran-

---

[3]   The situation is even worse: Lewis's method of evaluating counterfactuals ensures that the counterfactual $P \;\Box\!\!\rightarrow \sim\!Q$ should have the value of truth. This obviously makes the locality condition (L1) satisfied by fiat, as $\sim\!Q$ is assumed to be true in the actual world.

teed to match the actual world, and in this case all violations of the condition expressed in (SLOC) will amount to the genuine breaching of locality. Thus, the "one miracle only" approach seems to be a serious alternative to the approach developed and defended in this book.

Let me illustrate the main differences between those two approaches using the example considered in (Clifton *et al.* 1992). In their article Clifton, Pagonis and Pitowsky (CPP) selected a GHZ-state example in order to prove that the EPR argument is not sound, as both of its assumptions (locality and the criterion of reality) fail independently of the issue of the completeness of quantum mechanics. While I have already mentioned the second part of their work (regarding the issue of the elements of reality—cf. sec. 6.4), I haven't yet analyzed their argument in favor of the first claim that locality fails in the three-particle GHZ example. This argument consists of two steps. In the first step, CPP show that the assumptions of result determinism (in a counterfactual interpretation) plus setting-to-result locality lead to a contradiction with quantum-mechanical predictions. This is the result which confirms what we have already learned from the counterfactual version of Bell's theorem (sec. 6.3). The second step purports to show that the assumption of result-to-result locality together with quantum-mechanical predictions lead to result determinism. Putting these two results together we obtain the straightforward conclusion that the joint assumptions of setting-to-result and result-to-result localities imply a contradiction with quantum-mechanical predictions regarding the GHZ state.

Comparing CPP's results with the conclusions of my analysis based on the C1 approach to counterfactuals, we should immediately notice that they are fully congruous. Their step two corresponds to my counterfactual version of the original EPR argument given in chapter 6, according to which the quantum-mechanical predictions regarding the singlet-spin state, and the assumption of QM's completeness (which implies the negation of result determinism) do entail a violation of outcome-induced locality (in CPP's terminology "result-to-result" locality). And, as we have noted earlier, step one is in agreement with the counterfactual reinterpretation of Bell's theorem advanced in sec. 6.3. However, their method for arriving at these conclusions differs substantially from the method followed in this book, as they do not formulate any condition similar to (GLOC) which would be applicable to the result-to-result case of non-locality. Below, I will briefly review CPP's step two, stressing its dissimilarities with my own approach as well as its weak points.

CPP's derivation relies on the initial presupposition that in the actual world no measurement has been performed on any of the three GHZ particles. However, when we counterfactually consider the joint measurement of $X_1$, $Y_2$ and $Y_3$ (for an explication of the symbols used in the current reconstruction see sec. 4.1.1), we know that quantum mechanics predicts that the product of the three outcomes $x_1y_2y_3$ has to equate $+1$. This leads to the following counterfactual prediction:

$$(7.1) \qquad X_1Y_2Y_3\lambda \;\Box\!\!\to [(x_1 = +1 \wedge y_2 = +1 \wedge y_3 = +1) \vee$$
$$(x_1 = -1 \wedge y_2 = -1 \wedge y_3 = +1) \vee$$
$$(x_1 = +1 \wedge y_2 = -1 \wedge y_3 = -1) \vee$$
$$(x_1 = -1 \wedge y_2 = +1 \wedge y_3 = -1)]$$

where $\lambda$ as usual represents the complete description of the initial state of the three particles. The standard interpretation of (7.1) implies that there have to be up to four types of the closest possible antecedent-worlds, each containing a different combination of permitted outcomes. And now CPP claim (pp. 118-119) that if we assume that none of these four worlds is closer to the actual world than the other three, as befits the completeness assumption (or the negation of result determinism), the following two counterfactuals are derivable:

$$(7.2) \qquad (X_1Y_2Y_3\lambda \wedge y_2 = +1 \wedge y_3 = +1) \;\Box\!\!\to x_1 = +1$$
$$(X_1Y_2Y_3\lambda \wedge y_2 = -1 \wedge y_3 = +1) \;\Box\!\!\to x_1 = -1$$

Subsequently, CPP state that (7.2) implies the Lewisian causal (counterfactual) dependence between space-like separated events (in this case, the outcomes $y_2$ and $x_1$), and that "such dependence can only be blocked by abandoning our supposition that *both* pairs of worlds, defined by the result combination $(+1, +1, +1)$ and $(-1, -1, +1)$ are amongst the closest $X_1Y_2Y_3\lambda$-worlds to @ (i.e. the actual world—addition mine)" (p. 119). While I agree that the truth of (7.2) does imply, under Lewis's "miracle-permitting" semantics, that the locality requirement is violated (the truth of (7.2) in fact comes very close to violating the locality condition (L2) presented in sec. 6.1), I question that its derivation has anything to do with the issue of result determinism. Under the assumption that there are four $X_1Y_2Y_3\lambda$-worlds with four combinations of outcomes, the counterfactuals (7.2) come out true independently of whether some of these four worlds are closer to the actual one than the others, or all of them are equally close. To see this, let us suppose that the world containing the combination $(+1, +1, +1)$ is closer to the actual world than the world $(-1, -1, +1)$, reflecting the fact that the first combination of outcomes is predetermined in the actual world. Still, the second counterfactual in (7.2) would come out true, according to the standard Lewisian truth conditions, since its truth is to be evaluated not in the closest $X_1Y_2Y_3\lambda$-world, but in the closest $X_1Y_2Y_3\lambda$-and-$(y_2=-1)$-and-$(y_3=+1)$-world, and the world with the combination of outcomes $(-1, -1, +1)$ is obviously such a world.[4] Consequently, it looks like CPP can validly replace their result with the stronger claim that result-to-result non-locality follows from quantum-mechanical predictions alone, regardless of the interpretation of quantum-mechanical formalism. But this surely seems suspicious. Such a strong result is highly unlikely to be derivable in such a simple way.

Indeed, the fact that we were able to reach this surprising conclusion results from the insufficient care with which CPP treat the paramount issue of the counterfactual semantics that underlies their arguments. They should decide whether they want to follow the "miracle" semantics (either in its full, unrestricted version, or according to the "only one miracle" approach) or the "no-miracle" semantics. Let us assume first that their intended approach was the one that uses one small miracle in order to ensure the perfect match in the past of the antecedent-event. In that case (7.2) does indeed require the assumption of indeterminism in order to go through. For let us suppose that the combination of outcomes $(+1, +1, +1)$ is predetermined in the actual world, and that the determining factor lies in the common past of all three measurements. Then, in order to evaluate the second counterfactual in (7.2), we have to consider the situation in which a small miracle before the $Y_2$-measurement ensures that its result will be $-1$, without altering the initial state. In such a case the outcomes of the two other measurements will have to remain the same (as they are determined by the initial state of the three particles), and the entire counterfactual will turn out false. Note, however, that the world in which the truth value of the second counterfactual is decided is not the $(-1, -1, +1)$-world, but rather the world with the law-breaking combination of outcomes $(-1, +1, +1)$.

If, on the other hand, we decide to follow the no-miracle semantics of counterfactuals advocated in this book, then both counterfactuals in (7.2) will have to be accepted as true, independently of the issue of determinism. Strictly speaking, when we assume that the complete initial state symbol-

---

[4] Pagonis, Redhead and LaRivière apparently overlooked this flaw in their critical analysis of CPP's argument (see Pagonis *et al.* 1996).

ized by $\lambda$ determines the outcomes of the measurements to be $(+1, +1, +1)$, the second counterfactual in (7.2) will become vacuously true, for the statements in the antecedent are clearly contradictory (it cannot be the case that $\lambda$ coexists lawfully with the results $y_2 = -1$ and $y_3 = +1$). But even if we modify CPP's counterfactuals a bit by eliminating the factor $\lambda$ from the antecedent altogether, still their truth will be preserved. This is the case, because in order to evaluate the second counterfactual in (7.2) with $\lambda$ crossed out, we have to consider a lawful possible world in which $y_2 = -1$ and $y_3 = +1$, and the only way to achieve this is to "go back in time" and change the initial state into a different one $\lambda'$ such that it determines the combination of outcomes to be $(-1, -1, +1)$. Obviously, in this world the consequent of the counterfactual holds true.

It should be clear now why the extended locality condition (GLOC) is needed. The truth of the counterfactuals (7.2) no longer automatically guarantees the existence of non-local correlations in this case, because this truth can result from a common cause acting in a perfectly classical, sub-luminal way. Lewisian counterfactual dependence ceases to be a universal criterion of causation. In order for non-local causation to manifest itself, the possible world in which the second counterfactual in (7.2) is evaluated would have to coincide with the actual world within the joint past of all three measurements. But we know that this cannot occur. The lawful character of this possible world, together with the presupposition of determinism, imply that the past of the measurements *has* to be changed. Consequently, the closest possible world in which the antecedent of the second counterfactual in (7.2) is satisfied has one primary point of divergence located at the point of the creation of the three particles, and the condition (GLOC) remains satisfied. We have, therefore, finally confirmed CPP's claim that the violation of locality indeed follows only under the assumption of indeterminism.

One of the main reasons why I decided to follow the no-miracle approach to quantum counterfactuals instead of the "one miracle only" approach is that the applicability of the latter is restricted to well-localized antecedent-events only, whereas the former can be generalized to virtually all types of counterfactuals with the help of either the C1+ or C2+ semantics (cf. chapter 5).[5] In the "one miracle only" semantics it is not clear how

---

[5]    Maudlin in his (1994, p. 129) gives an analysis of a situation involving billiard balls which confirms that his approach to counterfactuals is exactly like mine. He explicitly accepts the fact that counterfactual dependence between distant events

to evaluate counterfactuals with complex antecedents, consisting for example of finite conjunctions or disjunctions of single-event statements (compare this situation with the analyses done in sections 5.2 and 5.4 which show how (C1+) and (C2+) handle these cases).[6] Even more troublesome are the general statements that require alterations of many individual facts of the matter at once (as in Lewis's famous example "If kangaroos had no tails, they would topple over", whose antecedent implies not only many individual statements of the form "Kangaroo $x$ has no tail", "Kangaroo $y$ has no tail", etc., but most likely also entails certain contrary-to-fact statements about kangaroos' ancestors, the way they evolved, their impact on the environment, etc.). For in such a case we would be at a complete loss to determine where to insert a miracle keeping the past (of what exactly?) intact.

Another significant distinction that was made in this book is the specification of two possible semantic interpretations of counterfactuals (C1) and (C2) with their appropriate generalizations (C1+) and (C2+). This distinction in turn leads to the differentiation between two available ways of interpreting quantum property attributions, which I referred to as "conservative" and "liberal" (see sec. 6.3). The conservative interpretation of quantum properties is based on the C2 reading of counterfactuals and roughly states that for a quantum system to have a definite measurable property, the same outcome has to be consistently revealed in all the possible worlds that share the absolute past of the measurement. The liberal property attribution, on the other hand, presumes that the outcome is preserved in all the worlds which agree with each other in the entire area outside the absolute future of the measurement (this obviously stems from the C1 version of the counterfactual semantics). From these characteristics it follows directly that if a system possesses the conservative property with respect to a given outcome $a$ of observable $A$ (meaning that the counterfactual $M(A) \; \Box \rightarrow_{C2} \; O(A) = a$ is true), then it also possesses the corresponding liberal property (expressed in the true counterfactual $M(A) \; \Box \rightarrow_{C1} \; O(A) = a$), but not *vice versa*. It is possible, then, that because of a no-

---

sometimes does not indicate that they are directly causally connected, but shows the existence of a common cause.

[6] For example, when the antecedent has the form of a conjunction of two statements $P_1$ and $P_2$, referring to two distinct point-like events, it is not clear whether we should consider a possible world with two miracles for each contrary-to-fact event separately, or only one miracle in the common past of both $P_1$ and $P_2$. It is even more hopeless to expect this approach to work in the case of such natural-language antecedents as, for instance, "Everybody hates somebody who does not hate them".

mological connection between space-like separated events we can infer the existence of a liberal property pertaining to a given system, but this connection cannot guarantee that a conservative property is present as well.

We have made every effort not to prematurely eliminate either of the two readings of counterfactuals, so all the subsequent analyses were carried out in two versions. Fortunately the condition of locality, although in principle expressible with the help of counterfactuals, was freed from the ambiguity connected with the two possible choices of the underlying semantics, thanks to the universality of the formulations (SLOC) and (GLOC). Thus, the remaining dependence on the selected semantics affected only the property attributions (and, as a result, the meaning of the counterfactual version of realism of possessed values), as well as counterfactual statements regarding the selection of alternative measurement settings.

Surprisingly, the results of the analyses of the two most important arguments in the conceptual study of quantum-mechanical non-locality, i.e. the EPR argument and Bell's theorem, turned out to be relatively independent on the underlying semantics. Both C1 and C2 counterfactual reinterpretations of Bell's theorem, for instance, confirmed the validity of its conclusion, according to which the counterfactual assumption of realism and the locality assumption (SLOC) are inconsistent with quantum-mechanical predictions. Similarly, the counterfactual EPR argument turned out to be invalid under both counterfactual reconstructions, albeit for different reasons. When assuming interpretation (C1), the invalidity of the EPR is a result of the rejection of Einstein's criterion of reality in its counterfactual reformulation. However, under the C2 interpretation, no such premise is necessary, as the derivation fails at its initial step that unsuccessfully attempts to infer the property attribution of one system from the outcome of the remote system. Consequently, Einstein's criterion of reality may be preserved under the stricter reading of property attribution. And it is actually quite reasonable to expect that while counterfactuals of the form $M(A) \; \Box \rightarrow_{C1} O(A) = a$ do not have to be associated with an existing categorical property of the system when they are derived from the outcomes revealed in the remote system, still the truth of the stronger counterfactual $M(A) \; \Box \rightarrow_{C2} O(A) = a$ may give us good grounds to believe in the existence of some sort of categorical property of the local system. But obviously Einstein's criterion of reality applied to the C2 property attributions does not seem to be likely to lead to inconsistencies with quantum-mechanical formalism, as was the case with the C1 interpretation (see sec. 4.2.6).

However, there seems to be one important discrepancy between the reconstructions based on (C1) and (C2). At the end of chapter 6 (sec. 6.6) we noted that even though the counterfactual EPR argument fails to establish that the completeness of the probabilistic description of quantum mechanics entails a violation of EPR-locality (locality that asserts that the physical state of the local system is independent of the distant measurement), still under the C1 reading of counterfactuals it is possible to derive some sort of outcome-to-outcome non-locality from the EPR analysis. This residual form of non-locality results as a corollary to the negative conclusion of the counterfactual analysis of the validity of EPR. In other words, the EPR argument indeed fails to establish its intended conclusion, but the price which is to be paid for this result is the acceptance of the fact that the alteration of the outcome in one system can change the distant outcome, *while everything inside the past light cone of the distant measurement remains the same.* This obviously contradicts the locality condition (GLOC). But it seems that in the case of semantics (C2) no such price has to be paid, for the EPR argument is rejected at its preliminary step. Consequently, it looks like counterfactuals (C2) afford us a means of formulating a fully local interpretation of the standard anti-realist quantum mechanics, with no outcome-to-outcome non-locality present. Or do they?

Unfortunately (or fortunately, depending on your perspective) this is not the case. It turns out that the aforementioned discrepancy is spurious, and that in fact the interpretation (C2) leads to the same sort of violation of outcome-independence as (C1). To see this, let us consider the following argument. Suppose that we have created two particles in the singlet-spin state, which implies that there is a perfect correlation between spin-components measured in the same direction on two particles. If the locality condition (GLOC) is to be preserved, we have to assume that for every possible world $w(\sigma_x^L = +1, \sigma_x^R = -1)$ in which the $x$-component of spin is measured on both particles with the outcomes given, the closest world $w(\sigma_x^L = -1, \sigma_x^R = +1)$ with the opposite outcomes will differ from $w(\sigma_x^L = +1, \sigma_x^R = -1)$ somewhere in the common past of both measurements. But this in turn implies that for every world $w(\sigma_x^L = +1, \sigma_x^R = -1)$ there is *no* world $w(\sigma_x^L = -1, \sigma_x^R = +1)$ which would have exactly the same absolute past of the $L$-measurement as $w(\sigma_x^L = +1, \sigma_x^R = -1)$ (if there were such a world, it would obviously be closer to $w(\sigma_x^L = +1, \sigma_x^R = -1)$ than the worlds with the "common cause" in the past, and hence (GLOC) would be violated). However, this last statement leads to the conclusion that in the world in which no left-hand side measurement is performed, there is one value $a$ (equal either +1 or −1) for which the counterfactual $M(\sigma_x^L) \; \square \rightarrow_{C2}$ $\sigma_x^L = a$ is true. For, to evaluate this counterfactual we have to select all possible worlds that share the absolute past of the $\sigma_x^L$-measurement, and we have just established that there can be no two such worlds with two different outcomes +1 and −1. In conclusion, we have proven that (GLOC) leads to the assumption of the incompleteness of quantum-mechanical formalism, and by transposition this shows that when we assume that the probabilistic description of standard quantum mechanics is complete, we have to accept the violation of (GLOC) with respect to the outcomes of space-like separated measurements.

We have now achieved an almost perfect congruity between the results produced by both interpretations (C1) and (C2) of quantum counterfactuals. Let us then finally summarize them for quick reference. In its most condensed form, the main conclusion of the book is that no matter what available interpretation of counterfactuals we decide to follow, there is no need in standard quantum mechanics for measurement-induced non-locality. Unraveling the meaning of this compact thought we may repeat what has already been said several times: all attempts at showing that there exists some sort of superluminal influence between a selection of local measurement and a distant physical system, including Stapp's counterfactual proofs and EPR's famous reasoning, fail. The reasons for their failure are multitudinous, the majority having something to do with requiring unreasonably strong premises for the argument. Those premises may be: a hidden assumption of realism, a questionable form of the locality condition, or Einstein's criterion of reality which, even though it looks innocuous, can be shown to lead by itself to a conflict with quantum-mechanical predictions. Consequently I believe that there are no reasons for accepting any of the locality violations that were presented in the first column of the table in sec. 1.6, including the famous Einstein-nonlocality.

However, our counterfactual analysis confirms the view that is held by many commentators[7]: some sort of non-locality is indeed necessary in order to account for the observable phenomena in quantum mechanics. This non-locality manifests itself in the violation of the generalized condition (GLOC) applied to the results of measurements. More specifically, it can be claimed that a change in the outcome revealed in a local measurement is sometimes accompanied by a change in the physical situation of a remote system which cannot be accounted for by the common cause hypothesis. We have proved that when a standard, anti-realist interpretation of quan-

---

[7] For instance by Maudlin (1994).

tum mechanics in the counterfactual form is accepted, the outcome-induced non-locality follows under both available interpretations of counterfactuals. And because Bell's result establishes that realistic interpretations of quantum mechanics are doomed to imply even stronger version of non-locality (Bell-nonlocality), it looks like there is no escape from some sort of superluminal influence in the quantum realm. What precisely are the consequences of this claim for the relations between quantum mechanics and special theory of relativity, is an altogether different topic, which lies beyond the intended scope of this book.[8]

---

[8] The book (Maudlin 1994) that we referred to many times here offers a deep analysis of the problem of the relations between quantum mechanics and relativity. For more recent development of this subject see e.g. (Myrvold 2002, 2003).

# Bibliography

Aharonov, Y., Bergmann, P.G., and Lebowitz, J.L.: 1964, "Time-Symmetry in the Quantum Process of Measurement", *Physical Review* 134B, 1410-1416.

Albert, D.: 1992, *Quantum Mechanics and Experience*, Harvard University Press, Cambridge (Mass.).

Albert, D. and Loewer, B.: 1988, "Interpreting the Many Worlds Interpretation", *Synthese* 77, 195-213.

Bedford, D and Stapp, H.P.: 1995, "Bell's Theorem in an Indeterministic Universe", *Synthese* 102, 139-164.

Bell, J.: 1964, "On the Einstein-Podolsky-Rosen Paradox", *Physics* 1, reprinted in (Bell 1987), 14-21.

Bell, J.: 1987, *Speakable and Unspeakable in Quantum Mechanics*, Cambridge University Press, Cambridge.

Bell, J.: 1987a, "On the Problem of Hidden Variables in Quantum Mechanics", in: (Bell 1987), 1-21.

Bell, J.: 1987b, "The Theory of Local Beables", in (Bell 1987), 52-62.

Bell, J.: 1987c, "Bertlmann's Socks and the Nature of Reality", in: (Bell 1987), 139-157.

Bennett, J.: 1984, "Counterfactuals and Temporal Direction", *The Philosophical Review* XCIII (1) 57-91.

Bennett, J.: 2003, *A Philosophical Guide to Conditionals*, Clarendon Press, Oxford.

Bigaj, T.: 2001, "Three-valued Logic, Indeterminacy and Quantum Mechanics", *Journal of Philosophical Logic* 30, 97-119.

Bigaj, T.: 2003a, "The Common Cause Explanation for Quantum Correlations of the EPR Type", *Justification, Truth, and Belief*, www.jtb-forum.pl

Bigaj, T.: 2004a, "Counterfactuals and Spatiotemporal Events", *Synthese* 142 (1), 1-20.

Bigaj, T.: 2004b, "Counterfactual Logic and the Hardy Paradox: Remarks on Shimony and Stein's Criticism of Stapp's Proof", preprint, *Philosophy of Science Archive*, Pittsburgh, http://philsci-archive.pitt.edu/archive/00001771/

Bigaj, T.: 2005, "Counterfactual Locality and EPR Arguments", in: A. Brożek, J.J. Jadacki and W. Strawiński (eds.), *Logic, Methodology and Philosophy of Science at Warsaw University*, vol. 2, WN Semper, Warsaw, 149-159.

Bigaj, T.: 2006, "Counterfactuals and Non-locality of Quantum Mechanics: The Bedford-Stapp Version of the GHZ Theorem", *Foundations of Science*, forthcoming.

Bird, A.: 1998, "Dispositions and Antidotes", *The Philosophical Quarterly* 48 (191), 227-234

Bohm, D.:1951, *Quantum Theory*, Prentice-Hall, Englewood Cliffs.

Bohr, N.: 1935, "Can Quantum Mechanical Description of Reality Be Considered Complete?", *Physical Review* 48, 696-702.

Bub, J.: 1997, *Interpreting the Quantum World*, Cambridge University Press, Cambridge.

Busch, P.: 2002, "EPR-Bell Tests with Unsharp Observables and Relativistic Quantum Measurement", in: (Placek & Butterfield 2002), 175-193.

Butterfield, J.: 1992, "David Lewis Meets John Bell", *Philosophy of Science* 59, 26-43.

Clauser, J.F., Horne, M.A., Shimony, A. and Holt, R.A.: 1969. "Proposed Experiment to Test Local Hidden-Variable Theories", *Physical Review Letters* 23, 880-884.

Clifton, R., Pagonis, C. and Pitowsky, I.: 1992, "Relativity, Quantum Mechanics and EPR', in: D. Hull, M. Forbes and K. Okruhlik (eds.), *PSA 1992*, Vol. 1, East Lansing, Michigan, 114-128.

Clifton R., Butterfield, J., and Redhead, M.: 1990, "Nonlocal Influences and Possible Worlds", *British Journal for the Philosophy of Science* 41, 5-58.

Collins, J., Hall, N., and Paul, L.A. (eds.): 2004, *Causation and Counterfactuals*, The MIT Press, Cambridge (Mass.)-London.

Cushing, J. and McMullin, E. (eds.): 1989, *Philosophical Consequences of Quantum Theory. Reflections on Bell's Theorem*. University of Notre Dame Press, Notre Dame.

Čapek, M. (ed.): 1976, *The Concepts of Space-Time*, D. Reidel, Dordrecht.

Dalla Chiara, M., Giuntini, R., Greechie, R. (eds.): 2004, *Reasoning in Quantum Theory*, Kluwer, Dordrecht.

Dickson, M.: 1994, "Stapp's Theorem Without Counterfactual Commitments: Why It Fails Nonetheless", *Studies in the History and Philosophy of Science* 24 (5), 791-814.

Dickson, M: 1998, *Quantum Chance and Non-locality*, Cambridge University Press, Cambridge.

Dickson, M: 2002, "Bohr on Bell: A Proposed Reading of Bohr and Its Implications for Bell's Theorem" in: (Placek & Butterfield 2002), 19-35.

Dickson, M, Clifton, R.: 1994, "Stapp's Algebraic Argument for Nonlocality", *Physical Review* A 49(5), 4251-4256.

Earman, J.: 1986, *A Primer on Determinism*, D. Reidel, Dordrecht.

Eberhard, P.H.: 1977, "Bell's Theorem without Hidden Variables", *Il Nuovo Cimento* 38B (1), 75-80.

Eberhard, P.H.: 1978, "Bell's Theorem and the Different Concepts of Locality", *Il Nuovo Cimento* 46B (2), 392-419.

Einstein, A., Podolsky, B., and Rosen, N.: 1935, "Can Quantum-Mechanical Description of Physical Reality Be Considered Complete?", *Physical Review* 48, 696-702.

Elga, A.: 2001, "Statistical Mechanics and the Asymmetry of Counterfactual Dependence", *Philosophy of Science* 68, S313-S324.

Esfeld, M.: 2001, "Lewis' Causation and Quantum Correlations", in: W. Spohn, M. Ledwig and M. Esfeld (eds.), *Current Issues in Causation*, Parderborn, Mentis, 175-189.

Esfeld, M.: 2004, "Quantum Entanglement and a Metaphysics of Relations", *Studies in the History and Philosophy of Modern Physics* 35B, 601-617.

Fellows, F.: 1988, "Comment on 'Bell's Theorem and the Foundations of Quantum Physics'", *American Journal of Physics* 56 (6), 567-568.

Field, H.: 2003, "Causation in a Physical World", in: M.J. Loux, D.W. Zimmerman, *The Oxford Handbook of Metaphysics*, OUP, Oxford, 435-460.

Fine, A.: 1981, "Correlations and Physical Locality", in: P.D. Asquith and R.N. Giere, *PSA 1980*, East Lansing

Fine, A.: 1986, *The Shaky Game: Einstein, Realism, and the Quantum Theory*, University of Chicago Press, Chicago.

Fine, K.: 1975, review of D. Lewis, *Counterfactuals*, *Mind* 84, 451-458.

Finkelstein, J.: 1998, "Yet Another Comment on Nonlocal Character of Quantum Theory", preprint quant-ph/9801011

Finkelstein, J.: 1999, "Space-time Counterfactuals", *Synthese* 119, 287-298.

Ghirardi, G. and Grassi, R: 1994, "Outcome Predictions and Property Attribution: the EPR Argument Reconsidered", *Studies in the History and Philosophy of Science* 25 (3), 397-423.

✟Gibbins, P.: 1983, "Quantum Logic and Ensembles", in: R. Swinburne (ed.), *Space, Time and Causality*, D. Reidel, Dordrecht, 191-205.

Greechie, R.J. and Gudder, S.P.: 1973, "Quantum Logics", in: C.A. Hooker (ed.) *Contemporary Research in the Foundation and Philosophy of Quantum Theory*, Reidel, Dordrecht, 143-173.

Greenberger, D.; Horne, M.; Shimony, A., and Zeilinger, A.: 1990, "Bell's Theorem without Inequalities", *American Journal of Physics* 58, 1131-1143.

Griffiths, R.B.: 1999, "Consistent Quantum Counterfactuals", *Physical Review A* 60 (1), R5-R8.

✟ Griffiths, R.B.: 2001, *Consistent Quantum Theory*, CUP, Cambridge.

Guy, R.A. and Deltete, R.J.: 1988, "Note on 'Bell's Theorem and the Foundations of Quantum Physics'", *American Journal of Physics* 56 (6) 565-566.

Haack, S.: 1996, *Deviant Logic, Fuzzy Logic*, 2nd edition, The University of Chicago Press, Chicago.

Hardy, L: 1992, "Quantum Mechanics, Local Realistic Theories, and Lorentz-invariant Realistic Theories", *Physical Review Letters* 68, 2981-2984.

Hawthorn, J. and M. Silberstein: 1995, "For Whom the Bell Arguments Toll?", *Synthese* 102, 99-138.

Healey, R.: 1991, "Holism and Nonseparability", *Journal of Philosophy* 88, 393-421.

Healey, R.: 1994, "Nonseparability and Causal Explanation", *Studies in History and Philosophy of Modern Physics* 25, 337-374.

Healey, R.: 2004, "Holism and Nonseparability in Physics", *The Stanford Encyclopedia of Philosophy (Winter 2004 Edition)*, Edward N. Zalta (ed.), URL = <http://plato.stanford.edu/archives/win2004/entries/physics-holism/>.

Horwich, P.: 1987, *Asymmetries in Time*, The MIT Press, Cambridge (Mass.), London.

Howard, D.: 1985, "Einstein on Locality and Separability", *Studies in History and Philosophy of Science* 16, 171-201.

Howard, D.: 1989, "Holism, Separability, and the Metaphysical Implications of the Bell Experiments", in: (Cushing & McMullin 1989), 224-253.

Howard, D.: 1997, "Space-time and Separability: Problems of Identity and Individuation in Fundamental Physics", in: R.S. Cohen, M. Horne and J. Stachel (eds.),

*Potentiality, Entanglement and Passion-at-a-Distance*, Kluwer, Dordrecht, 113-141.

Hughes, R.I.G.: 1989, *The Structure and Interpretation of Quantum Mechanics*, Harvard University Press, Cambridge (Mass).

Jammer, M.: 1974, *The Philosophy of Quantum Mechanics: The Interpretation of Quantum Mechanics in Historical Perspective*, John Wiley, New York.

Jarrett, J.: 1984, "On the Physical Significance of the Locality Condition in the Bell Arguments", *Noûs* 18, 569-89.

Jarrett, J.: 1989, "Bell's Theorem: A Guide to the Implications", in: (Cushing & McMullin 1989), 60-79.

Kastner, R.E.: 1999, "Time-symmetrized Quantum Theory, Counterfactuals, and 'Advanced Action'", *Studies in the History and Philosophy of Modern Physics* 30 (2), 237-259.

Kastner, R.E.: "The Three-Box "Paradox" and other Reasons to Reject the Counterfactual Usage of the ABL Rule", quant-ph/9807037 v3.

Lange, M.: 2002, *An Introduction to the Philosophy of Physics: Locality, Fields, Energy, and Mass*, Blackwell Publishing, Oxford.

Lewis, D.: 1973, *Counterfactuals*, Harvard University Press, Cambridge (Mass.)

Lewis, D.: 1977, "Possible-World Semantics for Counterfactual Logics: A Rejoinder", *Journal of Philosophical Logic* 6, 359-363.

Lewis, D.: 1981, "Ordering Semantics and Premise Semantics for Counterfactuals", *Journal of Philosophical Logic* 10, 217-234.

Lewis, D.: 1986a, "Counterfactual Dependence and Time's Arrow" with Postscripts in: *Philosophical Papers Vol II*, Oxford University Press, Oxford, 32-66.

Lewis, D.: 1986b, "Causality" in: *Philosophical Papers Vol II*, Oxford University Press, Oxford.

Lewis, D.: 1986c, "Counterfactuals and Comparative Possibility" in: *Philosophical Papers Vol II*, Oxford University Press, Oxford, 3-31.

Lewis, D. : 1986d, *On the Plurality of Worlds*, Basil Blackwell, Oxford.

Lewis, D.:1997, "Finkish Dispositions", *The Philosophical Quarterly* 47, 143-58.

Lewis, D.: 2000, "Causation as Influence", *Journal of Philosophy*, reprinted in (Collins *et al.* 2004), 75-106.

Lowe, E.J.: 1995, "The Truth About Counterfactuals", *The Philosophical Quarterly* 45 (178), 41-59.

Martin, C.B.: 1994, "Dispositions and Conditionals", *The Philosophical Quarterly* 44 (174), 1-8.

Maudlin, T.: 1994, *Quantum Non-locality and Relativity*, Blackwell, Oxford.

Maudlin, T.: 2003, "Distilling Metaphysics from Quantum Physics", in: M.J. Loux, D.W. Zimmerman, *The Oxford Handbook of Metaphysics*, Oxford University Press, Oxford, 461-487.

McCall, S.: 1984, "Counterfactuals Based on Real Possible Worlds", *Noûs* 18, 463-477.

Mermin, D.: 1998, "Nonlocal Character of Quantum Theory?", *American Journal of Physics* 66(10), 920-924.

Mumford, S.: 1994, "Dispositions, Supervenience and Reduction", *The Philosophical Quarterly* 44 (177), 419-438.

Mumford, S.: 1998, *Dispositions*, Oxford University Press, Oxford.

Müller, T.: 2002, "Branching Space-Time, Modal Logic and the Counterfactual Conditional", in: (Placek & Butterfield 2002), 273-291.

Myrvold, W.C.: 2002, "On Peaceful Coexistence: Is the Collapse Postulate Incompatible with Relativity?", *Studies in History and Philosophy of Modern Physics* 33, 435-466.

Myrvold, W.C.: 2003, "Relativistic Quantum Becoming", *British Journal for the Philosophy of Science* 54, 475-500.

Noordhof, P.: 2000, "Ramachandran's Four Counterexamples", *Mind* 109, 315-324

Nute, D.: 1975, "Counterfactuals and the Similarity of Worlds", *The Journal of Philosophy* LXXII (21), 773-778.

Pagonis, P., M. Redhead and P. La Rivière: 1996, "EPR, Relativity and the GHZ Experiment", in: R. Clifton (ed.) *Perspectives on Quantum Reality*, Kluwer, 43-55.

Percival, P.: 1999, "A Note on Lewis on Counterfactual Dependence in a Chancy World", *Analysis* 59 (3), 165-173.

Pearl, J.: 2000, *Causality*, Cambridge University Press, New York.

Placek, T.: 2000a, *Is Nature Deterministic? A Branching Perspective on EPR Phenomena*, Jagiellonian University Press, Kraków.

Placek, T. : 2000b, "Stapp's Arguments for Non-locality are Wrong", *Reports on Philosophy* 20, 131-167.

Placek, T. and Butterfield, J. (eds.): 2002, *Non-Locality and Modality*, Kluwer, Dordrecht

Plantinga, A.: 1976, "Actualism and Possible Worlds", *Theoria* 42, 139-160.

Price, H: 1996, *Time's Arrow and Archimedes' Point*, Oxford University Press, Oxford.

Putnam, H.: 1969, "Is Logic Empirical?", in: R.S. Cohen and M.W. Wartofsky (eds.), *Boston Studies in the Philosophy of Science* Vol. 5, D. Reidel, Dordrecht.

Quine, W.V.O.: 1974, *The Roots of Reference*, Open Court, La Salle.

Redhead, M.: 1987, *Non-locality, Incompleteness and Realism*, Oxford University Press, Oxford.

Redhead, M., La Rivière, P.: 1997, "The Relativistic EPR Argument", in: R.S. Cohen, M. Horne and J. Stachel (eds.), *Potentiality, Entanglement and Passion-at-a-Distance*, Kluwer, Dordrecht.

Reichenbach, H.: 1944, *Philosophical Foundations of Quantum Mechanics*, University of California Press, Berkeley.

Reichenbach, H.: 1956, *The Direction of Time*, University of California Press, Berkeley.

Sharp, W.D., Shanks, N.: 1993, "The Rise and Fall of Time-Symmetrized Quantum Mechanics", *Philosophy of Science* 60, 488-499.

Shimony, A.:1984, "Controllable and Uncontrollable Non-locality", in: S. Kamefuchi *et al.* (eds), *Foundations of Quantum Mechanics in the Light of New Technology*, Tokyo, The Physical Society of Japan. Reprinted in (Shimony 1993), 130-139.

Shimony, A.: 1986, "Events and Processes in the Quantum World", in: R. Penrose and C. Isham (eds.), *Quantum Concepts in Space and Time*, Oxford University Press, Oxford, reprinted in (Shimony 1993), 140-162.

Shimony, A.: 1990, "An Exposition of Bell's Theorem", in: A. Miller (ed.), *Sixty-two Years of Uncertainty*, Plenum Publishing, New York, reprinted in (Shimony 1993), 90-103.

Shimony, A.: 1993, *Search for a Naturalistic World View. Vol. II Natural Science and Metaphysics*, Cambridge University Press, Cambridge.

Shimony, A.: 2001, "The Logic of EPR", *Annales de la Fondation Louis de Broglie* 26, 399-410.

Shimony, A., Stein, H.: 2001, "Comment on 'Nonlocal Character of Quantum Theory' by Henry P. Stapp", *American Journal of Physics* 69, 848-853.

Shimony, A., Stein, H.: 2003, "On quantum non-locality, special relativity, and counterfactual reasoning", in: A. Ashtekar *et al.* (eds.), *Revisiting the Foundations of Relativistic Physics*, Kluwer, Dordrecht, 499-521.

Sklar, L.: 1970, "Is Probability a Dispositional Property?", *The Journal of Philosophy* LXVII (11), 355-366.

Sklar, L.: 1979, "Probability as a Theoretical Concept", *Synthese* 40, 409-414.

Sklar, L.: 1993, *Physics and Chance. Philosophical Issues in the Foundations of Statistical Mechanics*, Cambridge University Press, Cambridge.

Skyrms, B.: 1982, "Counterfactual Definiteness and Local Causation", *Philosophy of Science* 49, 43-50.

Sosa, E. and Tooley, M.: 1993, *Causation*. Oxford University Press, Oxford.

Stalnaker, R.C.: 1968, "A Theory of Conditionals", in: N. Rescher (ed.), *Studies in Logical Theory*, Blackwell, Oxford, reprinted in: E. Sosa (ed.), *Causation and Conditionals*, Oxford University Press, Oxford, 165-179.

Stalnaker, R.C.: 1976, "Possible Worlds", *Nous*, 10, pp. 65-75.

Stalnaker, R.C: 1978, "A Defense of Conditional Excluded Middle", in: W. Harper, R.C. Stalnaker and G. Pearce (eds.), *Ifs*, Dordrecht, Reidel.

Stapp, H.P.: 1971, "S-matrix Interpretation of Quantum Theory", *Physical Review D* 3, 1303-20.

Stapp, H.P.: 1977, "Are Superluminal Connections Necessary?", *Il Nuovo Cimento* 40B (1), 191-205.

Stapp, H.P.: 1985, "Bell's Theorem and the Foundations of Quantum Physics", *American Journal of Physics* 53 (4), 306-317

Stapp, H.P.: 1988a, Reply to "Note on 'Bell's Theorem and the Foundations of Quantum Physics'", *American Journal of Physics* 56 (6), 567.

Stapp, H.P.: 1988b, Reply to "Comment on 'Bell's Theorem and the Foundations of Quantum Physics'", *American Journal of Physics* 56 (6), 568-569.

Stapp, H.P.: 1989, "Quantum Nonlocality and the Description of Nature", in: (Cushing & McMullin 1989), 154-74.

Stapp, H.P.: 1990, "Quantum Measurement and the Mind-Brain Connection", in: P. Lahti and P. Mittelstaedt (eds.), *Symposium on the Foundations of Modern Physics 1990*, World Scientific, Singapore – New Jersey – London – Hong Kong.

Stapp, H.P.: 1990a, "Comments on 'Non-local Influences and Possible Worlds", *British Journal for the Philosophy of Science* 41, 59-72.

Stapp, H.P.: 1992, "Noise-Induced Reduction of Wave-Packets and Faster-than-Light Influences", *Physical Review* A 46 (11), 6860-6868.

Stapp, H.P.: 1993, "Significance of an Experiment of the Greenberger-Horne-Zeilinger Kind", *Physical Review* A 47 (2), 847-853.

Stapp, H.P.: 1994a, "Strong Versions of Bell's Theorem", *Physical Review* A 49 (5), 3182-3187.

Stapp, H.P.: 1994b, "Reply to 'Stapp's Algebraic Argument for Nonlocality'", *Physical Review* A 49(5), 4257-4260.

Stapp, H.P.: 1997, "Nonlocal Character of Quantum Theory", *American Journal of Physics* 65, 300-304.

Stapp, H.P.: 1998, "Meaning of Counterfactual Statements in Quantum Physics", *American Journal of Physics* 66(10), 924-926.

Stapp, H.P.: 1999, 'Comments on 'Non-locality, Counterfactuals, and Quantum Mechanics', *Physical Review A* 60(3), 2595-2598.

Stapp., H.P.: 2001a, Response to "Comment on 'Nonlocal Character of Quantum Theory'" by Abner Shimony and Howard Stein', *American Journal of Physics* 69(8), 854-859.

Stapp, H.P.: 2001b, "Bell's Theorem without Hidden Variables", Lawrence Berkeley Laboratory Report No. LBNL 46942, quant-ph/0010047

Stapp, H.P.: 2004, "A Bell-type Theorem without Hidden Variables", *American Journal of Physics* 72 (30), 30-33.

Tichý, P.: 1976, "A Counterexample to the Stalnaker-Lewis Analysis of Counterfactuals", *Philosophical Studies* 29, 271-273.

Tittel, W., Brendel, J., Gisin, B., Herzog, T., Zbinden, H. and Gisin, N.: 1998, "Experimental Demonstration of Quantum Correlations over More than 10 Kilometers", *Physical Review* A 57, 3229-3232.

Unger, P.: 1984, "Minimizing Arbitrariness: Toward a Metaphysics of Infinitely Many Isolated Concrete Worlds", *Midwest Studies in Philosophy* 9, 29-51.

Unruh, W.: 1999, "Nonlocality, Counterfactuals, and Quantum Mechanics", *Physical Review* A 59, 126-130.

Unruh, W.: 2002, "Is Quantum Mechanics Non-local?", in: (Placek & Butterfield 2002), 125-136.

Vaidman, L.: 1999a, "Time-symmetrized Counterfactuals in Quantum Theory", *Foundations of Physics* 29 (1999) 755-765.

Vaidman, L.: 1999b, "Defending Time-Symmetrized Quantum Counterfactuals", *Studies in the History and Philosophy of Modern Physics* 30 (3), 373-397.

Vaidman, L.: 1999, "The Meaning of Elements of Reality and Quantum Counterfactuals—Reply to Kastner", quant-ph/9903095 v1

van Fraassen, B.C.: 1973, "Semantic Analysis of Quantum Logic", in: C.A. Hooker (ed.) *Contemporary Research in the Foundation and Philosophy of Quantum Theory*, D. Reidel, Dordrecht, 80-142.

van Fraassen, B.C.: 1982, "The Charybdis of Realism: Epistemological Implications of Bell's Inequality", *Synthese* 52, 25-38.

van Fraassen, B.C.: 1991, *Quantum Mechanics: An Empiricist View*, Clarendon Press, Oxford.

van Inwagen, P.: 1986, "Two Concepts of Possible Worlds", *Midwest Studies in Philosophy* 11, 185-213.

Wigner, E.P.: 1970, "On Hidden Variables and Quantum Mechanical Probabilities", *American Journal of Physics* 38, p. 1005-1009.

Williams, D.C.: 1967, "The Myth of Passage", in: R. Gale (ed.), *The Philosophy of Time*, New York 1967.

# Index

# Epistemische Studien
## Schriften zur Erkenntnis- und Wissenschaftstheorie
Herausgegeben von / Edited by
Michael Esfeld • Stephan Hartmann • Mike Sandbothe

**Vol. 1**
Volker Halbach / Leon Horsten
**Principles of Truth**
ISBN 3-937202-45-5
2. Aufl., 228 pp • Paperback € 49,00

**Vol. 2**
Matthias Adam
**Theoriebeladenheit und Objektivität**
*Zur Rolle der Beobachtung in den Naturwissenschaften*
ISBN 3-937202-11-0
274 Seiten, • Hardcover € 59,00

**Vol. 3**
Christoph Halbig / Christian Suhm
**Was ist wirklich?**
Neuere Beiträge zur Realismusdebatte in der Philosophie
ISBN 3-937202-28-5
446 Seiten • Paperback € 32,00

**Vol. 4**
André Fuhrmann / Erik J. Olsson
**Pragmatisch denken**
ISBN 3-937202-46-3
321 Seiten • Hardcover € 84,00

**Vol. 5**
Pedro Schmechtig
**Sprache, Einstellung und Rationalität**
*Eine Untersuchung zu den Rationalitätsbedingungen von Einstellungs-Zuschreibungen*
ISBN 3-937202-56-0
330 Seiten • Hardcover € 89,00

**Vol. 6**
Christian Suhm
**Wissenschaftlicher Realismus**
*Eine Studie zur Realismus-Antirealismus-Debatte in der neueren Wissenschaftstheorie*
ISBN 3-937202-48-X
ca. 250 Seiten • Hardcover € 69,00

**Vol. 7**
Bernward Gesang
**Deskriptive oder normative Wissenschaftstheorie?**
ISBN 3-937202-69-2
ca. 240 Seiten • Hardcover € 76,00

**Vol. 8**
Jiri Benovsky
**Persistence Through Time, and Across Possible Worlds**
ISBN 3-937202-99-4
281 pp., Hardcover, € 84,00

**Vol. 9**
Thomas Sukopp
**Naturalismus**
Kritik und Verteidigung erkenntnistheoretischer Positionen
Mit Vorworten von Gerhard Vollmer und Werner Callebaut
ISBN 3-938793-13-9
348 pp., Hardcover, € 84,00

**ontos verlag**
P.O. Box 15 41
63133 Heusenstamm
Tel. ++49 6104 66 57 33
Fax ++49 6104 66 57 34
info@ontosverlag.com
www.ontosverlag.com

ontos verlag

Frankfurt • Lancaster